PATERNOSTER BIBLICAL MONOGRAPHS

A Prophet Like Moses?

A Narrative-Theological Reading of the Elijah Stories

PATERNOSTER BIBLICAL MONOGRAPHS

A full listing of all titles in this series appears at
the close of this book

PATERNOSTER BIBLICAL MONOGRAPHS

A Prophet Like Moses?

A Narrative-Theological Reading of the Elijah Stories

Havilah Dharamraj

Foreword by R.W.L. Moberly

MILTON KEYNES · COLORADO SPRINGS · HYDERABAD

Copyright © Havilah Dharamraj 2011

First published 2011 by Paternoster

PO Box 6326, Bletchley, Milton Keynes, MK1 9GG, UK

www.authenticmedia.co.uk

15 14 13 12 11 10 09 7 6 5 4 3 2 1

The right of Havilah Dharamraj to be identified as the Author of this Work has been asserted by her in accordance with the Copyright, Designs and Patents Act 1988

All rights reserved. No part of this publication may be reproduced, stored in a retrieval system, or transmitted in any form by any means, electronic, mechanical, photocopying, recording or otherwise, without the prior permission of the publisher or a license permitting restricted copying. In the UK such licenses are issued by the Copyright Licensing Agency, Barnard's Inn, 86 Fetter Lane, London EC4A 1EN.

British Library Cataloguing in Publication Data
A catalogue record for this book is available from the British Library

ISBN 978–1–84227–533–7
978-1-78078-389-5 (e-book)

Typeset by SAIACS Press
www.saiacs.org

Series Preface

One of the major objectives of Paternoster is to serve biblical scholarship by providing a channel for the publication of theses and other monographs of high quality at affordable prices. Paternoster stands within the broad evangelical tradition of Christianity. Our authors would describe themselves as Christians who recognise the authority of the Bible, maintain the centrality of the gospel message and assent to the classical credal statements of Christian belief. There is diversity within this constituency; advances in scholarship are possible only if there is freedom for frank debate on controversial issues and for the publication of new and sometimes provocative proposals. What is offered in this series is the best of writing by committed Christians who are concerned to develop well-founded biblical scholarship in a spirit of loyalty to the historic faith.

Series Editors

I. Howard Marshall, Honorary Research Professor of New Testament, University of Aberdeen, Scotland, UK

Richard J. Bauckham, Professor of New Testament Studies and Bishop Wardlaw Professor, University of St Andrews, Scotland, UK

Craig Blomberg, Distinguished Professor of New Testament, Denver Seminary, Colorado, USA

Robert P. Gordon, Regius Professor of Hebrew, University of Cambridge, UK

Tremper Longman III, Robert H. Gundry Professor and Chair of the Department of Biblical Studies, Westmont College, Santa Barbara, California, USA

Stanley E. Porter, President and Professor of New Testament, McMaster Divinity College, Hamilton, Ontario, Canada

To the memory of my mother, Leela.

"Her children rise up and call her blessed."
Proverbs 31:28

Contents

	Foreword by R. W. L. Moberly	xiii
	Abbreviations	xv
	Chapter 1	
	Introduction: What May be Expected of a Prophet Like Moses?	1
1.	A Prophet Like Moses	1
2.	The Critical Method Applied	4
3.	The Text Under Study	5
	Chapter 2	
	1 Kings 16:29-17:24: The Drought	7
1.	Ahab Begins his Reign	7
2.	The Drought	9
2.1.	1 Kings 17: 1-7: Elijah Predicts a Drought	9
2.2.	1 Kings 17:8-16: The Oil and the Flour	13
2.3.	1 Kings 17:17-24: The Widow's Son	15
3.	Conclusion	19
	Chapter 3	
	1 Kings 18: The Resolution of the Drought	21
1.	Towards the Resolution of the Drought	21
1.1.	1 Kings 18:1-16: Ahab and Obadiah (vv.1-6); Obadiah and Elijah (vv.7-16)	21
1.2.	1 Kings 18: 17-19: Ahab and Elijah	25
2.	The Contest at Carmel	27
2.1.	1 Kings 18:20-24: Either/Or Rather than Both/And	27
2.2.	1 Kings 18:25-40: The LORD vs. Baal	30
2.3.	1 Kings 18:30-46: The Covenant Affirmed	35
3.	Conclusion	40

Chapter 4
1 Kings 19: Horeb — 42

1.	1 Kings 19:1-10: Moses, Elijah and the Death Wish	42
1.1.	Moses and the Death Wish	42
1.1.1.	Moses' Intercession at Sinai (Exodus 32:31-32)	42
1.1.2.	Moses' Complaint at Kibroth-hattaavah (Numbers 11:4-15)	45
1.2.	Elijah and the Death Wish (1 Kings 19:1-10)	47
1.2.1.	Elijah's Complaint under the Broom Tree (1 Kings 19:1-4)	47
1.2.2.	Towards Elijah's Second Complaint (1 Kings 19:5-9a)	50
1.2.3.	Elijah's Complaint at Horeb (1 Kings 19:9b-10)	53
1.3.	Revisiting the Resonance between the Death Wish Narratives	68
2.	1 Kings 19:11-13a: The Earthquake, Wind, Fire and קוֹל	70
2.1.	The Text of 1 Kings 19:11-13a	70
2.1.1.	Verbal and Story Level Correspondences with Exodus Narratives	70
2.1.2.	Resolving the Grammar of the Text	71
2.1.3.	The "Still, Small, Voice"	73
2.1.3.1.	"Voice"	74
2.1.3.2.	"Small"	75
2.1.3.3.	"Still"; Job 4:12-16	77
2.1.3.4.	The Two "Voices"s	84
2.2.	The LORD's Absence and Presence in vv.11-13a	88
2.3.	Reconsidering the LORD's Absence and Presence in vv.11-13a	94
2.3.1.	Exodus 19-20	99
2.3.2.	Exodus 33-34	100
2.4.	Conclusion	102
3.	1 Kings 19:13-18: Elijah Receives his Commission	102
3.1.	1 Kings 19:13: The Second Question	102
3.1.1.	"When Elijah heard it he wrapped his face in his mantle"	102
3.1.2.	"And went out and stood at the entrance of the cave"	104

3.1.3.	"'What are you doing here, Elijah?'," with Respect to Jotham's Fable, Israel's Demand for a King and the "Death" of Joseph	105
3.2.	1 Kings 19:14: The Second Response	112
3.3.	1 Kings 19:15-18: The Commission	118
3.3.1.	"Under" and its Implications	119
3.3.2.	The Root "Remain" and the Remnant Motif	125
3.3.2.1	Noah: Genesis 7:17-24	126
3.3.2.2.	Joseph: Genesis 45:4b-8a	128
3.3.2.3.	An Israel Within Israel	130
3.4.	Comparing the Story Outlines of Exodus 32-34 and 1 Kings 19	135
3.5.	The Reliability of the Character Elijah	136
3.5.1.	Levels of Knowledge	137
3.5.2.	Time – Objective and Internal	140
3.5.3.	Conclusion	143
4.	1 Kings 19:19-21: Elisha becomes Elijah's Minister	144
4.1.	The Question of Elijah's "Lapses"	144
4.1.1.	The Appointments of Hazael and Jehu	144
4.1.2.	The "Anointing" of Elisha	149
4.2.	Mosaic Resonances	151
5.	Concluding Summary to 1 Kings 19	152

Chapter 5
1 Kings 22:51-2 Kings 1:18: Elijah and Ahaziah — 154

1.	1 Kings 22:51-53: Regnal Resumé	154
2.	2 Kings 1: The Themes Revisited	155
2.1.	Baal versus the LORD	155
2.2.	The Affirmation of the Prophet	160
3.	2 Kings 1 in the Context of the Elijah-Elisha Cycles	163

Chapter 6
2 Kings 2: Elijah's Ascension and Elisha's Succession — 166

1.	2 Kings 2	166
1.1.	Elijah's Ascension and Elisha's Succession	166
1.1.1.	2 Kings 2:1-6: Elisha accompanies Elijah	166
1.1.2.	2 Kings 2:7-8: Elijah parts the Jordan	174

1.1.3.	2 Kings 2:9-10: Elisha asks a "hard thing"	177
1.1.4.	2 Kings 2:11-12: Elijah is "taken"	183
1.1.5.	2 Kings 2:13-15: "The spirit of Elijah rests on Elisha"	189
1.1.6.	2 Kings 2:16-18: The Search for Elijah	193
1.2.	Structure and Focus of the 2 Kings 2 Narrative	196
1.3.	Interim Conclusion	199
2.	Exodus 14-15 and Joshua 1, 3-5	200
2.1.	The Two Great Water Crossings	200
2.1.1.	Verbal Parallels	200
2.1.2.	Story Level Parallels	203
2.2.	Interim Conclusion	204
3.	The Red Sea Crossing, the Jordan Crossing and 2 Kings 2: Conceptual Parallels	205
3.1.	The Dynamics of Authoritative Leadership: Moses and Joshua; Elijah and Elisha	205
3.2.	The War Theme in Exodus 14-15 and Joshua 1-5; Implications for 2 Kings 2	209
4.	Conclusion	217

Chapter 7
Conclusion: Is Elijah a Prophet Like Moses? 218

Appendix 226

Bibliography 229

Author Index 248

Scripture Index 251

Foreword

Elijah is one of the most famous and mysterious figures in the Old Testament. Such is his continuing significance in an ancient context that he appears with Moses to Jesus on the Mount of Transfiguration. Here Moses and Elijah together appear to represent the Law and the Prophets, and thereby symbolize the fullness of Scripture as the informing context for Jesus' journey to Jerusalem and coming passion.

Why such continuing significance? Within his Old Testament context Elijah appears abruptly and unannounced, and at the end he does not die – somewhat like Melchizedek, whose brief narrative appearance is closely read by the writer to the Hebrews (Heb. 7:1-3). In between Elijah is involved in two of the most enduring and engaging of Old Testament narratives, the contest on Mount Carmel and the encounter with the "still, small voice" at Mount Horeb.

What kind of scholarly work can best illuminate such narratives? Although there is a great variety of possible approaches and questions, a narrative-theological approach, such as Havilah Dharamraj practises, has more imaginative potential than most. She closely reads the given text and seeks to catch and tease out its nuances and resonances in its canonical context, in such a way as to preserve and enhance the qualities of the original.

Although we have here a fresh reading of the Elijah narratives as a whole, particular interest is likely to attach to Dharamraj's interpretation of I Kings 19, Elijah's journey to Mount Horeb. What is the nature of the "still, small voice", and is that in fact a good construal of the Hebrew? Is Elijah only at Horeb because of a major failure on his part, or are there other ways of reading the text? How does this episode contribute to the overall profile of Elijah, such that his being taken up to heaven at the end can be seen to be of a piece with what precedes?

Whether or not one agrees with all Dr Dharamraj's detailed interpretations, I am confident that every reader of this book will be challenged and stimulated to attend more closely to the scriptural text, and will come away with a renewed appreciation of the richness of Old Testament narrative in general, and the Elijah narratives in particular.

R. W. L. Moberly

Abbreviations

AB	Anchor Bible
ABR	*Australian Biblical Review*
AJSL	*American Journal for Semitic Languages and Literature*
Ant.	*Jewish Antiquities*
ASV	American Standard Version
ATANT	Abhandlungen zur Theologie des Alten und Neuen Testaments
BAR	*Biblical Archaeology Review*
BDB	Brown, Francis, S.R. Driver and Charles A. Briggs. *The Brown-Driver-Briggs Hebrew and English Lexicon*. Boston: Houghton, Mifflin and Company. 1906. Reprint, Peabody, Mass.: Hendrickson. 2000.
Bib	*Biblica*
BSC	Bible Student's Commentary
CBC	Cambridge Bible Commentary
CBQ	*Catholic Biblical Quarterly*
CC	Continental Commentaries
ETL	*Ephemerides theologicae louvanienses*
EvT	*Evangelische Theologie*
EVV	English versions
ExpTim	*Expository Times*
FAT	Forschungen zum Alten Testament
FOTL	Forms of Old Testament Literature
GKC	Gesenius, William and E. Kautzsch. *Gesenius-Kautzsch Hebrew Grammar*. Translated by Collins, G. W. Revised by A. E. Cowley. Oxford: Clarendon. 1898.
HAT	Handbuch zum Alten Testament.
HBD	*HarperCollins Bible Dictionary*
HSAT	Die Heilige Schrift des Alten Testaments
HTR	*Harvard Theological Review*
HUCA	*Hebrew Union College Annual*
ICC	International Critical Commentary
ISBE	*International Standard Bible Encyclopedia*
JANESCU	*Journal of the Ancient Near Eastern Society of Columbia University*

JAOS	*Journal of the American Oriental Society*
JB	Jerusalem Bible
JBL	*Journal of Biblical Literature*
JBQ	*Jewish Bible Quarterly*
Joüon-Muraoka	Joüon, Paul. *A Grammar of Biblical Hebrew*. Translated and revised by T. Muraoka. Vol. 1. Reprint of 1st edn. with corrections. Subsidia biblica 14/1. Rome: Pontifical Biblical Institute. 1993.
JNSL	*Journal of Northwest Semitic Languages*
JPS	Jewish Publication Society
JPSA	Jewish Publication Society of America
JSOT/ *JSOT*	*Journal for the Study of the Old Testament*
JSOTSup	Journal for the Study of the Old Testament: Supplement Series
JSS	*Journal of Semitic Studies*
JTC	*Journal for Theology and Church*
JTS	*Journal of Theological Studies*
JTSA	Jewish Theological Seminary of America
KJV	King James Version
L.A.B.	*Liber Antiquitatum Biblicarum*
LCL	Loeb Classical Library
LXX	Septuagint
MT	Masoretic Text
NAB	New American Bible
NASV	New American Standard Version
NCB	New Century Bible
NEB	New English Bible
NIBC	New Interpreter's Bible Commentary
NICOT	New International Commentary on the Old Testament
NIV	New International Version
NRSV	New Revised Standard Version
OT	Old Testament
OTL	Old Testament Library
OTS	*Oudtestamentische Studiën*
PEQ	*Palestine Exploration Qtly*
Per	*Perspectives*
Proof	*Prooftexts: A Journal of Jewish Literary History*
Rom. Ant.	The Roman Antiquities of Dionysius of Halicarnassus
RSV	Revised Standard Version
SBLMS	Society of Biblical Literature Monograph Series
SBT	Studies in Biblical Theology

Schol	Scholastik
Sem	Semeia
sg.	singular
SJOT	Scandinavian Journal of the Old Testament
SR	Studies in Religion
T. Benj.	Testament of Benjamin
TDOT	Theological Dictionary of the Old Testament
Tg. Jon.	Targum Jonathan
Tg. Onq.	Targum Onqelos
Tg. Ps.-J.	Targum Pseudo-Jonathan
TLOT	Theological Lexicon of the Old Testament
TOTC	Tyndale Old Testament Commentaries
VT	Vetus Testamentum
VTSup	Supplements to Vetus Testamentum
vv.	verses
WBC	Word Biblical Commentary
WC	Westminster Commentaries
WMANT	Wissenschaftliche Monographien zum Alten und Neuen Testament
ZAW	Zeitschrift für die alttestametliche Wissenschaft
ZTK	Zeitschrift für Theologie und Kirche
1QS	Dead Sea Scrolls; Rule of the Community

CHAPTER 1

Introduction:
What May be Expected of a Prophet Like Moses?

1. A Prophet Like Moses

Deuteronomy's epitaph to Moses declares him the prophet unsurpassed: "Never since has there arisen a prophet in Israel like Moses"; ולא קם נביא עוד בישראל כמשה; (Deut. 34:10a). The pronouncement suggests that Moses was the paradigm that prophets were to follow; their performance was to be benchmarked by his. While Moses forever remains a prophet without equal, hope that the prophetic line would yield another of Moses' fibre rests on the LORD's promise through Moses, made in response to Israel's request for a mediator between them and God (Deut. 18:15-22). The promise assures Israel a prophet "like" Moses, and in this text, the accent is on mediation of the divine word to the people. The prophet will deliver this word faithfully, and the people will be held accountable should they not heed it. They will know the word and the prophet who spoke that word as true in retrospect, by virtue of it fulfilling itself.

While the OT associates Moses with Samuel in the context of intercession (Jer. 15:1; Ps. 99:6), the comparative field opens up to include the entire life and work of Moses in the stories of the Elijah cycle as recounted in 1 Kgs 17-21 and 2 Kgs 1-2. Though the narrative does not once mention Moses by name, the richness of the intertexuality between this set of stories and the Moses stories set down in Exodus, Numbers and Deuteronomy invites a comparison of these two prophets. The resonance spills over into the succession stories, encouraging a secondary setting up of parallels between Elisha (2 Kgs 2) and Joshua (Josh. 1-6), which reinforce and accentuate the primary comparison.

Lists of these parallels between Moses and Elijah abound, a Midrashic compilation possibly being the earliest of the more exhaustive ones.[1] On setting up these correspondences, a comparative evaluation becomes possible, and indeed natural. Thus, for example, Walsh concludes his remarkably comprehensive engagement with the intertexuality as follows:

---

1. Piska 4.2, *Pesikta Rabbati*. See Appendix.

The effect of the pervasive allusions to the Moses traditions, then, is to depict Elijah as *almost the equal* of Moses [emphasis added], but as ultimately failing to meet the standards Moses set. This redounds to the glory of Moses in that he remains the unquestioned paradigm of prophecy in Israel. Ironically, it redounds to the qualified glory of Elijah as well, since he is many ways, though not all, a Moses *redivivus*.[2]

This is a possible line of approach, but not the only one, and sometimes it may subtly skew the reading of the text in that it may distract the reader's attention from the more significant issue of the purpose that the resonance works in its immediate textual context.[3]

Here, we recognize that the resonance is mediated to the reader through two channels—the character Elijah, and the narrator. In the Hebrew narrative tradition of the self-effacing and covert narrator, the character Elijah is brought to the foreground in the Kings stories; his speech and actions convey the parallels. The narrator sustains and augments the resonance by creating the correct background. This he does by carefully selecting the material for the narrative, by skilfully orchestrating the structure and progression of his plot, and by adding evocative story detail. The end to which the character and narrator work in tandem is—as is usual in Hebrew narrative—to lead the reader to adopt the narrator's point of view and espouse his evaluation of characters and situations. The key component of this leading, it appears, is the evoking of a paradigmatic event in Israel's history (namely, the Exodus) and its principal player (namely, Moses); hence the need to pay close attention to the function of these resonances within the discourse.

Given the resonance with stories in Exodus, Numbers and Deuteronomy, Deut. 18:18 becomes relevant as a possible handle to reading the Mosaic resonance. This returns us to the key preposition, כ, here used as the (often poetic) variant כמו.[4]

---

2. Walsh, (1996), 288-89.
3. A good example of such distraction is provided by one strand of early Jewish engagement with a certain instance of parallelism between the Moses and Elijah stories, namely, the passing of the two prophets. Here, labour is directed towards reconciling the death of Moses with the exception made for Elijah, the underlying assumption being that non-death is the ultimate affirmation of a life of extraordinary virtue. Thus, disregarding the biblical account of Moses' death, it argues that he was translated. *Sotah* 13b; cf. *Sifre to Deuteronomy* 357. Philo follows this interpretative tradition in *Sac. Of Abel* 8, arguing that "the end of virtuous and holy men is not death but a translation and migration (*Ques. on Gen.* 1.86)." Josephus, more subtly, links Moses with Enoch with the unusual expression ἀναχώρησε πρὸς τὸ Θεῖον (he "returned to the divinity") (*Ant.* 1.85; *Ant.* 4.326, cf. 3.96), and Moses with Elijah with the verb ἀφανίζομαι (to "disappear") (*Ant.* 4.326; *Ant.* 9.28). Thus, reading a sense of competition into the resonance may create more problems than it solves.
4. BDB, כ, 453-56.

כ has a more pronounced substantival character than do the other prepositions,[5] and "expresses a relation of either perfect (equality), or imperfect (resemblance) similitude; the meaning may therefore be exactly like, or more or less like, but in many cases without any precise nuance."[6] Relevant here is Fishbane's study of inner-biblical typological exegesis, not only because he identifies כ as a lexical indicator of this exegetical procedure,[7] but because the procedure itself is of interest to our undertaking. He explains these typologies as follows:

> ...inner biblical typologies constitute a literary-historical phenomenon which isolates perceived correlations between specific events, persons or places early in time with their later correspondents...[I]n so far as the 'later correspondents' occur in history and time, they will never be precisely identical with their prototype, but inevitably stand in a hermeneutical relationship with them. The reasons for this are twofold. On the one hand, while it is in the nature of typologies to emphasize the homological 'likeness' of any two events, the concrete historicity of the correlated data means that no new event is ever merely a 'type' of another, but always retains its historically unique character. Moreover, and this is the second factor, nexuses between distinct temporal data are never something simply given; they are something which must always be exegetically established. Indeed, in the Hebrew Bible such nexuses are the product of a specific mode of theological-historical speculation—one which seeks to adapt, interpret, or otherwise illuminate a present experience...by means of an older datum...By this means it also reveals unexpected unity in historical experience and providential continuity in its new patterns and shapes.[8]

By way of example, he demonstrates the role of Deut. 18:18 in typologies of a biographical nature. A prophet "like" Moses is evoked in the motif of the preparation of the prophet's mouth to speak the divine word; it has its origin with Moses (Exod. 4:10-16), and re-emerges in the commissioning accounts of Isaiah (Isa. 6:5-8), Jeremiah (Jer. 1:9) and Ezekiel (Ezek. 2:8-3:3).[9] The homology creates "spiritual-historical continuities."[10]

In the task that lies ahead, that of studying the parallel texts, Fishbane's approach is worth bearing in mind, though any

---

5. Joüon-Muraoka, §133g. Cf. GKC, §101a, §102.2; Waltke and O'Connor (1990), 11.2.9a-b.
6. Joüon-Muraoka, §133g.
7. Fishbane proposes this function for fixed rhetorical terms such as כאשר...כן and non-technical variants using כ. (1985), 352-53.
8. Fishbane (1985), 351-52.
9. Fishbane (1985), 374. At a critical juncture, Elijah is affirmed by the truth of the word of the LORD in his mouth; 1 Kgs 17:24.
10. Fishbane (1985), 373.

conclusions we draw with respect to the compositional intention in the Elijah stories can only be submitted as a tentative construct. In the present context, Fishbane's remarks inform us on the possible function of the preposition כ, directing us to conclude thus: the Elijah material in Kings does lend itself to being read against the corresponding Moses stories, and provokes an evaluation of Elijah vis-à-vis the promise of Deut. 18:18. A reasonable approach to evaluating Elijah as a prophet would be, not in terms of whether he is a Moses *redivivus*, but rather, in terms of how he does or does not reflect in the practice of his calling the qualities and virtues that mark Moses.

Further, we remind ourselves that the prophet's discharge of his duties is in the context of the covenant that binds Israel and the LORD. As such, our starting point is the history of Israel as recounted under the Omride kings, Ahab and Ahaziah. It is a troubled period, and one that creates opportunities for prophetic intervention towards the securing of Israel's relationship with God. Perhaps Elijah's moves will recall Moses' in analogous situations either in favourable comparison or contrast. All along, the need is to keep the ear sensitive to the pattern of the resonance; its rise and falling mark out the episodes key to the evaluation of Elijah. When we conclude our study of the implications of the intertexuality, we will return to answering the question of whether Elijah is a prophet like Moses. We may be able then to appreciate fully how distracting is the exercise of deciding who is the greater of the two.

2. The Critical Method Applied

We propose to engage in a narrative reading of the Elijah and Moses stories. Any comparison of texts immediately raises historical questions of composition, namely, source, dating and redaction. These are valid questions, and attempting answers to them would contribute to our understanding of the background of the text and inform our reading of it. However, the literary approach, privileging the received text and the canonical order, has been established as an alternate primary line of inquiry. It recognizes the primary story covered by Genesis-2 Kings as a complex discourse, regulated by the skilful interplay of ideological, historiographic and aesthetic concerns. This discourse, as we have noted, is inherently "dialogic" in nature, the restraint of the narrator inviting the reader's response. Locating the Elijah narratives within Genesis-2 Kings, we may read and respond to them vis-à-vis the "earlier" Moses stories. While conceding the subjectivity of such a strategy, as against the self-claimed objectivity of the historical methods, we operate within the demands of the discipline and rigour of the literary approach, attempting a close reading of the text, staying sensitive to its theological implications.

As concerns the Elijah corpus itself, we acknowledge the compositional and textual issues. There is disagreement on the unity of the main body of the prophetic narrative, namely, 1 Kgs 17-19;[11] and 2 Kgs 1 is customarily regarded as two independent narratives reworked into one.[12] As regards textual problems, 2 Kgs 1:17-18 presents difficulties with regnal synchronization between Israel and Judah.[13] More significantly to our reading, there is debate on 1 Kgs 19:9-14 on the issue of sequence, as posed by the doublet of question and answer.[14] Preferring to privilege the final form of the text, we will not engage with these issues. However, traditio-historical and form critical proposals will be drawn upon where they nuance the narrative reading.

In our exegesis, we compare the MT with the LXX, noting how this earliest rendering construes the Hebrew text. Largely, we do not engage in translation issues; thus, for convenience, we note the NRSV (unless specified otherwise). We have not included the MT because of constraint of space.

We will find ourselves identifying in the Elijah stories theological emphases from Deuteronomy, and this is relevant considering that Deuteronomy belongs to the Mosaic corpus; and, of course, this is compatible in historical-critical terms with the compositional hypothesis of the Deuteronomistic History.

3. The Text Under Study

We recognize 1 Kgs 16:31-1 Kgs 22:40 as the chronicle covering the reign of the Omride, Ahab. It records the famine in Ahab's reign, his wars against Aram, the irregularities in his administration (as in the incident of Naboth), and his joint campaign with Judah against Aram, which results in his death. As in most other regnal accounts in Kings, in each of these accounts Yahwist prophets play a part; some named, like Elijah and Micaiah ben Imlah, some anonymous; some operating individually, some in groups; some straightforward,

---

11. For attempts to recover the history of the text/the historical Elijah, see e.g., Seebass (1973), 121-36, on 1 Kgs 18; Jepsen (1971), 298-99 on 1 Kgs 18; Stamm (1966), 327-34 on 1 Kgs 19; Nordheim (1978), 154-59 on 1 Kgs 19. Smend (1975²), 525-43 treats the redaction of the section 1 Kgs 17-19. Cf. Carlson (1969), 416-39. Arguing literary unity are, e.g., Cohn (1982), 333-50, on 1 Kgs 17-19; Jobling (1978), 63-86, on 1 Kgs 17-18; Hobbs (1984), 327-34, on 1 Kgs 1-2.
12. Koch (1969), 187-88; DeVries (1978), 62.
13. See Hobbs (1985), 3-4.
14. For a survey of proposals, see Würthwein (1970), 152-166.

and some, like the 400 consulted before the battle of Ramoth-gilead, not so straightforward.

1 Kgs 22:51-2 Kgs 1:18 is the account of the reign of Ahab's successor Ahaziah, and this account also contains a prophetic component, forming part of the Elijah narratives. 2 Kgs 2, curiously, stands outside the flow of regnal history, between reigns, and relates a story of prophetic succession.

We will pick out the Elijah "cycle" from this general framework of regnal chronicle, and not engage with the other prophet of significance in the Ahab narrative, Micaiah. Our interest lies in tracking resonance with the Moses stories, and we find that 1 Kgs 19 and 2 Kgs 2 are richest in this respect. Thus, we will treat these at greater length. Of the textual chapters in which Elijah appears, 1 Kgs 21 will not be studied on its own, but referred to in the course of discussion on 2 Kgs 2, since the Naboth incident is more Ahab's story than Elijah's.

There are two OT texts outside the Elijah-Elisha cycles where Elijah finds mention, namely, 2 Chron. 21:12 (which is textually problematic) and Mal. 4:5. We shall not engage with these, since neither would contribute to our particular study.

CHAPTER 2

1 Kings 16:29-17:24: The Drought

As is common in the regnal accounts in Kings, the prophetic narrative is embedded within the account of the king's reign. Given the tenor of his opening speech, Elijah's entrance is forceful and dramatic; it adds to the tension of the narrative that he is introduced with neither antecedent nor title. It becomes the reader's task to work out his reliability as the narrator develops Elijah's character in the context of the plot. Alongside this exercise, we keep our ear sensitive to any resonance with the Moses stories, to see how this would nuance our reading of the text.

1. Ahab Begins his Reign

Ahab's reign is introduced with the usual regnal resumé (1 Kgs 16:29-33), expanded to accommodate instances in proof of the increasing wickedness of the Omrides. His taking of Jezebel of Sidon for queen recalls the narrator's censure of Solomon's Sidonian wives (1 Kgs 11:1-5). The association anticipates a severe political corollary (cf. 1 Kgs 11:9-13).

The narrator selects for attention the cultic consequences of the alliance, namely, a series of projects,[1] and brackets the list with the assessment of Ahab's sins as unprecedented (vv.30, 33b): "more than all before him"—מכל אשר לפניו. Indeed the concentric structure of the resumé heavily emphasizes Ahab's cultic sins.[2] It fits the logic of the larger narrative of Kings that the entrance of Elijah, pronouncing prophetic judgment, should almost immediately follow the inclusio of indictment.

V.34 is the briefly narrated episode of the rebuilding of Jericho, seemingly unconnected with the narrative in progress, since, it is neither part of the introductory regnal resumé, nor of the extensive prophetic traditions that follow.[3] Conroy argues for both lexical and

---

1. Emerton (1997), 295.
2.   A v.30   General religious evaluation
    B vv.31-33a Specific instances of irreligious behaviour
    A' v.33b   General religious evaluation
    Conroy (1996), 213.
3. So Jones (1984²), 298; Tov (1992), 346-47.

thematic links. At the verbal level, both Ahab and Hiel are seen to engage in construction projects, and both projects are contrary to the will of the LORD. If Ahab's buildings directly contravene the covenantal obligations, Hiel's is in defiance of the ancient curse on the rebuilder of Jericho (Josh. 6:26). Both Ahab and Hiel are each the subject of three verbs that belong loosely in the semantic field of "construction"—√קום, √בנה, √עשה and √בנה, √יסד, √נצב respectively. Thematically, Conroy argues three parallels which emerge in the larger narrative. First, like Hiel's sons, two of Ahab's sons and successors die untimely deaths.[4] Secondly, there is the motif of the prophetic word. Both sets of sons die by the fulfillment of it (2 Kgs 1:17; 9:26). Thirdly, the town names Bethel and Jericho recur in 2 Kgs 2, a narrative that revolves around Elijah and Elisha, each prophet having to do with the death of one of Ahab's sons.[5] Thus, concludes Conroy, the Hiel incident performs at once, both an analeptic and a proleptic narrative function. It links back to Josh. 6:26, and more immediately to the preceding section, namely, 1 Kgs 16:29-33. The latter contact sets up an analogy between Ahab and Hiel which, in turn, may be read as proleptic as regards various aspects of the Elijah-Elisha material.[6] Conroy's thesis is not implausible.

Another possibility is that this construction is an addendum to the list of Ahab's other prohibited projects, stated earlier, in the sense that it would have required the king's patronage, or at the very least, his overriding permission.[7] Certainly, a deep sense of foreboding is created by the stirring up and actualization of this ancient curse, reaching far back into the history of Israel. Long's summary is appropriate: "It is as though the editor saw that the troubles that were to beset Ahab's reign were anticipated in this little event. With irony, perhaps, normally praiseworthy building activity revives a dormant curse as a sort of omen for the regime."[8]

---

4. Thus, following the general practice for Israelite kings who die unnatural deaths, neither Jehoram nor Ahaziah are given burial notices. (Ahab is an exception). Halpern and Vanderhooft (1991), 192.
5. "...we would propose that the function of this building notice in 1 Kgs 16, 34 is to pave the way for the mention of Jericho in the 'Ascension of Elijah' unit in 2 Kgs 2." Bailey (1990), 166-67, n.145.
6. Conroy, (1996), 214-16.
7. E.g., Wiseman (1993), 163; Rice (1990), 138-39; Fretheim (1999), 92. Brueggemann may be cited to represent another angle: if by Hiel, a building project sponsored by Ahab is intended, and if the sons are seen as "foundation sacrifice," then, "the function of this verse is to make clear how Ahab has degraded covenantal practice, how cheap life is, and how arrogant royal practice has become." (2000), 204.
8. Long (1984), 174.

2. The Drought

2.1. 1 Kings 17: 1-7: Elijah Predicts a Drought

The reticence of the narrator is a striking feature of the introduction of Elijah into the story of Ahab's reign. He is introduced "midcareer, at an indeterminate age, with no biographical details preceding or to follow."[9] Though his name itself is suggestive of the direction of his religious loyalties (אליהו—"my God is YHWH"), at this point, the reader has only Elijah's word to assess him by. The narrator allows ambiguity by preferring not to use the usual introductory titles ("prophet"/"man of God") for such a person. Since he claims intimacy with and obedience to the LORD (as the phrase "before whom I stand" implies),[10] the implication is that his communication (לפי דברי/"the mouth of my word") is of the LORD. Moreover, Elijah covers the content of his message with a grave oath, which offers, as Long observes, a divine sanction for the truth of what the prophet is about to say. "Like a prophecy, the oath announces to King Ahab an irrevocable state of affairs bound to weigh on his rule."[11] However, there is opacity here that the narrative to come must dissolve, and indeed, Elijah's relationship with and representation of the LORD will form one of the themes of this chronicle, culminating in 2 Kgs 2:12 with his being "taken." The narrator prefers to tell Elijah's story subtly; rather than lead the reader with his own assessment of Elijah, as he has done with Ahab, he prefers to create a string of opportunities for the reader to work out for himself the reliability of Elijah's opening declaration.

A second case in point of the narrator's reticence is that he neither confirms nor denies either by his own comment or through Elijah that the drought follows on the list of the sins drawn out earlier.[12] It is for the reader to make the connection between the sins catalogued and the announcement of the drought, not only because of their juxtaposition, but from the deuteronomic echoes created. "The LORD will change the rain of your land into powder and only dust shall come down from the sky until you are destroyed" (Deut. 28:24) should Israel forsake (עזב√) the LORD (Deut. 28:20) and follow other

---

9. Brichto (1992), 123.
10. Elijah will use the expression again with the same asseverative force in 1 Kgs 18:15, as does his successor Elisha (2 Kgs 3:14; 5:16).
11. Long (1984), 179. Blank (1950/51), 73-95; Lehmann (1969), 74-92.
12. Fretheim is representative of the consensus that the "spirited stories about Elijah…address directly issues of idolatry that have been raised in the preceding chapters, but the narrator…is less visible; the stories themselves carry the freight of his concerns." (1999), 94.

gods (אחרי √הלך) (Deut. 28:14).[13] These echoes become keenly relevant to this particular apostasy, for Elijah's declaration not only reminds that the LORD he champions is "the God of Israel," but makes abundantly clear who is in control of rain.[14] Ahab's choice to serve another "lord," Baal of the thunderstorm, is challenged head on.[15] Indeed, the belief that the absence of rain means the absence of Baal is not only invoked, but also ingeniously deployed against him; this will turn out to be the first strike in an elaborate deconstruction of Ahab's favoured deity.[16] As for the deuteronomic formulaic verbs for apostasy √עזב and אחרי √הלך, the narrator will introduce them at key points in the narrative to come (1 Kgs 18:18), confirming the connections the reader is making at this early stage.

A third subject on which the narrator is covert, yet creates anticipation of, is that of the people since they, ultimately, will be the primary casualties of the punishment pronounced by Elijah. In the light of the deuteronomic caveat that Israel's apostasy will invite the punishment of drought, the reader is invited to ponder Israel's culpability. The critical role of the "character" Israel in directing the route of the narrative emerges gradually (1 Kgs 18; 19:10, 15-18), and comes to a resting point with Jehu's purge of the Omrides and Baalists (2 Kgs 9-10).

Thus, in opening his narrative with the announcement of the drought, the narrator brings together his three key characters. The

---

13. "In nothing did the ancient world recognize the hand of God more directly than in the giving and withholding of rain." Skinner (n.d.), 223. In OT belief, the LORD is the only God who can give rain (Jer. 14:22; cf. Isa. 30:23; Jer. 10:13; 30:23; 51:16; etc). Obedience to him brings the blessing of abundant rain (Lev. 26:4), but sin causes him to withhold it (Deut. 11:10-17; 1 Kgs 8:35-36; Jer. 5:24; 14:3-4). Thus, Jeremiah's confession on behalf of Judah (Jer. 14: 1 ff) and Zechariah's urging to ask the LORD for rain (Zech. 10:1). Patai (1939), 252-53.

    Jer. 14 laments the great drought on the land, confessing the cause to be Israel's sins (v.7). Cf. 2 Sam. 21:1-10.
14. Extrabiblical evidence on Canaanite myth helps set the story within its ancient context: "The Canaanites' equating of fertility with the presence of a live and vibrant Baal, who as the storm god sent the life-preserving rains onto the land, and their equating of drought and famine with the periodic death of Baal, set the stage for the stories in 1 Kings 17-19." Hauser and Gregory (1990), 11. Bronner (1968) pursues this polemic exhaustively over the motifs of oil and corn (77-85), rain (65-77), resurrection (106-122) and fire (54-65), all relevant to the stories of 1 Kgs 17-18. Cf. Cross (1973), 147-194.
15. See footnote above. Also, Ap-Thomas (1960), 151-52.
16. That Baal, who appears to be the target of the polemic that permeates 1 Kgs 17, is never mentioned is noteworthy, especially with reference to the narrator's "reticence," since appreciating this style of storytelling will have a significant bearing on our reading of the larger narrative, especially of Elijah at Horeb.

narrative following will play out their interactions with each other within the covenantal framework that relates their destinies.

Elijah's announcement of the drought is immediately followed by the divine command to go into hiding. Not only does this seal the authority of God on the subsequent action, but the reader is also alerted that Elijah's representation before the crown has been at the risk of his life.[17] The narrator records Elijah's obedience in what Walsh calls a "'command and compliance' pattern," not uncommon in Hebrew narrative. "The effect of the verbatim repetition," he elaborates, "is to emphasize that the obedience is absolute and complete: Elijah fulfills Yahweh's commands to the letter."[18]

לך מזה ופנית לך קדמה ונסתרת בנחל כרית אשר על פני הירדן
וילך ויעש כדבר יהוה
וילך וישב בנחל כרית אשר על פני הירדן

Elijah is sustained at Cherith in exactly the way he had been promised. The period comes to an end with the wadi drying up, a reminder that in the larger world of the story, the drought is well under way.

Even at this early stage of the Elijah narrative, the reader may pick up resonance with the Moses traditions, basically prompted at the lexical and story levels. First, both "careers" open with the hero making himself persona non grata with the existing political structures. Moses unadvisedly and criminally interferes with Egyptian authority and has to flee the country to save his life (Exod. 2:11-15). Elijah's challenging of the crown is apparently in obedience to his calling, but the result is the same; he too must flee. Both halt their flight by a watering hole in the wild; Moses by a well (Exod. 2:15), and Elijah by the wadi Cherith.[19]

Secondly, the stream that sustains Elijah over his stay in the desolate country "before" (perhaps, east of) the Jordan reminds of Israel's experiences in the desert beyond the Jordan of miraculous provision of water in times of great need, namely, the sweetening of the bitter water (Exod. 15:22 ff) and the water from the rock (Exod. 17:1-7; Num. 20:1-13). Strengthening this resonance is the food parallel set up with Exod. 16 (cf. Num. 11). The food arrives from an unexpected direction; in Elijah's case, birds bring it to him out of the sky, and in the case of Israel, the sky rains it down. Walsh rightly

---

17. E.g., Montgomery (1951), 294; House (1995), 213; Hauser and Gregory (1990), 13-14. Ahab will later put Micaiah into prison for his oracle against him (1 Kgs 22:26-27).
18. Walsh (1996), 228.
19. Fretheim picks up a different (but just as valid) resonance: "Elijah is a towering figure, a new Moses, who bursts upon the scene from outside normal channels (Gilead is east of the Jordan, away from the centres of power) and confronts the power structures in uncompromising terms." (1999), 95.

recognizes the significance of the lexical correspondence in operation between Exod. 16 and 1 Kgs 17.[20] In Exod. 16, Israel craves a return to the time "when we sat by the fleshpots and ate our fill of bread" (Exod. 16:3).[21]

בשבתנו על סיר הבשׂר באכלנו לחם לשׂבע

In response, the LORD promises "At twilight you shall eat meat, and in the morning you shall have your fill of bread," and without delay delivers as promised (Exod. 16:12-13; cf. v.8).

בין הערבים תאכלו בשׂר ובבקר תשׂבעו לחם

Elijah's menu and the times of the delivery of his meals recall Israel's supply, for Elijah too gets bread and meat in the morning and in the evening (1 Kgs 17:6):

לחם ובשׂר בבקר ולחם ובשׂר בערב

Further, the regular and miraculous provision of bread ("morning by morning"; Exod. 16:21) continued for Israel till they came to a habitable land, namely, to the borders of Canaan (Exod. 16: 35; cf. Josh. 5:12), just as Elijah's supply of bread and meat continued unfailingly until it was time for him to move to an inhabited place, namely, Zarephath.

Thirdly, there is the parallel of the prophet's obedience to divine command. This is not as obvious at this point in the narrative as it will be in retrospect, at the end of the Elijah narrative. Even so, one may note that the "command and compliance pattern" that Walsh sees as significant in the delineation of the contours of Elijah's service as prophet is very much the same as in the Plague narrative. There too the narrator relates the divine command to Moses and Moses' compliance thereof in parallel, and this could be read as a literary device employed to call attention to Moses' obedience. Examples may be found in the episode of the plague of frogs (Exod. 8:5-6), the plague of gnats (8:12-13; EVV 16-17), the plague of boils (9:8-10), the plague of darkness (10:21-22) and in the crossing of the Red Sea (ch. 14: cp. vv.16 and 21; and vv.26 and 27). In the plague of the water turning to blood, the description of the aftermath of Moses' act of obedience closely follows the prediction (ch.7: cp. vv.17-18 with vv.20-21).[22] In both the Exodus and the 1 Kings stories,

---

20. Walsh (1996), 228, 285. Walsh also rightly recognizes the significance of deviations from verbatim repetition, and notes here that the expansion of the LORD's statement that ravens will feed Elijah to the detailed notice in 17:6a is in order to set up an analogy with Exod. 16:8, 12. Cf. for example, Skinner (n.d.), 224; Fretheim (1999) 97.
21. Besides Exod. 16, Elijah at Cherith also recalls the episode recounted in Num. 11 where again, supply of meat is an issue and is mentioned along with manna.
22. Earlier examples are in the call narrative in the episodes of the staff turning into a snake (Exod. 4:3) and the leprous hand (4:6-7). In a conversation punctuated with Moses' reluctance to be obedient, these two events

the prophet's obedience is in essence an act of faith, and as such, an endorsement of the prophet's service. The episode closes with the first indication that the word of Elijah has taken effect; the rains have failed and the wadi dries up.

2.2. 1 Kings 17:8-16: The Oil and the Flour

The two Zarephath stories, arranged as they are in ascending climactic order, progressively build on the existing tension. Rather unexpectedly and ironically, Baal country is to be Elijah's next hiding place;[23] and rather illogically, a widow, among the weakest and most vulnerable socio-economically, is to be his host. That he cannot return yet to Israel speaks of the continuing risk to his life from Ahab. As commanded, Elijah sets off for Zarephath. Continuing his compliance, he seeks out a widow. The ensuing dialogue reveals the full effect of Elijah's calling down a drought. There was no prior indication that it would distress the surrounding peoples, least of all Baal's home country. Here, a woman juxtaposes verbs in disquieting paradox, speaking of a meal: "...we will eat it and we will die" (ואכלנהו ומתנו). This is more an inverted funerary meal than a meal for sustenance. Even before Carmel, Baal has lost.

Elijah's response unveils a further glimpse of the contours of his prophetic service. He employs the classic divine formula of encouragement, used regularly where the one encouraged is being called to exercise faith under threat to life,[24] and follows it up with the authoritative prophetic formula "thus says the LORD" which functions as preface to his salvation oracle. But more significantly, for the first time in the Elijah narrative, the narrator affirms the validity of Elijah's role as the LORD's agent and spokesperson. He does this both implicitly and explicitly. To begin with, he re-employs the literary device used in the previous episode (vv.4, 6) of creating a lexical parallel between prediction and outcome (vv.14, 16).

---

particularly stand out; Moses obeys without question and the LORD's point is proved.
23. Fensham asserts that in fact the main purpose of these two stories set in Sidon is "to demonstrate on Phoenician soil, where Baal is worshipped, that Yahweh has power over things on which Baal has failed." (1980), 234. Thus, in Zarephath, the LORD provides food while the god of fertility and vegetation lies impotent in the netherworld, and what is more, even prevails over Baal's slayer Mot in reversing death.
24. Though sometimes used by persons in authority to assure safety to life — e.g., David to Abiathar (1 Sam. 22:23), David to Mephibosheth (2 Sam. 9:7), Elisha to his manservant (2 Kgs 6:16) — it is regularly a divine guarantee of life — e.g., to Jacob, as he prepares to go to Egypt in his old age (Gen. 46:3), to Moses, challenged by Og of Bashan (Num. 21:34), to Joshua before the second battle with Ai (Josh. 8:1) and the battles with the Amorite and Canaanite coalitions (Josh. 10:8; 11:6), and even to Elijah himself, as he hesitates to face Ahaziah (2 Kgs 1:15).

כד הקמח לא תכלה וצפחת השמן לא תחסר
כד הקמח לא כלתה וצפחת השמן לא חסר כדבר יהוה אשר דבר ביד אליהו

Sandwiched between word and event, in both episodes, is a summary statement of obedience.

17: 5a

וילך ויעש כדבר יהוה

17:15a

ותלך ותעשה כדבר אליהו

Thereby, an auxiliary parallel is created between the two episodes, and specifically between the two prediction makers, which is sharpened by the commonality that both predictions concern miraculous sustenance in the face of famine. As the LORD is to Elijah, so Elijah is to the widow; and as much as the widow's unquestioning obedience is to her credit, so is Elijah's. Through these intersecting equations, the narrator skillfully orients the reader as regards Elijah's reliability as prophet.

In addition, the narrator concludes the episode with an explicit coalescing of the prediction makers—Elijah's word is "the word of the LORD that he spoke by Elijah" (17:16b). This assertion has implications for the previous prediction that the reader has heard Elijah make. Elijah's "my word" before Ahab is now placed beyond doubt as regards its origin.

As regards the resonance with the Moses stories, the continuing theme of drought recalls again the stories cited earlier, namely, from Exod. 16 and Num. 11. In the wilderness of Sin too, as in Zarephath, the dreaded expectation of Israel is of death by starvation: "you have brought us out into this wilderness to kill us with hunger" (להמית את כל הקהל הזה ברעב; Exod. 16:3). Walsh brings up here, "less obvious verbal allusions that connect the stories of manna with the second episode in 1 Kings 17." He points to the words "cake" (עגה) and "oil" (שמן) in the dialogue between prophet and widow, as recalling Num. 11:8: "and they made cakes of it; and the taste of it was like the taste of a dainty made with oil."

ועשו אתו עגות והיה טעמו כטעם לשד השמן

Further, says Walsh, the unique word צפיחת used to describe the flat round shape of the manna (Exod. 16:31) recurs in צפחת, the (possibly flat and round) juglet in which the widow kept her oil.[25] Indeed, since the word צפחת itself is rare,[26] it is interesting that the

---

25. Walsh (1996), 285.
26. It occurs in only one other place outside the Elijah stories, namely, in 1 Sam. 26:11-16. Within the Elijah corpus it recurs in 1 Kgs 19:6, where again, the circumstances immediately recall the miraculous feeding of Israel in the wilderness.

narrator uses it in connection with the food that saw this Sidonian household through the drought, and the possibility cannot be ruled out that he intends a subtle link with the food that stood between Israel and starvation over the wilderness years. And, just as in the case of Israel, where there was sufficient manna for all those lodged in a given tent (קהל; Exod. 16:16) for a great length of time (the idiomatic "forty years"; Exod. 16:35) till Israel came to Canaan, so also, the oil and flour sufficed for the widow and those of her house (בית) for (many) days (ימים), presumably (following Elijah's prediction) till the rains returned.

2.3. 1 Kings 17:17-24: The Widow's Son

This final episode in the drought series continues to explore the theme of Elijah's legitimacy as prophet. In fact, the narrator appears intent on leading the reader to a decision on the issue before he opens up the narrative to allow in the two other characters in his "triangle," namely, Ahab and Israel.

The widow's son takes ill and dies.[27] The narrator's development of his characterization of Elijah proceeds through the creation of another parallel, this time, of dialogue. The widow addresses Elijah thus:

ותאמר אל אליהו
מה לי ולך איש האלהים
באת אלי להזכיר את עוני
ולהמית את בני

Elijah relays the widow's need to God thus:

ויקרא אל יהוה ויאמר
יהוה אלהי
הגם על האלמנה אשר אני מתגורר עמה הרעות
להמית את בנה

---

27. It is regularly, though not always (e.g., Gray (1964), 342, following Josephus, *Ant.* 8.325) noted that any ambiguity in the narrator's description of the boy's condition—לא נותרה בו נשמה—is clarified by the widow's and Elijah's use of √מות, and by the narrator's account of his revival: ותשב נפש הילד על קרבו ויחי.

28. Given the context of Canaanite myth, it is not unexpected that the boy should die while the land labours under the rule of Mot, Baal's triumphant adversary. The biblical narrator then exploits this with polemical intent: in reviving the lad the LORD neutralizes Mot. See Hauser and Gregory (1990), 1-2, 19-20.

The widow's opening phrase minimizes the relationship between herself and the prophet;[28] Elijah opens his address with an acknowledgement of the personal and intimate relationship between him and the LORD. The distraught mother turns upon her guest, the "man of God," accusing him of unjustly visiting her sins upon her son. The prophet, in turn, berates the LORD for treating the widow, and indirectly him, with (undeserved) malevolence. Both are in agreement that a certain agency is responsible for the lad's death; the widow places the culpability on Elijah, and Elijah in turn projects it on the LORD.

If the woman speaks her frustration out to Elijah, Elijah cries out to the LORD. In this, the narrator exploits the opportunity to reveal the reciprocity in the relationship between God and prophet. Walsh comments: "Just as Elijah receives and acts upon Yahweh's word, so Yahweh in turn is responsive to Elijah's."[29] He argues that since the phrase "to listen to the voice of" (שמע√ בקול) is the usual idiom for "to obey," the "command and compliance pattern" seen hitherto is now reversed so as to make the LORD the one complying.[30] As Elijah requests, so it comes to pass, and the narrator reports it in almost identical language, just as he did with Elijah's compliance with the LORD's instructions:

תשב נא נפש הילד הזה על קרבו
ותשב נפש הילד על קרבו ויחי

This insight into the dynamic of the liaison between Elijah and God anticipates the occasions to follow when the LORD will hearken to the voice of this prophet at Carmel and atop an unnamed hill. In less unambiguous situations, such as at Horeb (1 Kgs 19), there is the possibility that the prior instances of the LORD honouring Elijah's representation by acting in accordance with it could bias the reading of the story in Elijah's favour.

This second episode at Zarephath creates an anti-parallel to previous one. Earlier, Elijah's position as prophet is affirmed in that he successfully represents the LORD to the widow. Here, he is affirmed in that he successfully represents the widow to the LORD. The two stories complementarily delineate Elijah's mediatory role as prophet, and prepare the reader for the narrative that follows, in which he will play out that role on a far grander scale.

As we noted, the telling of the miracle of the meal and oil is neatly rounded off by narratorial comment recognizing Elijah's authority as prophet. With this next miracle, the narrator takes the

---

Literally, "What do you and I have to do with one another?" Cf. 2 Kgs 3:13; Judg. 11:12; 2 Sam. 16:10; 19:23 EVV 19:22. In all contexts the idiom expresses the speaker's dissociation with the addressee.

29. Walsh (1996), 235.
30. Walsh (1996), 235.

acknowledgment further, by having a character articulate it. Though the narrator is on a higher level of knowledge, and generally his statement carries the greater force, the widow's confession is particularly significant for two reasons. First, the confessor is non-Israelite. When she was first introduced, the reader noted that she immediately recognized and honoured Elijah's religious affiliation, as evidenced by her oath (חי יהוה אלהיך). Later, the reader hears her address Elijah by the title "man of God," and understands that she is conscious of her sinfulness vis-à-vis this his position. Thus, her pronouncement following the revival of her son is rather unexpected:

עתה זה ידעתי כי איש אלהים אתה ודבר יהוה בפיך אמת

It appears that her second experience with Elijah has impacted her belief system in a way the first had not. This spontaneous confession forms an inclusio with the opening verse of the chapter where Elijah claims authority for the word he speaks (לפי דברי). Long is right in observing, "Structurally and thematically, the narrative comes to rest in this woman's recognition and confession."[31] This arrangement moves the climax from the restoration of the boy to the statement of faith, suggesting that the thrust here is to lead the reader to consolidate his decision on Elijah's integrity.[32]

Provan raises a point here that should be interacted with. He thinks that, in a way, the story ends strangely, since the widow's faith is focused on Elijah rather than on God himself. "It is Elijah's credentials as a man of God that have been validated (v.24) by the miracle, rather than God's ability to act."[33] There is something in this. The woman's experiences of the God of Israel are completely mediated by Elijah; as far as she sees, it is at his word that the food does not run out, and it is at his hands that she receives the lad revived. She is excluded from the knowledge that the LORD had designed that she should feed Elijah just as much as she is excluded from the event in the upper chamber. It is only reasonable then, that Elijah is the focal point of the expression of her faith. It is essential however, to see that her faith per se rests in the "word of the LORD"; it is that which has proved itself to her as trustworthy. As 1 Kgs 17 demonstrates so skillfully, this is the word that Elijah unleashes as "my word" (and it does his bidding) and also the word that "comes to him" (to which he deferentially submits). The

---

31. Long (1984), 186; cf. Brichto (1992), 127. The LXX glosses the opening verse to correspond even more closely with the final verse, deliberately strengthening the inclusio, and indicating the interpretative emphasis on it: διὰ στόματος λόγου μου—"through the word of *my mouth.*"
32. So, e.g., Long (1984), 187; De Vries (1985), 207; Nelson (1987), 108-09.
33. Provan (1995), 134.

dynamic operating between God and his representative is too intricate an enmeshing to be teased into isolated strands. The issue will be contested for much higher stakes at Carmel (18:36). Meanwhile, at Zarephath, the widow has already put her finger on a complex truth. [34]

Secondly, the declaration carries proleptic hints.[35] The Sidonian woman recalls the other daughter of Sidon the narrative has introduced earlier, "Jezebel daughter of King Ethbaal of the Sidonians" mentioned together with the account of Ahab's servitude of Baal. The narrator will later cast Jezebel against Elijah, and this Sidonian widow's putting herself on Elijah's side seems a blow already dealt against the queen. Looking to the narrative immediately following, the widow's reproach anticipates that of Ahab (1 Kgs 18:17). Further, the indisputable control that the LORD and his champion exercise over the spectrum of natural order and over human life and death, presage both the issue and outcome of the confrontation at Carmel. Most significantly, the events in Sidon look ahead to an Israel pressed to declare their religious allegiance, and the mood of the Zarephath story may be extrapolated to foreshadow a victory for Elijah; at Carmel, as in Zarephath, the operative verb with respect to confession will be knowing (√ידע; 1 Kgs 18:37).

As regards resonance with the Moses narratives, Walsh proposes that the allusions are not drawn randomly, but that each chapter echoes specific passages, and that 1 Kgs 17 recalls precisely, Exod. 16 and Num. 11. Walsh's case for Num. 11 is based on two lexical links. Firstly, Num. 11:8, as noted earlier, uses two words for manna, which are also found in the episode of the meal and oil; secondly, immediately following this description of manna, is Num. 11:10-12, which "has verbal and thematic links with the third episode in 1 Kings 17. In both the prophet accuses Yahweh of mistreating someone who deserves better; the prophet's complaint in both cases is *hărē'ôtā*, literally 'have you done evil?' Moses compares the Israelites to a child carried in the bosom; Elijah takes the child from his mother's bosom."[36]

Walsh's second verbal correspondence is weakened somewhat by the fact that Moses uses the same term to express a similar frustration at what he sees as the LORD's unfair treatment of the Israelites (הרעתה; Exod. 5:22). More comprehensively, as we will argue later, the highlight of Moses' expressed frustration in Num.

---

34. It is regularly noted that the widow's statement of faith recalls the confessions of other notable non-Israelites who come to know the LORD's power even more directly. E.g., Rahab (Josh. 2:9-11), Jethro (Exod. 18:11) and Naaman (2 Kgs 5:15).
35. Cf. e.g., Long (1984), 187; Nelson (1987), 112; Cohn (1982), 348.
36. Walsh (1996), 285.

11:11-15 is his death wish, and as such, this sequence is readily recalled in 1 Kgs 19 where Elijah expresses a desire to die at the LORD's hands.

3. Conclusion

In a shift that undermines the house of Omri, what began as a regnal account has quickly turned into a prophet narrative. Ahab's following after other gods proves to be his undoing. In the face of the deuteronomic curse, he is discredited as king in that he is now unable to secure the well-being of his people, and that prerogative has passed to Elijah.

The nature of the curse on the land reveals the intent of Elijah. On behalf of the God he serves, he has opened the first round of hostilities against the god Ahab has given himself to in servitude. However, the collage of stories so far is not to be reduced to preparatory work for the major event of chapter 18. These stories have their own integrity.[37] On one hand, they introduce and witness to Israel's God, and on the other, they establish Elijah's authenticity to the reader. As regards the latter, we note that form critically, the three stories are regularly placed in the category for stories that "extol the admirable qualities of the prophets and...inculcate proper attitudes towards them and the power they represent."[38] In 1 Kgs 17 Elijah's credentials are gradually built up: in the first story he is the obedient, yet passive, beneficiary; in the second, he mediates the oracle of salvation between God and the widow; in the third, he aggressively petitions God and is listened to:[39] "...as though there might be some question in the reader about the reliability of a prophet's word that propels the main drama (17:1), the events in vv.2-16 and 17-24 attest to Elijah's truth."[40] Having accomplished that objective, the narrative is now ready for the re-introduction of Ahab in 1 Kgs 18.

---

37. Cf. Fretheim (1999), 96.
38. Nelson (1987), 109; See Long for a detailed survey. (1984), 181-82, 186. However, one must avoid the temptation to centre the narrative on Elijah just so as to make one's point as does, e.g., DeVries. He classifies the first two drought stories as "prophet-authorization narrative"—"a marvelous story demonstrating the power of a prophet to prevail over institutional rivals, enhancing belief in prophetic authority to challenge usurpations of Yahweh's supremacy"—and the third as "prophet-legitimation" narrative— "a marvelous story demonstrating the scope and nature of a prophet's empowerment, identifying that prophet as genuine." DeVries (1985), 207.
39. E.g., Nelson (1987), 108.
40. Long (1984), 187. Cf. Cohn (1982), 335.

With respect to Mosaic resonance, the narrative framework immediately establishes nascent associations—it would be unrealistic to expect exact correspondences—with that of the Moses stories (Exod. 2-6). Both the protagonists open their careers with an offensive against the existing political structures; both flee the repercussions and find refuge at watering places in the wilderness.

1 Kgs 17 with its motif of miraculous provision of food (at Cherith and Zarephath) primarily recalls Exod. 16. That said, the secondary resonance with the Plague narratives (Exod. 7-12) must not go unmentioned. In both cases, the calamity descends at the prophet's word. A distinction is made for Israel as the plagues increase in severity (Exod. 8:18 EVV 8:22, 9:4-6; 9:26; 10:23; 11:7; 12); in the end, Israel's firstborn escape death. This finds a faint echo in the peculiar providential preservation, in the midst of life-threatening circumstances, of the prophet and the household that honours him; even death is defeated as the lad is revived.

Thematically, the confrontation, as in the Moses stories, is between a disobedient king and an obedient prophet, with the prophet being at risk from royal reprisal (cf. Exod. 10:28). A second plane of confrontation is emergent, namely, that between the LORD and his rival deity/deities (cf. Exod. 12:12); this theme will gradually occupy centre stage in the course of the episodes recounted in 1 Kgs 18.

CHAPTER 3

1 Kings 18: The Resolution of the Drought

The narrative thus far sought to establish to the reader the reliability of Elijah through the narration of a series of displays of power; the last of these elicits a confession, and the reader is led to understand this as the appropriate response to Elijah as a "man of God." The narrative also introduced associations with the Exodus stories, generating expectancy of a development of these parallels. The narrative now re-introduces Ahab, so that the story of the drought may be resolved. In the course of its three episodes, 1 Kgs 18 develops the characters of Ahab and Elijah, bringing them face-to-face once again. The conflict logically creates opportunity for the introduction of the party bearing the consequence of the drought, namely, Israel. With this, the resolution of the drought becomes compounded with the issue of Israel's allegiance, and with a demand for Israel to decide the reliability of Elijah and his God as against that of Ahab and Baal.

1. Towards the Resolution of the Drought

1.1. 1 Kings 18:1-16: Ahab and Obadiah (vv.1-6); Obadiah and Elijah (vv.7-16)

The narrative technique employed in 1 Kgs 17 is recognizable in the opening verses of chapter 18. For the third time, the word of the LORD is used to dislodge the plot from its current resting point and drive it forwards. The explanation following the customary imperative לך is however, not as straightforward as in the previous cases. The purpose of Elijah's showing himself to Ahab is in order that the LORD may send rain (ואתנה מטר) on the earth, but how the one will bring about the other is not clarified. However, the reader recalls that in the case of Zarephath, though the LORD assured that he has ordained a widow to feed Elijah, the unfolding story of Elijah's compliance revealed Elijah's own initiative in actualising this arrangement. Extrapolating this model, the likelihood is that it is up to Elijah now to work out the modus operandi for bringing the drought to an end.¹

As before, the prophet's submission to the order is immediate and complete, and this is indicated—again, as before—in the use of parallel language to describe command and compliance (here, the verbs √הלך and √ראה).

Obadiah's role is significant in that it develops the characterisation of the two main players of the larger narrative, namely, Ahab, an account of whose reign it is, and Elijah, whose life work it becomes to counter Ahab and his house. Obadiah is introduced by his official position at the palace, and with a summary theological evaluation; the latter is immediately supported with an example of his deeds—a hundred Yahwist prophets owe him their lives (vv.3-4).² It invites comparison with Ahab's regnal summary, and Ahab does not come off well. Neither does Jezebel. The mention of Jezebel appears incidental to the recounting of Obadiah's zeal for the LORD, but two other purposes are served. Mainly, it introduces the darkest actor in the affairs of the house of Ahab, and that on a suitably disquieting note. Secondarily, it creates a lexical link with Ahab through the verb √כרת (vv.4-5). While she "cuts off" Yahwist prophets, the concern that occupies Ahab is that his livestock is not "cut off." Ahab's culpability is amplified by this juxtaposition³ and by being linked with his viciously Baalist queen.

Next, Obadiah's long and distraught response to Elijah's command does nothing to improve Ahab's image. Rather than follow the path of repentance that Solomon sets out for a nation distressed by drought (1 Kgs 8: 35-36), Ahab is seen to be turning his energies to seeking out Elijah, and that not with kind intent, as the LORD's protective hiding of his prophet suggests.⁴ This means that unlike Obadiah or even the Sidonian widow, Ahab is unable to make the connection between his own sin and the threat of death

---

1. Cf. Rice (1990), 147.
2. Like Elijah, Obadiah bears a theophoric name, declaring he is in the LORD's service. True to his name, his behaviour mirrors the LORD's. He protectively hides prophets, and sustains them with bread and water.
3. "On the surface of it, the king's concern is admirable...[b]ut...the narrator creates a context that puts Ahab in a very bad light...[in] contrast between himself and Obadiah: because of the drought, Ahab is unable to provide sustenance for his animals; despite the drought, Obadiah is able to provide bread and water for the prophets of Yahweh." Walsh (1996), 239.
4. The LXX makes an exegetical substitution into Obadiah's statement reflecting its particularly severe characterisation of Ahab as one capable of wanton destruction: "...and if they said, He is not [here], then has he set fire to the kingdom and its territories, because he has not found thee" (18:10).

that lies over his land.⁵ From his own mouth, the reader will hear him deflect the troubles of Israel onto Elijah. Obadiah's fear is not so much that he must inform Ahab of Elijah's reappearance—indeed, he would welcome clues to his whereabouts—but that Elijah may disappear as is his wont.⁶ Ahab's rage at having his raised expectations unmet, would seek satisfaction, even if it meant the death of an apparently trustworthy and high-ranking official (v.12a). Obadiah repeatedly endeavours to impress this on Elijah (vv.9, 12, 14); indeed he uses it to both open and conclude his defence of his reluctance to obey Elijah. Of the three references Obadiah makes to his death at Ahab's hands, it is interesting that he uses the verb √הרג twice (vv.12, 14), and these occurrences frame the use of the same verb for his account of the actions of Jezebel (v.13). This is a brutal synonym of the euphemism √כרת that the narrator used earlier to link husband and wife, and creates a second lexical association between the royal couple along the lines of the first. Ahab's sword, it appears, can be as unrestrained and as misdirected as Jezebel's. Indeed, as Walsh observes, "Obadiah parallels his own likely fate at Ahab's hands to the persecution of other faithful Yahwists perpetrated by Jezebel."⁷

Though the object of Obadiah's frantic speech—with its grisly refrain, "he will kill me!"—is self-preservation, it ends up being all about Ahab and Jezebel. Not a statement but refers to their deeds and intentions, and the picture that emerges is of a crown flagrantly consolidating its apostasy by raw abuse of power. Faithful Israel, rather than the ambivalent Israel at Carmel, whom Obadiah and his hundred prophets represent, cowers in caves and under cloaks of anonymity, their fear of the LORD (cf. Obadiah's claim; v.12b) totally eclipsed by their dread of Ahab and Jezebel.

It appears, then, that the narrator has mainly set up the two interactions (Ahab and Obadiah; Obadiah and Elijah) not so much to advance the plot as to set the scene for the Carmel episode by developing the characterisation of king and prophet using Obadiah. Long sums up well:

---

5. The three-year famine reminds of the one in David's time. Contrary to Ahab, David "inquired of the LORD" in order to set right any failings of which the famine could have been a consequence (2 Sam. 21:1). Wiseman (1993), 167. Cf. Rand's exploration of the contrast between David and Ahab in the matter of the murders of Uriah and Naboth—(1996) 90-97—and Chinitz's paralleling of 1 Kgs 21 with 2 Sam 11-12—(1997) 108-113.
6. Provan (1995), 137; House (1995), 216-17; Rice (1990), 148; Hauser and Gregory (1990), 108.
7. Walsh (1996), 242.

The two scenes together…retard the decisive action in the interest of narrative complexity and suspense. We now know how severe is the drought, and how thoroughly powerful is Elijah's word (17:1). We recognize how deadly earnest is Ahab's pursuit of Elijah, and how necessary was his secretive existence east of the Jordan (17:3)…It is clear that Elijah's pursuit of God's word threatens his own person as much as it does King Ahab and the land. Gradually, the contours of confrontation have taken shape, sketched in dialogue, suggested in circumstance, implicit, foreboding.[8]

The result is that the dramatic tension now centres on Elijah's final word to Obadiah. Knowing that he has been in hiding from possible hostile repercussions to his calling down the drought, the reader waits to see how he will react to this gruesome bulletin from Obadiah. It appears that there is all the more reason now—now that the crown's negative reactions have actualised—for Elijah to return to a safe house. His response to Obadiah crowns the drama of the first two scenes, and sets the tone for the one to come. Elijah swears with solemn force that his intention is to appear before Ahab the selfsame day.

חי יהוה צבאות אשר עמדתי לפניו כי היום אראה אליו

This is the third time that the oath חי יהוה is heard since Elijah used it in his declaration to Ahab (17:1). The widow and Obadiah, fearful of death, have used it to assert their inability to comply with Elijah's command; Elijah uses it to affirm his determination to comply with the LORD's command in the face of a very real threat to his life. (The verb ראה√ links back to v.1, as does the idiom for obedience "before whom I stand"; היום suggests the keenness to comply without delay.) Further, since the reader has encountered this oath twice already, the change Elijah introduces to it leaps out. He swears by the LORD of Hosts, referring to God by his military title.[9] The battle for the loyalty of Israel has moved to the next higher level.[10]

---

8. Long (1984), 192. One tends to agree less with his reading of the Elijah-Obadiah encounter as a "proleptic evocation of the prophet-king confrontation to come." He thinks that Obadiah, like Ahab, assumes the worst of Elijah; under his polite and circumspect language lies the fear that "Elijah wants to have *me* slain by catching *me* up in his devious escape from Ahab's net!" (1984), 191. It appears more likely, as we have argued, that the narrator's intent to censor Ahab is better served by setting up Obadiah as a foil.
9. Treated in the sections on 1 Kgs 19 (v.10) and 2 Kgs 2 (v.2). Elisha uses it as well, and in a military context; 2 Kgs 3:14.
10. The contest that follows recalls 1 Sam. 17, the story of David and Goliath. There too, the battle lines are clearly drawn; a challenge is issued; the terms of the contest, that is, the obligations of the defeated, are agreed upon; and,

1.2. 1 Kings 18:17-19: Ahab and Elijah

The first words the reader hears Ahab speak reveal his opinion of Elijah, and in so doing, carry Ahab's characterization further. Here, one last opportunity is seized to stand Obadiah in the spotlight of narratorial favour, his shadow darkening Ahab. The latter's question on recognition, as Walsh observes, is identical in structure to Obadiah's but opposite in tone:[11] האתה זה עכר ישראל he asks, as against Obadiah's האתה זה אדני אליהו. Ahab does not use the label "troubler" lightly.[12] The word always describes a negative action, one which has a social dimension in that it has a harmful consequence on another person, or even the entire nation.[13] A likely possibility is that the Baalist Ahab believes that Elijah's intransigent stance re the LORD has offended Baal and caused him to withhold Israel's rain,[14] and eliminating this "Achan"[15] might be the solution (cf. Jeroboam and the prophet from Bethel; 1 Kgs 13:1-10).[16] There is something in this possibility, especially since Elijah immediately turns the accusation against Ahab, and faults him for the trouble of drought, in that he has given himself to the service of the wrong deity. (Here is a hint of the Achan-like fate that awaits Ahab; in the immediate context, as Provan points out, the state-subsidised Baalist prophets reap the fatal consequences of bringing trouble on Israel.[17])

The language of Elijah's indictment is characteristically deuteronomic: Ahab and his father before him have abandoned (עזב√) the LORD's commandments (מצות יהוה) and he, particularly, is guilty of following after Baal (cf. הלך√ אחרי אלהים אחרים). (E.g.,

---

the LORD is invoked by his military title, יהוה צבאות. The LORD's representative is clearly disadvantaged but triumphs resoundingly, following which Israel slaughters the enemy. If the reader should make these associations, it adds to the other proleptic hints of a victory for Elijah at Carmel.

11. Walsh (1996), 243; Nelson (1987), 115.
12. Cf. Brueggemann (2000), 222; Jones (1984²), 315; Nelson (1987), 116. DeVries translates, "Is that you, O Israel's hex?" and perhaps takes it too far in suggesting that עכר implies "one who is consorting with dark supernatural forces in order to do harm." (1985), 217.
13. Mosis (2001), 70; Jobling (1978), 70. Cf. its use of Simeon and Levi (Gen.34:30), and Achan (Josh. 7:25).
14. Walsh (1996), 243; Rice (1990), 148-49.
15. The noun form that Ahab uses of Elijah is used of Achan in 1 Chron. 2:7, which, curiously, names him עכר, rather than עכן. Saul is one other instance of a "troubler" (עכר√) in the instance of his handicapping the army with his ill-advised oath (1 Sam. 14:29).
16. Provan (1995), 137.
17. Provan (1995), 139.

Deut. 28:13-14.)[18] Elijah takes his life in his hands in standing up to a powerful monarch, especially considering the ad hominem nature of the argument.[19] Further, he demands rather than solicits Ahab's cooperation in requiring that "all Israel"[20] is to be gathered to him [Elijah], along with the sundry prophets that Jezebel patronizes. Having heard of Jezebel's murderous activities from the narrator and more vividly from Obadiah, and with this fresh information that she promotes the worship of Baal and Asherah at state expense,[21] the reader appreciates the scale of Elijah's demand. Thus, it is as unexpected as this new turn of events set in motion by Elijah's instructions that the ferocious Ahab of the episodes past meekly complies (v. 20).

The general note of resonance with the Moses stories is that of the confrontation between king and prophet. Like Pharaoh, Ahab is stubborn. The "plague" of drought called down by the LORD's representative does not prompt self-searching. He continues unrepentant, his anger directed misguidedly at the prophet (cf. Exod. 10:28). Meanwhile, as in Egypt, the land, the people and the livestock bear the brunt of the "plague." Like Moses, Elijah presents himself before the king repeatedly, persevering undaunted in the face of severe resistance. As with Moses, his obedience to the divine command is to the letter, and his representation of the LORD is authoritative. The issue at stake continues to be the LORD's people, Israel.

---

18. The case of the Omrides recalls Israel following the death of Joshua, as recounted in the summary introduction to the book of Judges. They recurrently and regularly abandoned the LORD and served Baal and the Ashtaroth (ויעזבו את יהוה ויעבדו לבעל ולעשתרות). Therefore, "the hand of the LORD was against them to bring misfortune, as the LORD had warned them and sworn to them; and they were in great distress." (Judg. 2:13, 15). This theological logic underlies the regnal accounts in Kings, and drives the climactic oration over the fall of Israel (2 Kgs 17:5-23).
19. Gray (1964), 349.
20. Cohn comments on the repeated "all" (כל) Israel in 1 Kgs 18:19-21, 24, 30, 39 as stressing hyperbolically, the historic significance of the event now taking place. (1982), 340, n.17. See Flanagan (1976) for a traditio-historical hypothesis of the Deuteronomist's use of the phrase כל ישראל as a technical term.
21. Cf. 2 Sam. 9:9-11; 1 Kgs 2:7.

2. The Contest at Carmel

2.1. 1 Kings 18:20-24: Either/Or Rather than Both/And

As repeatedly seen over the narrative, compliance is once more indicated lexically. Elijah's imperatives are obeyed—Ahab "sends" and "gathers" (שלח√, קבץ√) the two groups (הנביאים, כל ישראל) to the designated place (אל הר הכרמל).[22] When used with a pair as unlikely as Elijah-Ahab, the command-compliance pattern is richly ironical. As concerns characterisation, the effect is to reinforce the authority of the prophet, and somewhat weaken Ahab's portrayal as Pharaoh to Elijah's Moses. The latter could be intentional, for it prepares the reader for a new face to play Pharaoh. Ahab will drop into the role of non-participant at the contest and then continue in compliance with Elijah, moving over for Jezebel.[23] The sharing out of this role between the royal pair is consistent with the narrator's portrayal of Jezebel as Ahab's active partner in crime.

Elijah's opening statement at once clarifies that the party that is foremost in his concerns is Israel, and that the issue that moves him is their religious loyalty. It also spells out Elijah's position—he is intolerant of the idea that Israel may accommodate more than one deity into their religious allegiance, and imposes that view upon the people, challenging them to a choice. Fretheim's puts it well when he says, "This story might be called a dramatized form of the First Commandment..."[24]

Walsh correctly evaluates the situation thus: "Since Yahweh is on the side of exclusivism and Baal is not, even a willingness to consider choosing moves one toward Yahweh." Thus, Israel's silence communicates not only their refusal to be drawn into choice, but also their inability to see the two deities as rivals. Elijah then proceeds to address the latter by setting up a contest that will pit the two against one another. The expectation is that one of the two will emerge victorious, again a Yahwist premise. Significantly, this draws Israel into responding favourably. "They begin, without

---

22. It is regularly noted with puzzlement that the 400 prophets of Asherah receive no mention. However, it is not explicitly stated that they are absent, either. It is possible that they are included in the group of prophets Ahab has gathered at Carmel. Cf. Long (1984), 193. One surmises that since the immediate issue is the return of rains, it is germane that the Baalist prophets (representatives of the god of rain) merit the narrator's focus. They are pitted against Elijah, who proves them false and enforces on them the penalty for false prophets (Deut. 13:1-11; 18:20).
23. See Trible for a provocative discussion on the relationship between Elijah and Jezebel in terms of complex polarities. (1995) 3-19.
24. Fretheim (1999), 102-03.

realising it, to adopt a Yahwistic point of view," foreshadowing which party will soon emerge victor.[25]

The scene is strongly evocative of deuteronomic texts at various levels. First, at the story level, the assembling of Israel with the purpose of rehearsing their covenant obligations is reminiscent of Moses' addresses to the people in Deuteronomy. Secondly, and of critical significance, is the conceptual resonance, embedding within its matrix, the linguistic. A brief reference to two texts will help make the point.

In Deut. 11:26-28, Moses succinctly brings to focus the alternatives he has been setting out so painstakingly (starting Deut. 5:1). Relevant to 1 Kgs 18 is that one of the motivations that Moses uses to force a choice concerns seasonal rain. The promise of Canaan as one "watered by rain from the sky, a land that the LORD your God looks after...from the beginning of the year to the end of the year" is turned into a conditional blessing and curse. If Israel serves the LORD, "then he will give rain for your land in its season"; but if Israel allows itself to be seduced into serving other gods, "the anger of the LORD will be kindled...and he will shut up the heavens, so that there will be no rain and the land will yield no fruit." (Deut. 11:11-17). Underlying the proposition is a vein of polemic. Nelson observes, "The subject of rain and fertility seems to lead naturally to the topic of 'other gods,' to whose power these good things might be credited."[26] The warning is communicated in no uncertain terms, as is Moses' summing up of the alternatives: blessing for obedience; curse for turning away to follow new gods.

Moses returns to amplify this theme as he ties up the threads that have run through his exhortations. It is, as Wright observes, a "powerful summary...charged with evangelistic energy, emotion and urgency (cf. Ezek. 18:30-32)."[27] The repetition of "today" (היום; thrice in Deut. 11:26-28; four times in Deut. 30:15-20) emphasizes the immediacy of the decision. He lays out the choices in polar opposites so as to rule out any possibility of ambiguity whatsoever: life (חיים) as against death (מות) (v.15); prosperity (טוב) as against calamity (רע) (v.15); to increase (רבה√) as against to perish (אבד√) (vv.16-17); blessing (ברכה) rather than curse (קללה) (v.19); in short, the LORD (יהוה) rather than "other gods" (אלהים אחרים) (vv.16-17). Yet, as forcefully as Moses champions the choice of יהוה, he can do no more than set the choice before Israel; the decision-making rests with Israel.[28]

---

25. Walsh (1996), 245-46. Cf. Nelson (1987), 117, 121-22.
26. Nelson (2002), 139; cf. Wright (1998), 155.
27. Wright (1998), 291.
28. The summoning and gathering together of all Israel at Carmel reminds too of the assembly at Shechem (Josh. 24). There also, a prophet initiates the

1 Kings 18: The Resolution of the Drought

At Carmel, in the third year of a life-threatening drought brought on by apostasy, Elijah's address to Israel is marked with an urgent and piercing minimalism reminiscent of Moses' (עד מתי אתם פסחים על שתי הסעפים).[29] He makes precisely the same unequivocal demarcations as Moses did before, confronting Israel with a choice between the LORD and the "other god," Baal, (אם יהוה האלהים לכו אחריו ואם הבעל לכו אחריו), and draws the lines clearly between the two camps of prophets—himself all alone (נביא ליהוה)[30] and the group of 450 (נביאי הבעל).

The reader notes here that Elijah moves on the assumption that his God will prove himself. The reader also notes that the narrator (presumed "omniscient") has preferred not to notify the reader as to whether Elijah's project is at the LORD's prompting or if not, whether it has, at least, the LORD's authorization. But if, for the interim, we assume that Elijah operates under the licence granted to initiate moves towards a divinely decreed end, then his actions are indicative of the vigour of the interdependence and co-operation that drives the partnership between prophet and God. Simultaneously, the episode is also indicative of the intense evangelistic zeal that constrains Elijah (he speaks of it in 1 Kgs 19:10, 14) to appeal to Israel in the most persuasive manner available to him. Both features are so powerfully evocative that this point in the Kings narrative becomes the first of the key superimpositions the

---

meeting, the solemn purpose of which is to lead Israel to choose whom they will serve—the LORD or "other gods." Joshua mediates a renewal of the covenant, as (we will argue) does Elijah. There is no altar here, as in Exod. 24 and 1 Kgs 18, but a stone plays a part in the ceremony.

29. It is debated whether or not there are two distinct verbs in biblical Hebrew with the consonants פסח. BDB, 820, suggests there are, and discusses פסח I, "to pass over" and פסח II, "to limp." *KB*, 769, does not differentiate between roots I and II.

There are only three uses of פסח II in the OT. (1) 2 Sam 4:4, "and he (Mephibosheth) fell and 'became limp/lame'." (2) 1 Kings 18:21, "How long will you go limping with two different opinions?" (3) 1 Kings 18:26, "and they (the priests of Baal) 'leaped' upon/'hobbled' upon the altar," presumably in a reference to ritual dance.

Walsh cites Lev. 21:18, where פסח is listed among the disqualifying defects for priesthood. "As long, then, as the people continue to [פסח], they will be unfit for membership in Yahweh's cultic community. And so Elijah insists on a clear, exclusive choice between Yahweh and Baal." Further, the word creates a verbal link between the Israelites and the Baalist prophets, "underscoring that the people's 'limping with two different opinions' is in effect a Baalist stance." (1996), 245, 248.

Elijah uses the verb √יתר, "remain," to describe his survival of Ahab's dishonourable intent and Jezebel's pogrom. We will note its contextual significance vis-à-vis its synonym √שאר in 1 Kgs 19.

narrator mediates between the characters Elijah and Moses. The reader cannot but check his stride and turn his head for a second glance at this prophet so "like" Moses (Deut. 18:18).

As we move further into the story of the contest, this setting up of Elijah as one like Moses becomes increasingly evident. This is accomplished through two motifs: the LORD as Israel's God (vis-à-vis Baal), and the covenant.

2.2. 1 Kings 18:25-40: The LORD vs. Baal

The story of the contest, especially in retrospect, is seen to be thick with proleptic hints as to the outcome. These clues, carefully planted by the narrator, consistently expose the inadequacy of Baal as an option for the position of "God." Let us follow this theme through the Carmel story.

It was noted earlier that the first intimation comes when Israel accedes to the contest. In doing so, they unconsciously adopt the Yahwistic presupposition that one of the parties will prove himself at the expense of the other. Jobling calls this "the volitional turning point."[31] Another hint comes when the command-compliance pattern is turned against the proponents of Baal, this time, his 450 prophets.[32] Just as he directs them to, they ready the sacrifice and call on the name of their god (עשׂה√; קרא√—cf. vv. 25-26). While Elijah needed to dialogue with Israel and obtain their consent for his proposal, with the Baalist prophets there are no such courtesies recorded. Elijah turns to them with orders, and they wordlessly act upon those orders, establishing the norm for the proceedings that follow.

An indicator of Elijah's attitude towards the opposing deity may be seen in vv.24-25. The reader notes that in repeating instructions to the Baalist prophets, as in his laying out the rules of the contest before Israel, Elijah refers to Baal, not by name, but in relation to the addressee. Thus in v.24, he requires that Israel must call on the name of their god—

וקראתם בשם אלהיכם ואני אקרא בשם יהוה

—as in v.25, he requires that the prophets do similarly:

וקראו בשם אלהיכם

The namelessness of the opposition's deity, when juxtaposed with the name of Elijah's God creates a verbal imbalance in favour of the latter. There is a subtle dilution of the nameless one's potency, a potency his name would have conferred on him (Baal: "lord"/"master"). Elijah's disregard for Baal reflects on Israel's choice when he pointedly alludes to Baal as "your god" when

---

30. Jobling (1978), 71, 73-74.
31. Walsh (1996), 247.

addressing them. It subtly entrenches the charge that they have chosen unwisely.

Elijah's disregard shortly turns to open contempt. Half a day has passed since the Baalists have prepared their sacrifice, and called on Baal unceasingly, accompanying their cries with ritual perambulation of their altar. Elijah flagrantly provokes the Baalists with bawdy humour, egging them to cry louder to catch the attention of a god whose energies are directed towards other activities. The command-compliance pattern is deployed with devastating irony (cf. vv.27 and 28: קרא√ בקול גדול). On its heels comes an ominous note of anticipation. The Baalists gash themselves till blood pours out (שפך√) from them in futile libation, a clever prolepsis of the slaughter to come.[33]

The Baalist endeavour climaxes in a two-stage negation (vv.26, 29). Leading up to this is the motif of the Baalist advantage over Elijah, which is played out, first subtly and then in increasingly bolder tones, by intersecting similarities with contrasts. The motif emerges even as Elijah draws up sides: he stands outnumbered, one against 450. The procedures for both parties are laid out in laboriously repetitious terms (vv.23-34), but the verbal parallels serve to throw Elijah's handicapping of himself into relief. He allows the opposition the first choice of sacrificial beast[34] (and the risk here is that Elijah may be left with a substandard animal), and chooses to let them take their turn first (giving Baal the clear opportunity to preempt Elijah). As the contest progresses, he will further stack the odds against himself: he allows the Baalists to encroach into his half of the day (v.29); he soaks his sacrifice, wood and all, till his altar stands islanded in a pool of water. Against these contrasts is the lexical correspondence between the prayers of the opposing parties: "O Baal, answer us!" (הבעל עננו) and "Answer me, O LORD, answer me!" (עננו יהוה עננו). The climactic contrast that the plot is leading up to is the responses to these two prayers. Here, commentators rightly identify the verb "answer" as a keyword (cf. vv.21, 24, 26, 29, 37).[35] Baal's answer is recounted at two points. At midday, there was "no voice, and no answerer" (ואין קול ואין ענה; v.26). Walsh makes some significant observations here on the implications of this statement for Baal:

---

32. Holt suggests prolepsis in the Baalists' ritual self-mutilation in that the rites being forbidden in Israel (Lev. 19:28; 21:5; Deut. 14:1), they put themselves under penalty. (1995), 89.
33. Perhaps the procurement of the animals is also up to the Baalists: "Let them give us..." (v.23), but this is difficult to harmonize with "And they took the bull which he gave them..." (v.26).
34. E.g., Provan (1995), 138; DeVries (1985), 226.

> ...the narrator does not say, "Baal did not answer," as if Baal exists and can answer but for some reason remains silent. By phrasing the sentence in terms of absence ("There is no") rather than presence, the narrator hints at Baal's nonentity...the sequence "no voice, no answerer"...implies a causal relationship: there is no voice because there is no one to answer when Baal is invoked.[36]

Still, Baal is generously offered an extension of time to prove himself.[37] The conclusion is the same, and the narrator's repetition of the words ring with a damning finality. It powerfully moves the reader to pause to assess if this is to be understood as an isolated instance of Baal's non-cooperation, or moving beyond it, as an unqualified judgment on the nonexistence of Baal. "There was no voice, and no answerer, and no one paying attention (ואין קול ואין ענה ואין קשב; v.29)."[38] Brueggemann cites the poem of Isa. 41:21-29, presented as an imagined court case in which the claims of the other gods are examined and demolished.[39] The verdict, as at Carmel, is to nullify them into a state of nothingness: הן אתם מאין (v.24; cf. v.29).

The third item in the negation—ואין קשב—not only reiterates the absence of the deity being invoked, but may also be applied in another direction—the Baalists have lost their audience; even Israel has stopped paying attention. This would lead smoothly into the next contrast: Elijah summons Israel to draw near and they, who had rewarded his challenge with sullen silence, now promptly heed him. Symbolically, the gap between Elijah and Israel begins to close.

The climactic contrast, as we have said, is the one between Baal's non-answer and the LORD's spectacular response. The second half of Elijah's prayer is relevant here. He asks that he be answered so that Israel might come into knowledge on two counts: (a) "that you,

---

35. Walsh (1996), 248. Cf. e.g., Parzen (1940), 69-96; Nelson (1987), 121.
36. While the MT grants Baal the possible status of deity at least till he is proved otherwise, Tg. Jon. is less generous, eliminating it at the very start. Elijah challenges Israel: "How long are you to be divided into two divisions? Is not the Lord God? Serve before him alone. And why are you going astray after Baal in whom there is no profit?"
37. The LXX departs from the MT in v.29: "And they prophesied until the evening came; and it came to pass as it was the time of the offering of the sacrifice, that Elijah the Tishbite spoke to the prophets of the abominations, saying, Stand by for the present, and I will offer my sacrifice. And they stood aside and departed." Though the departure of the Baalist prophets would contradict their availability in v.40, their removal seems to follow logically on the removal of Baal from the competition: the god is proved nonexistent, his adherents disappear.
38. Brueggemann (2000), 223.

O LORD, are God"; (b) "that you, you have turned their heart backward."

ענני יהוה ענני וידעו העם הזה כי אתה יהוה האלהים
ואתה הסבת את לבם אחרנית

The correspondence of the first part to the rules of the contest is plain enough—"the god who answers by fire is indeed God (v.24)":

והיה האלהים אשר יענה באש הוא האלהים

Thus, unlike the non-answering Baal, the LORD answers and proves himself. The fire, falling from above, "eats" (√אכל) the sacrifice and the wood; then it goes beyond what a fire would naturally consume, devouring the very stones of the altar and not sparing even the dust that remains in its place. Reaching the trench, it just "licks up" (√לחך) the water. The verbs used of the activity of the heavenly fire are loaded with polemic against the Baal myth. While his rival lies lifeless in the grip of Mot, unable to receive the sacrifice his prophets prepare for him, the LORD is vigorously alive; he "eats" and "drinks" heartily of the "meal" offered him.

Though with this Baal has been more than sufficiently demolished, perhaps there yet is one further strike against Baal, embedded in the (b) half of Elijah's prayer. Elijah attaches a corollary to the proof that the LORD is God, and this is as intriguing and ambiguous as it is unexpected. Nelson sets out the two possible readings:[40] "While the natural assumption is that this means God will have turned the people back to fidelity,[41] it could also be taken as an assertion that God had previously caused their apostasy to Baal[42]." The latter reading is the more sensitive and sophisticated, and Walsh's engagement with it is representative. He notes that the verb √סבב is in the past tense though Israel has not yet come back to the LORD, and further, that this expression is not the usual one for the sense of conversion.[43] Indeed, √שוב is regularly used in this sense.[44]

---

39. Nelson (1987), 118.
40. So Tg. Jon.: "…may this people know by your doing for them the sign, that you, Lord, are God, and by your loving them you are asking for them by your Memra to bring them back to fear of you."
41. E.g., Montgomery, citing Rashi ("Thou gavest them place to depart from thee, and in thy hand it is to establish their heart toward thee") adds, "the divine Providence, not the heathen Baal…was the cause of the people's backsliding, all *ad majorem gloriam Dei*, as in the 'hardening of the heart of the people' in Egypt, and the temptations in the desert." (1951), 305; cf. DeVries (1985), 230.
42. Walsh (1996), 252.
43. BDB, שוב, 997; Graupner and Fabry (2004), 484-512.

Furthermore, the emphatic pronoun suggests that without this revelation, the people will probably credit the turning of their minds to Baal rather than to Yahweh. Startling though it may be, Elijah seems to be attributing to Yahweh the popular confusion of Yahweh and Baal that the contest is intended to resolve. If the people of Israel have been turned away from Yahweh, only Yahweh himself could have done it. In other words, Elijah does not even credit Baal with enough reality to be an effective rival to Yahweh.[45]

With the devastation of Baal accomplished, attention turns to his prophets. Elijah brings them down to Wadi Kishon and slaughters them there,[46] demonstrating a double victory: not only has he dispatched Baal's prophets to join Baal in non-existence, but also, he has proved Israel's conversion in that they seize the Baalists on his orders.[47] House proposes that perhaps there is here, on Elijah's part, obedience to Moses' injunction that prophets who lead the nation astray should be dealt with thus.[48] If so, it contributes to the growing evidence that Elijah models his role as prophet after his paradigmatic predecessor.

In essence, the Carmel episode is an encounter between Israel and their God. In story detail, the scene incredibly echoes another encounter, indelible in Israel's memory (Exod. 19). There is the mountain, at which Israel is gathered at a prophet's leading; the expectation of an experience of God; and the supernatural fire that grips the people with dread (cf. Deut. 5:4-5, 22-27). Carmel becomes Horeb as the fire of God falls:[49] "And the appearance of the glory of

---

44. Walsh supports his reading with examples that show that "the idea is not unusual in Hebrew thought. Yahweh can lead a people into error to trap them (1 Kgs 22:19-23), to gain glory through their downfall (Exod. 7:1-5), to chastise them (2 Sam. 24), to test their faithfulness (Deut. 13:1-3), and even for reasons unknown (Isa. 63:17). The underlying theological principle is that since Yahweh is the only God of Israel, all that happens to Yahweh's people is ultimately his responsibility." Walsh (1996), 252-53.
45. Ap-Thomas relates the slaughter to 2 Sam. 21:8 ff where seven Saulides are ritually executed to end a three-year famine. (1960), 154. In such a case, the technical term √שחט which is used of the act is particularly relevant.
46. The Canaanite myth is applied ironically: figuratively, Baal "dies" at Carmel, and in actuality, so do his prophets. The death however, is meted out not by Moth, but by the LORD's prophet and people.
47. Deut. 13:1-11. E.g., House (1995), 220; Nelson (1987), 119. Thus, it is relevant to their fate that the Baalists "prophesy"—ויתנבאו (1 Kgs 18:29).
48. Here, Exod. 19:18 is often cited for the theophanic associations of fire that descends from heaven. E.g., Fretheim (1999), 104. Others cite examples of theophanic consuming fire—Lev. 9:24; 10:2; Num. 16:35; Judg. 13:20; 2 Chron. 7:1-3. E.g., Rice (1990), 153; Long (1984), 195. Particularly resonant are Lev. 9:24 and 2 Chron. 7:1-3: the fire of the LORD "eats" (√אכל) the

1 Kings 18: The Resolution of the Drought

the LORD was like a devouring fire on the top of the mountain in the sight of all Israel (Exod. 24:17)."

ומראה כבוד יהוה כאש אכלת בראש ההר לעיני בני ישראל

Ahab's Israel participates, even if only in part and for a fleeting moment, in the experience of their forefathers.

Significantly for the 1 Kgs 18 narrative, there is a conceptual, theological overlap between Horeb and Carmel. Both are designed to be a faith-defining moment for Israel. The awesome divine self-revelation is intended to crystallize Israel's loyalty to this one God. While at Horeb this commitment is secured as a preemptive strike against Israel choosing any other god (cf. Deut. 4:10, 15ff), at Carmel, this commitment must be won vis-à-vis Baal. Thus, while at Horeb, the requirement is that Israel must be satisfied that the LORD is God, here at Carmel, it must be demonstrated to them that the LORD is God alone. This is done, as we have noted, by systematically demolishing the rival god and his adherents. The evoking of the Horeb narratives is of value in that no other background could better set off the non-negotiable and irreducible tenet on which Israel's faith was birthed, "The LORD, he is God."

The secondary effect of the resonance developed is to call attention to the Mosaic quality of the figure of Elijah. He is the prophetic mediator, standing between the theophanic, consuming fire and an awestruck people, his purpose being to lead Israel into knowledge of their God—who he is, and what choosing him entails. The functional semblance is strengthened by the other motif that runs through the Carmel story, that of the covenant.

2.3. 1 Kings 18:30-46: The Covenant Affirmed

In drawing attention to texts parallel to the Carmel story, Walsh picks two: Exod. 24 as a primary parallel and Exod. 32 as secondary. Let us first examine the latter briefly.

At the story level, Walsh equates Moses' argument in Exod. 32:11-13 (that the LORD will destroy calf-worshipping Israel at the risk of his own reputation) with Elijah's (that the LORD must demonstrate his supremacy for his own glory's sake). Following both prayers, he notes, is a "bloody scene in which the prophet, with the help of faithful Israelites, executes a large number of sinners. Moses enlists the Levites and together they kill three thousand unfaithful Israelites (Exod. 32:25-29); Elijah enlists the people of Israel and slaughters the prophets of Baal."[50] The chief difficulty with these parallels is that

---

    sacrifice, and the people on witnessing it recognize it as theophany and fall on their faces.
49. Walsh (1996), 286-87. So also, e.g., Cross (1973), 192; Roberts (2000), 637; Long (1984), 193; Cohn (1982), 341.

they are drawn from a story of covenant violation and as such, sit uncomfortably with the primary parallel Walsh sets up with Exod. 24, where the thrust is covenant making. Besides, Walsh traces out but an epidermal resemblance. In Exod. 32, the LORD's expressed desire is to annihilate Israel for faithlessness; 1 Kgs 18 opens with the LORD explicitly announcing the lifting of the penalty for apostasy, namely, the ongoing life-threatening drought. Equating the bloody deaths of "a large number of sinners" in the two plots is inexact, since the Exodus group consists of Israelites who were only recently covenanted, and the other of Baalist prophets (who, if we assume were "imported" by Jezebel, never had anything to do with Israel's God). A more convincing parallel to the purge of Exod. 32, as we shall argue in our discussion of 1 Kgs 19, is the purge declared by the LORD on Baal-worshipping Israelites (who had but recently confessed the LORD to be God at Carmel and then lost no time in turning to apostasy, much like their forefathers at Sinai). We conclude that a more distinct and cleaner note of resonance is obtained on comparing the Carmel episode with Exod. 24 alone, and turn to examine this.

The term "covenant" (ברית) does not appear in the Carmel story, nor are there any references to either the law or the commandments. However, (a) the announcement of the contest, and thus the rationale for holding it, flows out of Elijah's accusation of the house of Omri in general and Ahab in particular of forsaking the commandments of the LORD, and (b) at least three features in the narrative shape it so as to recall Exod. 24, the account of Israel's entering into covenant with the LORD at Horeb.

The most graphic component of the covenant motif is the structure central to the contest, namely, Elijah's altar. The narrator slows down the pace to note its state of disrepair and describe Elijah's rebuilding of it. As regularly noted, "the images rivet this moment to deeply traditional Israelite sensibilities."[51] Twelve stones are used, and the narrator pauses to make explicit that these are "according to the number of the tribes of the sons of Jacob," "stones symbolic of Israel's covenantal constitution."[52] The act and the explanatory detail recall Moses' covenant sealing ritual: he "built an altar at the foot of the mountain, and twelve pillars, corresponding to the twelve tribes of Israel" (Exod. 24:4).[53]

---

50. Long (1984), 193.
51. Long (1984), 193. The four jars filled thrice with water is also read as symbolic of all Israel. E.g., Ap-Thomas (1960), 153; Long (1984), 193.
52. Cf. Joshua's stone witnessing to a covenant renewal ceremony (Josh. 24:26-27). Walsh notes the drenching of the altar with a "libation." Moses dashes sacrificial blood against his altar, and Elijah uses a liquid no less symbolizing life, particularly under the prevailing condition of drought.

ויבן מזבח תחת ההר ושתים עשרה מצבה לשנים עשר שבטי ישראל

In Exod. 24, the purpose of the altar is to seal the concord between Israel and God (vv.7-8).[54] In 1 Kgs 18, the altar is a means to re-establish that concord by confession of its fundamental article, namely, the LORD's position as the God of Israel.

The altar and its function set up the second and most significant parallel between the two stories, namely, Israel's collective response to their understanding of the LORD. At Horeb they speak with one voice (ויען כל העם קול אחד) declaring their acceptance of the covenant and their willingness to obediently discharge their part in it (Exod. 24:3; cf. v.7). When this mood is evoked at Carmel, the effect is particularly dramatic because of the marked difference in context. At Carmel, the people have compromised the covenant and are clearly resistant to Elijah's efforts to change the status quo. Thus, when the conversion happens, it points to the depth of the impact of the experience undergone. Jobling calls it "the epistemological turning-point," the logical progression from the "volitional turning point" when they agreed to Elijah's proposal for the contest.[55] Spontaneously, all the people (כל העם) fall to the ground on their faces as one, declaring in one voice their recognition of the truth that thus far they have been unable to discern.

Embedded into Israel's response to God, both at Horeb and at Carmel, is Israel's respect of God's prophet. At Horeb, Israel listens carefully to Moses' every word, as he sets before them "all the words of the LORD and all the ordinances" and pronounce their willingness to complete obedience (Exod. 24:3, 7). At Carmel, it is hard not to notice that Israel's confession is made in the very same words that Elijah had used in setting out the terms of the contest. Here, Fretheim seems to miss the point when he comments that the words follow the traditional confession (cf. Ps. 95:7), and notably, nothing is said about the prophet.[56] One sees in 1 Kgs 18:39 an affirmation that goes beyond "The LORD is our God" of Ps. 95:7. The complete congruence with Elijah's words prior (even the definite article is retained—האלהים) is noteworthy on two counts. First, it is a credal acclamation of the LORD's absolute and universal

---

One notes, however, the functional dissimilarities of the two liquids. Walsh also takes as significant that the prophet "draws near" (√נגש; Exod. 24:2; 1 Kgs 18:36) as intermediary between God and the people. Walsh (1996), 286. In itself, the last is a very minor detail, but perhaps it does contribute towards the overall resonance.

53. Childs reads Exod. 24:3-8 as a ceremony of covenant **renewal** because of the emphasis on a ceremony at the foot of the mountain and on the people's acceptance of the covenantal law. (1974), 500-02.
54. Jobling (1978), 71.
55. Fretheim (1999), 104.

sovereignty,[57] affirming what has been proved over Elijah's years in hiding. Secondly, in its careful adherence to Elijah it automatically, succinctly, and undeniably affirms the prophet. Indeed, to say any more would be redundant, and even detract from the impact achieved by this striking, dramatic minimalism.

The third feature of the covenant motif carries over into the last section of 1 Kgs 18. This is Ahab's implied eating and drinking on the mountain (√אכל; √שתה), often read as a parallel to Exod. 24:9-11, where the institutional representatives of Israel eat and drink (√אכל; √שתה) on Horeb in the presence of God.[58] Roberts treats this subject at length.[59] She begins with Elijah's command to Ahab to "Go up!" (√עלה). The imperative clarifies the location of his meal, as in the case of the elders at Horeb, who are likewise commanded to ascend the mountain (√עלה). Both parties comply, going up to the place of theophany (Exod. 24:9; 1 Kgs 18:42). To illustrate Ahab's role in covenant renewal as sacral king[60] Roberts then cites the examples of Josiah and Hezekiah. Josiah's covenant renewal procedures[61] included a purge wherein the priests of the high places were slaughtered, a removal from the temple of all items of pagan cultus which were then burned in the Wadi Kidron, and the keeping of a covenant meal in terms of the Passover (2 Kgs 23; 2 Chron. 34:29-35:19). Hezekiah's desire to renew the covenant[62] results in the cleansing of the temple, bringing out the unclean items to the Wadi Kidron, the demolition of pagan shrines, and the celebration of the Passover (2 Chron. 29-31:1). Ahab's case is certainly well removed from that of these two reformist kings, and his meal is no Passover (the text does not even clarify if he did eat and drink, using only the infinitives of purpose to say that he went up "to eat and to drink"). Even so, Roberts' appeal to these two examples to make out a case for Ahab being prompted to a covenant sealing ritual meal is not wholly without justification, especially in the context of the resonance with Exod. 24. On another track, she cites the cases of two other kings, Saul (1 Sam. 9) and David (2 Sam. 6-7), to further her

---

56. "The point of the narrative is not just that Yahweh is the God of Israel, but that Yahweh is God, period." Nelson (1987), 120.
57. E.g., Walsh (1996), 286; Provan (1995), 139.
58. Roberts (2000), 637-44.
59. Cf. Widengren (1957), 1-32; McCarthy (1981), 285-87.
60. "The king…made a covenant before the LORD, to follow the LORD, keeping his commandments, his decrees, and his statutes, with all his heart and all his soul, to perform the words of this covenant that were written in this book. All the people joined in the covenant." 2 Kgs 23:3; cf. 2 Chron. 34:31-32.
61. "Now it is in my heart to make a covenant with the LORD, the God of Israel, so that his fierce anger may turn away from us." 2 Chron. 29:10.

argument that a ritual meal legitimates the enthronement of a human king and confers divine approval.

Ahab, Roberts argues, is not just a subservient compliant. "The active participation of the king in covenant renewal requires Ahab's sincere cooperation and devotion. Just as the people are able to recognize, at that moment, the power of Yahweh in the fire, Ahab is able to reaffirm his loyalty to Yahweh."[63] The LORD's acceptance of Ahab, she concludes, is confirmed by the coming of the rain. There is something in this. Ahab's readiness to submit to correction from a prophet is clearly affirmed in the Naboth incident (1 Kgs 21:17-29), and is a possibility at Carmel as well. It fits with the not entirely negative portrayal of Ahab,[64] and the narrator's efforts to consistently show up Jezebel as the "blacker" one. It prepares the reader, as we have noted earlier, for Ahab's role as neo-Pharaoh to be gradually taken over by Jezebel till at the start of 1 Kgs 19, she completely replaces him. Also, it prepares for the logic in the progression of Ahab's story, when he appears next in 1 Kgs 20. There, he is clearly under divine favour, twice being granted victories in unequal combat against Aram.[65] All said, Ahab's implied eating and drinking in the sacred place of theophany makes a significant contribution to the covenant motif.

The postscript to the motif is the return of rain upon the land. It was announced in prolepsis in 1 Kgs 18:1, in anticipation of Israel's and Ahab's return to the prescribed faith. Thus, it arrives once both people and king have been shown, in their own ways, to have renewed their covenantal bond with the LORD. It concludes the contest in a final and decisive statement for the LORD.[66] As House

---

62. Roberts (2000), 643. Cf. Appler (1999), 60. Contra Brueggemann (2000), 227: "Ahab is no player. Ahab has done nothing to turn curse to blessing."
63. Holt argues Ahab's similarity to Ahaz and Zedekiah, good kings too lacking in backbone to do as counselled by their respective prophets. (1995), 95-96. See Parzen's listing of biblical evidence for the Omrides' not being wholly unfaithful—(1940), 78-81; Waldman for the rabbinic view favouring Ahab—(1988), 41-47; Feldman for Josephus' picture of an honourable Ahab—(1992), 368-84.
64. The LXX has variants in three passages, which combine to paint Ahab even more sympathetically than does the MT—more weak than wicked, grieved at Jezebel's crimes and quick to repent of his misdeeds. Thus, "Ahab *wept* and went to Jezreel" (καὶ ἔκλαιεν καὶ ἐπορεύετο Αχααβ εἰς Ιεζραελ, rather than "rode and went"; 1 Kgs 18:45b); tears of repentance perhaps? If so, they fit with his reaction at the news of Naboth's death: "And it came to pass, when Ahab heard that Naboth the Jezreelite was dead, that *he rent his garments, and put on sackcloth*"; 1 Kgs 21:16 (LXX 20:16). Similarly, at Elijah's denunciation of his deed, the LXX's account of his repentance is more elaborate (1 Kgs 21:27-29; LXX 20:27-29). See Gooding, (1964), 269-80.
65. Cf. Fretheim (1999), 104.

observes, "Rain is not just rain here but evidence of the Lord's absolute sovereignty over nature and human affairs."[67]

The covenant theme, even more than the anti-Baal motif, showcases Elijah's role as covenant mediator. Moses-like, he initiates the assembly of "all Israel"; his altar is built to represent the people whom he leads into a confession of allegiance; he himself commands the obedience of Israel even as he mediates their obedience to the LORD; and, he leads the institutional representative into a meal celebrating the event. Thus, while 1 Kgs 18 is consonant with the relationship between prophets and kings, where the former are messengers who call the latter into account for failure to keep the covenant, the Carmel story particularly makes space to display Elijah as a prophet after Moses.

3. Conclusion

Looking back over 1 Kgs 17 and 18, the reader recognizes the enrichment of the narrative with Mosaic motifs. Taken individually, these may often be recognized in other regnal accounts as well. It is when they are woven together thick and close as in this chronicle that a remarkable resemblance to the Moses stories emerges.

First, there is the theme of confrontation between the LORD's representative and political structures. Ahab's people suffer a bondage they themselves do not recognize, even though they groan under the oppression of the drought. Elijah challenges this neo-Pharaoh to desist from "troubling" Israel. Ahab, however, is shown as persisting in his hardness of heart; the "plague" of drought and resultant famine does not prompt remorse and obedience, rather, it fuels his misdirected rage against the prophet (cf. Exod. 10:28-29).[68] Thus, the crown's defiance of God becomes a foil for the consistent and complete obedience of the prophet.

Secondly, there is the polemical nature of the narrative, re the rival "god" (cf. Exod. 12:12). The "plague" and the miracles associated with it strike a crushing blow to the credibility of Baal. Rain withheld by Israel's God brings Baal-country to its knees; the dead is raised in Sidon at a time when the state deity himself lies "dead" in the underworld; the faithful are miraculously protected from the "plague." The challenge of Baal heightens to a climax in the Carmel episode. The contest pits prophet against a state-sponsored

---

66. House (1995), 221.
67. The effort to bring Ahab into "knowing" the LORD (cf. Exod. 9:14) continues into 1 Kgs 20 (vv.13, 28). In the end, the erring ruler (Ahab/Pharaoh) will be ruined in battle (1 Kgs 22; Exod. 14), the ultimate disgrace for a king, while the prophet (Elijah/Moses) departs from the world with the highest honours (2 Kgs 2; Deut. 34).

faction, echoing the exchanges between Moses and Pharaoh's coterie of wise men (cf. Exod. 7:11; 7:22; 8:3, EVV 8:7) who eventually stand defeated (Exod. 8:14, EVV 8:18). Like the Sidonian widow, these Egyptians recognize the power of Israel's God (Exod. 8:15, EVV 8:15).

These two Mosaic strains create a third, that of the prophet in dual relationship with God and people. The Carmel story is as much an affirmation of the God of Israel as it is of his prophet. Nelson demarcates the story using the five proposals Elijah makes—sequentially, to Israel twice, to the Baalist prophets, to God, and once more to Israel. Except for the first one, which receives a non-committal response, all the others are promptly endorsed.[69] In addition, there are the proposals he makes to Ahab on either side of the contest story proper, and these too are received with submissive obedience. Especially in the light of Obadiah's building up of reader expectation of a ruthless and relentless Ahab, the manner in which Elijah dominates Ahab from the start is an index of his authority as representative of a party superior to the crown.

Nelson observes that Elijah is called "prophet" only well into the cycle of stories, that is, in 1 Kgs 18:36, as he approaches the altar to petition his God, and as the plot approaches the climactic moment of truth. Perhaps this is deliberate, "emphasizing his authority at this moment and underscoring the emptiness of the claim of the Baal prophets to that title,"[70] so-called prophets from the beginning. Elijah's own claim to be true prophet is implicitly bound up with the contest, since who he is, is dependent on who the LORD is proved to be. He makes this explicit in his prayer: "Let it be known ($\sqrt{ידע}$) this day that you are God in Israel, that I am your servant, and that I have done all these things at your bidding" (1 Kgs 18:36). As in the case of the Sidonian widow, Israel's coming into knowledge will be in terms of two integrally enmeshed components, the LORD and his prophet. If, as DeVries does, we may parallel this episode with 2 Kgs 1, where also Elijah requests fire from heaven, then these are both narratives of prophet authorisation,[71] for clearly, in the latter story, the fire is to come down "if I am a man of God" (2 Kgs 1:10, 12). The pattern is not unfamiliar, for this is the case in the Moses stories as well. At the Red Sea and again at Sinai, the integrity and dependability of God is meshed with that of his prophet (Exod. 14:31; 19:9). Like Moses, Elijah is proved to be as reliable as his God.

1 Kgs 18 ends with Elijah outrunning Ahab's chariot to the capital. Enabled by God he continues, as in the rest of the narrative till this moment, one step ahead of the Omride.

---

68. Nelson (1987), 117.
69. Nelson (1987), 118.
70. DeVries (1985), 230.

CHAPTER 4

1 Kings 19: Horeb

In 1 Kgs 19, the resonance between the Moses and Elijah stories is at its richest. The settings are brilliantly evocative, taking the reader from the edges of the inhabited world deep into trackless wilderness and on to the holy mountain. Here is the only story outside the Pentateuch to use Sinai/Horeb as locale; here again is the theophanic triad of earthquake, wind and fire, so significant in Israel's traditions; and on this mountain once more, a prophet holds dialogue with God. This section of the Elijah narrative, therefore, merits close examination.

The unity of this chapter with the previous Elijah corpus is argued both ways,[1] one of the points of debate being Jezebel's role; with the story having reached a resting point after Carmel, Jezebel sets the plot in motion again, but is then never mentioned over the rest of the chapter, even (as we shall discuss) at a point that would warrant it. However, we continue our close reading of the final form of the text.

1. 1 Kings 19:1-10: Moses, Elijah and the Death Wish

The key event in this section is Elijah's request that his life be ended. This finds parallels—largely conceptual—in two similar requests of Moses. It suits the flow of our argument to treat the Moses texts first.

1.1. Moses and the Death Wish

1.1.1. MOSES' INTERCESSION AT SINAI (EXODUS 32:31-32)
Moses' first request to die comes in the aftermath of the golden calf episode. Moses has already interceded to stay the LORD's intention to consume Israel. He has destroyed the image and overseen a bloody purge. His expressed purpose now in returning up Sinai is to make atonement.

---

1. E.g., Steck (1968), who demonstrated the redaction of four prophetic stories into the narrative of 1 Kgs 17-19. For arguments for the unity of this text see, e.g., Cohn (1982).

In admitting the degree of Israel's sin, Moses states it, as Moberly points out, in the language of the prohibition in Exod. 20:23:[2]
Exod. 20:23:

ואלהי זהב לא תעשו לכם

Exod. 32:31:

ויעשו להם אלהי זהב

Yet, in the face of Israel's flagrant law-breaking and deliberate rejection of the LORD, Moses pleads forgiveness. As Cassuto explains, the apodosis of the conditional sentence ועתה אם תשא את חטאתם—"well and good"—is not expressly stated, because it is self-understood, cf. 1 Sam. 12: 14-15.[3] But if the LORD will not forgive, מחני נא מספרך אשר כתבת—"blot me out of the book that you have written."

We may rule out the possibility that this is an "audacious challenge to Yahweh—"If you won't do what I want, just kill me!";[4] or that it is an "audacious threat" through which Moses submits his resignation.[5] Either tone is hardly likely, given his tentative approach—the אולי—into the divine presence, and given the tenor of entreaty in the intercessions of Exod. 32-24. Thus, Tg. Onk. paraphrases: "And Mosheh returned, and prayed before the Lord, and said, I supplicate of Thee, Thou Lord of all the world, before whom the darkness is as light!..."

As to how we are to understand Moses' request, there are still at least three possible readings. The wider view is that Moses could have been requesting to die in the place of an Israel out of favour with God. Fretheim suggests that Moses probes if one may stand in for many, with a vivid, though not literal reference to those who are God's elect people (cf. Ezek. 13:9; Mal. 3:16) and "offers up his place among God's elect for the sake of the people's future."[6] The concept of vicarious sacrifice is best associated with Isa. 53, where the Servant makes himself, or may be made, a guilt offering. The idea of vicarious sacrifice is unambiguously articulated in the Hellenistic Jewish text, 4 Maccabees. Charlesworth comments: "Doctrinally, the most significant contribution of 4 Maccabees is the development of the notion that the suffering and death of the martyred righteous had redemptive efficacy for all Israel and secured God's grace and pardon for his people."[7] In 6:28f. Eleazar says: "Be merciful to your people and let our punishment be a satisfaction on their behalf. Make my blood their purification and take my life as a ransom for

---

2. Moberly (1983), 57.
3. Cassuto (1967), 423.
4. Kirsch (1998), 272.
5. Coats (1993), 65-66.
6. Fretheim (1991), 290. Cf. e.g., Childs (1974), 571; Enns (2000), 577.
7. Charlesworth (1985), 539.

theirs." (Also 17:12f; cf. 2 Macc. 7:30-38). Charlesworth adds that the concept, though sufficiently well attested in apocalyptic literature (e.g., T. Benj. 3:8) and at Qumran (e.g., 1QS 5:6; 8:3f., 10; 9:4), was neither normative nor widespread in Judaism.[8] Though this does not rule out the possibility of an occurrence of this idea earlier in the canonical order, it weakens it somewhat.

A second alternative is that Moses could be asking to die along with unpardoned Israel. Cassuto sees Moses as saying, "I do not wish my fate to be better than that of the rest of my people."[9] The assumption here is that Israel still remains under the peril of destruction—en masse or otherwise. Moses' first round of intercession has won a concession from the LORD in that he has changed his mind on the annihilation of Israel. Moses fears that the LORD would destroy Israel over a period of time, either by his own hand, or by withdrawing his protection and leaving them vulnerable to being picked off by other peoples.

A third possibility is that Moses was asking for his death, independent of whatever fate might befall an unforgiven people. Thus McNeile: "It is sometimes thought that Moses here rose to a great spiritual height of self-renunciation, in asking God to erase his name from his book rather than leave his people unforgiven." Rather, "[I]f God will not grant his request, Moses despairingly asks that he may die; cf. Num. xi.15."[10] Similarly, Driver: "Moses would rather not live than that his people should remain unforgiven."[11] Such a reading would resonate with 1 Kgs 19, where Elijah requests death out of despair at his inadequacy.

All three readings are possible, the second and the third more so. The point we shall return to later is that here Moses is on a mission of overwhelming magnitude, namely, to gain atonement for Israel; not through the known route, that is, the prescribed cultus, for the High Priest himself stands implicated in the sin of idolatry, but by his own standing with the LORD. "The basis of all such intercession," says Barr, "is the sense of the freedom of God, the knowledge that even in his wrath he is not tied legalistically to a precise penalty which he is forced by his own nature to exact, or a procedure which he cannot but follow."[12] Should his attempt fail, Moses will have reached the end of a cul-de-sac. And he sees no alternative beyond failure other than death for himself, and so requests that death.

---

8. Charlesworth (1985), 539.
9. Cassuto (1967), 423.
10. McNeile (1908), 209.
11. Driver (1918), 356.
12. Barr (1963), 77 in the context of Jer. 15:1-4, which suggests that the intercession of a Moses or Samuel might have averted God-sent disaster.

1.1.2. Moses' Complaint at Kibroth-hattaavah (Numbers 11:4-15)

Moses' other death wish comes about in the course of yet another of Israel's complaints about provision. This time, they complain, not because they have nothing to eat, but because the manna bores them. Understandably, "the anger of the LORD was kindled greatly." The situation is "evil in the sight of Moses." (v.10.) On the other occasions that Moses loses his temper, the object of his anger is clear (e.g., Exod. 16:20; 32:19; Lev. 10:16; Num. 16:15; Num. 31:14). Here, it has to be inferred from his address to the LORD.

Moses opens with למה הרעת לעבדך—"Why have you dealt ill with thy servant?" He uses the same verb in another context, that of Pharaoh multiplying Israel's labour, asking the LORD, למה הרעתה לעם הזה—"Why have you done evil to this people?" (Exod. 5:22). Moses reasons that he has inadvertently needled Pharaoh into treating Israel with greater severity than before (5:23); since the LORD is Moses' commissioner, it is the LORD's door at which the evil treatment of Israel must be laid. Thus the LORD has used Moses to ill-treat Israel.

Moses uses a similar logic here, in reverse. He accuses the LORD of treating him ill, in that he has laid the burden of Israel upon him. Thus the LORD has used Israel to ill-treat Moses.[13] These two parallel cases of reasoning happen in parallel situations. In Exod. 5 he is caught between a recalcitrant Pharaoh and accusing Israelite supervisors, and he is unable to deal profitably with either. In Num. 11 he finds himself having to mediate between a demanding Israel and an angry God. This situation is different in that, in previous situations of physical demands, either the LORD directly answers with provision (Exod. 16:12) or Moses takes the case to the LORD who then makes provision (Exod. 15:25; 17:4-6). Here, however, both the LORD and the people are displeased simultaneously. It is likely that Moses' own displeasure is at this new and perplexing situation.

Moses opens his complaint with the erroneous assumption of ill-treatment which he states using the two parties as subject: "Why have you...?" and "Why have I...?" There is a sense here that he considers the LORD arbitrary and unfair. He can see no reason why the LORD must ill-treat him, or why he should not find favour before the LORD. This drawing of battle lines, and the arranging of him and the LORD on opposite sides forms the matrix to his monologue.

Jewish lore agrees that Israel could be particularly "spiteful" in its treatment of Moses:

---

13. In both Exod. 5 and Num. 11, it is striking that though the accusation is aimed at God, all the activity happens at the human level.

"If Moses went out early they would say: 'Behold the son of Amram who betakes himself early to the gathering of manna, that he may get the largest grains.' If he went out late, they would say: 'Behold the son of Amram, he ate and drank, and hence slept so long, that he had to get up late.' If he went through the thick of the multitude, they said: 'Behold the son of Amram, he goes through the multitude, to gather in marks of honour.' But if he chose a path aside from the crowd, they said: 'Behold the son of Amram, who makes it impossible for us to follow the simple commandment, to honour a sage.' Then Moses said: 'If I did this you were not content, and if I did that you were not content! I can no longer bear you alone.'"[14]

The implied accusation in Moses' opening questions is that he was never willing to take on responsibility for them; it was laid on him uninvited.

He strengthens his argument (v.12) with the most compelling reason for a person to take responsibility for another, namely, the obligation of a mother towards her newborn. In asking if he has conceived and birthed them, Moses leaves the unasked question hanging, demanding answer. Who then is Israel's parent? The emphatic use of the personal pronoun twice— האנכי הריתי...אם אנכי ילדתיהו—makes it plain that whoever the parent may be, it is certainly not Moses. Since he is not responsible for the two steps that bring a child into the world, it is entirely unreasonable that he should be saddled with the duty of nursing it. Then he explicitly states the LORD's responsibility in this affair: it is the LORD who promised the land to Israel's ancestors.[15]

Further, Moses adds, he is inadequate for this responsibility. He does not have the means to feed the people according to their desires (vv.13-14); by himself, he is totally unable to bear "all these people" and their demands. His sense of being overwhelmed comes through in his emphatic use of personal pronouns לא אוכל אנכי לבדי; he sums up with כי כבד ממני, the מן in ממני being an elative, expressing the ultimate degree, "too heavy."[16]

In closing (v.15), he revisits his opening words, not to repeat his accusations, but to extrapolate from them the answers to his ills.

Problem: לָמָה הֲרֵעֹתָ לְעַבְדֶּךָ
Resolution: וְאִם־כָּכָה אַתְּ־עֹשֶׂה לִי הָרְגֵנִי נָא הָרֹג
Problem: וְלָמָּה לֹא־מָצָתִי חֵן בְּעֵינֶיךָ
Resolution: הָרְגֵנִי נָא הָרֹג אִם־מָצָאתִי חֵן בְּעֵינֶיךָ
Problem: ...לָשׂוּם אֶת־מַשָּׂא כָּל־הָעָם הַזֶּה עָלָי

---

14. Ginzberg (1911), 69.
15. Later, Moses recalls the LORD's caring relationship with Israel using the very same images (Deut. 1:31; 32:18). Cf. also, Exod. 4:22.
16. Williams (1976), 318.

1 Kings 19: Horeb

Resolution: וְאֵלֵךְ־אֶרְאֶה בְרָעָתִי
The personal pronoun is strengthened by double usage, אֵת עֹשֵׂה. In the request for death, the use of the infinitive absolute following the imperative indicates immediacy; and there is a trace of black humour too, in appealing for death "if" he has "found favour" in the LORD's sight. In formulating his demand, Moses deploys the full force of language.

1.2. Elijah and the Death Wish (1 Kings 19:1-10)

1 Ahab told Jezebel all that Elijah had done, and how he had killed all the prophets with the sword.
2 Then Jezebel sent a messenger to Elijah, saying, "So may the gods do to me, and more also, if I do not make your life like the life of one of them by this time tomorrow."
3 Then he was afraid; he got up and fled for his life, and came to Beer-sheba, which belongs to Judah; he left his servant there.
4 But he himself went a day's journey into the wilderness, and came and sat down under a solitary broom tree. He asked that he might die: "It is enough; now, O LORD, take away my life, for I am no better than my ancestors."
5 Then he lay down under the broom tree and fell asleep. Suddenly an angel touched him and said to him, "Get up and eat."
6 He looked, and there at his head was a cake baked on hot stones, and a jar of water. He ate and drank, and lay down again.
7 The angel of the LORD came a second time, touched him, and said, "Get up and eat, otherwise the journey will be too much for you."
8 He got up, and ate and drank; then he went in the strength of that food forty days and forty nights to Horeb the mount of God.
9 At that place he came to a cave, and spent the night there. Then the word of the LORD came to him, saying, "What are you doing here, Elijah?"
10 He answered, "I have been very zealous for the LORD, the God of hosts; for the Israelites have forsaken your covenant, thrown down your altars, and killed your prophets with the sword. I alone am left, and they are seeking my life, to take it away."

The third death wish under consideration is Elijah's. This stretch of narrative is vigorously evocative of the Moses stories at multiple levels, and may be treated in two sections, each dealing with a "complaint." In each section, we shall note the Mosaic resonance in the setting of the scene, and within the world of the story. More significant, however, are the conceptual parallels between the three sets of death wish narratives. These are best set out once we have studied both complaints.

1.2.1. ELIJAH'S COMPLAINT UNDER THE BROOM TREE (1 KINGS 19:1-4)

The flow of the story, with its various stopping points, recalls Israel's wilderness wandering. Elijah moves from Jezreel to Beer-sheba to an unknown point in the Negev, marked only by a tree, and then deeper still into the wasteland till he reaches the cave at Horeb, from where he must go on to the wilderness of Damascus. At Beer-sheba he voluntarily enters into alone-ness. It is suggested that he seems to be turning his back on more than his servant here—perhaps his country and his call.[17]

A second level at which the discourse resonates with the Moses stories is within the world of the story. Here, the character of Jezebel steps out of the shadows. Given the development of her character thus far, one is not surprised to learn, at the start of 1 Kgs 19, that the higher authority Ahab reports to is his wife. (Jewish legend notes that "Jezebel was not only the daughter and wife of a king, she was also co-regent with her husband, the only reigning queen in Jewish history except Athaliah."[18]) Not surprising too, is the vehemence of her reaction.[19] She goes on to swear a dreadful oath, made the more terrible because she swears it against herself, to personally see to his death "by this time tomorrow." That she can set a time for his death, and then give him a day's notice bespeaks her unqualified confidence in her ability to keep the promise she makes to herself. House describes her as being "as worthy an opponent as God's servants ever face in Scripture."[20] Indeed, in her disdain for the LORD and his representatives, in her incredible immunity to the recent evidence at Carmel, the reader sees a new Pharaoh pitting herself against the LORD's prophet. Like him, she may threaten death ("Take care…the day you see my face you shall die"; Exod. 10:28); if her circle of power is smaller, her vicious use of it makes up the difference.

It is arguable whether Elijah's response to Jezebel is a desperate flight or a calculated retreat. The MT pointing favours "to see" (√ראה) as the first verb describing Elijah's response to Jezebel's message,[21] while the LXX prefers to read "he was afraid" (√ירא), making explicit the reason for the departure. Regularly, readings lean towards the LXX. Thus, Hauser, for example: "a rapid-fire sequence of three verbs depicts sudden, animated, terrified activity by Elijah…fleeing without even a slight hesitation."[22] While this

---

17. E.g., House (1995), 222; De Vries (1985), 235.
18. Ginzberg (1913), 189.
19. As noted, the LXX prefaces her speech with a declaration that is at once an arrogant challenge and a caustic belittling: "If you are Elijah, I am Jezebel." Burney proposes that the force and character of the phrase speak for its genuineness. Burney (1903), 229. Cf. Eissfeldt (1967); Simon (1997), 199-200. Since we will not engage with source issues, we merely note that the LXX's characterization of Jezebel seems appropriate.
20. House (1995), 222.
21. However, given that the verb lacks the object, the MT pointing looks "apologetic" in favour of Elijah.
22. Hauser and Gregory (1990), 62. Contra, e.g., Allen (1979), who argues that Elijah was broken, not frightened by Jezebel.

behaviour conflicts with the characterization of Elijah thus far, it anticipates what follows under the broom tree.

Following the MT punctuation, Elijah's death wish is in two parts, one setting out an imperative, and the other justifying it:

רב עתה יהוה קח נפשי
כי לא טוב אנכי מאבתי

In the first part, the phrase עתה is linked to יהוה with a conjunctive accent, leaving the רב as a terse expostulation. (LXX: ἱκανούσθω νῦν; "let it now be enough.") Tg. Jon. paraphrases, "And he said, "It is long enough for me. How long am I being knocked about like this?", reading fatigue and a deep frustration at the events that have led to this situation. Less ambiguous is the death wish itself, with the rationale clearly explained. He wishes to die at the hand of the LORD because of failure. He states that failure in comparative terms—he is no better than his fathers/forebears. This is usually understood as a reference to his predecessor prophets.[23] If so, Fretheim may be correct in reading here what the narrator does not make explicit at any point in the narrative, namely, that Israel's confession has been followed quickly by backsliding.[24] Like the prophets before him, he has not been able to make a difference to Israel's tendency to apostasy. Alternately, if Elijah is referring to his national heritage, he is likening himself to Israel, ever a disappointment to God.

While conceding that "psychologizing" is usually an exegetical mistake, Nelson sees this episode as warranting it. The lone broom tree could be "a careful psychological touch"—the double mention of it frames the death wish—emphasizing Elijah's isolation and consequent "depression."[25] Deep dissatisfaction is understandable, especially in the context of the spectacular triumph at Carmel over Jezebel's prophets. Now, it has taken very little, it would appear, for Jezebel to reduce Elijah to such as those Baalist prophets were. Even if she has not removed him by death, she has effectively eliminated him from the arena. In embracing the desire for death, Elijah executes Jezebel's mandate upon himself. The irony brings out the magnitude of the defeat.

Along another line, Walsh reads into Elijah's death wish, a "challenge":

> If Yahweh accepts Elijah's prayer and allows him to die, he releases the prophet from the task of Israel's conversion and implicitly admits that his demands on Elijah were excessive. If, on the other hand, Yahweh does not

---

23. E.g., Fretheim (1999), 108; Rice (1990), 157.
24. Fretheim (1999), 108.
25. Nelson (1987), 126. Cf. Wiener (1978). Burney (1903), 209, comments on the force of אחד, cf. 1 Sam. 6:7.

accede to Elijah's request, then he must address the underlying causes of the prophet's despair and act even more forcefully to bring Israel back. In either case, Elijah himself no longer bears responsibility for the outcome.[26]

Elijah's introspective absorption with his own performance as prophet weakens somewhat the suggestion that he is challenging God. Further, if God were to act on Elijah's request, it need not necessarily imply his mismanagement of Elijah. There is something, however, in the second half of Walsh's argument. As in Num. 11, the prophet has addressed his death wish to the LORD, and the progression of the plot hangs on his response.

1.2.2. TOWARDS ELIJAH'S SECOND COMPLAINT (1 KINGS 19:5-9A)

Here in the wilderness, details that call to mind Israel's desert wanderings come thick and fast. The food and water is provided by miracle, and the bread comes as Elijah sleeps, just as the manna fell at night (Num. 11:9). He wakes, and behold (הנה), it is there; there is a wonderment here, echoing that of Israel, when they first saw "the bread that the LORD has given you to eat (Exod. 16:15)."

A messenger is introduced into the story, who, on the second appearance is identified as the angel of the LORD—מלאך יהוה; מלאך, observes Eichrodt, is "a peculiarly equivocal expression speaking of God's personal activity in veiled language."[27] Circumstantially and functionally, this מלאך יהוה puts the reader in mind of the angel promised to Israel—in whom the LORD's name is—with the purpose of guarding Israel on the way and bringing them to a place prepared (Exod. 23:20):

הִנֵּה אָנֹכִי שֹׁלֵחַ מַלְאָךְ לְפָנֶיךָ לִשְׁמָרְךָ בַּדָּרֶךְ וְלַהֲבִיאֲךָ אֶל־הַמָּקוֹם אֲשֶׁר הֲכִנֹתִי:

Israel must not rebel against him. Rather, they are enjoined to obey him, for then, the LORD will be an enemy to their enemies, will bless their bread and water, remove sickness and enable them to increase till they possess the land (Exod. 23:20-33; cf. 33:2). Elijah's angel goes some way in being a functional counterpart of the one promised Israel in the capacity of guardian and guide. He provides Elijah a cake and water, cures the sickness of tired body and mind, and appears to know the way (הדרך) ahead of Elijah, a whisper of a suggestion that Elijah will go to a place in some way prepared and awaiting him. When Elijah responds with obedience to the messenger's prompting, the reader notes that Elijah's story has subtly reverted into the familiar pattern of divine command and

---

26. Walsh (1996), 268.
27. Eichrodt (1969), 39.

prophet's compliance, and suspects that a reversal of Elijah's fortunes may be at hand.

While the events under the broom tree throw up points of equivalence between Elijah's circumstances and Israel's wilderness years, the reader discerns a gradual shift as the prophet moves closer to Horeb. Here, the Mosaic parallels begin to take over. Elijah travels for an idiomatic forty days and nights. At first, this might recall Israel in their aimless wandering, for here is a man wandering as deep, and apparently, as aimlessly, in the wilderness. However, the description of Elijah's arrival at his destination clarifies the new direction of the resonance with its lexical reminiscence of Moses' first approach to the same place:

אל הר האלהים חרבה (Exod. 3:1);
עד הר האלהים חרב (1 Kings 19:8).[28]

Significantly, these are the only two occurrences of Horeb described as the mountain of God. Immediately, the idiomatic forty days and nights of travel "in the strength of that food" evokes Moses' periods of fasting on Horeb (Exod. 34:28; cf. Deut. 9:9, 18, 25) rather than Israel's forty years.[29]
Exod. 34:28:

ארבעים יום וארבעים לילה לחם לא אכל ומים לא שתה

As if to complete the parallel, there is the detail of the cave that serves for Elijah's lodging. Here, the definite article becomes a consideration. Simon, for example, dismisses it as "meaningless," citing "the" cave in which Obadiah reports he stowed away prophets (1 Kgs 18:4, 13).[30] Indeed, grammarians note the peculiar employment of the article in Hebrew, "to denote a single person or thing (primarily one which is as yet unknown, and therefore not capable of being defined) as being present to the mind under given circumstances."[31] However, commentators regularly consider the article here as significant intertexuality.[32] A parallel use of the definite article re a location is 1 Kgs 13:11; the old prophet from Bethel finds the Judahite man of God under "the" oak tree. In both places, it would seem the narrator is making reference to places made famous by association. Indeed, Jewish legend insists that "the cave in which Moses concealed himself while God passed in review

---

28. The LXX omits "the mountain of God" in both texts. Tg. Onq. and Ps.-J. (Exodus) and Tg. Jon. (Former Prophets) have "the mountain on which the glory of the LORD was revealed, to Horeb."
29. E.g., Wiseman (1993), 172; Provan (1995), 145; Nelson (1987), 128.
30. Simon (1997), 322, n.124. Cf. Montgomery (1951), 313.
31. GKC, §126q-r; Joüon-Muraoka, §137n-o; Thus, e.g., the raven and the dove (Gen. 8:7-8) and the donkey (Exod. 4:20).
32. E.g., Wiseman (1993), 172; Rice (1990), 158; Fretheim (1999), 109; Nelson (1987), 128; add Gray (1964), 364.

before him with his celestial retinue, was the same in which Elijah lodged when God revealed himself to him on Horeb."[33] Thus, though EVV substitute with an indefinite article, we note that the LXX and the Targum retain it in this text. Certainly, it can be read so as to contribute to the resonance that is taking shape. A last detail in the 1 Kgs narrative is that Elijah tarries the night in the cave. The LORD meets with him, presumably, early next morning, reminiscent of the timing of two Exodus theophanies (Exod. 19:16-17; 34:2).

Meanwhile, the text does not clarify the motivation for the trip to Horeb. It could not have been Elijah's destination from the start, since his words ("Enough!...take away my life...") and actions (he sleeps/lies down to die) under the broom tree indicate he desires to go no further, either literally or figuratively. The first hint of a second phase to Elijah's journey comes from the angel, though with no mention of the terminus. Commentators choose between two possibilities: (a) the LORD draws Elijah towards Horeb; (b) Elijah directs himself towards Horeb. With regards to the first possibility, Fretheim sees God as leading the prophet to Horeb "for the sake of the right context for the confrontation";[34] Provan suggests the LORD has a didactic purpose, namely, to impart knowledge of himself beyond what Elijah had experienced at Carmel.[35] With respect to the second possibility, House sees Elijah journeying to Horeb to "decide for himself if the Lord is God";[36] Hauser suggests he is still fleeing from Jezebel and comes to Horeb despondently seeking the LORD's pity;[37] Coote thinks that since Moses returns to Horeb after the slaughter in the camp (Exod. 32), the parallel story here demands Elijah's travelling to Horeb post the slaughter of the Baalists.[38]

Regarding the itinerary itself, it seems reasonable to postulate it as driven by both characters. The angel presents a rigorous journey as the next step, and prepares Elijah towards it. Yet, in the absence of a clear directive, as was usual thus far in the narrative, it appears that Horeb is Elijah's decision. Elijah's purpose can only be construed from the events related. At the broom tree in the wilderness, he is without leading, both personally and professionally. There is no direct response to his death wish; he is refreshed with food, which indicates God's rejection of his request; yet, there is no leading for what he must do next in his capacity as prophet. Since, at Horeb, he is ready with a statement of his case, we may assume that his purpose in travelling to Horeb is to present it.

---

33. Ginzberg (1911), 137.
34. Fretheim (1999), 109.
35. Provan (1995), 145-46.
36. House (1995), 222.
37. Hauser and Gregory (1990), 67.
38. Coote (1992), 25.

We must now study Elijah's second complaint before we return to how it bears on the two death wishes of Moses.

1.2.3. Elijah's Complaint at Horeb (1 Kings 19:9b-10)

1 Kings 19:9b
The narrative now slows into dialogue mode. The word of the LORD comes asking the question מה־לך פה אליהו—"What concerns you here, Elijah?" (19:9). How is this question to be understood? One way is to stress the "here" of the question and read it as a severe reminder that Elijah is in the wrong place; he should be "there" in Israel, his post of service, not "here" at Horeb. The contrast is between responsibility and escape.[39] This need not be the case, for at least two reasons. First, the angel hints of a long journey ahead, and this could not be the way Elijah had come for he was only a day's journey from Beersheba into the wilderness. What is more, the angel implicitly sanctions the journey with a provision of food and drink, urging Elijah to strengthen himself for the journey. Secondly, there are several instances where the narrator has God opening the conversation with a question, and significantly, the characters addressed invariably read the question as an invitation to dialogue, and either choose or refuse to do so.[40]

Coming to the idiom מה־לך: when the verbless interrogative clause is used with the lamedh of interest, the object of the lamedh is usually personal, and concerns the object in a loosely or elliptically defined way.[41] Simon explains that this idiom can be part of a genuine question (as Caleb's מה־לך asked of Achsah; Judg. 1:14), or a rebuke that is part of a rhetorical question (as the captain's question to Jonah in Jon. 1:6). In Elijah's context, it is more likely that it is a genuine question and, as Seybold observes, could be in line with the מה־לך common to audiences with a king, of which he lists four occurrences: David and the woman of Tekoa (2 Sam. 14:5), David and Bathsheba (1 Kgs 1:16), the king of Israel and the woman whose son had been eaten in famine (2 Kgs 6:28), and Ahasuerus and Esther (Esth. 5:3).[42] In each case, the question opens the audition,

---

39. Nordheim (1978), 61; DeVries (1985), 237; Rice (1990), 158.
40. Cf. Adam ("Where are you?" Gen. 3:9), Cain ("Why are you angry..? Gen. 3:6 and "Where is your brother Abel?" 3:9), Hagar ("...where have you come from and where are you going?" Gen. 16:8), Balaam ("Who are these men with you?" Num. 22:9) and Jonah ("Is it right for you to be angry about the bush?" Jon. 4:9).
41. Waltke and O'Connor (1990), 18.3b.
42. Seybold (1973), 8, n.30. He makes out the Elijah passage to belong to the sphere of juridical proceedings and lists elements in support, among them, the opening question—מה־לך—which is an enquiry into the intentions of the person seeking justice.

signalling the petitioners to state the case that has caused them to seek the king's presence.⁴³ If this usage of the idiom is represented in Elijah's case, then the "here" appended to מה־לך would draw attention to the place. Just as much as this could be in rebuke, it could also be in reference to the unusual locus Elijah has chosen for this audience. Elijah's reply, whose major content is Israel's abandoning of the covenant pacted at Horeb, would then answer the "here" of the question. The question could then be explained as asking, "What troubles you that brings you here?" or more concisely, "What concerns you here?"

1 Kings 19:10 aα

קנא קנאתי ליהוה

Elijah emphatically states his zeal. In the immediate context, this zeal cannot be denied (other than perhaps in 19:3-4). Since his first appearance on the scene, Elijah's involvement in his mission is wholehearted and unambiguous. His obedience to the LORD's directives is prompt and courageous, his prayers are passionate, his confrontation of a powerful establishment is at the risk of his own life, and it appears there is nothing he will stop at in his ardent desire to effect the turning back of a wayward people.

The setting, and the aural associations stirred up by the word √קנא evoke a wider context. A prophet goes up to Horeb for audience with the LORD; there is mention of a rocky shelter; a theophany follows; the prophet presents Israel before God. The scene of Exod. 34 is instantly recognizable, setting up a parallel between the two prophets. Olley well represents the comparison drawn: "Moses, in a parallel situation 'on the mountain,' interceded for the people, arguing for YHWH's continuing relationship. Elijah's relationship to the people is controlled by 'zeal', not compassionate identification."⁴⁴ Here, zeal is set against intercession, making out the latter to be the more desirable in a prophet.

The most appropriate locus for comparison however, is not "on the mountain" but at the point of the prophets' demonstration of zeal—Exod. 32 and 1 Kgs 18. In both cases, Israel's worship of other gods is the trigger; in both cases, the prophets take to the sword, purging the people of the chief offenders. However, the decision on whether Elijah's zeal is to be commended or condemned must take into account the usage of the word itself.

---

43. The other two instances of genuine question within a narrative text—Gen. 21:7 (Hagar and the angel of the LORD); Judg. 18:23-24 (Micah and the Danites)—are akin to the royal audition opener, in that the question may be rendered, "What troubles you?/What is your problem?"
44. Olley (1998), 41.

1 Kings 19: Horeb

√קנא, occurring only in the piel, carries implications of both zeal and jealousy. Since the verb expresses a very strong emotion whereby some quality or possession of the object is desired by the subject, it is often translated "envy." Thus, for example, it expresses the reaction of barren Rachel towards Leah, the mother of many sons (Gen. 30:1), and that of Joseph's brothers towards their father's favourite son (Gen. 37:11). However, the analogy between divine and human jealousy lies in the demand for exclusive possession or devotion and the central meaning of √קנא relates to jealousy as applicable to a marriage relationship, this relationship being used metaphorically to describe the bond between Israel and their God. Though most strongly developed in Hos. 1-3, Jer. 3 and Eze. 16 and 23, the language of conjugal jealousy sometimes describes God's feelings for Israel in Pentateuchal texts.

The intensive nominal forms קַנָּא and קַנּוֹא are used only in reference to God's jealousy: אֵל קַנָּא (Exod. 20:5; Deut. 5:9—as punishing those who hate him; Exod. 34:14; Deut. 4:24; 6:15—as demanding exclusive service; and Exod. 34:14, as naming himself with the attribute—קַנָּא שְׁמוֹ) and אֵל קַנּוֹא (Jos. 24:19—as one not forgiving transgression; Nah. 1:2—as taking vengeance on his enemies).[45] The Pentateuch/Joshua occurrences above are very specifically in the context of Israel's following after other gods, for which the consequences will be severe (God will consume them—Deut. 4:25, 6:15; Josh. 24:19; God will punish the sin over generations—Exod. 20:5; Deut. 5:9). Weinfeld notes that the expression הלך אחר —"follow after"—has conjugal connotations and, more forcefully, √זנה is used to describe the worship of other gods (Exod. 34:15-16).[46] The law provides a fit end for the justified jealousy of a husband, and Israel is warned that they may have to pay for spiritual adultery with annihilation.

The display of divine קנא in these texts being punitive, the tendency is to contrast the title אל קנא with אל רחום, since the latter entails forgiveness of sin (Exod. 34:6-7), while the former, very explicitly, rather entails zero tolerance of sin (Josh. 24:19). However, divine action accomplished with קנא has another side—it is directed against the nations on Israel's behalf and effects good for Israel (e.g., Nah. 1:2; Isa. 42:13). Further, as Fretheim explains, jealousy, by definition has both an inner and outer reference, the inner being the prior one. God cares deeply about Israel, therefore he cares about what they do with their allegiances.[47] His aggressive response to their rejection of him is an index of his passionate love for them.

---

45. BDB, קנא, 888.
46. Cf. Jer. 2:2, 25; Hos. 2:7, 15 (EVV 2:13). Weinfeld (1991), 295.
47. Fretheim (1999), 310.

Examining the word in Exod. 34, one finds that the LORD's pronouncement of zeal is part of the restatement of covenant law. "The point of these laws," Moberly points out, "is not to renew the covenant on conditions different from those previously obtaining (Ex. 20-24)—their continuing validity is taken for granted—*but to select and emphasize those particular aspects which are relevant to the sinful tendencies which Israel has displayed.*" Thus the cultic emphasis in the laws of vv.11-26 is a reaction to the cultic sin of the golden calf, and it may be this "god" that is referred to in v.14 in unique singular, and in the "molten gods" (אלהי מסכה) of the second commandment (preferring it over "idol"—פסל—of Exod. 20:4). The declaration of divine jealousy in Exod. 20:5 is restated far more emphatically, making the point that unfaithfulness as in the recent past is incompatible with the LORD's nature as zealous God. Looking ahead to Canaan, space is given to warning against the many temptations to accommodate to or adopt the religious practices of the peoples there.[48] Childs notes that the injunctions against worshipping, eating, sacrificing and playing the harlot in Exod. 34:14-16 recall the activities of Israel in 32:6.[49] Thus, "As Yahweh renews the covenant he does so by demanding obedience in the area where Israel has already failed and where they will be under continual temptation in the promised land to sin again."[50]

The correspondence emerges: the LORD presents his zeal as the reason why Israel must not give herself over to idolatry: Exod. 34:14:

לא תשתחוה לאל אחר כי יהוה קנא שמו אל קנא הוא

Elijah submits that he has been zealous because of Israel's forsaking of the covenant.[51] The only other incidence of the expression is found in Deut. 29:24 (EVV v.25)—עזבו את־ברית. And here, Israel is said to have forsaken the covenant in that she "turned and served other gods (v.25; EVV v.26)." Like the LORD's, Elijah's zeal is triggered by Israel's preference for other gods, in this instance, Baal.[52]

---

48. Moberly (1983), 95-98. Cf. Fretheim (1991), 308-9; Janzen (2000), 260-61.
49. Childs (1974), 613.
50. Moberly (1983), 96.
51. We note that the word order in the MT is irregular in כי עזבו בריתך בני ישראל. The LXX has ἐγκατέλιπόν σε, an even more forceful rendering of Israel's sin.
52. Traces this rare locution are to found in Elijah's rebuke of Ahab and his house in 1 Kgs 18:18, again in the context of idolatry: "You have forsaken the commandments of the LORD and followed the Baals"— בעזבכם את־מצות יהוה.

Looking for comparisons within biblical narrative, we note that Jewish tradition has long associated Phinehas and Elijah,[53] the former celebrated for his zeal.[54] It may be useful to study this case to see what similarities, if any, it has with Elijah's.

Num. 25 relates how at Shittim, Israel began to "play the harlot" (√זנה) with Moabite women. The verb, frequently used as a metaphor for Israel's engagement in idolatrous worship,[55] portends a cultic corollary, and the next verse describes how the nation bound itself to the worship of Baal-Peor. With this the LORD's anger was kindled and a deadly plague swept through the camp. Even as Moses takes steps to deal with the disaster, and Israel weeps at the tent of meeting, an Israelite man openly brings a Midianite woman in, and the scene is set to narrate Phinehas' act of zeal. Phinehas gets up, arms himself with a spear, follows the Israelite into the קבה, and pierces the two through. Opinion is divided over the nature of Zimri's sin, and commentators variously propose that it could have been illicit sex,[56] marriage to a non-Israelite,[57] a cultic offence,[58] or a combination; v.6 does not specifically point in the direction of any particular one. However, the story provides clues.

First, the hapax legomenon קבה. Three distinct suggestions are that קבה could have meant a regular tent,[59] the tent of meeting,[60] or a portable shrine.[61] The second suggestion is the least likely, since in

---

53. Extra-biblical sources equate Phinehas with Elijah, some going so far as to state explicitly that Phinehas and Elijah are the same person, e.g., *LAB* 48:1-2; Targ. Ps.-J. to Exod. 6:18: "He (Qohat) lived until he saw Phinehas, the same is Elijah the high priest, who is to be sent to the Dispersion of Israel at the end of days." One dimension of this equation is zeal for God. See Hayward (1978), 22-34.
54. Thus, Mattathias "burned with zeal for the law, just as Phinehas did against Zimri son of Salu (1 Macc. 2:26)." "Phinehas son of Eleazar ranks third in glory, for being zealous in the fear of the Lord, and standing firm, when the people turned away, in the noble courage of his soul; and he made atonement for Israel." Sir. 45:23; cf. 4 Macc.18:12.
55. See Bird (1989), 75-94.
56. Cook and Espin (1871), 750; Keil (1869), 205.
57. Binns (1927), 178; Noordtzij (1983), 241; Noth (1968), 198; Sturdy (1976), 184; Budd (1984), 280.
58. Wenham (1981), 187; Milgrom (1990), 212, 214, 476-80; Cross (1973), 201-3; Reif (1971), 200-6.
59. Cook and Espin (1871), 750); Keil (1869), 206; Noordtzij (1983), 241); Noth (1968), 198.
60. Sturdy (1976), 184-5.
61. Budd (1984), 280; Reif (1971), 200-6; Cross (1973), 201-3. These follow Morgenstern, who proposes a parallel between the אהל מועד and the pre-Islamic קבה, a sacred tent. (1942-43), 153-265; (1943-44), 1-52.

v.6 it is at the door of the אהל מועד that the congregation (and Phinehas) is assembled, but it is into the קבה that Phinehas follows the offenders in v.8. It is unlikely that two different terms would be used for the same structure within the space of three verses. On the contrary, they possibly distinguish between one tent and the other. The suggestion that it is neither more nor less than a regular tent is weakened somewhat by the narrator's preference for an unusual term over the usual אהל. This leaves the possibility that the tent was in some way associated with cultus.

Secondly, Moses' order is to "kill any of your people who have yoked themselves to Baal of Peor (v.5)." If one assumes that Phinehas acts on this command issued to the שפטים, it favours the presence of a cultic component in Zimri's act of defiance, in addition to any others there might be.

Thirdly, Zimri is "Zimri son of Salu, head of an ancestral house belonging to the Simeonites"—נשיא בית־אב לשמעני (v.14). This recalls v.4, in which the LORD commands punitive action against "all the chiefs of the people"—ראשי העם. This could be either because of their direct involvement with Baal, or because of their failure to keep their people from apostasy, or both. What is significant is that the punishment is to effect the turning away of divine wrath, and since the wrath of the LORD is juxtaposed with Israel's association with Baal of Peor (v.3), the offence of the ראשים is strongly linked to Israel's apostasy.

Fourthly, Zimri's death immediately stays the plague explicitly tied with Israel's worship of Baal of Peor (cf. Num. 31:16; Josh. 22:17). This again points to a connection between Israel's collective sin and Zimri's.

The likelihood is that Zimri, a leader in Israel, has set up a קבה among the tents of his clan (since he brings the woman אל־אחיו), within sight of the אהל מועד. While Moses and the congregation wait on the LORD at the door of the אהל מועד, Zimri brazenly continues his liaison with Baal of Peor as evidenced by his bringing Cozbi into the camp; or worse, as Organ and Reif stress, Zimri, being a member of a chieftain's family, takes responsibility in time of crisis, and seeks recourse to another oracle so as to find an alternative solution to the plague.[62] Either way, Zimri flagrantly challenges the singular worship of the LORD, and this is what stirs Phinehas to his deed. "The immediate cessation of the plague proves the rightness of Phinehas' actions and the reliability of Yhwh."[63]

The story brings out the significance of Phinehas' voluntary act in several ways. First, as several commentators note, the narrative bears parallels to the only other instance of Israel's apostasy in the

---

62. Reif (1971), 205; Organ (2001), 208-9.
63. Organ (2001), 209.

course of the exodus and the wilderness wanderings, namely, the incident of the golden calf (Exod. 32).[64] At the level of story, both narratives have the same contrast between events on the mountaintop and in the plain below; while God works towards binding Israel to himself in covenant relationship, Israel turns to worship another god. Smaller correspondences in the stories are: (a) In both cases, the idolatry has a foreign connection—the Egyptian gold that was used to create the image (Exod. 12:35; 32:2-4), and the women of Moab/Midian. (b) Both offences are punished by a plague (Exod. 32:35). (c) At Sinai, Moses orders the Levites to kill their fellow Israelites (Exod. 32:27); at Shittim, he orders the judges to execute any engaged in Baal worship. (d) The Levites are rewarded for voluntarily taking the LORD's side and avenging him, with being ordained as priests for the service of the LORD (Exod. 32:29); Phinehas, who similarly avenges the LORD, is granted a perpetual priesthood. These correspondences increase the significance of Phinehas' display of zeal beyond the narrative of Num. 25. The two instances of apostasy function as bookends, demarcating the story of the generation that had been led from Egypt. The plague at Shittim consumes the last of them, and immediately following, a census is taken of the new generation that will enter Canaan (Num. 26:1-2, 64-65). If Moses' zeal for Israel had kept them from being consumed by God's wrath when they had barely been formed into a nation, then Phinehas' zeal for Israel saves a generation that will form a new Israel.

A second way the story attaches value to Phinehas' deed is by the use of √קנא. It is enormously to Phinehas' credit that the LORD sees his own zeal active in Phinehas: בקנאו את־קנאתי בתוכם. McNeile describes the satisfaction wrought: "His [Phinehas'] jealousy was so deep and real that it adequately expressed the jealousy of Jehovah, rendering it unnecessary for Jehovah to express it further by consuming Israel."[65] At this point, Phinehas' character becomes subsumed into the LORD's; he is more than merely God's representative; his zeal, for that moment, is the very zeal of God, and thus, even though the deed is not commissioned by the LORD, it meets with full, and even extravagant, approval. Indeed, the fact that Phinehas acts voluntarily only adds to his merit.

Here, in 1 Kgs 19, another story that evokes Exod. 32-34, Elijah presents his zeal. Against the background of Carmel, where he has had 450 Baalists put to the sword letting none escape, Elijah's zeal takes a shape that recalls Phinehas'. In the absence of any instruction from the LORD, his act appears as spontaneous as Phinehas'. The reason for the killing is the same, that is, to expunge the threat to

---

64. E.g., Olson (1996), 153-4; Wenham (1981), 185.
65. McNeile (1911), 144.

Israel's true faith and cultus. However, unlike Phinehas' case, there is no divine affirmation of Elijah's self-avowed zeal. His slaughter of the 450 Baalist prophets is neither criticized nor explicitly affirmed. However, there is a verbal suggestion of implicit validation. 1 Kgs 19:1, which opens the Horeb episode, includes a detail missing in the earlier account of Elijah's purge—a sword (חרב). The חרב reappears with triple intensity at the close of the story (v.17)—even if partly in metaphor—as one divinely unleashed. The LORD's dealing with Israel's apostasy not only matches Elijah's but also carries it further. By this, Elijah's zeal is implicitly validated at the highest level.

...ליהוה אלהי צבאות
In affirming his zeal, Elijah uses the LORD's militaristic title ליהוה אלהי צבאות (cf. his oath to Obadiah in 18:15— חי יהוה צבאות). Within the wider sense of service,[66] the verb √צבא specifically has connotations of service in war (e.g., Num. 31:7).[67] The noun צבא is translated host/army and can refer to any company, including among others, organized militia (e.g., Judg. 4:2), the forces of heavenly beings (e.g., 1 Kgs 22:19), or the collection of celestial bodies (e.g., Deut. 4:19).[68] When in the form of a divine title, it occurs as either a two-part or as a three-part formula, as seen above. The latter shows that אלהים stands in construct relationship with צבאות but it is doubtful that יהוה is similarly in construct. If וֹת is taken as an abstract plural ending,[69] then צבאות may be taken as a noun in apposition to יהוה, thus making יהוה צבאות a technical term which may be rendered "the LORD Almighty/All-Powerful," a possibility supported by the LXX's frequent rendering of the two-part formula as κύριος σαβαωθ/κύριος παντοκράτωρ, and the three-part formula as κύριος παντοκράτωρ/κύριος ὁ θεὸς ὁ παντοκράτωρ.[70] However, the few

---

66. Cf. cultic service rendered by the Levites (e.g., Num. 4:23; Num. 8:24).
67. A basic point of agreement among most scholars is that this divine title, in its earliest stages, is to be associated with the Ark, the palladium of holy war. See Miller (1973), 152.
68. BDB, צבא, 838-9.
69. GKC (1898), §124d.
70. "When nouns which the usage of language always treats as proper nouns occasionally appear to be connected with a following genitive, this is really owing to an ellipse whereby the noun which really governs the genitive, i.e. the appellative idea contained in the proper name, is suppressed. So evidently in the case of יְהוָה צְבָאוֹת." GKC, §125h. So also, Joüon-Muraoka, §131o; BDB, צבא, 839; Eichrodt (1961), 194.

occurrences of κύριος τῶν δυνάμεων (common to the Psalter) leave open the possibility of reading יהוה as in construct with צבאות.⁷¹

These connotations to this title of Israel's God are fleshed out in the belief that Israel's military victories resided in the fact that the LORD fought for them (Ps. 44:9; Prov. 21:31) joining his heavenly forces (embracing heavenly armies and astral arrays) to Israel's hosts (Josh. 5:13ff.; 2 Kgs 6:15ff.).⁷² Something of this comes through in David's speech before Goliath, the one other narrative where this formula occurs (1 Sam. 17:41-51).

The Philistine, in disdain for his rival, for his rival's presumed weapon and, implicitly for his god, curses him "by his [Goliath's] gods." (v.43). Edelman reminds that the last, a customary procedure, takes on significance because now Goliath specifically pits himself against David's God.⁷³ David's response is couched in "impeccable terms of standard Israelite belief"⁷⁴ (vv.45-47)—he names the LORD as the affronted party who now, as Goliath's real rival, will best him. Cartledge notes that the narrator makes a point of having the compound name explained by paraphrase,⁷⁵ יהוה צבאות אלהי מערכות ישראל, and in this it has a specificity missing in the reference to the un-named Philistine gods.⁷⁶ In David's use of it, Brueggemann reads an allusion to the entire memory of the LORD's deliverance of Israel in the past.⁷⁷

The Philistine "embodies a belief in armaments, an ideology of reliance on military force, and the desire for invulnerability."⁷⁸ Thus the irony when David fells the Philistine, and even as Goliath lies on the ground trapped by the weight of his 5000-shekel armour, uses the Philistine's own sword against him. Ironically, the very bronze

---

71. The title is clearly associated with kingship. E.g., Isa. 6:5— המלך יהוה צבאות; Ps. 84:4 (EVV 84:3). In Amos 4:13 the title is accorded in the context of the LORD creating the mountains and the wind. McClellan argues that צבאות is a generic term (including arrays of stars, priestly service) of which the military connotation is one species. (1940), 300-307. Ross holds that the title denotes a God whose principal attribute was royal majesty and any military connotations it may have had were overwhelmed by this other, even from its earliest usages. (1967), 76-92. While this position is debatable, the argument underscores the wide acceptance of the universal scope of this title.
72. Imschoot (1954), 20-22; Eichrodt (1961), 192-94; Wambacq (1947), 279; Miller (1973), 155-56.
73. Edelman (1991), 132.
74. Alter (1999), 108.
75. Cartledge (2001), 220.
76. Brueggemann (1990), 130.
77. Brueggemann (1990), 130.
78. Fokkelman (1986), 148.

and iron that suggested his invincibility account for his destruction.⁷⁹ Victory comes, not only because of David's daring, but because he is faithful to his understanding of the LORD in relation to Israel and to the world. Because of this understanding, he could prophetically project the defeat onto the Philistine army and the victory onto Israel (ונתן אתכם בידנו), and looking beyond the boundaries of the two warring countries, declare that the knowledge of Israel's God is for "all the earth." Thus the title יהוה צבאות אלהי מערכות ישראל invokes the irresistibility of this all-powerful deity.

In 1 Kgs 19, when Elijah uses this militaristic title, the informed reader hears a resonance of aggression, especially in the context of the ongoing hostilities between the deities over Israel's allegiance. It functions as an apposite overture to the statement of Elijah's concern, that Israel has forsaken the covenant. Further, because of its associations, it creates anticipation that this situation will be overcome.

כי

The clauses in v.10aα are linked with כי.
Frank sees parallelism here

ליהוה אלהי צבאות   קנא קנאתי
בני ישראל   כי עזבו בריתך

and the inference he draws is representative of a common reading of this text: "The prophet's fidelity and zeal for the LORD is set against the infidelity of the Israelites."⁸⁰ The answer to the question of whether Elijah is using Israel as a foil to present himself as commendable depends on how one understands כי.

Pedersen calls כי the most comprehensive of all Hebrew particles.⁸¹ It is understood to have, originally, a non-connective demonstrative character.⁸² It came to be used in Biblical Hebrew not only as a conjunction but also as a clausal adverb; there are two main

---

79. Ariella Deem (1978), 349-51, argues that 1 Sam. 17: 49 should be rendered "…and he struck out at the Philistine, at his greave, and the stone sank into his greave [מצח, cf. v.6, מצחה], and he fell on his face to the ground." Thus the stone would sink into the knee, the space that must be left open to enable the warrior to walk. As he awkwardly makes his way towards David, the stone penetrates into this vulnerable place, locking his leg and causing him to fall forward (rather than backward, as would have been the case if he had been hit in the forehead).. Fokkelman agrees that this is a "more effective and telling point of denouement." (1986), 186.
80. Frank (1963), 413.
81. Pedersen (1926), 118.
82. BDB, כי, 471; Joüon-Muraoka, §164d.

clause-adverbial uses of כִּי—the emphatic and the logical/causal.[83] As for the emphatic usage the debate ranges from insisting that all usages of כִּי (including the causal) are emphatic in some way,[84] to rejecting the emphatic function of כִּי altogether.[85]

Aejmelaeus rightly warns, "in the case of a multipurpose particle that appears in different contexts, one must be aware of the fact that it is only from the context in which the particle occurs and from the contents of the clauses involved that the function of the particle and its rendering...may be inferred."[86] In the text under study, the LXX's rendering of this particle is causal, using the subordinating conjunction ὅτι. Further, the best-known use of כִּי is that of a subordinating conjunction introducing a causal clause.[87] Additionally, the self-asseveration אַל קְנָא which has been shown to bear on 1 Kgs 19:10, in all its five occurrences as cited above, is made in a text that involves כִּי and it is agreed across the spectrum that in these texts it has a fundamentally causal function.[88] These considerations direct the investigation towards causal כִּי clauses following the main clause, and here the term "causal" is used to include such nuances as cause, reason, motivation and explanation.

These causal functions may be divided between two types of conjunction—"because" and "for." There is the proposal that the position of the causal clause before or after the main clause decides its rendering—"because" if before, and "for" if after,[89] which are further understood as involving subordination and coordination respectively.[90] Schoors objects, observing that most occurrences of כִּי following the main clause can be rendered "because" as well.[91] Aejmelaeus abandons the position-oriented criterion for rendering כִּי in favour of paying attention to the "logical relationship of the clauses involved, to their dependence on one another; ...the tightness and directness or looseness and indirectness of causality correlates positively with the dependence of the clauses on one

---

83. Waltke and O'Connor (1990), 39.3.4e. Lesser clause-adverbial functions include temporal, conditional and concessive.
84. E.g., Muilenberg (1961) 136, 160. So also, e.g., Pedersen (1926), 118; Gordis (1943), 176-78; Meek (1959/60), 45-54. More cautiously, Schoors (1981), 240-76; BDB, כִּי, 472; Joüon-Muraoka, §164b; GKC, §148d.
85. Aejmelaeus (1986),193-209; Claassen (1983), 29-46.
86. Aejmelaeus (1986), 195.
87. Schoors (1981), 264; Joüon-Muraoka, §170d.
88. E.g., Muilenberg (1961), 150-52; Aejmelaeus (1986), 202.
89. E.g., BDB, כִּי, 473.
90. Aejmelaeus (1986), 202.
91. Schoors (1981), 264-65.

another."⁹² Thus, the greater the dependence, the stronger the case for rendering כי as "because."

כי introduces the clause in each of the five אל קנא texts. These appear to fall somewhere mid-spectrum between strictly causal⁹³ and loosely causal,⁹⁴ and are in the category of motivational causal clauses, a characteristic feature of the law collections—casuistic law is expanded by motivations⁹⁵ and apodictic law⁹⁶ frequently receives the motive clause.⁹⁷ The LXX oscillates between the subordinating conjunction ὅτι (Deut. 4:24; 5:9; 6:15) and the coordinating conjunction γάρ (Exod. 20:5; 34:14) in the five אל קנא texts (all apodictic law),⁹⁸ showing the difficulty of gauging the dependence of the causal clause on the main, and therefore, the difficulty of locating the כי on the strict-loose continuum of causality. However, the narratives of the Pentateuch—notably the instance of the golden calf and the Baal-Peor episode—clarify the strength of the connection between the clauses in these texts by making abundantly clear that Israel's service of other gods surely ignites the jealousy of God.

Comparing the אל קנא instances of כי with 1 Kgs 19:10, one finds that in Elijah's statement the logical link between the main and causal clauses is as strong as in the אל קנא cases, if not grammatically stronger. The LXX's construal here of כי as ὅτι rather than γάρ would move the sense towards cause/reason (strictly causal/subordinating) rather than explanation (loosely

---

92. Aejmelaeus (1986), 202.
93. Where the main clause demands the causal clause; e.g., Num. 27:4: "Why should the name of our father be taken away from his clan כי he had no son?" Aejmelaeus (1986), 203.
94. Where the causal clause does not state the cause for *what* is said in the main clause but rather the *reason for saying it*, or does not refer to the full statement of the main clause but perhaps only to one word of it. E.g., Exod. 12:39: "They baked unleavened cakes of the dough that they had brought out of Egypt כי it was not leavened כי they were driven out of Egypt..." Aejmelaeus (1986), 203.
95. E.g., Exod. 22:25f (EVV 22:26f): If you take your neighbour's cloak in pawn, you shall restore it before the sun goes down כי it may be your neighbour's only clothing..."
96. E.g., in the אל קנא texts.
97. Muilenburg (1961), 150-52; Aejmelaeus (1986), 204.
98. While both conjunctions may be used in a causal sense, γάρ is more explanatory and inferential, and so, often has diminished causal force. But then, ὅτι, though strongly causal, may also involve so loose a subordination that the translation "for" recommends itself. This makes it hard to draw the line between strongly and loosely causal usage of ὅτι. Arndt and Gingrich (1957), pp. 151, 593-4.

causal/coordinating). Indeed, Elijah's emphatic expression of zeal calls for a correspondingly vigorous reason for the ignition of that zeal.

The issue of emphasis reintroduces the emphatic interpretation of כי, referred to above. Muilenburg insists, "it is characteristically associated with emphatic words or clauses, that it frequently appears in a strategic position in the poem or narrative...and that it often confirms or underlines what has been said, or, at times, undergirds the whole of the utterance and gives point to it."[99] However, Aejmelaeus rejects this, reasoning that the main role of כי is as a causal connective, and that כי could not normally be used as an emphatic particle in connections where its use as a connective was possible, simply because it would have been impossible to distinguish between the two kinds of cases.[100]

Steering between the two, one may cautiously subscribe to the possibility that כי may occasionally have emphatic usage,[101] and that "the two clausal uses [namely, emphatic and causal] should not be too strictly separated."[102] If the causal כי in Elijah's speech does indeed have an undertone of emphasis, then, it ties up the sin of Israel very closely with Elijah's zeal, augmenting the effect already obtained by reading the כי as strictly causal. A step further is to read inter-textually, and relate the prophet's zeal to the nation's sin with the same degree of interconnectedness as in the case of God's zeal in the instance of Israel's idolatry, the zeal being strongly dependent on the idolatry. Thus, the possibility that Elijah is boasting of his own faithfulness, using Israel as foil, (i.e., with כי used concessively) is weakened. Elijah's zeal is a proven fact, and is, basically, a true prophet's correct and expected response in the face of Israel's service of other gods.

19:10aβ, γ
The punctuation of the sentence suggests that Elijah presents the razing of the LORD's altars and the slaying of his prophets by the sword as two concrete examples of Israel's fundamental error of breaching the covenant.[103] In 1 Kgs 18, the reader has encountered examples of both—Jezebel's slaughter of the LORD's prophets (it is reasonable to presume the people's co-operation) and the ruined altar at Carmel. Israel had been directed, in the most forceful terms, to break down pagan sancta—הרס תהרסם מצבתיהם (Exod. 23:24), so that the service of foreign gods would be wiped out. Ironically,

---

99. Muilenburg (1961), 150.
100. Aejmelaeus (1986), 205.
101. BDB, כי, 472; Joüon-Muraoka, §164b; Waltke and O'Connor (1990), 39.3.1d.
102. Waltke and O'Connor (1990), 39.3.4e.
103. Walsh (1996), 272-3; Simon (1997), 206.

Israel was directing this injunction—√הרס—against the LORD's altars, presumably with similar intent; the verb implies destruction by tearing down,[104] and thus, is a deliberate and violent act. To ensure further the elimination of their faith, Israel had taken the sword to the LORD's prophets, contrary to the injunction that it is a prophet "who speaks in the name of other gods" who deserved to be removed from the sphere of Israel's religion (Deut. 18:20). √הרג implies ruthless violence and is used primarily for the brutal slaying of humans by other humans; thus its usage in describing massacres.[105] With both altars and prophets removed, and Baalist substitutes in place, the forsaking of the covenant would be complete.

19:10b
Elijah finishes with ואותר אני לבדי ויבקשו את־נפשי לקחתה.

Redaction[106] and literary critics attempt, in different ways, a solution to the oddity that Jezebel, the immediate threat to Elijah's life, goes unmentioned. The latter psychologize, attributing to the depressed Elijah a selective memory.[107] While this is not improbable, we note that at Carmel Elijah circumvented Ahab to appeal to the people. In this context, the possibility is that Jezebel is eclipsed by a superior concern, namely, Israel and the covenant.

In military contexts, יתר frequently indicates the survivors of people who have been defeated (Josh. 12:4; 23:12), or to those who have survived a conspiracy (Judg. 9:5).[108] If Elijah wants to continue the allusion to war, this word fits well, in the sense of survival against great odds. He alone is remnant.[109] We noted that at Carmel Elijah used the phrase לבדי in the context of identifying the sides in the contest that ends in the slaughter of the deafeated. The context at Horeb is not dissimilar with its terminology of war, the mention of

---

104. BDB, הרס, 248.
105. E.g., the massacre of Jews planned by Haman (Est. 3:13; 7:4); massacres following battles (e.g., Num. 31:7; Josh. 8:24; Judg. 7:25). BDB, הרג, 247.
106. See DeVries (1985), 234-35.
107. Provan (1995), 145; cf. Nelson (1987), 126.
108. BDB, יתר, 451.
109. A concern here is the reliability of Elijah's claim, numerically speaking, that he alone remains. It is pointed out that later the LORD rebukes him with the information that 7,000 remain faithful (v.18). E.g., Gregory and Hauser (1990), 75; DeVries (1985), 237. Others read v.18 as a promise or a word of encouragement given to a prophet despondent in his alone-ness. E.g., Fretheim (1999), 110; Provan (1995), 147; House (1995), 224. (Either reading could be accommodated into Paul's use of this episode in Rom. 11:2-5. Is it possible that Paul puts his own slant on the text in order to make his point on "a remnant, chosen by grace"?) We will treat the issue later.

killings, casualties and survivors. Obadiah's hundred, having withdrawn from the arena of battle, may not be counted, leaving Elijah the only (cf. the force of the LXX's superlative μονώτατος) prophet remaining in the field.[110]

A "plain" reading of Elijah's statement, then, would be that he is stating the fact that he is the last item on Israel's murderous list. Scholarly comment reads further, and takes up either one of two positions. (a) This statement is Elijah's indulgence in self-pity and self-doubt, continuing from the episode of the death wish.[111] (b) This is a request for guarantee of safety, born of his sense of self-importance.[112]

Robinson is representative of position (b): the idea of going to Horeb, he says, is of Elijah's own devising. He sees himself as a Moses-like figure, and so, deliberately spins the journey out to make it last 40 days, eating nothing en route. His purpose in coming to Horeb is to call the LORD "to account" over the ills that have beset him. "Devoured by egotism" he makes "the mistake of…thinking of himself as indispensable"; "He is the last prophet left, and (he implies) self-interest should therefore ensure that God take special steps to preserve him."[113]

Several points in this thesis need clarification. First, Elijah's state of mind, as may be reconstructed from the text: there is general agreement among commentators that Elijah under the broom tree is demoralized and feels deeply inadequate. He has lost his sense of perspective, and considers himself worthy of nothing less than death. "Forty days" later, at Horeb, it is odd that he should swing to the other end of the spectrum of a lost sense of perspective, considering himself crucial to God's plans for Israel. Robinson offers no reason for such a metamorphosis.

Secondly, Robinson proposes that Elijah continues to be preoccupied with himself, just as he was under the broom tree. This is common to position (a) as well, and so both (a) and (b) may be engaged with simultaneously here. Let us agree, provisionally, that

---

110. Coote reads significant narratorial intent into the omission in Elijah's self-description: "…in contrast to his statement in 18:22, he omits the word 'prophet,' precisely because it is questionable whether at this point Elijah is a prophet." He observes that Elijah at Horeb, like Obadiah's hundred, is now concealed in a cave, too. (1981), 117. This is debatable. The contest context of Carmel necessitates his self-identification as a נביא ליהוה; at Horeb, in dialogue with God the phrase is unnecessary and even redundant.
111. E.g., House (1995), 224; Hauser and Gregory (1990), 68-73.
112. E.g., Fretheim (1999), 109; Provan (1995), 145; Robinson (1991), 528-30, 534-35.
113. Robinson (1991), 518-35.

Elijah's concern at Horeb is indeed solely Elijah. Elijah, it is generally agreed, has deliberately chosen Horeb for his audience with the LORD, making an arduous journey to get there. If Elijah indeed desired to plead his case, he need not necessarily choose Horeb for this; Horeb has no previous associations with a prophet seeking to plead his own case. Horeb does, however, immediately call up recollections of Moses and of Israel immediately post-Exodus, very specifically with respect to the giving of the law, the sealing of the covenant and the first act of national apostasy. And when the narrator adds in details that specifically evoke these narratives, leading up to a theophany evoking the Sinai tradition, it begins to appear that the narrator and Elijah have more than Elijah in mind. Sandwiched between the Mosaic details and the Sinaitic theophany, is Elijah's first response, the central section of which is given to a statement and an elaboration thereof of Israel's abandoning of the covenant. Bookending this core are an assertion of zeal, and a report of alone-ness. If, as argued earlier, the former is best interpreted as linked to Israel's apostasy, then it would make Israel's turning away the burden of all but the concluding statement of Elijah's speech. This weakens the proposition that Elijah's key concern at Horeb is himself. Certainly, there remains the possibility that Elijah is concerned for his personal safety, but it is likely that this is not the principal motivation behind his speech.

Further, the case that Elijah has only himself as his concern would have gained support had Elijah explicitly pleaded his own security or demanded it from God, considering he is given that opportunity at Horeb, prompted by a question. Even if in declaring his alone-ness, he is implicitly requesting protection, the fact that he does not plainly bring up the matter, as he does with his concern at the broom tree, points to the possibility that apprehension over personal protection is eclipsed by a deeper concern; the bias of his speech—covenant, altars, prophets—is a reasonable indication (even if provisional at this point in the narrative) that this concern is in the direction of Israel's faith.

1.3. Revisiting the Resonance between the Death Wish Narratives

Standing back from the three death wish narratives, we try to put our finger on the common factor precipitating the death wishes. It is perhaps that the prophet encounters an unprecedented crisis. In Exod. 32, Moses seeks to make atonement and obtain the LORD's forgiveness for an extraordinary sin of national proportions employing, without precedent, a route outside of the divine prescriptions, namely, intercession. In Num. 11, Moses finds himself, for the first time, sandwiched between a rebellious people and an angry God. In 1 Kings 19, for the first time in the narrative, Elijah behaves contrary to his norm of intrepid obedience. Both prophets

1 Kings 19: Horeb

respond by requesting a cessation of life and ministry—Moses with rhetorical questions and expostulations, Elijah with symbolism, gesture[114] and weary request.

Here, we note that a striking verbal parallel between Elijah's speech at Horeb and Moses' at Kibroth-hattaavah is the expression of alone-ness אנכי לבדי (Num. 11:14). The loneliness of the leader runs through all three narratives. In Exod. 32, Moses is of the people and yet not of them, for he is their leader, but not part of their trespass. On Horeb, he wrestles alone with a God whose responses he is unsure of. The possibility that faces him if divine forgiveness is not granted is the ultimate loneliness of shouldering responsibility for a rebellious people no longer in relationship with God. In Num. 11, Moses separates himself from God on the one hand with his emphatic "thou" and "I" (especially as he brings his complaint to a finish; vv.14-15), and on the other seeks to disengage with Israel, too burdensome to bear. In 1 Kings 19, Elijah brings about his isolation by physically removing himself from people and land. Eventually, he separates himself from his servant, and has naught for company but the "solitary broom tree." At Horeb he expresses this alone-ness with the powerful and evocative phrase אנכי לבדי.[115]

Besides creating the conceptual resonance of the loneliness of the leader, the phrase אנכי לבדי draws attention to the two texts it links. Looking over them, we notice a pattern in the contours of the two "complaints."

A. Prophet presents account of service	Num. 11:10-12	1 Kings 19:10aα1
B. Prophet presents Israel's sin	Num.11:13/Exod.32:31	1 Kings 19:10aα2-β
C. Prophet summarizes situation	Num. 11:14	1 Kings 19:10b
D. Prophet requests redress	Num.11:15/Exod.32:32	(1 Kings 19:4)

This allows the possibility that the character Elijah shapes his speech on the Mosaic template.[116] Tentatively: Elijah's crisis is compounded when his complaint under the broom tree receives no direct answer. In need of guidance, he determines to journey to Horeb, for that is

---

114. Thus Coote sees more than weariness in Elijah's desire to sleep: "The man who twice before has claimed 'I have stood (in service) before Yahweh' and who will again stand before Yahweh now wants only to lie down." (1981), 116.
115. As noted before, the LXX powerfully renders it with a superlative—μονώτατος, a hapax legomenon.
116. There is a similar textual correspondence between Elijah and Jonah in comparable situations of distress. Brichto notes the correspondence. (1992), 141. Indeed, Jonah seems clearly to be modelling himself on Elijah.
Jon. 4:8: ועתה יהוה קח נא את נפשי ממני כי טוב מותי מחיי
1 Kings 19:4: עתה יהוה קח נפשי כי לא טוב אנכי מאבתי

surely the place the God of Moses, the prophetic model, may be found. Reassessing the issue at stake, he formulates its presentation to the LORD along the lines of Moses' complaint in a similarly frustrating situation—that of Israel's stiff-neckedness. First, he submits his credentials as faithful prophet. From this ground, he presents Israel's sin; Israel seeks to annul the covenant by taking on other gods, and to effect this, they shut off the two channels of communication with God, namely, altars and prophets. In closing, Elijah presents the predicament of his alone-ness vis-à-vis rebellious Israel. He refrains from recommending the solution Moses proposed, for he has already tried it on impulse, and found the LORD as unreceptive to it as he was when Moses mooted it. He leaves to the LORD the task of finding answers.

2. 1 Kings 19:11-13a: The Earthquake, Wind, Fire and קול

First, we will examine 1 Kgs 19:11-13a with the focus on issues of grammar and the usage of words and phrases, so as to arrive at the best possible rendering of the text. After this, we shall consider the import of the text for the narrative of 1 Kgs 19, seeking assistance in this from the two passages that it evokes, namely, Exod. 19-20 and 33-34.

2.1. The Text of 1 Kings 19:11-13a

11 And he said, Go forth and stand upon the mountain before the LORD
And behold, the LORD [is/was] passing by and a great and strong wind [is/was] rending mountains and breaking rocks in pieces before the LORD
Not in the wind, [is/was] the LORD
And after the wind, an earthquake
Not in the earthquake, [is/was] the LORD
12 And after the earthquake, a fire
Not in the fire, [is/was] the LORD
And after the fire
קול דממה דקה
13 And it was that when Elijah heard [it], he hid his face in his mantle
And went forth and stood at the entrance of the cave.[117]

2.1.1. VERBAL AND STORY LEVEL CORRESPONDENCES WITH EXODUS NARRATIVES

It is widely recognized that this text is strongly evocative of two Exodus narratives, namely, Exod. 19-20 and 33-34. We will briefly

---

117. Drawn from NRSV and Fox (2002), 163.

1 Kings 19: Horeb

list the resonances at the verbal and story detail levels, and make reference to them later.

The awesome phenomena at Horeb in Exod. 19-20 so became a part of the retelling of the earliest history of Israel that their God became traditionally associated with them; thus the theophanic triad of storm cloud, fire and earthquake in, for example, Ps. 97:2-5. The wind, earthquake and fire 1 Kgs 19 immediately recall the events of the making of the covenant. With respect to Exod. 33-34, at the verbal level, the LORD's commands to the prophets bear correspondence re location: 1 Kgs 19:11 corresponds to Exod. 34:2 (ונצבת לי שם על ראש ההר; צא ועמדת בהר לפני יהוה). The theophanic moment is described with the same verb: ויעבר יהוה (34:6); יהוה עבר (1 Kgs 19:11).

Correspondences of story detail, as noted previously, are the forty days of fast, the time of the day at which the theophany occurs and the cave/rock-cleft. Considering the last mentioned feature: though Elijah is commanded to go out and stand on the mountain before the LORD, the most he does is to go out and stand at the entrance of the cave. In Exodus, Moses is commanded to present himself before the LORD "on top of the mountain" (34:2) but according to the LORD's spoken account, at the climax of the theophany he stands in the cleft of a rock (33:21-22a).[118] It is plausible that having Elijah stand at the cave-mouth is the narrator's device to increase the parallel with Moses' physical position in the theophany of Exod. 33-34.[119]

2.1.2. RESOLVING THE GRAMMAR OF THE TEXT

The demarcation between direct discourse and narration in this text presents a dilemma, and this matter of grammatical ambiguity must be addressed first.[120] It is clear that the passage opens with the LORD's command to Elijah; but it remains to be decided at what point, if at all, the direct speech becomes narration.

Robinson points out that typically, translations take the verb עבר√ as equivalent to a continuous past tense, construing the text from 11aβ on as narrative.[121] Robinson's problem with such a rendering is that we would have a theophany culminating in a קול, and then

---

118. Cf. Simon (1997), 204.
119. Cf. Rice (1990), 160.
120. Wurthwein discusses the issue of the integrity of the text, and surveys suggestions for its reordering. (1970), 152-166.
121. Thus: "And behold, the LORD passed by, and a great and strong wind rent the mountains, and broke in pieces the rocks before the LORD, but the LORD was not in the wind; and after the wind an earthquake, but the LORD was not in the earthquake; and after the earthquake a fire, but the LORD was not in the fire; and after the fire a קול דממה דקה."

almost immediately and awkwardly, a second קול in v.13. To solve this, he falls back on the LXX's translation of עבר with a future tense, παρελεύσεται "as is grammatically equally possible"; but it is not clear, he concedes, whether the remainder is to be taken as narrative or prediction. "I suggest," he says, "that we go the whole hog and take all of 11b-12 as prediction, continuing YHWH's speech." (Thus, "The LORD will pass by and a great and strong wind will rend the mountains...") כשמע אליהו would then refer, not to the קול of v.12, but to the LORD's words, predicting the theophany to come. So, in response, Elijah goes to the entrance of the cave. The theophany is telescoped in v.13b; "it takes for granted the preliminaries, in which YHWH is *not* to be found...and proceeds at once to the positive element, the divine voice and what it says. Thus there is only one *qôl*: v.12 foretells it; v.13 narrates it."[122]

Robinson's solution, however, would have the LORD repeatedly referring to himself in the third person (six times in 11-12). Though this feature is not at all uncommon, the occurrence of six repeats in two verses does seem rather excessive and more awkward than having two occurrences of קול in two successive verses, and this weakens Robinson's solution. Further, re Robinson's complaint against the double usage of קול, it is not necessary to understand both the occurrences as referring to exactly the same phenomenon; we shall return to this in the next section, when we study the phrase קול דממה דקה.

Meanwhile, there are alternative possibilities for demarcating direct speech from narrative in vv.11-13a, and Walsh sets out two other choices.[123]

(a) Following the brief imperative צא ועמדת בהר לפני יהוה the rest of vv.11-12 are read as a narrated account of the theophany.[124] Elijah recognizes the presence of the LORD at the קול דממה דקה and moves to the mouth of the cave.

(b) V.11aa and the first phrase following is read as the LORD's spoken command—צא ועמדת בהר לפני יהוה והנה יהוה עבר—and the rest as narrative.[125]

Walsh rightly assesses alternative (b) as less plausible since the participle form of the verb characterizes the theophany, and it seems arbitrary to divide up these vivid present constructions between the LORD and the narrator. Further, the MT punctuation does not favour such a division. This leaves us with option (a). However, Walsh widens the range of possibilities further with an attractive

---

122. Robinson (1991), 521.
123. Walsh (1996), 274-5.
124. So, Tg. Jon., KJV, NAS, RSV.
125. So, LXX, NIV, NRSV.

"compromise" between the option (a) and a rendering such as Robinson's.

> The description may fulfil a double function: it contains Yahweh's words anticipating the theophany; but it also serves as an implicit description of the events as they unfold, in order to avoid a repetition of details that would no doubt weaken the power of the images. (For a comparable use of this technique, see Exodus 9:13-21, where Yahweh's speech to Moses imperceptibly becomes Moses' repetition of the speech before Pharaoh and his court.)[126]

Simon gives an example of a similar "ellipse of scriptural narrative" within the Elijah corpus itself: in 1 Kings 21:17-20, the LORD tells Elijah what to say to Ahab; without a pause we read Ahab's response.[127] Further, as Walsh points out, the "compromise" evokes the narrative technique in Exod. 33, a text that resonates with 1 Kgs 19 in other ways as well as further discussion will show, where the LORD's announcement (rather than a narrative of the actual occurrence) of a forthcoming theophany is recorded.[128] We shall settle, then, for Robinson's proposal as modified using Walsh's creative input, as one that best resolves the difficulty posed by the text: vv.11-13a are at once both the LORD's prediction of what is to follow *and* a description of the theophany in actual occurrence.

2.1.3. THE "STILL, SMALL, VOICE"

Next, we take up the more complicated issue of what the text articulates; we make the evocative phrase קול דממה דקה our starting point.

Here, Fox makes a helpful conversation partner, in that he surveys translations of the phrase over the past thirty years or so, and sets out the possibilities for the translation of each of theˆthree words. He divides renderings to date into four schools.

(a) It is understood as the expression of a natural phenomenon—"a sound of a gentle blowing" (NASV, 1995 Update) and "the sound of a gentle breeze" (JB).

(b) It is the divine voice itself, even if rather muffled—"a gentle whisper" (NIV) and "the breath of a light whisper" (Moffat). Robinson, whom we shall interact with in the next section concerning the import of the קול דממה דקה, refers to it as "a gentle whispering qol" which is "the voice of YHWH."[129]

---

126. Walsh (1996), 274-5.
127. Simon (1997), 214.
128. Walsh (1996), 274-5.
129. Robinson (1991), 534.

(c) A third school steers a course between the two, leaving the origin of the קוֹל—whether animate or inanimate—unclear: "a low murmuring sound" (NEB) and "a tiny whispering sound" (NAB).

(d) Lastly, there is what Fox calls "the paradoxical approach, which understands the phrase as a mysterium, albeit not traemendum [sic]"—"a sound of sheer silence" (NRSV).[130]

Following Fox's observations on each of the three words helps to set out the choices one has for translation and interpretation.

2.1.3.1. "Voice"

קוֹל, Fox agrees, "can certainly mean either "sound" or "voice," yet it is the latter which is almost always indicated in biblical theophany scenes." Further, he argues, "in the Carmel scene of ch. 18, the word has already played a prominent role, so that would seem to be the logical choice."

To take his second point first: at Carmel, the Baalist prophets receive "no קוֹל, no answerer" (Kgs 18:26, 29); the word קוֹל here would best translate as "voice," since an intelligible response from an "answerer" seems anticipated. Later on, in the same chapter, Elijah forewarns Ahab of the deluge to come using the expression קוֹל הֲמוֹן הַגֶּשֶׁם (1 Kgs 18:41). Here, קוֹל can only be translated as "sound." Besides having both renderings of קוֹל, one finds that קוֹל/voice is used with respect to Baal, the non-answerer. If one is seeking to find at Horeb a God who answers with a קוֹל, in contrast to Baal who does not answer with a קוֹל, one need not look for it in 1 Kgs 19:12; rather, one naturally finds it in v.13. But even this exercise is misdirected, since, in 1 Kgs 18, the contest is not about an answer (ענה/) by קוֹל, but rather, by fire (v.24); indeed, when Elijah pleads for an answer (עֲנֵנִי; v.37), the response is fire.

Returning to Fox's first point that biblical theophany scenes almost always indicate a קוֹל/voice: a relevant text to examine this in would be Exod. 19, since the theophanic phenomena of 1 Kgs 19 evoke the parallel. In Exod. 19:11 the LORD promises to descend on Sinai in the sight of all the people on the third day. In Exod. 19:16, the events of the third day are described, and among the phenomena is a קוֹל/sound, the קוֹל שֹׁפָר חָזָק. More significant to the discussion is Exod. 19:19:

ויהי קול השופר הולך וחזק מאד משה ידבר והאלהים יעננו בקול

Here there are two aural phenomena, one from the trumpet and the other from the LORD, making the former a קוֹל/sound (as in 1 Kgs 19:16), while the latter is a קוֹל/voice, since it is part of the

---

130. Fox (2002), 164.

conversation between Moses and the LORD.¹³¹ Thus, this theophany's description employs קול in both senses, and it is not too difficult to determine which sense is intended in a given usage.

One concludes then that there are no compelling reasons to follow Fox's preference for "voice" against "sound." A preference to read "sound" for קול would depend on how the two remaining words in the expression are interpreted, but before we move on to that, there is the issue of whether the word קול here is in the absolute or construct state. קול in the absolute frequently occurs linked to a single adjective, often גדול. When in construct with other nouns, it stands as the first noun in a series of nouns, sometimes up to 4 nouns, as for example "the voice of the cry of the daughter of my people" (קול שועת בת עמי; Jer. 8:19). A not uncommon construction is for קול in the construct state to be followed by a noun which is followed by an adjective: thus, קול התרועה הגדולה (the sound of a great shout; 1 Sam. 4:6), קול חיל גדול (a sound of a great army; 2 Kgs 7:6), קול המולה גדלה (a sound of a great tempest; Jer. 11:16), קול רעש גדול (a sound of a great quaking; Eze. 3:12), קול המון שלו (a sound of a carefree multitude; Eze. 23:42). This is the pattern in קול דממה דקה, and the likelihood is that קול here is in the construct rather than in the absolute. This would correspond with the genitives of the LXX —φωνὴ αὔρας λεπτῆς.

With this we move on to the next word, and since דממה will entail more discussion than דקה, let us examine דקה first.

2.1.3.2. "Small"

דקה is the most intriguing of the three words because of its usage here. The verb √דקק means to crush, pulverize, thresh, be fine.¹³² As an adjective, דק, it is used to describe kine and ears of corn in Pharaoh's dream, manna, hair, incense, a person withered and shrunk, and dust¹³³—all of which are tangible objects. Thus 1 Kgs 19:12 remains the only instance where the adjective does not refer to something that can be felt. "Why," asks Fox, "would a writer utilize

---

131. Thereafter, the LORD speaks to Israel—Exod. 20:1, 19, 22—implying a divine קול/voice. Cf. Deut. 5:4, 22ff. It is of interest that the LXX uses the plural with respect to the trumpet—φωναὶ τῆς σάλπιγγος—and the singular with respect to God—θεὸς ἀπεκρίνατο αὐτῷ φωνῇ—though earlier, in 19:16, it uses the singular for the trumpet blast—φωνὴ τῆς σάλπιγγος. Perhaps the intention is to differentiate between the sound of the trumpet and the voice of God in Exod. 19:19?
132. BDB, דקק, 200-01.
133. Gen. 41:3, 4, 6, 7, 23, 24; Exod. 16:14; Lev. 13:30; Lev. 16:12; Lev. 21:20; Isa. 29:5; 40:15.

'thin' to describe a sound?"[134] He then offers Coote's proposal as a possible answer. Coote singles out the use of דק in the case of manna, as being particularly significant. He contrasts the קול of 1 Kgs 19 with the קול of Deut. 5:22-26. The latter betokened the danger of death—"If we hear the voice of the LORD our God any longer, we shall die" (v.25). The former קול, being described as דקה, recalls the דק manna. Thus, Coote submits, the קול is a "voice-bread." It presages life rather than death, and offers the word of the LORD as the prophet's sustenance.[135] The association appears far-fetched, and even Fox, though he does not discount it, observes that it only "hearkens back ever so slightly to nurturing images from Israel's past."[136]

Since cross-checking with the usage of דק as an adjective does not yield very decisive results, one returns to the verb.[137] Here the usage is remarkably consistent. The majority cases are in the context of idolatrous images and altars being pulverized (Exod. 32:20; 2 Chr. 15:16; 34:4; 34:7) and several of them use the word dust (עפר) to indicate the degree to which the objects are ground down (Deut. 9:21; 2 Kgs 23:6; 23:15). Two other concrete usages are the beating fine of incense (Exod. 30:36), and the crushing of grain (Isa. 28:28). Further, the verb is extended to metaphoric use: in 2 Sam. 22:43, Israel's enemies are beaten to עפר (cf. Mic. 4:13) and in Isa. 41:15, Israel will thresh mountains, making the hills as chaff (מוץ). Thus, the associations are all with finely dividing an object to the greatest possible degree; of something tangible being ground down till it is barely so.

This sense is carried quite clearly in several of the adjectival usages listed above, certainly in the case of the incense, hair and dust. The case of manna is not too far removed, either. It is described as דק מחספס דק ככפר (Exod. 16:14); as דק as a scaling or flake, and as דק as frost; the similes try to communicate its delicate thinness and smallness. Again, here is something that is at the limits of being discerned by touch.

To return to Fox's question—why would a writer use such a word to describe a קול? Perhaps the answer is that the writer does not, and דקה better describes the other word, דממה. So, we will return to דקה after having studied דממה.

---

134. Fox (2002), 165.
135. Coote (1981), 115-20.
136. Fox (2002), 165.
137. BDB, דקק, 200-01.

2.1.3.3. "STILL"; JOB 4:12-16

Fox offers the choices for דממה: it can mean "silence," or by extension, the "calm after the storm" as in Ps. 107:29; or, based on cognates and applied to passages such as Lam. 2:10 and Job 4:16, it is taken as the verbalization of mourning and understood to mean "wailing" or "murmuring."[138] Fox, preferring "voice" over "sound," and using "thin" for דקה, remains rather undecided on how to render דממה. Finally, he offers:

> At the risk of abandoning the comforting and the familiar (and the inspiring)...I would suggest that the wind/earthquake/fire sequences encourage us to understand the phrase as something on the order of 'the voice of a thin whisper' or 'a thin, murmuring voice'. I should add that I find this solution both emotionally unsatisfying and aesthetically inadequate...[139]

Fox does not justify his choice in rendering דממה; however, Schick, in his study of the stems דום and דמם makes the same choice, and may be consulted for the argument in favour of this rendition.[140] Schick begins by citing sources to show that "a comparison of the translations which the leading Hebrew dictionaries give for the stem דמם shows that they unanimously assign to it the meaning *to be silent*."[141]

For example, BDB gives the verb √דמם three categories of meaning. (a) "be silent": e.g., למען יזמרך כבוד ולא ידם (Ps. 30:13). (b) "be still," as opposed to both speech and motion: e.g., ואדם לא אצא פתח (Job 31:34). (c) "be struck dumb" in amazement and fear: e.g., ידמו כאבן describes the state of the peoples, overcome with terror and dread, as Israel passes by (Exod. 15:16).[142]

Against this, and following Paul Haupt,[143] Schick proposes that such a stem does not exist; rather, biblical Hebrew uses two other stems. First, and more commonly used, is the stem דום, which "is a poetic synonym of the more prosaic עמד," and means, by derivation from Arabic and Ethiopian cognates, and from cases in post-Biblical Hebrew: (1) *to stay, halt, remain*; (2) *to remain immoveable, be rigid*; (3) *to wait*; (4) *to stop, cease*; (5) *to come to an end, perish*.[144]

The second stem, דמם, has two usages.

---

138. Fox (2002), 164.
139. Fox (2002), 165.
140. Schick (1913), 219-243.
141. Schick (1913), 219.
142. BDB, דמם, 198-99; Baumann (1978), 260-61; 64-65.
143. Haupt (1909), 4ff. See also Levine (1993), 89-106; Dahood (1960), 400.
144. Schick (1913), 221, 242.

(1) "דמם, to moan, must be compared with Assyrian *damâmu*, to weep, lament, sigh."[145] Schick adds that this stem דמם, is "an entirely different stem from דום" but "occurs far less frequently in the OT than דום, and some of the passages in which it is found are extremely difficult, not to say desperate"; he identifies Ps. 4:5 (EVV 4:4) and 30:13 as the only two such passages. Proceeding from this, Schick resolutely states that from the stem דמם, *to whisper*, is derived the noun דממה. Accordingly, he translates 1 Kgs 19:12, "and after the fire the sound of a soft whisper"; Ps. 107:29, "He hushes the storm to a whisper"; and Job 4:16, "A form was before my eyes/A whispering voice I heard."

(2) An alternate usage of דמם is "in connection with mourning or bewailing some misfortune, either the death of some person, a national calamity, or some grievous moral evil encroaching upon a nation."[146] So, in Amos 5:13 (*to sigh*) and Isa. 23:2 and 47:5, Lam. 2:10 and 3:28 (*to moan*).[147] Since the context described above is not the context of 1 Kgs 19, Job 4:12-16 or Ps. 107:27, any shade of this usage in the דממה of these texts becomes rather unlikely.[148] That leaves one with the first usage, *to whisper*, which, as mentioned, is to be located in two texts.

Ps. 4:5 reads אמרו בלבבכם על משכבכם ודמו. English versions render it, "Commune with your own hearts upon your beds and be still/be silent." Schick argues that if דמו is understood as being derived from דמם, *to whisper*, "the passage becomes clear without resorting to emendation." למען יזמרך כבוד ולא ידם in Ps. 30:13 is usually rendered "so that my glory may sing praise to you and not be silent." Schick would have דמם here mean *to speak in a subdued, hardly audible voice*. Thus, ולא ידם is to be read "and will not mutter subdued."

Both these cases, as Schick would translate them, have the implications of indistinctly heard speech. Adding the further description of דקה with its implications of "thin," "fine" or "barely perceptible" carries the aural aspect of קול דממה דקה to the point where, for all practical purposes, דממה is a hush/silence/stillness. Further, the senses of דמם as Schick would have them, with their

---

145. BDB, דמם, 199 offers this as a second sense of the stem דמם, "to groan, wail, lament" and cites Isa. 23:2 as a possible case, adding that "most, however, assign this to I. דמם," in which case it would mean "to be struck dumb, be silent."
146. Schick (1913), 222, 238-39.
147. Schick (1913), 239.
148. Koehler and Baumgartner (1994), 226 give II. דמם as "to wail," but then links דממה to I. דמם, giving possible meanings of "calm, cessation of strong movement of air" (Ps. 107:29) and "vibrant silence" (1 Kgs 19:12).

1 Kings 19: Horeb

two proposed usages, do not make any substantial difference to the reading of the texts he lists, and he himself attests to the difficulty of the texts which use דמם, *to whisper*. Rather, the basic sense of √דמם as silence/stillness, as overwhelmingly used in translation, quite satisfies all the texts Schick lists.

Thus, Fox's two choices for דממה, "whisper"/"murmuring" are, in fact, not too far removed from the one he initially recommends as serving the context better—"silence"/"calm after the storm." A firmer approach, compared to one that uses rather uncertain cognates with a confusingly wide range of senses, is to examine the two other texts in which דממה figures, namely, Job 4:16 and Ps. 107:29. Of the two, the Job passage merits attention since it contains two common words, קול and דממה, these being used in an appreciably similar context.

Job 4:12-16
12 Now, to me a word (דבר) was spoken in secret (√גנב)
and my ear caught (√לקח) something (שמץ) of the message;
13 Amid thoughts (שעפים) from visions (חזיון) of the night
when deep sleep (תרדמה) falls upon men,
14 Dread (פחד) came upon me, and trembling,
which caused all my bones to shake.
15 Then a spirit (רוח) glides (√חלף) past my face
making the hair of my flesh stand on end./A storm makes my flesh bristle.
(ורוח על פני יחלף תסמר שערת בשרי)
16 It stands still (יעמד)...
but I cannot recognize its appearance (מראה)
A form (תמונה) is before my eyes;
a hush—then I hear a voice:/And I hear a murmuring voice: [149]
(דממה וקול אשמע)

The text creates a scene of vision and audition. Notable is the "extensive use of indeterminate language" that "underlines the mysterious, transcendental nature of Eliphaz's vision."[150] The speaker opens with a prepositional phrase "to me," underlining that this is a testimony of personal experience. The word דבר need not take on oracular implications as it does in the phrase דבר יהוה used in divine disclosures to prophets, though in this context, such a connotation is readily evoked. The matter is brought to Eliphaz by

---

149. Drawn largely from NRSV and Dhorme (1967).
150. Hartley (1988), 112 n.18.

stealth; the use of √גנב in the Pual,¹⁵¹ as Hartley observes, "connotes the clandestine setting of the experience and the privileged nature of the information received" and also reiterates the nature of prophetic vision in the OT in that the initiative for revelation originates outside the recipient; the human party does nothing to induce the vision. Adding to the idea of stealth and secrecy is the following word, the verb √לקח, which carries the extended meaning of stealing (e.g., Judg. 17:2; 18:17, 18, 24; cf. Jer. 23:20).¹⁵²

שֵׁמֶץ, found only here and in Job 26:14 in the OT, may be argued to mean "a little" or "fraction"¹⁵³ rather than the more preferred "whisper."¹⁵⁴ Either way, the general sense is that what the recipient's ear catches is only a partial knowledge of God's ways— "something wholly inadequate."¹⁵⁵

שְׂעִפִּים is yet another unusual word, with only one other occurrence and that, in the same book (Job 20:2). By some unclear semantic process this noun סָעִיף/שָׂעִיף means both "branch" (e.g., Isa. 17:6) and "thought."¹⁵⁶ Rowley attempts a connection: "Just as the boughs branch off from the trees, so thoughts and opinions can branch off in more than one direction...Eliphaz is here thinking of the confused medley of thoughts that come to one in sleep"¹⁵⁷ or in "night visions." חזיון is yet another word used infrequently, four of its ten occurrences being found in Job alone (7:14; 20:8; 33:15). Its usage suggests that Eliphaz here receives a divine communication¹⁵⁸ (cf. the technical sense of √חזה), and the following noun, תרדמה, reiterates this. Though תרדמה may describe a deep natural sleep (e.g., Prov. 19:15), and Eliphaz speaks of it falling generally "on men," most other usages of √רדם suggest a divinely induced stupor (Gen. 2:21; Ps. 76:7; Dan. 8:18; 10:9), with the purpose of divine communication (Gen. 15:12; Isa. 29:10). The most significant usage is Gen. 15:12. A similar תרדמה falls upon Abraham as the sun goes down, during which he is overwhelmed by dread—אימה and

---

151. Werblowsky proposes that the form may be a technical or semi-technical term used in connection with nocturnal revelations, and thus "describe a specific kind of reception of the dabhar." (1956), 105-06. Cf. Robertson (1960), 416-17.
152. Hartley (1988), 111.
153. Based on the usage in Sir. 10:10 and 18:32. E.g., Gordis (1978), 48; Dhorme (1967), 49; Rowley (1970), 53; KJV.
154. From the Arabic cognate meaning to "speak rapidly and indistinctly." BDB, שֶׁמֶץ, 1036; most EVV.
155. BDB, שֶׁמֶץ, 1036.
156. BDB, סָעִף, 972; Gordis (1978), 48.
157. Rowley (1970), 53.
158. Used of visions in the ecstatic state, of night visions and of divine communications in a vision, oracle or prophecy. BDB, חזה, 303.

1 Kings 19: Horeb

darkness; these are preambles to the LORD opening communication with him. Eliphaz too, in the course of his nighttime תרדמה is seized by dread—פחד (used alongside אימה in Exod. 15:16), prior to receiving the divine word. Terror "encounters"[159] him, penetrating his very bones.[160]

Now the verbs change from descriptive perfects to historic presents, "vividly describing his experience as though he is passing through it again."[161] A רוח sweeps by (√חלף) Eliphaz's face. רוח, notably, is nowhere used of disembodied spirits,[162] and seldom in the masculine, in which case it is used more often of air in motion. However, if רוח is taken to be the subject of the next verb, √סמר, רוח appropriates both genders;[163] as subject of יחלף it would be masculine in the first stich, and as subject of תסמר it would be feminine in the second stich. Though this grammatical phenomenon is not uncommon, being attested to in Job 1:19 and also in 1 Kgs 19:11 (רוח גדולה וחזק), it adds to the ambivalence.

Coming to the verbs themselves, the verb √חלף is used both to describe the swift passing by of both the wind (Hab. 1:1) and of the LORD (Job 9:11; 11:10). As for √סמר, it ocurrs twice: here, in the Piel and in Ps. 119:20 in the Qal; opinion is divided over which noun is its subject.

(a) One proposal is that the subject of תסמר is שערת, where שערה is an alternate spelling for סערה/storm,[164] and the -ת ending is taken as the older form of the absolute.[165] Thus שערת/storm would be parallel to רוח/wind as in, for example, Isa. 41:16. Thus: "A storm makes my flesh bristle" (as in "gooseflesh").[166] Dahood sees here a certain poetic device known as "the breakup of a stereotyped phrase." Thus, the stereotyped phrase רוח סערה (Ps. 148:8; Ezek. 1:4) has its two

---

159. The verb root here is possibly קרה rather than קרא (Gordis (1978), 49; see GKC, §75rr), and Gordis notes that the same verb is used of the encounter of God with the gentile prophet Balaam in Num. 23:3 (Gordis (1978), 49).
160. "Affections, and even emotions, pervading or affecting strongly a man's being, are particularly attributed to them [the bones], or conceived as operating in them." Driver and Gray (1921), 45.
161. Rowley (1970), 54.
162. Clines (1989), 111; Rowley (1970), 54; Driver and Gray (1921), 46.
163. See Albrecht (1896), 42-44.
164. As in Job 9:17 and Nah. 1:3; however, elsewhere spelt סערה, cf. Job 38:1.
165. GKC, §80 g.
166. So, for example, (following the Targum—"Then a strong wind passes before my face;/A storm makes my flesh glow."), Gordis (1978), 49; Dahood (1967), 544-45; Blommerde (1969), 40-41.
167. ורוח תשאם וסערה תפיץ אותם.
168. Dahood (1967), 544-45.

elements separated (cf. Isa. 41:16)¹⁶⁷ making equivalents between the two lines, which seems a possibility:¹⁶⁸

פני	יחלף	רוש
בשרי	תסמר	שערת

(b) An alternate proposal is to take שערת as the construct form of שערה, meaning "hair", where the feminine singular is understood as a generic term and not a nomen unitatis. The verb תסמר could then be read either as an intransitive, as in Ps. 119:20, with שערת בשרי as its subject ("the hair of my body stands on end")¹⁶⁹ or it could take רוח as its subject ("a spirit/wind causes the hair of my body to stand on end").¹⁷⁰

Paul suggests that both proposals (a) and (b) are equally possible, and perhaps the ambiguity is deliberate, a double entendre on both meanings being intended, with overtones of the storm theophany of Job 28.¹⁷¹ This could well be, considering the unusual extent of indeterminate language in this text. This feature continues into the next verse; it begins with יעמד—"it/one stands still," the subject being indefinite, though there is general agreement that it refers to the תמונה. The vagueness heightens the awe and terror of the moment. Significantly, תמונה is invariably used either with reference to God or to some representation that Israel may substitute for God in worship.¹⁷² Moses sees the תמונה of God (Num. 12:8), while at Sinai, Israel categorically does not see any תמונה (Deut. 4:12). Thus, it is not surprising that Eliphaz's claim to have both seen and heard God is negated in part by the LXX.¹⁷³ Significantly, common to Job 4:16 and Num. 12:8 are both תמונה and מראה, both nouns used in the context of divine communication. A further point of note is the shortness of the line which consists of יעמד; it has a single word instead of the usual three. Besides the suggestion that there are words missing here, it is proposed that this could be deliberate, a dramatic device to convey Eliphaz's fearfulness even at the recollection of the moment.¹⁷⁴

---

169. E.g., Rowley (1970), 54; Clines (1989), 111.
170. E.g., Dhorme (1967), 50-51.
171. Paul (1983), 119-21.
172. Used of God in Num. 12:8; Deut. 4:12, 15; Ps. 17:15: used of substitutes in worship in Exod. 20:4; Deut. 4:16, 23, 25; Deut. 5:8.
173. LXX: ἀνέστην καὶ οὐκ ἐπέγνων εἶδον καὶ οὐκ ἦν μορφὴ πρὸ ὀφθαλμῶν μου ἀλλ' ἢ αὔραν καὶ φωνὴν ἤκουον. The reading of יעמד as אעמד is probably out of dogmatic considerations—the desire to avoid any approximation of an image of God. Gordis (1978), 49. Similarly, תמונה.
174. See Rowley (1970), 55; Clines (1989), 111-12; Hartley (1988), 109.

The visual now becomes the aural: דְּמָמָה וָקוֹל אֶשְׁמָע. Besides Job 4:16 and 1 Kgs 19:12, the only other occurrence of דממה is in Ps. 107:29:

יָקֵם סְעָרָה לִדְמָמָה וַיֶּחֱשׁוּ גַּלֵּיהֶם

Here the meaning of דממה is less clouded, because of the seafarer context (vv.23-32). The LORD commands the stormy wind (רוח סערה) and the waves are lifted up (v.25); he then commands the storm (סערה) into a hush (דממה) and the waves are stilled; the sailors are glad because they (i.e., the waves) have been quieted— √שׁתק, used of the sea in Jon. 1:11, 12—and are brought to their desired haven (v.30). This usage of the rare word דממה directs the assumption that it is derived from √דמם "to be or grow dumb, silent, still."[175] Such a "calm after the storm" reading would be relevant to both the Job and Kings texts: in the latter, there is a devastatingly "great and strong wind" (1 Kgs 19:11) succeeded by similarly violent natural phenomena; in the former, there is the possibility of reading שערת as storm (Job 4:15).

This leaves the problem of the relationship between דממה and קול in the line דְּמָמָה וָקוֹל אֶשְׁמָע, and here opinion is evenly divided. Either one privileges the MT accentuation and dissociates קול from דממה, reading "silence/a hush—and/then I hear a voice";[176] or, one privileges the MT pausal vocalization of וָקוֹל, and links קול to דממה, and reads it as a hendiadys, "I hear a murmuring voice."[177] Both being possible, one refers to the earliest rendering of the unpointed text, the LXX, which reads: αὔραν καὶ φωνὴν ἤκουον. Here a difference is made between קול and דממה, one being a breath (perhaps of air), and the other being a cognizable voice, and this appears to favour disjunction. We will go with this reading since, as we shall see, it ties in with the only other passage in which a theophany is described in similar terms.[178]

In summary, two features stand out in Job 4:12-16, both comparable with 1 Kings 19. First, as mentioned before, there is an extensive use of indeterminate, infrequently used language, possibly compounded by the use of double entendre. The combined weight

---

175. BDB, דמם, 198-99.
176. So, for e.g., Rowley (1970), 55; Hartley (1988), 109; Gordis (1978), 50; RSV, KJV, JB, ASV.
177. NEB, NAB, NIV, JPS. Dhorme does not see a hendiadys, but parallels this text with 1 Kgs 19:12 to conclude that "the word דממה in our text has simply been detached from its context to be thrown into relief. In fact, it is וקול which should open the hemistich...the last hemistich is therefore simply: 'And I hear a whispered voice'." 1967), 51-52.
178. We note that in variation from Kings, the Job text has the words קול and דממה in the reverse order and connected by a copula.

of the words and the phrasing is an index of the struggle to render into human language a supernatural experience—here, an intimate encounter with the divine. In Kings too, language is pushed to the limits to describe an intensely private encounter between prophet and God; thus the mysterious קול דממה דקה. The change of tense in Job 4:15, 16 to the imperfect vivifies the description just as does the change to participles in 1 Kgs 19:11.

Secondly, the vision and audition account in Job follows the OT pattern in that hearing dominates over seeing. There is a form, but it is unrecognisable; however there is a voice, and the words it speaks are readily and perfectly identifiable. In Kings, once the procession of phenomena in which the LORD is not is ended, Elijah's hearing takes over from seeing; it is a sound/voice that he responds to, as if in recognition of the divine presence.

Flowing from this, there arises the question of the double usage of the word קול in 1 Kgs 19:12, 13; are both usages identical, and if not, how are they related to each other?

2.1.3.4. The Two "קול"s

In Ps. 107:29, דממה is clearly the opposite of סערה, and is therefore a phenomenon of nature; a gentle breeze/a calm. As suggested earlier, this could well inform the interpretation of the scene at Horeb. The violence of the stormy mountain-rending and rock-splitting רוח, and the further violence of the earthquake and the fire are followed by a sudden, eerie calm. The idea that דממה is no more than a barely discernible breath (of wind), a hush, an uncanny stillness in nature, a vibrant silence, fits well as an unexpected and dramatic climax to the parade of the elements of nature in 1 Kgs 19. Fox remarks that such a reading (as "calm after the storm") makes "eminent sense" here.[179] קול would then best read "sound" and the phrase would then approximate "sound of a (דקה) calm." (This would correspond with the genitives of the LXX, φωνὴ αὔρας λεπτῆς.) דקה, as we have seen, defines that which is fine and delicate, barely discernible by touch. Putting all three words together one arrives at "sound of a fine/sheer calm/hush/silence." Walsh makes a similar choice in rendering the phrase "sound of sheer silence," and we may borrow his rationale to round off our line of argument and the choices we have settled on:

---

179. Fox (2002), 164. In spite of acknowledging this in his discussion on דממה, Fox, as already quoted, concludes with the translation, "the voice of a thin whisper"/"a thin, murmuring voice." He does not properly justify his choice for rendering דממה, other than to mention that "wailing" or "murmuring" "clarifies Job's vision in 4.16…I heard a *droning voice*."

The numinous power of the image lies precisely in our inability to grasp it—a quality utterly lost by translations that render it "a thin whispering sound" or the like; the NRSV's "sound of sheer silence" captures the senses perfectly with losing any of its mysterious paradox.[180]

(Walsh's understanding is that the קול דממה דקה, with its rich chiastic sound (*q-d-m*/*m-d-q*) and mysterious paradoxical sense is the phenomenon that "*contains*" the divine presence,[181] a point we will return to later.)

If our choice of translation/s is valid, the קול of v.13 would be a speaking קול, a voice. That the קול of v.13 is not identical with the קול of v.12 is supported by the narrator's choice not to use an article—"And behold! A voice comes to him!" If the narrator had meant the same aural phenomenon as in v.12, the likelihood is that he would have used "*the* voice comes to him."

This scheme makes two points, both with reference to Exod. 19:19, which we have commented on earlier. (a) It gives a reasonable explanation for the double usage of the word קול in two successive verses, the difference in the usage corresponding to the pattern in Exod. 19:19. (b) 1 Kgs 19:13 need not have used the word קול; it could have used instead the usual formula that the rest of the Elijah narrative uses, namely, the word of the LORD [came] to him— דבר יהוה אליו (1 Kgs 17:2, 8; 18:31; 19:9; cf. 18:1). However, 1 Kgs 19:13 has a variation—קול אליו. Considering that the previous verses have described a theophany much in resonance with Exod. 19, the variation takes on significance. In Exod. 19, the description of physical phenomena, the קול/sound of the "trumpet" included, climaxes with the speaking voice of God himself. Extrapolating this sequence to 1 Kgs 19, one has a description of physical phenomena, the קול/sound of the "hush" included, leading to the speaking voice of God. Thus Elijah's being addressed by a קול/voice recalls Moses' first experience at Horeb.

There is, however, a marked difference between the Exod. 19 and 1 Kgs 19 theophanies. The former has a longer list of natural phenomena (vv.16-18: thunder and lightning, thick cloud, smoke, fire, quake) than the latter. More significantly, where the latter has a hush just before the speaking voice, the former has a trumpet sound growing louder and louder (v.19). These two differences correspond to the difference in situation. In Exod. 19, it is all Israel, standing beyond the set boundaries, which is the intended beneficiary of the theophany (vv.9-17). The event is so that Israel may meet God (v.17), and trust Moses, seeing that he mediates between God and them (v.9). However, in 1 Kgs 19, the situation is vastly different in that it

---

180. Walsh (1996), 276.
181. Walsh (1996), 276.

is intensely private. Thus, one has a hush, rather than a loud trumpet sound, and this is in line with the Job 4 theophany, granted privately to Eliphaz. Having discussed the various key words in these two private theophanies, we may now set them out against each other.

Job 4:15-16	1 Kgs 19:11-13
שׂערת/רוח	אש/רעש/רוח גדולה וחזק
a wind/a storm	a great and mighty wind/earthquake/fire
דממה	קול דממה דקה
a hush	a sound of a sheer calm
וקול אשמע	אליו קול
and I hear a voice	a voice [came] to him

The Job 4 and 1 Kgs 19 theophanies reinforce each other re the order of events: tumultuous phenomena, associated with nature; a profound hush; finally, the speaking voice of God. What Fox says of his rendering applies with this proposal as well, namely, that it risks "abandoning the comforting and the familiar (and the inspiring)." He speaks with special reference to the KJV's "still, small voice," a rendering which "has stood up remarkably well for almost four hundred years."[182] However, as Fox's categorizations of renderings show, translators over the past thirty years have taken that risk, opening up the exploration of alternatives. The rendering argued here, for reasons submitted, would disagree only with the approach that considers קול דממה דקה as an indication of God speaking ("a gentle whisper"/"the breath of a light whisper"). It would have no serious quarrel either with the approach that understands it as the expression of a natural phenomenon ("a sound of a gentle blowing/breeze"), or with the "non-committal" approach that leaves the source of the phenomenon unclear ("a low murmuring sound"/"a tiny whispering sound"). It falls in line, however, with the "paradoxical approach" — "a sound of sheer silence."

In the Kings narrative, as in Job, this evocative phrase describes the divine presence, and this is signalled in four ways. First, the disclaimer that trails in the wake of each of the physical phenomena speaks by its sudden absence here. Implicitly, the LORD is in this fourth phenomenon, a point that the LXX emphatically draws attention to with the insertion κἀκεῖ κύριος.

Second, language, which so articulately described the first three events, now strains to find ideograms to "represent" what von Rad

---

182. Fox (2002), 165.

describes as "the extreme limit of apprehension by the senses."[183] In the endeavour, two aural words are followed by a tactile one. Similarly, Moses' bush burns—הסנה בער באש—but does not burn —לא יבער הסנה (3:2, 3). Ezekiel falls back on strings of qualifiers (Ezek. 1:26-38); ultimately, all that he will claim is that he saw "the *appearance* of the *likeness* of the glory of the LORD (Ezek. 1:28)." Rendering this ineffable phrase faithfully—a continuing challenge—is less important than recognizing it as an announcement of the actual and real presence of the LORD.[184]

Third, it is this last phenomenon that provokes the hitherto apparently passive observer into activity. One understands that Elijah has been waiting, watchful for the moment he must go out and present himself. As soon as he discerns the divine presence, he covers his face. "The gesture," Terrien observes, "is an acknowledgement of the inward certainty of the presence, and at the same time, the recognition of the *mysterium traemendum* [sic] of holiness."[185]

Fourth, it is from the womb of this קול דממה דקה that a speaking קול emerges and it asks the question that the "word of the LORD" had asked earlier. Elijah's response confirms to the reader that the prophet sees no difference in the two media, דבר and קול. Both are divine communications, only the קול is more intimate. If we are to read intertextually with Exod. 33-34 then, Elijah's experience of the divine recalls Moses': the LORD habitually spoke with Moses as familiarly as one speaks with a friend (Exod. 33:11) and Num. 7:89 explains further using the word קול to describe how the LORD "spoke" with Moses in private. In Exod. 34:5, in private theophany, there is an implicit speaking קול—the LORD "descended…stood with him there…proclaimed the name."

Thus, a clear contrast is created between the physical phenomena and the קול דממה דקה: A series of striking negations explicitly conveys the absence of divine presence in the former; the latter, as

---

183. Von Rad (1975), 20.
184. Thus, even an odd rendering of קול דממה דקה such as Lust's "a roaring and thunderous voice" —(1975), 110-15—is preferable to those that read it, for example, in terms of a Jungian framework, as does Wiener (1978), in that it acknowledges the concreteness of the theophany.
185. Terrien (1978), 232. Tg. Jon. reads: "…the Lord was revealing himself, and before him were armies of the angels" of wind, earthquake and fire respectively; in none of these was "the Shekinah of the Lord." But after "the army of the angels of fire was the voice of those who were praising softly." "Softly" has the sense of "whispering" or "stillness," and the Targums connect God with quiet or silent prayer. The implication seems to be that the Lord has finally revealed himself and thus, contact has been established between the Lord and his waiting prophet.

expressed by language, intertextual allusion and narrative detail, mysteriously, yet compellingly communicates the divine presence. "The invisibility of a God who yet speaks remains the cardinal tenet of a Hebraic theology of presence."[186] This leads to the question of the meaning of this theophany with its curious absence-presence feature, and its implications for the story of 1 Kgs 19.

2.2. The LORD's Absence and Presence in vv.11-13a

Robinson makes a profitable conversation partner in any discussion on the import of קוֹל דְּמָמָה דַקָּה since he casts his net wide, succinctly surveying the various interpretative moves from the Targums through patristic commentaries down to the present.[187] Most helpful is that, in conclusion, he offers a "synthesis" of the views that he deems "on the right lines," since his synthesis is representative of the major trends in interpreting this difficult text. We shall interact with this synthesis one half at a time. The first half reads:

> In ch. 18, YHWH has vanquished the power of Baal by his mastery of those natural elements which the pagan god was believed to control. In this chapter, the polemic against paganism is continued. It is true that the natural elements are often used by YHWH, but he remains beyond them, transcendent, mysterious, obscurely perceived.

There are two points of emphasis here; first, the polemic against paganism, and secondly, the divine self-revelation. On both points, Robinson concurs with Baumann, whom he quotes:

> If demamah is used in a particular way in Job 4:16 and 1 K. 19:12 to describe the reception of a revelation, a theophany, this is to be understood as a deliberate attempt to separate the Israelite concept of theophany from the religious ideas of the ancient Near East. At the same time, that which is totally imperceptible, intangible, and inaudible in the theophany is characterized most clearly.[188]

Let us consider the first point of emphasis—the polemic in the form of the LORD being categorically disassociated with natural phenomena. Here we may refer to J. Jeremias, who first proposed a polemical bias as underlying the text:

> Were there circles in Israel which spoke of the coming of Yahweh in the 'still, small voice (of the wind),' and which rejected the link, often made in

---

186. Terrien (1978), 112.
187. Robinson (1991), 522-535.
188. Baumann (1978), 264-65.

Israel, between Yahweh and the destructive forces of nature, because, in Israel's religious environment, the manifestation of the gods was usually just so linked with them? In this case it was not a more refined conception of God which characterized these circles, but their opposition to equating the religion of Yahweh with the religions of the world around. The polemic against the world around would necessarily lead to a polemic against Israel's own religious tradition. At the time of Elijah such a polemic would have been quite conceivable.[189]

The polemical tone of 1 Kgs 18 can be traced back into the start of the Elijah narratives. The stories in 1 Kgs 17 are strongly confrontational in nature—Elijah against Ahab, Elijah against famine, Elijah against death. The theme climaxes at Carmel, being pushed into relief by the plot of the narrative. Elijah sets up the "contest" with polemical intent, for Baal, to the knowledge of his audience, is the storm god, with thunderbolts at his command. As it turns out, it is the LORD who sends fire and "wins." Let us suppose that, as Robinson proposes, "the polemic against paganism is continued" into 1 Kgs 19.

In 1 Kgs 19, the narrative takes a dramatic, unexpected turn. The prophet who has hitherto single-handedly taken on the crown, the people and 450 Baalist prophets is himself on the run. The world of the story becomes small and intimate, peopled only with a prophet and his God. The overriding concern is the prophet's lapse and possible restoration. Such a story would not logically call for polemic against paganism as in the preceding two chapters, and if there was indeed such, it would then seem to be arbitrarily introduced, especially since Elijah himself does not need that lesson.

Secondly, at Carmel, the polemical feature is that the LORD demonstrates his superiority over Baal by associating himself with a natural element, fire. At Horeb, if we are to assume the polemic continues, it continues with the LORD dissociating himself from the same element. In 2 Kgs 1, he will once more polemically associate himself with fire, again in confrontation with a Baal-serving monarch. These shifts are too confusing to be plausible.

Thirdly, the theophany is not quite straightforward in its associations and dissociations. The three natural phenomena are not "natural" in the usual sense and therefore certainly in some way part of the theophany; yet the LORD is absent from this section of the "theophany." This could well convey the same sense as in other passages where the LORD is not identified with, but yet is associated with natural forces (for example, Ps. 97:2f: "Clouds and thick darkness are round about him...fire goes before him"). (On the other hand, it could have other implications, which we shall consider

---

189. Jeremias (1965), 115, translated by and cited in Wurthwein (1970), 155.

later.) Further, as we have discussed in the previous section, there is the possibility that קוֹל דְּמָמָה דַקָּה could have been understood as a natural phenomenon—a gentle breeze, and the story implies that this did contain the LORD's presence in some way that Elijah could readily discern. All this subtlety and ambiguity in the text makes it hard to postulate a clearly defined polemic against paganism.[190]

The second point of emphasis in Robinson's proposal for the import of the theophany is the self-revelation that God is beyond natural phenomena; he is "transcendent, mysterious, obscurely perceived."[191] This is the position of a number of patristic commentaries, in that they find the theophany to point to the impossibility of knowing God.[192] "The God of biblical faith, even in the midst of a theophany, is at once *Deus revelatus atque absconditus*. He is known as unknown."[193]

This is true not only of this theophany but also of the other two at Horeb that this theophany evokes. In Exod. 33-34, the closest parallel to Elijah's situation, there is the irony that even as the prophet is

---

190. A variation is the proposal that Elijah is being taught that the LORD henceforth dissociates himself from Baalist nature-related thaumaturgy. The LORD is concerned to correct the misconception that he is identical to the powers of nature and can be perceived only through them. (Cross (1973), 190-94; Rice (1990), 159. Cf. Bronner, (1968), 63.) This hypothesis however, makes it difficult to explain the second fire-from-heaven incident in 2 Kgs 1. And further, as Simon points out, 1 Kgs 18 "offers no substantive basis for the idea of fire as a manifestation of the godhead." Both Elijah's condition for the contest (v.24) and the narrator's description of the fire (v.38) speak of the element as being God-sent rather than as a materialization of the deity. So also, Israel's confession (v.39) does not contain the fear of death as it does at Horeb (Exod. 20:18-21; Deut. 18:16-17). (1997), 210-11.
191. A slightly different slant on the self-revelation theme is Fohrer's: "The being of Yahweh is not depicted with symbols of storm, earthquake and fire, which symbolize the sudden and frightening power of the holy and unapproachable God that scorns all efforts of self-defence by man. The divine being is rather described by the gentle stillness of the breeze." Thus, "there is a turning from the God of war and battles to the God whose being is not revealed in terrifying outbursts, but who can be compared to the gentle stillness of the breeze." (1957), 89, translated by and cited in Wurthwein, (1970), 154. However, this interpretation does not offer much towards engaging profitably with the narrative that follows, in which the LORD declares his plans to purge Israel with the very "war and battles" that Fohrer proposes he is turning away from.
192. Robinson quotes Paterius, notary of Gregory I, Claudius, bishop of Turin and Rupert of Deutz who offer this identical reflection, possibly all from the same patristic source: "Tunc ergo verum est quod de Deo cognoscimus, cum plene nos aliquid de illo cognoscere non posse sentimus." (1991), 525.
193. Terrien (1978), 119.

granted unparalleled access into the divine presence, he is covered (again, ironically, by God's own "hand") until God has passed by (Exod. 33:22). Even as the deity reveals, he conceals. In Exod. 19-20, where the theophany is attended by phenomena as in 1 Kgs 19, the self-disclosure is to a people. Yet, even though God spoke to them "face to face" they "saw no form" (Deut. 5:4; 4:12); at the core of Israel's most intimate experience of God, there is the paradox of non-experience.

However, there is a difference. These two theophanies both have the express purpose of divine self-revelation; one is given at the request of Moses to "see" God, and the other is at God's initiative and in order to bind a people to himself in covenant. Thus, both open with self-introductions—"The LORD, the LORD, merciful and gracious..." (Exod. 34:6ff.) and "I am the LORD your God, who..." (Exod. 20:2).[194] In 1 Kgs 19, when the prophet is asked what concern brings him "here" (to Horeb), he does not ask to be granted a theophanic self-revelation; rather, he states his problem re Israel. The LORD chooses to reply with a theophany. While it is quite possible that the LORD's reply (whatever it might articulate) *incorporates* the not unfamiliar theophanic paradox of immanence-transcendence, it is unlikely that self-revelation as a transcendent deity is a focal point thereof. However, let us assume with Robinson that in answer, the LORD grants Elijah a self-revelation in terms of his transcendence — "the gentle murmuring which is YHWH's self-expression in a specific form."[195] What purpose does it serve? This leads us to interact with the second half of Robinson's proffered "synthesis" of views that he sees as along the right lines.

Robinson proposes, "YHWH plans this subdued sound in part as rebuke to Elijah's megalomania." (The other reason, as discussed, is to repudiate any association with Baal.) Elijah believes himself to be "a worthy spiritual descendant of that great prophet," Moses,[196] and "is willing to continue to serve only on his terms; he requires a clear manifestation of YHWH's power and protection."[197] This megalomania is censured by the קוֹל דממה דקה in two ways: first, Robinson finds it plausible that the קוֹל is implicitly articulating that a spectacular theophany cannot or will not be given to Elijah. Here, he makes reference to Eichrodt, who traces the evolution of divine communication on a larger framework. Over time (Eichrodt proposes), fire, storm and earthquake

---

194. Cf. Exod. 3, a third theophany at Horeb, again with the express purpose of divine self-revelation, which opens with a formula of self-identification (v.6).
195. Robinson (1991), 527.
196. Robinson (1991), 519.
197. Robinson (1991), 534.

acquired a predominantly symbolic significance as a representation of God's intervention in history...and its function of making the invisible God concretely visible diminished in importance...*Elijah's encounter with God at Horeb provides the first clear indication of a changed attitude.*[198] Here it is expressly stated that God is not in the storm, nor in the earthquake nor in the fire...The manifestation of God in fire [cf. Ex. 3] had already betrayed a sense that the lineaments of the divine were not confined to any fixed forms, but were inconceivable by Man. Now they have passed completely into the invisible, out of which the divine word sounds forth as the only element of the divine nature which human senses can grasp. The elemental forces are no longer the means by which God is made visible, but have become phenomena accompanying the divine activity, his 'garment' [cf. Ps. 104:1], his glory [cf. Ex. 24:17], his messenger [cf. Ps. 104:4].[199]

Perhaps Robinson reads the text better by preferring to lay emphasis, not on the closure of the era of spectacular theophanies,[200] but to infer that "[i]t is possible...to be a spiritual son of Moses without experiencing the outward manifestation of YHWH's glory in a convulsion of natural forces as Moses did on Sinai."[201]

The assumption here is that Elijah's requirement of the LORD at Horeb is that he be awarded a theophany such as Moses experienced. This is not implausible, but in the absence of any help from the narrator on this issue, this need not be the only way to read the intentions of the character portrayed. The opposite holds an equal chance, namely, the postulation that Elijah may not particularly be in search of an Exodus-like theophany; he simply needs to seek out the LORD for direction in this his crisis of uncertainty, and his urgent need takes him to the place where, more than in any other place, a prophet who would emulate Moses may find him.

Further, in Exod. 19-20, the place of "the outward manifestation of YHWH's glory in a convulsion of natural forces," the phenomena are part of the great moment of the LORD binding himself with Israel in covenant, rather than about the inter-personal dynamics between Moses and God. As regards Moses, the theophany formally legitimates and establishes his office as covenant mediator. These elements are not part of the Horeb scene in 1 Kgs 19. Any endorsement of his status as true prophet and mediator Elijah has already requested and obtained at Carmel ("...let it be known this day that you are God...that I am your servant..." 1 Kgs 18:36) before

---

198. Italics added.
199. Eichrodt (1967), 19-20. Cf. Skinner (n.d.), 240; Gray (1964), 365.
200. As do Terrien (1978), 231-2; Hauser and Gregory (1990), 117.
201. Robinson (1991), 525-6.

all Israel. At Horeb, there is no Israel, only the prophet and God; thus, it might not be apposite to impute to Elijah the desire for Moses' experience in Exod. 19-20 per se.

However, what is awarded Elijah at Horeb that is reminiscent of the extraordinary relationship between Moses and the LORD is the speaking of the LORD to Elijah in a קול (1 Kgs 19:13, rather than v.12). "When Moses went into the tent of meeting to speak with him [the LORD], he would hear the voice (הקול) speaking to him" (Num. 7:89). Thus, in this situation of personal encounter at Horeb, Elijah's experience corresponds with Moses' own private moments with the LORD.

The other way the קול דממה דקה rebukes Elijah's "megalomania," Robinson holds, is that

> ...the theophany that he experiences on Horeb, while having Mosaic overtones, owes its climax more to the Ex 33-34 than to the Ex 19 tradition, and serves to remind Elijah of what had been the essence of Moses' experience, the commandments of God. It is the duty of a prophet to fulfil them, rather than look for a dramatic endorsement of his prophetic status and an unconditional guarantee of his personal safety.[202]

Here, one presumes that the "commandments of God" take the form of the question that the קול asks—"What concerns you here, Elijah?"—since Robinson understands the question to be a command that Elijah must return to where his work lies.[203]

In the section on 1 Kgs 19:9b, we have discussed that the question need not be a confrontational one; considering similar occurrences of the idiom in other narratives, we concluded that it could be a formal invitation to dialogue.

Next, Moses' experience in Exod. 33-34: this episode in Israel's history explores the consequences and possibilities following unfaithfulness to the covenant. Wilful disobedience to the commandments brings the covenant to breaking point; the LORD proposes to "consume" (Exod. 32:10) the very people he had taken as his "treasured possession" (Exod. 19:5). Moses' dogged perseverance in mediation ultimately results in a renewed covenant and a restored relationship. Possibly even more than Israel, it is Moses who learns from this experience that with the LORD, obedience is no small matter.

One characteristic of Elijah, as portrayed in the previous two chapters, is his unquestioning obedience to the commands of the LORD, often at great risk to his life. In chapter 19, Elijah does slip

---

202. Robinson (1991), 527.
203. Robinson (1991), 522, 534.

badly, the nadir being the point at which he asks to die. However, the reversal begins almost immediately, in that he obediently submits to being fed and strengthened towards a further task—a journey. As we have proposed previously, Elijah's journey to Horeb could well be interpreted as an attempt at self-restoration. It is to his credit if, in this endeavour, he retraces the footsteps of a model prophet, Moses. It is plausible to assume Elijah's appreciation of the fact that Moses' associations with Horeb are to do with the relationship between the LORD and Israel, and not with personal gain or glory. Thus, we may envisage that in coming to Horeb, Elijah is demonstrating obedience to his calling as a prophet and mediator between the LORD and his people. As such, a further exhortation to obedience (other than the subtle one received at the broom tree) such as Robinson proposes, may be redundant.

In summary, we have discussed reasons why the theophany at Horeb in 1 Kgs 19 is best not interpreted as a polemic against Baalism, or as a special case of divine self-revelation in terms of transcendence, or as a rebuke directed at Elijah. It is possible that there is another way to understand the text, which will make sense of the phenomenon of absence and presence both in its immediate and wider contexts.

2.3. *Reconsidering the LORD's Absence and Presence in vv.11-13a*

In 1 Kgs 19:8, Elijah arrives at Horeb; in v.19 he departs. The text in between, vv.9-18, is the dialogue between the prophet and the LORD. The latter initiates it and concludes it. The LORD opens by asking the reason for Elijah's presence at Horeb. Elijah's response in v.10 describes a problem, and since this problem is presented in answer to the LORD's question, it is reasonable to suppose that this is the reason for his presence at Horeb, namely, to present this predicament before the LORD. Similarly, it is reasonable to suppose that the LORD's command following in v.11 is directly in response to what Elijah has just said. Elijah is to stand on the mountain. The LORD then passes by and what follows is a description of his passing by. This would then be the LORD's answer to Elijah's statement in v.10.

Thus, the sense of the theophany lies within the context of the conversation between Elijah and God. What it articulates must be, first and foremost, relevant to the direction and flow of the dialogue. The burden of Elijah's presentation, as discussed previously, is Israel and her covenantal relationship to the LORD. So, perhaps this relationship is a good place to seek clues to unlocking the import of the LORD's absence and presence in the elements of the theophany.

The verb Elijah uses to describe what Israel is doing with the covenant, and thus with their relationship with the LORD, is √עזב. The basic meaning of √עזב is "leave"; there is a removal from an object, thereby dissolving connections with that object. "With regard to persons, this sort of turning away or separation also generates juridical, economic, political and emotional considerations." For example, "abandoning" a clan member "violates the elementary bonds of community and calls life itself into question." An abandoned sick slave (1 Sam. 30:13), David's abandoned concubines (2 Sam. 15:16), the abandoned wife (Deut. 24:1) are left to an uncertain and unhappy fate. When the LORD and Israel are the subject or object of √עזב, these societal obligations and implications are borrowed: thus, for example, no more can the LORD forsake his people than a mother her child (Isa. 49:14f.).[204]

Flowing from this general use, √עזב has special usage in law, where it refers to "the end of a relationship of solidarity between members of a community or group, with various legal consequences attaching to such 'leaving'." An extension of these general and special usages is in theology, as concerns the relationship between the LORD and Israel. Both the Deuteronomistic and the Chronicler's history use √עזב almost as a leitmotif in exilic-postexilic reflections on history: Israel has sinned and forsaken the LORD.[205] Similarly, texts in which the law, the covenant or the commandments are forsaken (√עזב) follow the same semantic model, and are thus understood as a violation of loyalty toward another person.[206]

A text which well illustrates this theological usage of √עזב, features both God and Israel as the subject of the verb, and which carries the various implications of its general use, is Deut. 31:16-17:

> The LORD said to Moses, "Soon you will lie down with your ancestors. Then this people will begin to prostitute themselves to the foreign gods in their midst, the gods of the land into which they are going; they will forsake me (√עזב) , breaking (√פרר) my covenant that I have made with them. My anger will be kindled against them in that day. I will forsake (√עזב) them and hide my face from them; they will become easy prey, and many terrible troubles will come upon them. In that day they will say, "Have not these troubles come upon us because our God is not in our midst?" (NRSV)

Several points are noteworthy. First, Israel's dealings with the covenant and Israel's dealings with God are held together by synonymity. Honouring the LORD entails honouring the covenant,

---

204. Gerstenberger (1990), 586-87.
205. Deut. 28:20; 31:16; Jdg. 2:12f; 10:6, 13; 1 Sam. 8:8; 2 Kgs 21:22; Isa. 65:11; Jer. 2: 13, 17, 19; 16:11; 19:4; Hos. 4:10. Gerstenberger (1990), 590-91.
206. 1 Kgs 18:18; 2 Kgs 17:16; Ezra 9:10; Ps. 89:31 [30]; Jer. 9:12 [13]; 22:9; Dan. 11:30. Gerstenberger (1990), 591.

and breaking the covenant is tantamount to forsaking him.²⁰⁷ Secondly, forsaking the LORD and his covenant are marked by Israel's worship of other gods; again, this is a connection that is frequently made, especially within the Deuteronomistic framework.²⁰⁸ Thirdly, the verb used to describe the breaking of the covenant is √פרר, which is nearly always used in the sense of "violation of" or "reneging on." The object of the verb could be a vow, advice or counsel, or God's commandments; however, of the 53 uses, in 23 the direct object is "covenant," and forms part of the comprehensive vocabulary relating to apostasy.²⁰⁹ Its use here reiterates the moral overtones of √עזב and anticipates the following verse, which describes the LORD's reaction. This leads into the fourth point: the LORD's anger at Israel's sin, for such it is, is demonstrated in a punishment that fits the offence. If Israel would forsake (√עזב) the LORD, he will in turn forsake (√עזב) Israel. Fifthly, this forsaking by the LORD of his people takes the form of leaving Israel prey to other nations, again, a not unfamiliar theme,²¹⁰ and Israel will recognize in this an absence of his presence—"God is not in our midst."

A feature of the text that deserves note is the operation of something like the lex talionis. The LORD forsakes Israel, as a reaction to her forsaking of him; and as we have noted already, this formula of requital recurs both within the Deuteronomistic and the Chronicler's history.²¹¹ And it is not the verb √עזב alone which is used in such a formula of logical condemnation.

In his book, *The Hidden God*, Balentine explores the usage of the expression "hiding of the face" (√סתר) as an "element from a large stock of language which gives expression to the hiddenness of God in the Old Testament."²¹² From his study of √סתר and related verbs

---

207. The linking together of covenant and God may be found in, for e.g., Exod. 19:5; Deut. 31:20; 33:9; Judg. 2:20; Ps. 44:17; 78:37.
208. For e.g., Josh. 24:20; Judg. 2:12, 13; 10:6, 10, 13; 1 Sam. 8:8; 12:10; 1 Kgs 9:9; 2 Kgs 17:16; 21:22; 22:17.
209. Ruppert (2003), 117-18, cf. 118-120.
210. Examples where Israel's misfortunes are linked with her forsaking (√עזב) of the LORD are: Deut. 28:20; 29:24 ff; Josh. 24:20; Judg. 2:12 ff; 10:6 ff; 1 Kgs 9:9; 2 Kgs 22:16ff.
211. The formula occurs in the Chronicler's history in several places. Rehoboam and Asa are reprimanded by prophets in these terms: "You abandoned (√עזב) me, so I have abandoned (√עזב) you to the hand of Shishak" (2 Chron. 12:5); "If you abandon (√עזב) him [the LORD], he will abandon (√עזב) you" (2 Chron. 15:2). In 2 Chron. 24:20, Zechariah indicts the nation with, "Because you have forsaken (√עזב) the LORD, he has also forsaken (√עזב) you."
212. Balentine (1983), 115.

1 Kings 19: Horeb

such as √שכח (to forget) and √מאס (to reject), he finds that in many of these texts in which God is the subject of the verb, the language and phrasing is suggestive of the lex talionis. Balentine offers Hos. 4:6 as an example, the object of the verbs (perhaps) being the priests:

> ...because you have rejected (√מאס) knowledge,
> I reject (√מאס) you from being a priest to me.
> And since you have forgotten (√שכח) the law of your God,
> I will also forget (√שכח) your children.[213]

Balentine points out that in Hos. 9:17, there is a similar logic, this time clearly against the nation: "Because they have not listened (√שמע) to him, my God will reject them (√מאס)." Even though the verbs used are different, the principle of the retribution fitting the offence holds; Israel's refusal to hearken is met with the LORD's refusal/rejection of them.[214]

Balentine concludes from his study that God's "hiding" of himself is neither arbitrary not capricious; in OT contexts other than the Psalms, "God's hiding comes as a result of collective unfaithfulness and thus effects an abandonment of the community as a whole."[215] One way in which this abandonment by God is manifest is by reference to the threat of death or destruction at the hands of their adversaries; e.g., Eze. 39:23—"I hid my face from them and gave them into the hand of their adversaries, and they all fell by the sword."[216]

Balentine's observations reiterate our comments on Deut. 31:16-17, and this returns us to the usage of the verb √עזב in 1 Kgs 19:10. Before we discuss the implications of √עזב in this text, we note that it has a prior occurrence in 1 Kgs 18:18. Here Elijah responds to Ahab's accusation with, "I have not troubled Israel; but you have, and your father's house, because you have forsaken (√עזב) the commandments of the LORD and followed the Baals." The associations are as in Deut. 31:16-17. Ahab has abandoned the commandments of the LORD (and hence, the LORD himself) in that he has given himself to apostasy; in reciprocation, the text implies, the LORD has

---

213. Another example is the LORD's rejection of Saul: "Because you have rejected (√מאס) the word of the LORD, he has also rejected (√מאס) you from being king" (1 Sam. 15:23; cf. v.26).
214. Balentine (1983), 146.
215. Balentine (1983), 68.
216. Similarly, when Israel "forgets" (√שכח) the LORD, judgement strikes: e.g., Jer. 13:25; 18:15ff; Eze. 22:12ff; 23:35. Again, her rejection (√מאס) of the LORD is an invitation to disaster: e.g., Lev. 26:15f; 2 Kgs 17: 15ff; Isa. 5:24; Amos 2:4.

abandoned Israel, as evidenced by the "trouble" that has befallen the land (cf. 1 Kgs 16:30-33; 17:1) in the form of a prolonged drought.

The schema is the same in 1 Kgs 19:10ff, only here, the subject of the verb is not an individual, but Israel. Israel has abandoned the covenant, and therefore, the LORD. There is ample evidence of this—they are tearing down the LORD's altars and killing off his prophets. It would only be according to the pattern set out, by sermon admonitions and in Israel's experience, that the LORD should respond by proposing that he will, in turn, abandon his part in the covenant obligations. In order to grasp the dynamics of such an abandoning, one refers to parallel episodes in Israel's history. The cycles of apostasy, abandonment, oppression, supplication, deliverance in the book of Judges serve well as demonstration. Judg. 2:11-23 is a summary introduction to the rest of the book, namely, to the record of the events that immediately follow the death of Joshua. Twice (vv.12 and 13) the verb √עזב is used in conjunction with the laying out of Israel's sin, namely, her following after the gods of the land. Vv.14-15 describes the LORD's reaction: he gave them over to their enemies, leaving them defenceless and in great distress. This manner of the LORD's abandoning of Israel follows the forewarning in Deut. 31:16-21 to the letter.

Another comparable forewarning is in Lev. 26. The first section of this chapter lays out the rewards for obedience; the second section describes the penalties for disobedience. In the latter, the principle of divine retribution is made abundantly clear by three repeated pairs of "if you walk contrary to me, I will walk contrary to you" (the noun קרי is used as the keyword) in vv.23-24, 27-28 and 40-41. The LORD's reaction becomes manifest in the land being laid waste; Israel, powerless before her enemies, will be scattered among the nations. (This is best exemplified in the Exile.)

However, there is an element in Lev. 26 that must not be missed. In vv.44-45, the LORD declares: "Yet for all that, when they are in the land of their enemies, I will not spurn them, or abhor them so as to destroy them utterly and break my covenant with them; for I am the LORD their God; but I will remember in their favour the covenant with their ancestors whom I brought out of the land of Egypt in the sight of the nations, to be their God: I am the LORD" (cf. Judg. 2:1). This enduring and indissoluble faithfulness of the LORD to his covenant (made and renewed at Horeb; Exod. 20 and 34 respectively) is demonstrated in both the examples considered above, namely, in the cycles in the period of the judges, and in the period of exile. Thus, it may be significant that though Israel forsakes the covenant, the LORD rather speaks of forsaking Israel (and as it happens, this is in chastisement, and therefore for a period only), and not his covenant with her (e.g., Deut. 31:17).[217]

The submission here is that in 1 Kgs 19, there is a similar abandoning by the LORD of his covenant obligations to Israel. This is communicated non-verbally by the "empty" theophany; the LORD is absent in the very theophanic elements that are traditionally thought of as the vehicle of his presence. In this particular context, this metaphor communicates with a power that the plainly spoken word could not have achieved, for this is Horeb, the place of the making of the covenant. The elemental phenomena of a sacred moment in sacred space are momentarily reassembled before human eyes once more at Horeb; only, the place of the making of the covenant is used, with extraordinary dramatic effect, to propose an abandoning thereof.

Besides drawing attention to the principle of divine retribution, there are three related points we are trying to make here: first, the text under study is a non-verbal statement that is graphic enough to make the message plain. Secondly, the LORD's abandoning of the covenant obligations is for a period and for a purpose, as in the rest of Israel's history. Thirdly, and we will argue this at length in the next section, what is communicated to Elijah is a proposal and not an irreversible decision.

Having studied the theophany in the context of the narrative in 1 Kgs 19, we must recognize that the shape of the theophany straightaway invites reading this text within a wider context, namely, the historic events at Horeb as related in Exod. 19-20 and 33-34. It is therefore necessary to see how these two texts direct the interpretation of the LORD's absence in the elements of the theophany in 1 Kgs 19.

2.3.1. EXODUS 19-20

In Exod. 19:16-18, there is thunder, lightning and thick cloud, which put together suggest a thunderstorm. This, along with the fire and the implied earthquake ("the whole mountain shook violently") makes the parallel for the violent wind, earthquake and fire of 1 Kgs 19. A detail to take note of is that while the theophanic elements in themselves are cause for Israel's awe, there is an element that they fear can bring death upon them. This is the holy being they understand as being present within the natural elements. Exod. 19:9 first speaks of this in the LORD's words to Moses: "I am going to come to you in a dense cloud." Then, the act itself is described

---

217. Cf. Eze. 16:59-60: "Yes, thus says the Lord GOD: I will deal with you as you have done, you who have despised the oath, breaking the covenant; yet I will remember my covenant with you in the days of your youth, and I will establish with you an everlasting covenant."

vividly, with preciseness as to the location: "Mount Sinai was wrapped in smoke, because the LORD had descended upon it in fire...to the top of the mountain (19:18, 20). That the LORD is, in some physical way, present on the mountaintop, is made abundantly clear by the two successive insistent repeats of an earlier injunction (19:12) not to break through the boundaries demarcating sacred space, on pain of instant death (19:21-22, 24).

That Israel recognizes and is overwhelmed by the actuality of the deity's presence is seen in their refusal to have the audience continue any further: "...do not let God speak to us or we will die" (Exod. 20:19). Thus, only the mediator, Moses, "drew near to the thick darkness where God was" (20:21). As Terrien comments on this theophany:

> The covenant played a significant part in this event, but it was initiated by the prior reality of presence. The covenant appears to be a ritual act of mutual obligation which is precisely intended to prolong in a modified form the most extraordinary, indeed a unique, perception of the holy; the self-manifestation of the creator...The covenant aims therefore at transcending the ravages of time, preventing the erosion of ancestral memories, and bringing to life for the children yet unborn the fathers' 'ancient rapture.' [218]

This is the historic and sacred event that is recreated in 1 Kgs 19 in the telling of the story of a later Israel. The arresting contrast is that, just as emphatically as the narrator in Exodus shows the LORD to be present in the midst of the theophanic elements, the narrator of Elijah's story shows the LORD to be absent in them. Thus, if the purpose of the LORD's presence in the theophanic fire (Exod. 19-20) was the personal issuing of the law and thus, the making of the covenant, then, the LORD's absence in the very same theophanic phenomena, at the geographical milieu to which the traditions of Israel forever ascribed the origin of their bond with the LORD, most likely signals the converse, namely, a proposal to abandon covenant obligations.

One must test this reading against Exod. 33-34, the other text that this narrative recalls.

2.3.2. EXODUS 33-34

Other than the parallels at the verbal and story detail levels that have already been listed, the most significant resonance is that of situation: the conversations, whether between Moses and the LORD, or between Elijah and the LORD, are about an idolatrous nation and their covenantal relationship with her God. Exod. 32-34

---

218. Terrien (1978), 121-2.

demonstrates that the covenant relationship can break down in the event of sin. Sin violates the law, and the Giver of the law responds by withdrawing his presence.[219] To restore the covenant relationship, the LORD must concede his presence to his people in as full and rich a manner as before the sin. This will distinguish them, once more, as being his people (Exod. 33:16; 34:9). It is possible, then, to understand the absence of the LORD in the theophany of 1 Kgs 19 as the proposal of a similar withdrawal, disclosed symbolically. However, the difference to take note of is that in Exod. 32-34, the violation of the covenant even in its moment of making elicits a response from the LORD unparalleled in severity; the covenant ruptures, and must be ceremonially renewed before the relationship between the LORD and his people is normalized. Following this event, the covenant continues to hold even in the face of Israel's repeated unfaithfulness, but as in the examples cited above, their abandoning of the LORD is paid for by a reciprocal abandoning of them by the LORD.

To encapsulate, the element in Exod. 20 that is strikingly relevant to the 1 Kgs theophany is the certitude of the divine presence in the physical phenomena at Horeb, and this contrasts strongly with the LORD's absence in the theophany given to Elijah. The element in Exod. 33-34 that is significant to 1 Kgs 19 is the absence of the presence of the LORD in the event of Israel's unfaithfulness.[220] It appears that both texts move the reading of the theophany in 1 Kgs in the direction we have proposed.

---

219. *L.A.B.* 9.17 has an interesting insertion in the description of Moses' immediate reaction to the sin of the golden calf. "And he looked at the tablets and saw that the writing was gone, and he hurried to break them." Cf. Tg. Ps.-J. on Exod. 32:19: Moses' anger blazed forth, and he threw the tables from his hands and broke them...but the sacred writing that was on them flew and floated in the air of the heavens." While the purpose here is to attenuate the enormity of Moses' impulsive destruction of that which had been inscribed by God himself, the tradition is relevant to our argument in that absence of the divine writing on the tablets is immediately understood by Moses as a rupture of the covenant. The tablets are of no more importance than any other stone, and Moses, realizing this, breaks them in frustration at Israel.

220. Cf. Deut. 31:16-17, which we have already examined, where Israel's forsaking of the LORD entails circumstances in which she will realize that "God is not in our midst." Related to this cause and effect sequence is 1 Kgs 6:13. Here, Solomon is promised that if he remains faithful to the LORD, "I [the LORD] will dwell (√שׁכן) among the children of Israel, and will not forsake (√עזב) my people Israel." Thus, the LORD's forsaking is equated with his absence, and his not forsaking with his presence.

2.4. Conclusion

In the first part of the discussion we examined the text with a focus on grammar and semantics. The phrase קול דממה דקה was studied with reference to Job 4:16. The inference was that קול דממה דקה signifies a natural phenomenon in the same sense as the other three elements of the theophany are "natural"; but as much as the latter are (explicitly) empty of the presence of deity, the former (implicitly) contains it.

In order to make sense of these absence-presence events, we considered 1 Kgs 19:11-12 as the LORD's response to the central issue in Elijah's statement in v.10, namely, Israel's resolve to forsake the covenant. Tracing the usage of the verb √עזב, it was noted that a principle of retribution (stated in language not unlike the *lex talionis*) is frequently encountered in the event of Israel's unfaithfulness to the covenant; the LORD in turn abandons Israel, and this is manifest by his withdrawing of his presence. Thus, the absence of the LORD could be read as his non-verbal communication to the prophet of his proposal to deal with Israel in this not unfamiliar manner. He then grants Elijah his presence, and the dialogue continues; now, face to face as it were.

3. 1 Kings 19:13-18: Elijah Receives his Commission

3.1. 1 Kings 19:13: The Second Question

When Elijah heard, he wrapped his face in his mantle and went out and stood at the entrance of the cave. And behold, there came a voice to him that said, "What concerns you here, Elijah?"[221]

3.1.1. "WHEN ELIJAH HEARD IT HE WRAPPED HIS FACE IN HIS MANTLE"

On hearing (it), Elijah covers his face with his mantle. Robinson, taking 1 Kgs 19:11b-12 to be prediction rather than narrative, deduces that Elijah performs this action before he experiences the theophany, and actually, in preparation for it:

> He [Elijah] is looking forward to a repeat of the Mosaic experience. He remembers that Moses had to be covered by the divine hand lest he should see God and die; that he was granted only a rear view of YHWH, namely the sound of the divine voice (Ex. 33:18-34:9); and that after the theophany Moses veiled his face before addressing Aaron and others since it glowed and he was in danger of dazzling them (Ex. 34:30-35). So full is Elijah with a sense of his own importance, that he hastens to cover himself

---

221. Drawn from NRSV.

1 Kings 19: Horeb

up even before the theophany occurs and without waiting to be commanded.[222]

We have previously argued 1 Kgs 19:11b-12 serves simultaneously as both prediction and narrative. Thus, what Elijah hears and responds to would be, not the LORD's prediction of the events to come, but the last of those events, the קוֹל דְּמָמָה דַקָּה. On hearing the קוֹל דְּמָמָה דַקָּה then, Elijah covers his face. How best may this action be understood?

Elijah's gesture of covering his face recalls human self-protective instinct in the face of encounter with the divine. Cases in point are Manoah and his wife, Gideon and Ezekiel.[223] The last mentioned is particularly relevant since the sequence matches that in 1 Kgs 19. Ezek. 1:28:

וָאֶרְאֶה וָאֶפֹּל עַל פָּנַי וָאֶשְׁמַע קוֹל מְדַבֵּר

The prophet Ezekiel experiences visual phenomena, which he understands to be the similitude of the glory of the LORD; he instinctively falls down on his face; then, he hears a קוֹל speaking. Similarly, Elijah experiences an aural phenomenon; he spontaneously responds by covering his face; then, a speaking קוֹל comes to him.

But here, the narrator may intend the detail to remind the reader of Moses hiding his face at Horeb in Exod. 3. As the Being in the burning bush reveals himself to be the God of Moses' forebears, Moses hides his face because he is afraid to look upon God — וַיַּסְתֵּר מֹשֶׁה פָּנָיו כִּי יָרֵא מֵהַבִּיט אֶל הָאֱלֹהִים (Exod. 3:6b). Both Moses and Elijah (and Ezekiel) act at the exact point of recognition of the divine presence. It is a reflexive response of self-preservation.

There is also, perhaps, an echo of Exod. 33-34; the other detail of cave/cleft recalls it. However, the difference is that in this Exodus incident, the LORD himself undertakes to protect Moses at the moment of greatest proximity to the divine glory; he will put Moses in a rocky cleft, and further, cover him with his "hand" (Exod. 33:21). Apparently, nothing that Moses himself can provide for his protection will be sufficient in the course of this intensely intimate encounter. If Elijah is indeed expecting a meeting with the LORD of this order, he should remember, as Robinson rightly points out,

---

222. Robinson (1991), 527-28.
223. On recognizing the messenger to be divine, Manoah and his wife "fell on their faces to the ground" (Judg. 13:20); Gideon, in a similar situation, expresses fear that he has seen the angel of the LORD face to face and must be reassured that he will not die (Judg. 6:22-23). So also, Daniel sinks to the ground face down at the vision of the heavenly messenger, and later averts his face as the messenger speaks, apparently fearing for his safety (Dan. 10: 9, 15-19).

"Moses had to be covered by the divine hand lest he should see God and die." It is probable then, that even in the event that he is taken over by a sense of self-importance, it is likely that the stronger, innate instinct for self-preservation should prevail.

Considering that this narrative does not restrict itself to parallels from one single Mosaic incident but rather creates a Mosaic environment recalling the entire range of Mosaic tradition,[224] the inclusion of the detail of Elijah's covering of his face most evokes Moses' similar gesture at his first encounter with deity, at the burning bush.

3.1.2. "...AND WENT OUT AND STOOD AT THE ENTRANCE OF THE CAVE"

That Elijah goes to the mouth of the cave is sometimes interpreted as disobedience to the command in 19:11 that he should "stand on the mountain." Robinson comments: "Though YHWH calls upon him to 'Stand on the mountain before YHWH' (19:11), he stands only at the entrance to the cave, fearing perhaps for his safety if he goes any further."[225] Similarly, Walsh. He proposes that both the divine questions imply disobedience. He suggests that in 19:9, God asked Elijah what he was doing "here," meaning, here at Horeb as against there in Israel. The second question continues its emphasis on location, but now God asks what Elijah is doing "here" in the cave when he should be standing there on the mountain.[226]

There could be another way to read ויצא ויעמד פתח המערה. Elijah discerns the exact moment when the LORD is about to pass by; the קול דממה דקה is the indicator (as in Job 4:15-16). Elijah's responses are described in a sequence of verbs. He hears, he wraps his face, he goes out and he stands. Standing, as he does, at the mouth of the cave, he could well be said to be standing on the mountain, and we have noted that this description of his location could be the narrator's device to position him simultaneously on the mountain and in the cleft, as Moses was in Exod. 33:21, 34:2.

Robinson comments further on the verb used, עמד√.

> When told to *stand* before YHWH on the mountain (19:11), he stays where he is, at the mouth of the cave. This despite the fact that he has twice proudly described his mission precisely as *standing* before YHWH (17:1; 18:15)![227]...Elijah will not venture away from the cave, which is an apt

---

224. The earthquake, wind and fire belong to Exod. 19-20, while the cleft/cave comes from Exod. 33-34, and the appellation "Horeb, the mountain of God" is unique to Exod. 3.
225. Robinson (1991), 521.
226. Walsh (1996), 276-77.
227. Robinson (1991), 529.

1 Kings 19: Horeb

symbol for, perhaps, the womb in which he wants to retreat; or at least for the safe condition of a closet-prophet.[228]

We recall here the "command and compliance" pattern frequent in the Elijah narrative thus far, where the LORD's commands and Elijah's compliance of them are recounted in almost identical words: e.g., the verbs √קום and √הלך (1 Kgs 17:9, 10); √הלך and √ראה (18:1, 2). Here, in chapter 19, in the sequence of verbs that describe Elijah's response to the קול דממה דקה, the last two verbs are identical to those in the command of 19:11—√יצא and √עמד. As in the earlier cases, this could well flag scrupulous obedience. Particularly in the event that there is no divine rebuke of his behaviour, let us conclude that the case for disobedience re this specific command is not particularly strong. We will address the larger question of Elijah's obedience as a prophet at a later point.

3.1.3. "WHAT ARE YOU DOING HERE, ELIJAH," WITH REFERENCE TO JOTHAM'S FABLE, ISRAEL'S DEMAND FOR A KING AND THE "DEATH" OF JOSEPH

This brings us the second asking of the question, מה לך פה אליהו. Commentators generally agree that the second question, since it is identical to the first, conveys an identical message, namely, that of reproof. It is also suggested that this repetition could be a case of the widely used ancient Semitic narrative device for emphasis;[229] thus, the repetition highlights the reprimand. In any case, the consensus is that it is a second chance for Elijah to come up with a different, and presumably, more acceptable answer—one sufficiently and suitably instructed by his experience of the theophany.[230]

At this point, it may be helpful to look briefly at three texts that use the literary device of repeated speech.

Jotham's Fable: Judg. 9:16-20

As rejoinder to the murder of his brothers by Abimelech, Jotham addresses the Shechemites. He tells a fable and appends an application. Ignoring the debate on how exactly the application ties in (or does not tie in) with the fable, we focus on the literary device employed in vv.16-20, namely, that of repetition.

The application takes the form of a curse. Rhetorically, the curse is conditional, and the conditional clauses describe two possible situations: one concerns the crowning of Abimelech as king, and the

---

228. Robinson (1991), 534.
229. E.g., Wiseman (1993), 173.
230. E.g., Robinson (1991), 522; Hauser and Gregory (1990), 134; Provan (1995), 146; Walsh (1996), 277; Simon (1997), 214; Nelson (1987), 125.

other concerns Gideon and his house. With respect to the first situation, the issue is whether the Shechemites have acted in truth and integrity in crowning Abimelech as king. With respect to the second situation, the issue is whether the Shechemites have recompensed good to Gideon and his house, as his deeds deserved.
v.16:

וְעַתָּה אִם־בֶּאֱמֶת וּבְתָמִים עֲשִׂיתֶם
וַתַּמְלִיכוּ אֶת־אֲבִימֶלֶךְ
וְאִם־טוֹבָה עֲשִׂיתֶם עִם־יְרֻבַּעַל וְעִם־בֵּיתוֹ
וְאִם־כִּגְמוּל יָדָיו עֲשִׂיתֶם לוֹ:

By collating phrases from each, these two situations are condensed into a single conditional clause (without pausal indication) in v.19, where the speech resumes after a parenthesis.
v.19:

וְאִם־בֶּאֱמֶת וּבְתָמִים עֲשִׂיתֶם עִם־יְרֻבַּעַל וְעִם־בֵּיתוֹ הַיּוֹם הַזֶּה
שִׂמְחוּ בַּאֲבִימֶלֶךְ וְיִשְׂמַח גַּם־הוּא בָּכֶם:

The content of the parenthetical aside colours the resumption of the interrupted construction (in v.19a). Jotham summarizes Gideon's deeds on behalf of Shechem: "my father fought for you, and exposed his life to great risk, and rescued you from the hand of Midian" (v.17). He then describes how Shechem has rewarded Gideon.

(1) "You have risen up against my father's house this day, and have killed his sons, seventy men on one stone" (v.18). Jotham lays the death of his brothers at Shechem's door, for they had with full cognizance furnished Abimelech the means by which to eliminate his brothers (Judg. 9:3-5, 24), namely, seventy pieces of silver from the temple treasury, with which he hired assassins. Thus they certainly shared the guilt in a crime from which both they and Abimelech jointly profited (Judg. 9:3).

(2) "[You] have made Abimelech, the son of his slave woman, king over the lords of Shechem, because he is your kinsman" (v.18). Shechem had chosen a bastard over Gideon's legitimate sons, and that for an unworthy reason, namely, because he was one of them (Judg. 9:1-3).

The parenthesis makes clear that both conditions in the protasis of v.16 have not been met. First, "truth and integrity" have been markedly absent in the choice of Abimelech for king; secondly, Shechem's dealings with Gideon and his house have in no way been what "his actions deserved"; as much as he had done them good, they had returned him evil. When Jotham resumes after this parenthetic review, he restates the conditional clause with phrasing borrowed from before the parenthesis. The words now have a totally different implication. They lose their previous neutral character, and now become loaded with irony and sarcasm. Because the crime has already been committed, the curse is now seen as being not so much

1 Kings 19: Horeb

conditional as a pronouncement of irrevocable and deserved judgement. Thus, the chapter goes on to relate the falling out between Abimelech and Shechem, and concludes the tale on a note of retribution: "on them came the curse of Jotham son of Jerubbaal" (Judg. 9:57). The point is that what is interpolated between the two statements of the protasis in vv.16 and 19a defines the way the second statement of the protasis is read, as also the apodosis in v.19b: "...then rejoice in Abimelech and let him also rejoice in you." The parenthetical review makes such an event remote; rather, it is the ruin of both parties that is being pronounced as imminent.

The Demand for a King: 1 Samuel 8:7-9

Another text in which an interpolation serves to nuance repetition is 1 Sam. 8:7-9. Samuel has grown old and appoints two sons as judges. The move is a failure. The elders of Israel seek audience with Samuel and present a case for the appointment of a king. Samuel is displeased and takes the matter to the LORD. He may not have wholly expected the response: שמע בקול העם לכל אשר יאמרו אליך (1 Sam. 8:7a). In v.9a the injunction is repeated in condensed form: ועתה שמע בקולם. Between the two is a parenthesis expressing significant reservations on two counts.

(1) The problem of monarchy is not political but theological in that Israel has rejected the LORD from being king over them (v.7b). Samuel is to understand the request for a king in terms of the far more fundamental relationship between the LORD and Israel rather than in terms of his and his sons' inadequacies, even though the elders have made this the immediate occasion of their demand for a king. The pronouns are made emphatic by their position: לא אתך מאסו כי אתי מאסו (v.7b). Thus, Samuel is urged to see this opposition as a part of the whole, namely, the far more serious rejection of the LORD himself.

(2) This rejection is nothing new, but one more step in the continuum of rebellion, begun at the time of the exodus itself. One implication that may be read into this is that if the LORD has tolerated Israel's contrariness over all this period, it is reason enough for Samuel to exercise patience, and allow Israel the freedom to choose to rebel.

Thus, when Samuel is instructed for the second time to listen to and comply with Israel, his perceived role in the affair is changed. He is no longer the aggrieved party, but rather, spokesman and witness for a greater aggrieved party: "Now then, listen to their voice; only—you shall solemnly warn them" (v.9). The content of the interpolation puts a significantly new implication on the repeated directive.

The two texts commented on above are different from the case of repetition in 1 Kgs 19 in two ways. First, the repetition occurs within the course of a single speech. Secondly, the parenthesis or interpolation is verbal, and part of the speech. In 1 Kgs 19, the repetition occurs as part of dialogue. Further, between the two sets of repeated dialogue, the "interpolation" is a linear progression of narrative itself. The narrative flow does not freeze between the repetitions, as it does in the case of Jotham and Samuel. An instance where the repetition is not part of the same speech and where the narrative progresses between the repetitions is in the Dothan incident in the Joseph cycle. Only, this case differs from 1 Kgs 19 in that two different speakers articulate the verbally identical construction.

The "Death" of Joseph: Genesis 37:19-34
At Dothan, Joseph's brothers spy him afar off, and decide to kill him. They will say (to whomsoever it concerns), חיה רעה אכלתהו (v.20). In v.33, the phrase occurs with verbatim repetition: חיה רעה אכלתהו. But here, it is not the collective voice of a group conspiring cold-blooded fratricide. The story has moved on. Joseph, even if he has not been murdered, has been removed permanently from the scene, or so the brothers think. The robe is now cunningly employed to lead the aged Jacob to arrive at his own inference. The words, which the brothers had planned to use to deceive their father, are deviously drawn out from Jacob himself, and therein lies the effectiveness of the repetition. The sentences, though wholly equivalent verbally, have totally different status, both because of the speakers and because of their locus along the linear axis of the unfolding narrative. The first time, the words are an angry mutter, part of an as yet unformulated conspiracy. The second time, they are a grief-stricken cry of certainty and finality. The altered context alters the sense and function of the words.

The relevance of these three examples to 1 Kgs 19 is that they demonstrate the effectiveness of a certain literary device common to Biblical narrative, namely, repetition. Here, Alter comments that in Biblical prose "word-for-word restatement rather than inventive synonymity [is] the norm for repetition;...the ideal reader (originally, listener) is expected to attend closely to the constantly emerging differences in a medium that seems predicated on constant recurrence."[231] Each text that employs this dialectic of similarity and difference, Fokkelman points out, ingeniously mixes the two in its own distinctive ratio.[232]

In summary, these three examples establish that at least in direct speech in a given narrative, total equivalence between identical constructions would generally not be the narrator's intention; nor is

---

231. Alter (1981), 97.
232. Fokkelman (1999), 122-23.

it realizable, considering the movement along the narrative's axis. Thus we set aside the reading that the second מה לך פה אליהו is identical to the first in sense and function, and thus a repeated reprimand; instead, we examine what nuances of difference there may be in the second asking of this question.

In our study of the previous section of the text, we considered that the LORD's question מה לך פה אליהו (v.9) is not uncommon, and where used it functions as a conversation opener; in several cases it is the formal preamble to a royal audience. Elijah's response (v.10) has as its central issue Israel's resolve to forsake the covenant. We proposed that the theophany (vv.11-12) is the LORD's rejoinder. Examining the usage of the verb עזב√, it was noted that a principle of retribution (stated in language not unlike the *lex talionis*) is frequently encountered in the event of Israel's unfaithfulness to the covenant where the LORD in turn abandons Israel, this being made manifest by the withdrawing of his presence. Thus, the absence of the LORD in the theophanic elements could be read as his non-verbal communication to the prophet of his proposal to deal with Israel in this not unfamiliar manner.

At the end of this intentionally symbolic "empty" theophany, the LORD grants Elijah his presence (signalled by the קול דממה דקה), which the prophet recognizes; the dialogue now returns to the verbal mode, and is, as it were, face to face. The LORD asks again, מה לך פה אליהו. Logically, the sense of the question may best be arrived at by probing the question's relationship to the non-verbal communication that has passed between the LORD and Elijah in the interval between the last dialogue and the current one. In the interval, the LORD has proposed punitive action in retribution against Israel. One expects that now the prophet (on the assumption that he has understood the symbolic communication) will intercede (cf. Amos 7:1-6). The prophet does not; or perhaps, before the prophet does, the LORD speaks. Before going further, let us make a short reference to the Mosaic environment in which this narrative is set. The parallel situation that is evoked is Exod. 32-34. Here also the theme is God's punitive action against Israel, which is worked out in the course of dialogue between God and his prophet. Thus it would be profitable to see if this text would help our understanding of 1 Kgs 19:13b.

The LORD's immediate reaction to Israel's idolatry is violent. He would annihilate them. The curious imperative that prefaces the declaration of his intention has provoked more comment than the declaration itself: ועתה הניחה לי (Exod. 32:10) —"let me be"/"let me alone," or less literally, "do not interfere with me."

Widmer, treating this phrase at length, arrives at three possible ways to read it. (1) It is a test to see if Moses would give up Israel in order to make way for his own exaltation to the position of patriarch. (2) It is the announcement of a determination; the LORD has fully made up his mind and will brook no interference by way of intercession. (3) It is an implicit invitation for Moses to intercede on behalf of endangered Israel.[233]

Position (1) is not plausible if we are to take seriously Moses' standing as the archetypal prophetic intercessor (cf. Jer. 15:1). It empties the dialogue of its two main thrusts—the awful gravity of the threat and the efficacy of genuine intercession. The Deuteronomy account (9:18,19) mentions forty days, an extended period of pleading before the LORD relents. To argue that this is a test is surely to miss the point of the amazing struggle between man and God, and within the mind of God (cf. Hos. 11:8, 9). Besides, Moses' intercession here merely averts the immediate danger of annihilation; he has to follow up with three more separate pleas in as many meetings (Exod. 32:31-34; 33:12-23; 34:6-9) before the covenant can be renewed. Thus, if the first case of intercession is not seen as a genuine act of intervention, the others cannot automatically be assumed to be so.

Widmer quite rightly argues that position (2) is unlikely as well; by asking Moses to leave him alone, Moses is implicitly given the option *not* to leave him. It becomes an "invitation by prohibition," analogous to the confrontational language of prophecy which by its very provocative nature seeks to elicit a response that will counter the coming to pass of the prophecy.[234] As Fretheim observes, God seems to anticipate that Moses would resist what is being said, and that he has absolute freedom so to do. Thus, at this point the decision has not yet reached an "irretrievable point" and "Moses could [as God seems to see it] conceivably contribute something to the divine deliberation that might occasion a future for Israel other than wrath."[235] This moves us in the direction of position (3); the imperative intimates and anticipates intercession in that it plants a possibility in Moses' mind that such mediation is allowed and can be effective;[236] at very least, "leave me alone" is an acknowledgement that the prophet may *not* leave God alone.

Another valuable approach to gaining appreciation of the phrase "leave me alone" is to survey the usage of √נוח. Gowan comments on the four other instances of √נוח in the hiphil imperative where the sense of the verb is "to let alone"/"refrain from interfering with"/"permit."[237] The blind Samson requests his guard to permit or leave him alone to feel the pillars supporting the house (Judg. 16:26);

---

233. Widmer (2004), 98-100.
234. Widmer (2004), 101-02.
235. Fretheim (1991), 283-84.
236. So, e.g., Sarna (1991), 205; Janzen (2000), 231; Childs (1974), 567.
237. See BDB, נוח, 629.

David prefers that his men let Shimei alone to continue cursing him (2 Sam. 16:11); Josiah orders that the bones of the prophet buried at Bethel be let alone and not moved (2 Kgs 23:18); God would let Ephraim alone to be joined to idols (Hos. 4:16-17). "In each case," Gowan points out, "someone who has the power to do something to another is asked to refrain." In the fifth and only instance (i.e., Exod. 32:10), "God is the one affected, as he asks of a human being, 'Let me alone, that…'. Who would dare write such a thing?"[238] The startling implication is that God has bound his resolve to his prophet's consent, making himself, in some way, subject to the will of his prophet.

This "vulnerability" of God is displayed once more in Exod. 33:5. He struggles within himself to "decide what to do" with Israel, and resolves the dilemma in the course of dialogue with his prophet. Gowan makes a discerning comment on the two interactions in Exod. 32:10 and 33:5 re the idea of "persuading" God:

> God does not stand aloof, making royal decisions without getting involved with the people concerned. God listens to Moses, and Moses' commitment to these people makes a difference. I do not read passages such as these as evidence [that] humans have to persuade, somehow, a reluctant God to do what is right. The picture of God presented to us throughout the Old Testament is that of a God who has chosen to work with, rather than just upon human beings, so that humans (in this case Moses) are given the chance, if they will accept the responsibility, to contribute to a future that will be different from what it would have been, had they remained passive.[239]

With that we return to 1 Kgs 19, to determine the import of the second asking of the question מה לך פה אליהו. Considering that one has no access to the tone of the question, one must use mainly the context, and secondarily consult parallel texts if any, for the best possible reading of it.

Within the context, there are two alternatives. (1) The question is rhetorical, the implied answer being that there is nothing that concerns Elijah further at Horeb, and therefore he may now leave; it implicitly terminates the on-going conversation. (2) The question is genuine and thus, an invitation to dialogue further; Elijah is given an opportunity to express himself in the light of the event that has just concluded, namely, the theophanic display.

Alternative (1) is less probable, considering that the question (as remarked on re other texts) is usually understood as a formal granting of audience, and here in v.13b would be a cue for Elijah to

---

238. Gowan (1994), 223.
239. Gowan (1994), 231-2. Thus, this imperative is often read as God's invitation to prophetic intercession. E.g., Childs (1974), 567; cf. Moberly (1983), 50.

speak. Indeed Elijah seems to react to it as such, since he promptly responds, just as was the case in 1 Kgs 19:9-10. Thus, the likelihood is that this is a genuine question, as was its predecessor, and anticipates a response.

If, as we have argued, the context of the question is that the LORD has only just communicated his intention to punitively and retributively abandon Israel, then it would not be unreasonable to propose that God is in dialogue with his prophet, comparable to Exod. 32-34. In formally asking if there is anything else that concerns Elijah here at Horeb, the implication could be that if Elijah has nothing more to say, the LORD will get on with implementing his proposal. Just as much as the "Now, let me alone" of Exod. 32:10, מה לך פה אליהו may be read as an invitation to the prophet to dialogue. Even more so perhaps, since the invitation is more explicit, being phrased as a formulaic conversation-opener rather than as a prohibition. The inference then, is that the decision, as in Exod. 32:10, has not reached a point of irreversibility; rather, it remains tentative till the prophet has been given opportunity to contribute to the future of the people whom he both represents to God and represents God to.[240]

We have not yet resolved the issue of why the narrator should choose to use repetition at this point in the narrative. Perhaps this is better investigated once the rest of the repeated dialogue has been studied, namely, Elijah's response.

3.2. 1 Kings 19:14: The Second Response

As noted earlier, the scholarly consensus is that the LORD's repeated question is Elijah's chance to redeem himself with a worthier response. The expectation is that he must repent of his self-righteous stance, intercede for Israel rather than condemn her and desist from misrepresenting himself as the last man standing. That he repeats himself word for word is indication of his inflexible resistance to divine instruction and grace.[241] As Robinson (reading 1 Kgs 19:11, 12 as prediction) puts it:

> Excited...by the Mosaic role in which he believes YHWH is to cast him, Elijah at once wraps his face in his mantle, and strains to hear the divine

---

240. In Amos 7:1-6, the prophet is confronted with two pictures of devastating judgment on Israel. In each case, the prophet pleads that God desist, arguing, "How can Jacob stand? He is so small!" God responds to each plea with relenting. This reiterates the dynamic of God's decision-making process re Israel as evidenced in Exod. 32-34 and argues the case for a similar dynamic in 1 Kgs 19.
241. E.g., Robinson (1991), 522; Hauser and Gregory (1990), 134; Provan (1995), 146; Walsh (1996), 277; Simon (1997), 214; Nelson (1987), 125.

> whisper...As promised, the qôl is then heard. But what a blow for Elijah: the qôl turns out to be the voice of YHWH simply asking Elijah for a second time what he is doing there, as if to say his work lies elsewhere. Elijah, though, is too self-preoccupied to fall in with YHWH's requirements. He has undergone no change of heart. He is in fact rather annoyed with YHWH for playing this trick of (sic) him. If YHWH can simply repeat himself in this way, so can he. So he re-iterates his whining self-justification. Cannot YHWH see that in justice he is obliged to provide him dramatic, miraculous protection, as he did of old to Moses? He is the last prophet left, and (he implies) self-interest should therefore ensure that God take special steps to preserve him.[242]

The assumption that buttresses the reading here is that the LORD's second question is totally equivalent in sense and function to the first. This is certainly a possibility, especially if the reason for the equivalence is didactic in nature, and the LORD repeats his question so as to elicit a "correct" answer from his prophet-student. However, there are a few points to mull over before we can accept this condition of equivalence.

First, if this usage of מה לך is, as we have shown, a formulaic and idiomatic one, and not a rebuke in terms of where Elijah is re location, then, there can be no "correct" answer, for Elijah is only being prompted to speak what is on his mind; the פה added to the usual formula would indicate that Elijah is welcome to unburden himself of that which has brought him particularly to Horeb, so out of his way. In this event, a second asking in order to educe a correction would seem unlikely.

Secondly, in the samples of repetitions in direct speech within narratives that we have considered, total equivalence of sense and function is seen *not* to be the norm. The repeated line becomes the locus of an emergent nuance that carries the reader forward into the story by way of anticipation. When the reader hears Jotham's conditional clause for the second time, he hears with a more discerning ear than when he heard it first. He has been reminded of the fact that Shechem has not demonstrated integrity in its dealings with Gideon and his house; he now hears the condition as an inexorable curse whose playing out, he anticipates, will constitute the remainder of the story of Abimelech and Shechem. Similarly, the LORD's speech to Samuel directs the reader's expectations on the route the narrative will take. Having been informed in an aside that Israel's demand for a king is but another marker in her history of rebellion, the reader expects to learn that Israel will pay the price for her choice. In the case of the Joseph story, the repeated line closes a cycle of deception as it moves from the mouths of the deceivers to

---

242. Robinson (1991), 534-35.

the deceived. In doing so, the repetition emphasises the fact that the deception is just that—a deception, and reminds the reader that with Joseph still being alive, the story must certainly move towards some dramatic denouement, in which the deceivers will be unmasked and the deceived receive relief.

Thus, it appears that repeated direct speech within narratives is normally incremental.[243] The argument for total equivalence that Robinson and others see in 1 Kgs 19:13b remains a possibility, but we note that it would not correspond to the normal use of the literary device of repetition.

Thirdly, if, as Robinson proposes, Elijah whiningly repeats himself, using repetition just so as to get back at God, what may we expect by way of divine rejoinder to such non-cooperation? A survey shows two kinds of divine response—reassurance[244] and rebuke. Gideon is a case for the first category (Judg. 6:14-16). God's "I hereby commission you" only frightens Gideon into an objection: "But sir, how can I deliver Israel? My clan is the weakest in Manasseh, and I am the least in my family." The LORD's response perfectly addresses the twin concerns of deficiency in the clan and in the individual. "But I will be with you" (the insufficiency of the clan is replaced with the implicit but unquestionable sufficiency of God) "and you shall strike down the Midianites, every one of them" (the prophetic assurance is that Gideon will rout the enemy, whether Gideon be least in his family or not).

A comparable case is that of Jeremiah (Jer. 1:5-9). His objection to his commission to be "a prophet to the nations" is "Ah, Lord GOD! Truly I do not know how to speak, for I am only a boy." The answer explicitly deals with both of Jeremiah's concerns, namely, his youth, and his lack of eloquence. "Do not say, 'I am only a boy'," the LORD responds, going on to assure him that his accompanying presence will make him equal to the task. Next, the LORD touches the deficient organ, symbolically putting his own words into Jeremiah's mouth.[245]

The LORD's other usual response to non-cooperation from his representative is rebuke, often strongly worded. When Moses replies, "O My Lord, please send someone else" (if that is the right reading of the Hebrew), the narrator makes clear that "the anger of

---

243. A far more common category is repetition with verbal increment, where the increment serves as a node for nuance. See Alter (1981), 88-113; Fokkelman (1999), 113-22.
244. Miller (1994), 141-77.
245. Isaiah could be cited as yet another example (Isa. 6:5-7). Even though his dismay at his unclean lips is not a balking or reluctance re his prophetic duty, the point of relevance is that the LORD specifically addresses his problem before commissioning him.

the LORD was kindled against Moses." Thus the reader is left in no doubt about the sharpness of tone in the alternate arrangement the LORD devises for Moses' public speeches (Exod. 4:13ff).

Jeremiah (Jer. 12:1-6) similarly comes under rebuke. He observes that the guilty thrive and flourish, and turns his deep discontent into a charge against God, indicting him of nurturing them; for how could they prosper but for divine sponsorship? He is promptly rewarded with a cutting comment on his lack of stamina of spirit: "If you have raced with foot-runners and they have wearied you, how will you compete with horses?" Similarly severe is the divine response to the complaint in which Jeremiah says he cannot understand why, in spite of his faithfulness to his commission as prophet, he must suffer affliction that seems to have no end (Jer. 15:10-21). The LORD declares that Jeremiah may serve as his mouth only on condition that he will "utter what is precious and not what is worthless."

One sees, then, that the LORD does not gladly suffer a noncompliant prophet. He makes his displeasure known. On the other hand, when the situation warrants it, he does not hesitate to reassure and encourage. Such unequivocal feedback, either by way of reassurance or by rebuke is absent in 1 Kgs 19. Elijah's doubly refractory attitude, if such it is, is met with a directive to appoint two heads of state and a prophet. How is the reader to understand this — as an implicit rebuke (in that Elijah is to be replaced by Elisha) or as an implicit show of confidence (in that Elijah is entrusted with a commission of clearly enormous import)? We shall return to this issue in the following section. For the interim, we observe that unambiguous divine reaction, such as may be seen in several other instances, is missing in Elijah's case. This weakens the position that Elijah's reply in 1 Kgs 19:14 may be clearly understood to be a case of non-cooperation, and censured as such.

Is there another way to read Elijah's repeated answer? Since we have not completely ruled out the plausibility of Robinson's reading, any alternate proposal must be heuristic.

We have proposed that the second divine question be read as Elijah's cue to express his opinion, if so he desires, on the proposal made non-verbally that the LORD wishes to punish Israel by abandoning her. This cue, being phrased as a formulaic question that has already been used once in this conversation, is neutral in that it does not presuppose a particular answer. Broadly, Elijah has two choices — he may speak, or he may remain silent, implying that he reserves comment on the proposal just intimated to him. If however, he chooses to speak, one expects that what he says must have some bearing on the proposal.

However, there is no trace of this in Elijah's answer. It is as if the theophany-proposal never happened. As the consensus of scholarly opinion construes it, Elijah deliberately ignores what has passed between the LORD and him since the last round of question and answer, and returns the same answer as further back in the conversation. The consensus sees in this Elijah's failure to appreciate and respond to what has just been presented him by way of theophany. But what if Elijah, having understood well enough the intent of the theophany, *chooses* not to respond, to deliberately ignore it? It would then mean that his ignoring of it is an expression of his refusal to consider the theophany-proposal. Instead, he repeats verbatim a remark from earlier in the conversation, and as consensus observes, this returns the conversation, and the story, to that earlier point on the linear axis of the narrative. From this point the narrative must move forward again, but taking a new path.

In short, the proposal is that Elijah's answer is an expression of non-concurrence. While he could have phrased this as explicit disagreement, he chooses to do it differently, and his choice is not illogical. Perhaps it is the LORD's repeated usage of the formula that decides the manner of the expression of his disagreement. He repeats his previous answer by design, so as to attain a desired end, namely, to return the conversation to a point prior to the proposal, in the process entirely sidestepping the proposal itself.[246]

Thus, certainly, as Robinson reads him, Elijah is being adamant and obstinate, but not, as Robinson proposes, in a negative sense. To best illustrate the dynamic between prophet and God in operation here, one must return to Exod. 32-34 to examine what Coats calls "the polar tension between intercession and revolution."[247] Moses, he claims, "behaves in a manner that is not always obviously distinct from the revolutionary action of the people."[248] He negotiates without himself conceding an inch, asks uncomfortable questions, impudently reminds the LORD that he must keep his promises, requests the LORD to take his life, and identifies with the people whom he himself has punished as rebels.

> Yet, the tradition carries no condemnation of Moses for such audacious behaviour. On the contrary, *Moses' revolutionary innovations before God, his refusals to take the directive as it stood, are understood consistently as obedience and faithful loyalty* [emphasis added]…The ambiguity in Exodus 32-34 suggests that the line between obedience and revolution can never be rigidly drawn. To do so reduces obedience to mechanical legalism. To the contrary, each new generation faces the necessity for determining where

---

246. This is common enough in everyday conversation. One expresses one's reluctance to be drawn into comment by ignoring the invitation and either abruptly changing to a fresh topic or by returning to an earlier one.
247. Coats (1977), 98.
248. Coats (1977), 105.

the line might be, and what loyalty to the right—or the left—side of the line should look like.[249]

If Elijah's intention at Horeb is to model Moses, his seemingly refractory behaviour is not unexpected. In this "revolutionary innovation before God" he, in his generation, is attempting to define and demonstrate loyalty to his God, his people and his calling. As Moses before him, he does not hesitate to use unconventional forms of intercession that appear more to be insubordination than intervention. By ignoring the LORD's tentative proposal, he forces him to take an alternative route in dealing with his rebellious people.

This alternative to Robinson's reading of the second exchange between the LORD and Elijah remains provisional till the LORD's response in 1 Kgs 19:15-18 is examined to see if it may convincingly be read as the LORD's alternative dealing with Israel. Meanwhile, we sum up this section with comment on the effect of the employment of the literary device of repetition in this narrative.

First, repetition, when used skillfully, is a dramatic way to make a point. This is true of the other narrative sections examined. In Jotham's speech, the repeated conditional clause immediately highlights the fact that the Shechemites have not demonstrated integrity in their dealings; in the LORD's directive to Samuel, the imperative to listen to the people dramatizes the danger to Israel that this acceding to their demand will entail. In 1 Kgs 19, the repetition strikes the point home that here dialogue has reached an impasse; there is a stalemate here that seeks a resolution.

Secondly, as we have already shown, repetition is a literary device that carries the reader back and forth along the axis of the narrative. As we have seen to be true of the Jotham, Samuel and Joseph narratives, it not only compels him to revisit a prior event but also to anticipate the future. At Horeb, the repeated exchange of words becomes the means by which to cause a backflow of the narration in progress. In so doing it stirs up reader anticipation in the direction of the LORD's dealings with rebellious Israel—if Elijah can prevail on him not to forsake Israel, how else will he deal with her sin?

Thirdly, the "dialectics of similarity and difference"[250] that must come into play in the repeat of a string of words in direct speech in a narrative is exploited to define the roles of the speakers. In the Joseph narrative, the words remain the same, but the speakers change; this brings out the complementarity between them—one speaker misleads and the other is misled. In 1 Kgs 19, a similar harmonious balance of roles emerges via the repeated dialogue. In

---

249. Coats (1977), 105-6.
250. Fokkelman (1999), 116, 121.

the first round, God is the one being consulted, since the implication of Elijah's pilgrimage to Horeb is that he desires audience with God. Indeed, God meets with him, and opens the consultation with an invitation for Elijah to speak his mind. This suggests that the LORD will hear Elijah out, and arbitrate on issues as necessary, just as one would expect of a king holding court. The second time round, however, there is a slide towards almost complete role reversal. The LORD is the one consulting; and, it appears, the prophet is now in the role of arbitrator. This subtly reiterates the dynamic of the relationship between God and prophet, and places this interchange in the continuum where belong the conversations of God with Abraham, Moses, Samuel and Jeremiah.

With this, we move on to the last exchange at Horeb, to see how that will influence the direction of our reading of this episode at Horeb.

3.3. 1 Kings 19:15-18: The Commission

15 And the LORD said to him, "Go return on your way to the wilderness of Damascus; when you arrive you shall anoint Hazael as king over Aram.
16 Also you shall anoint Jehu son of Nimshi as king over Israel; and you shall anoint Elisha son of Shaphat of Abel-meholah as prophet in your place.
17 Whoever escapes from the sword of Hazael, Jehu shall kill; and whoever escapes from the sword of Jehu, Elisha shall kill.
18 Yet I will leave seven thousand in Israel, all the knees that have not bowed to Baal, and every mouth that has not kissed him.

These four verses, which close the Horeb episode, are the LORD's final words to Elijah. They divide into two halves; the first two verses are a series of instructions to the prophet, and the last two describe Israel's future. The text has been interpreted in several ways. First, it is read as a termination of office.[251] Robinson explains:

> ...[Elijah] re-iterates his whining self-justification...He is the last prophet left and (he implies) self-interest should therefore ensure that God take special steps to preserve him...He [God] is not interested in continuing to employ this tetchy and arrogant prima donna of a prophet on these terms. He therefore lets him know that he has no longer any use for his ministry: the future lies with Hazael, Jehu and Elisha. The theophany represents Elijah's last chance; now that he has failed to respond, he receives notice of dismissal, and the initiative passes elsewhere.[252]

---

251. E.g., Robinson (1991), 528; Hauser and Gregory (1990), 142-47; Kissling (1996), 123-24; Brichto (1992), 144.
252. Robinson (1991), 535.

1 Kings 19: Horeb

Such a reading relies heavily on rendering the preposition תחת as "instead of," and needs to be reconciled with the narrative that follows on several scores. We shall return to this under the discussion of תחת.

Secondly, the text is read from a diametrically opposite point—it is not a termination of office, but a re-commissioning. Proponents of this view read Elijah's two replies as a resignation from office. The severe depression, which prompted the request that God take his life, has not lifted. He travels to Horeb to present his inability to continue in office, in "despondency…which neither logic nor the showiest theophany can cure."[253] However, God will not accept his resignation, and instead, effectively rehabilitates the severely depressed prophet by restoring his sense of purpose.[254] Simon sees more than just psychotherapy here: "…the LORD commands him to inaugurate a new epoch, in which the arena of the struggle will be transferred from nature to history, and the attempt to influence the people will be replaced by the annihilation of almost all of them."[255] Habel proposes that this is more than just a re-commissioning; it is has the elements of the genre of prophetic call narrative.[256] Reading the LORD's words as a re-commissioning is more plausible than reading it as a dismissal, chiefly because it fits in with the rest of the narrative without difficulty, a point we shall return to.

This returns us to considering the first proposal at greater length, and the particle תחת, being central to the reading of this text, serves well as a starting point.

3.3.1. "UNDER" AND ITS IMPLICATIONS

תחת is used here as a preposition. Sifting out the possibilities,[257] the following three senses are relevant to the text under study: (a) "under" in the sense of being under authority;[258] (b) "in place of" or "instead of," in a transferred sense; (c) in the same sense of transfer, it could also mean "to succeed to the place of."

---

253. Nelson (1987), 129.
254. Nelson 1987), 127, 129; Wiseman (1993), 173; House (1995), 224; DeVries (1985), 236-37; Simon (1997), 214-17; Coote (1981), 116.
255. Simon (1997), 217. Simon (1997), 209-10, compares this episode with Jer. 15:10-21, while Brueggemann compares it with Jer. 12:1-6. (2000), 237.
256. Habel (1965), 298. Habel makes a study of the calls of Moses, Gideon, Jeremiah, Isaiah and Ezekiel and II Isaiah.
257. BDB, תחת, 1065-66.
258. E.g., Hagar is instructed to place herself under Sarah's hands (והתעני תחת ידיה; Gen. 16:9); princes and warriors place themselves under Solomon (נתנו יד תחת שלמה המלך; 1 Chron. 29:24).

Sense (a) would apply, since, as the narrative unfolds, Elisha takes up service under Elijah (1 Kgs 19:21), and in 2 Kgs 2:3, 5, Elijah is recognized publicly to have been Elisha's master (אדון).

Sense (b), the one preferred by Robinson who reads the text as a dismissal of Elijah, is grammatically possible (cf. LXX: ἀντὶ σοῦ) and not at all uncommon in Biblical narrative.[259] However, to make it viable within the demands of a narrative reading as distinct from a historical-critical one, several issues would need explanation. First, Elijah's ministry continues without a break through 1 Kgs 21 and 2 Kgs 1, and, as before Horeb, the "word of the LORD" comes to him and he is asked to deliver messages of divine rebuke to the crown. Robinson does not explain this; Kissling, another proponent, offers with reference to the choice of Elijah to carry the message to Ahab: "Elijah has been somewhat rehabilitated in Yahweh's eyes since the events of Horeb."[260] This is rather inadequate, especially considering that it must be argued from silence. Further, it weakens the case for a dismissal of any seriousness and consequence, especially since in the same episode Ahab is rebuked severely, and pardoned only after "he has humbled himself before [the LORD]" (1 Kgs 21:29); if Elijah has been dismissed on account of his being an "arrogant prima donna," one would expect some indication of his "rehabilitation" in the post-Horeb narrative, before it becomes "business as usual" between him and the LORD.

Secondly, if this were a speech of termination of office, logically, it would suffice that Elijah is commanded to anoint Elisha as prophet in his stead. Even this would be a rather odd procedure, since dismissal would imply that from then on Elijah is divested of his position and authority as the LORD's prophet, and as such, automatically disqualified for cultic activities within a prophet's purview, such as anointing.[261] The additional onerous and risk-fraught commissions to appoint two heads of state by stealth against powerful incumbent monarchs appear even more anomalous if they

---

259. E.g., as it concerns individuals—

Seth is given in place of Abel (זרע אחר תחת הבל; Gen. 4:25); Judah offers himself in place of Benjamin (ישב נא עבדך תחת הנער; Gen. 44:33); the Levites are ordained instead of Israel's firstborn (לקחתי את הלוים מתוך בני ישראל תחת כל בכור פטר רחם מבני ישראל; Num. 3:12, etc.); Samson is offered his sister-in-law instead of his wife (תהי נא לך תחתיה; Judg. 15:2); a queen is sought to replace Vashti (תמלך תחת ושתי; Esth. 2:4).

260. Kissling (1996), 131.

261. The other case of removal from position that comes to mind is that of Saul. Once the LORD rejects him (1 Sam. 15:26), he cuts off all communication with Saul (1 Sam. 28:6, 15), and the initiative passes to the anointed successor, David.

are handed to an unmanageable prophet being relieved of his duties.[262]

Thirdly, neither Robinson nor any of the other proponents of the dismissal premise explain why a de-badged prophet is being requested for a double share of his spirit by the one who has supposedly replaced him already, why his departure carries all the marks of unprecedented divine favour, why in summary statement it is implied that he has been Israel's defence, and why, both to Elisha and the watching prophets, Elisha's success at re-enacting Elijah's miracle of parting the Jordan is taken as the sign that the prophetic spirit of Elijah has fallen upon Elisha (2 Kgs 2). Elijah continues as undiminished in stature as before Horeb, and unless this question is sufficiently addressed, the proposal that he has been terminated in office at Horeb is hard to sustain.

This brings us to the third sense for תחת, namely, "to succeed to the place of."[263] This has much wider usage than the other two senses and may be used of succession to an office,[264] of a generation or people group that succeeds another,[265] and of descendants that succeed their forebear.[266] However, the most copious usage by far is in routinely describing succession to the throne, where it becomes a technical term, part of the formulaic record of transition of kingship;[267] in the books of Kings alone it is used about forty five times (e.g., 2 Kgs 15:7-38). Its technical use in recording succession to the position of priest and king makes it very possible that the use of תחת in 1 Kgs 19:16 is with reference to prophetic succession, of which there are no other accounts for comparison, save the succession of Moses the prophet by Joshua the leader (which does not use the preposition).

A second reason why תחת here is better read with sense (c) is because its context is the appointment of two others to positions of high authority—Hazael and Jehu. This choice of another king to replace the incumbent recalls Saul and David. After Saul is rejected, David is anointed king-in-waiting, explicitly to replace Saul (1 Sam. 16:1-2). Similarly, Hazael and Jehu are anointed to occupy the throne

---

262. One recognizes that Elisha eventually performs the tasks. However the point here is that the LORD entrusts Elijah with the responsibility.
263. This involves the issue of the prophetic succession of Elijah by Elisha, which will be treated separately and at length, with reference to 1 Kgs 19:19-21 and 2 Kgs 2:1-18.
264. E.g., the office of priest (Exod. 29:30; Lev. 6:22; 16:32; Deut. 10:6; 1 Kgs 2:35) and commander of the army (2 Sam. 17:25; 1 Kgs 2:35).
265. E.g., Num. 32:12; Deut. 2:12, 21-23; 4:37; Josh. 5:7; cf. Eccl. 2:18.
266. E.g., Num. 25:13.
267. E.g., Gen. 36:33-39; 2 Sam. 10:1; 16:18; Isa. 37:38; Jer. 37:1; and extensive use in Kings and Chronicles.

at some later time (whether immediately succeeding the incumbent ruler or not). However, Elisha's appointment must be clarified, since the matter concerns Elijah personally; so, along with the extra details of parentage and hometown (given so that Elijah may readily locate him? Cf. "Jesse the Bethlehemite" among whose sons a successor to Saul might be found; 1 Sam. 16:1) it seems likely that Elisha is being specified as Elijah's immediate successor.

Thirdly, the narrative itself follows a route that supports the reading of תחת as "to succeed to the place of." Elisha puts himself under the authority of Elijah (sense (a) of תחת) and remains so until his assumption. Only following this does Elisha prove to himself and to the expectantly watching band of prophets that he is indeed Elijah's successor, and he does this by parting the Jordan following the same procedure as Elijah's. From this point on Elisha assumes the functions of a prophet and these include the trademark speaking on behalf of the LORD (2 Kgs 2:21). 2 Kgs 3:11 makes the distinction between his past role as Elijah's minister and his present status:

> Jehoshaphat said, "Is there no prophet of the LORD here, through whom we may inquire of the LORD?" Then one of the servants of the king of Israel answered, "Elisha son of Shaphat, who used to pour water on the hands of Elijah, is here."

It appears then that, in the context, sense (c) is the best fit for תחת. Appealing to the wider context, the only other account of the succession of a prophet is at once evoked, namely the succession of Moses by Joshua. The fact that it belongs to the same corpus that the 1 Kgs 19 narrative evokes at several other points adds to its significance. We will briefly examine the story level parallels; if these are significant enough, we may justifiably draw from this narrative in order to confirm or correct our reading of תחת.

Taking Num. 27:12-23 as the main "succession" text, one notes that the context of the succession is the impending death of Moses (vv.12-14). Though the exact day has not yet been intimated, this is the second reminder that Moses has not long to live (cf. Num. 20:12). His response to the situation is to request a successor be appointed so that there will be no vacuum in leadership on his departure, whenever that may be. Promptly, the LORD returns Joshua as the answer.

Elijah's situation at Horeb parallels this insofar as he believes uncertainty hangs over his life in the face of the systematic removal of the prophets of the LORD in progress. We have argued that his "I alone remain" is an expression of his concern for the continuing voice of true prophecy in Israel, which he believes is in jeopardy. Though this cannot be read as an implicit request for a true prophet to succeed him in the event of his death, it is possible such a solution be provided in answer to the problem. Such is the case in Num. 11; the LORD answers Moses' complaint that he is unable to bear alone the burden of Israel's leadership (v.14) with the immediate appointment of seventy elders who will share the task (vv.16-17). So, in 1 Kgs 19, the directive to anoint Elisha may serve a comparable cause-effect function.

Next, instructions are given for Joshua to be publicly and ceremonially commissioned (Num. 27:18-23), and this procedure is shortly carried out. The appointment is of a politico-military nature.[268] Not only is it the first transition in leadership, but it is also a transition that must be carefully handled if at all the objective of the exodus, namely, bringing Israel into Canaan, is to be achieved; for Israel to be convinced to accept him in the role of Moses, his appointment must be seen to have divine sanction (cf. Deut. 31:14, 23), must be promoted by Moses and must be meshed into the sacral component of Israel's leadership, here represented by Eleazar the high priest. For all these reasons, the installation is elaborately structured and its message subsequently reinforced on more than one occasion (Deut. 3:28; 31) till Moses departs and Joshua moves into his place.

Elisha's appointment, however, does not carry the wide-ranging implications of Joshua's, especially in the political and military senses. If he is God's answer to Elijah's concern for Israel, then his appointment is as a prophet who will fearlessly represent true prophecy after Elijah has passed on. Thus, it suffices that Elisha's appointment has only the people of Abel-meholah as witness, and is accomplished with two "ceremonies." These, however, in their symbolic content more than sufficiently express what has transpired; Elijah lays a personal item, his mantle, on Elisha signifying the latter's position as successor, and Elisha simultaneously bids farewell to both his profession and his people with a ceremonial meal.

---

268. Moses asks that the LORD "appoint someone over the congregation who shall go out before them and come in before them, who shall lead them out and bring them in..." (Num. 27:16-17). These expressions, though not necessarily military in reference (e.g., 2 Kgs 11:18), are predominantly so (e.g., Deut. 31:2-3; Josh. 14:11; 1 Sam. 18:13, 16; 29:6; 1 Kgs 3:7) and these military images are appropriate since Joshua's task is predominantly the conquest of Canaan. Milgrom notes that the second expression employs the same verbs as in the first but in the hiphil, thereby denoting the military officer who not only leads his troops but also plans its strategy, e.g., David in 2 Sam. 5:2. (1990), 235; cf., among others, Ashley (1993), 551; Budd (1984), 306. Thus Joshua appropriates Moses' duties of governance and defence (Deut. 31:2-3). The question of prophetic succession is addressed in Deut. 18.

Following the installation of Joshua, Moses continues in his duties as Israel's leader, and this underlines Joshua's position as leader in waiting.[269] This is no co-regency in the normal sense,[270] because further communication between the LORD and Israel still flows through Moses (Num. 28:1; 30:1), and even in the event of military action, it is Moses and Eleazar who play the pivotal roles (Num. 31:1-2, 13, 25-26, 51, 54). There is no mention of Joshua in the war against Midian.[271] This is how it continues till Moses departs. So also, Elijah carries on his prophetic responsibilities as before till the day of his assumption; there is no involvement of Elisha either in his confrontation with Ahab or with Ahaziah.

After both the older men, Moses and Elijah, depart, the younger men come into their own. "After the death of Moses the servant of the LORD, the LORD spoke to Joshua the son of Nun, Moses' assistant, (משרת) saying, 'My servant Moses is dead. Now proceed…'." (Josh. 1:1-2) A concrete event demarcates Joshua who was "the one who was serving Moses" and Joshua, leader of Israel. This is a situation not unlike Elisha's: following his installation, he is said to be in Elijah's service (√שרת; 1 Kgs 19:21); when for the first time he is spoken of as a "prophet of the LORD" it is after the departure of Elijah, and it is recalled then that before this he "used to pour water on the hands of Elijah" (2 Kgs 3:11).

A last resonance, remarkable for the similarity, is that both successors are proved in the eyes of the people by the miraculous parting of the Jordan. "On that day the LORD exalted Joshua in the sight of all Israel; and they stood in awe of him, as they had stood in awe of Moses, all the days of his life (Josh. 4:14)." In Elisha's case: "When the company of prophets who were at Jericho saw him at a distance, they declared, 'The spirit of Elijah rests on Elisha.' They came to meet him and bowed to the ground before him (2 Kgs 2:15)." Following this event, the successors are held in the same respect as the ones they succeeded.

Thus, it appears there is sufficient cause for reading תחת in 1 Kgs 19:16 to mean, "to succeed to the place of." We conclude that Elisha's appointment need not imply the termination of Elijah from office.

The alternative left, then, is to read the text as a re-commissioning. A re-commissioning would imply that Elijah's tenure in office has lapsed, either because the LORD has dismissed him or because he

---

269. So, for example, Ashley (1993), 555.
270. As suggested by Wenham. The ceremony of Num. 27 "inaugurates a co-regency, when Moses and Joshua were joint leaders of the people, a transition period that was terminated by the death of Moses on Mount Nebo." (1981), 195.
271. This would be particularly significant in the light of the military connotations in Joshua's job description, discussed earlier.

himself has tendered his resignation. There is no indication of the former up to this point in the narrative; as for the latter, we have argued that resignation from office is confined to the broom tree episode. Thus, rather than a re-commissioning, this could be read as a re-alignment of divine plans re Israel. If Elijah's second reply is taken as a refusal to accept the LORD's proposal for a punitive lapse of his covenant obligations, then in response to this refusal the conversation can move forward only in one of two directions: either the LORD insists on following through with his proposal, or he, in mercy, concedes a less severe alternative. The latter is not unfamiliar in the OT; in fact, it is arguably the norm rather than the exception. Within the Moses and Elijah narratives themselves the pattern is played out, not only at two key points in the story of Exod. 32-34 (32:10ff; 33:3ff), but several times over in the course of Israel's wilderness journey (Num. 14:10ff; 16:44ff; Num. 21:6ff) and in the case of Ahab (1 Kgs 21:17ff). 1 Kgs 19:15-18, may be taken as just such an alternative, and in this one God seizes the initiative to set right the covenant relationship with Israel.

A key term in this approach to reading the text is the root שאר and its role in the remnant motif.

3.3.2. THE ROOT "REMAIN" AND THE REMNANT MOTIF

The verb √שאר and corresponding noun שארית render the sense of "remnant," "rest," "residue," "remainder," "that which is left over" without any apparent variation of meaning.[272] "The basic meaning of the root שאר is to remain or be left over from a larger number or quantity which has in some way been disposed of."[273] As such, it may be used of the inanimate, such as wood or land;[274] otherwise, it is most often used with respect to Israel/Judah, though it is sometime descriptive of other peoples,[275] and even of all living creatures.[276] It may have a negative connotation, in that the magnitude of the catastrophe has been so great that any remnant that survives is of no consequence;[277] in many cases it has a positive implication — despite the cataclysm, a remnant survives, and functions as the seed of a restored community.[278] Sometimes the remnant survives despite the fact that the whole is worthy of

---

272. Widengren (1984), 240. Cf. in BDB, שאר, שארית, 985-86. Clements (2004), 273-77; Wildberger (1997), 1255.
273. Henton (1952), 28.
274. Isa. 44:17 and 15:9, respectively.
275. E.g., Isa. 14:30; 17:3; Amos 1:8; 9:12; Zech. 9:7.
276. Gen.7:23; cf. vv.1-5.
277. E.g., Isa. 17:4-6; Jer. 8:3; Amos 5:3.
278. E.g., Gen. 8:15-19, cf. 7:23; 45:7; Jer. 23:3; Mic. 2:12; 4:7; Zeph. 3:12-13.

destruction;²⁷⁹ sometimes, the remnant is described as faithful.²⁸⁰ Whether the catastrophe is seen as an act of divine judgement (which in most cases it is) or as a general calamity, the survival of a viable remnant is understood specifically as an act of divine mercy, or of divine grace and providence, respectively.²⁸¹

The idea of a remnant reaches fullness in the "writing" prophets, but may be found throughout the OT. Especially since the root שאר occurs in the course of a narrative in 1 Kgs 19, it may be fruitful to examine its occurrence and usage in other narrative contexts. Of these, the stories concerning Noah and Joseph are of particular significance to us, first, because they are prior to the Elijah narrative in canonical order, and so may help lead up to an understanding of the concept; secondly, because they deal with key events of survival through calamitous events—the survival of humankind and of incipient Israel, respectively.

3.3.2.1. Noah: Genesis 7:17-24

We will summarize from the wealth of comment that understands this climactic scene as a reversal of creation.²⁸² מים and על הארץ occur six times each, often in close conjunction, in strong reminiscence of Gen.1; the heavenly sea above the firmament empties downward into the sea gushing up from the great deeps below the earth (v.11), and separation of one from the other blurs as the world sinks into pre-creation barrenness; "the very verb of proliferation [√רבה; Gen. 1:28] employed in the Creation story for living creatures is here attached to the instrument of their destruction";²⁸³ the breath of life (נשמת חיים; Gen. 2:7) breathed into man's nostrils with face-to-face intimacy in the act of making now expires in the nostrils of all living things.

With alliteration and repetition, the narrator overwhelms the scene with the magnitude of the victory of the waters. The verb √גבר brings in undertones of a military conquest. The waters triumph (v.18) and triumph exceedingly (v.19), submerging the very mountain peaks; the eightfold repeat of כל underlines the totality of the devastation they inflict. And life does not merely die; God wipes clean the record (מחה)²⁸⁴ of all things living, fulfilling his stated

---

279. E.g., Jer. 5:10-18 (though the root שאר is not used here, the concept is evident).
280. E.g., Zeph. 3:12-13.
281. Jer. 23:3-4; 31:7-9; Amos 5:14-15; Mic. 4:6-7.
282. Wenham (1987); Alter (1996); Kidner (1967); Hamilton (1990); Westermann (1984), 438-40; von Rad (1972), 128-30; Sarna (1989), 55-57.
283. Alter (1996), 33.
284. Cf. Exod. 17:14; 32:32-33; sometimes the act used water (Num. 5:23).

1 Kings 19: Horeb

resolve (Gen. 6:7; 7:4). With paronomastic allusion, the verb √מחה looks forward to the mention of the one who escapes this obliteration, namely, נח. Ironically, the same death-dealing waters are the medium of rescue from death, for the flood's increase causes the ark to float. Hamilton points out that the contrast between the condemned and the spared is enhanced by two niphals, ימחו and ישאר—the former are blotted out from the earth, while the latter alone is left remnant (with those in the ark with him).[285] The suggestion is that the controlling agent here is God, and he deploys the waters to work his ends, simultaneously both extinguishing life and carefully conserving it.

Wenham comments that the absence of personal names, except for a "parenthetic" mention of Noah "enhances the desolation."[286] On the contrary, the introduction of Noah at the very end of the list of the blotted out, as one *not* blotted out but left remaining by design, is particularly noteworthy. There are two points of significance here.

First, we consider the purpose for the preserving of the remnant. Hasel in his *The Remnant: The History and Theology of the Remnant Idea from Genesis to Isaiah* comments:

> The remnant motif of primeval history is firmly grounded in unique events of the past, such as creation and flood, but directing its full attention to the future. Stress is actually placed on the fact that a remnant was actually preserved, that it survived the destructive cataclysm, and made possible the future existence of mankind…One can say that it contains in a real sense an inherent future expectation, which in the later development of this motif in Israelite religion becomes enriched and further developed to a considerable degree.[287]

The survived remnant, containing as it does, all the necessary seeds of life for the continuing existence of mankind, makes the future its purpose and goal.

Secondly, we consider the factor that makes possible the preserving of the said remnant. The flood, as stated unambiguously in the prologue to the story, was the effect of which sin was the cause (Gen. 6:5-7). Post-flood, the LORD must resolve "never again [to] curse the ground because of humankind, for the inclination of the human heart is evil from its youth" (Gen. 8:21). It is the will of God that prevails, and his gracious will is for salvation, not for judgement. As Hasel sums up:

---

285. Hamilton (1990), 297.
286. Wenham (1987), 182.
287. Hasel (1980), 140-41.

The remnant motif is from the start securely anchored in salvation history. Though the devisings of the heart of men are still evil, Yahweh's grace alone made possible the continuation of the existence of the human race by means of the righteous Noah and his family who constitute the remnant.[288]

The Flood story has given us three threads that weave together to form the remnant motif, and we will follow these into the Joseph story: one, a death-dealing catastrophe; two, the preservation of life through the catastrophe; and three, the gracious will of God operating to preserve that life.

3.3.2.2. Joseph: Genesis 45:4b-8a

וַיֹּאמֶר אֲנִי יוֹסֵף אֲחִיכֶם אֲשֶׁר־מְכַרְתֶּם אֹתִי מִצְרָיְמָה:
וְעַתָּה אַל־תֵּעָצְבוּ וְאַל־יִחַר בְּעֵינֵיכֶם כִּי־מְכַרְתֶּם אֹתִי הֵנָּה כִּי לְמִחְיָה שְׁלָחַנִי אֱלֹהִים לִפְנֵיכֶם:
כִּי־זֶה שְׁנָתַיִם הָרָעָב בְּקֶרֶב הָאָרֶץ וְעוֹד חָמֵשׁ שָׁנִים אֲשֶׁר אֵין־חָרִישׁ וְקָצִיר:
וַיִּשְׁלָחֵנִי אֱלֹהִים לִפְנֵיכֶם לָשׂוּם לָכֶם שְׁאֵרִית בָּאָרֶץ וּלְהַחֲיוֹת לָכֶם לִפְלֵיטָה גְּדֹלָה:
וְעַתָּה לֹא־אַתֶּם שְׁלַחְתֶּם אֹתִי הֵנָּה כִּי הָאֱלֹהִים

In 45:3, Joseph makes his statement of self-disclosure—"I am Joseph." His brothers are overwhelmed into silence. He repeats himself, this time adding information that nobody else could have possessed; he is Joseph whom they sold into Egypt. As if reading their dismay at this vocalization of the crime, he hastens to reassure them. Three times in the speech that follows he articulates it: "God sent me before you to preserve life"; "God sent me before you to preserve for you a remnant"; "It was not you who sent me here but God." Joseph, however, is not attempting to shield his brothers from their conscience with a euphemism. As von Rad emphasizes:

> Here in the scene of recognition the narrator indicates clearly for the first time what is of paramount importance to him in the entire Joseph story: God's hand, which in all the confusion of human guilt directs everything to a gracious goal...[I]t would be wrong to see only distracting friendliness in Joseph's remarks; rather, Joseph wants to state an objective truth, in which, to be sure, the enigma mentioned above, the question of how this activity of God is related to the brothers' drastically described activity, remains an absolutely unresolved mystery. The matter must rest with the fact that ultimately it was not the brothers' hate but God who brought Joseph to Egypt...[289]

---

288. Hasel (1980), 146.
289. Von Rad (1963), 393.

Just as important, if not more, is the reason why God sent Joseph ahead. Twice Joseph mentions it—it is so that the clan may not die, but live; להחיות/למחיה (vv.5, 7), and the first time, the term occupies an emphatic frontal position. Joseph will repeat it years hence post Jacob's death, in recapitulating for his fearful brothers the purpose of his hard experiences—to preserve alive a numerous people, as indeed may be demonstrated as having reached fulfilment "this day" (Gen. 50:20). It is also a phrase central to the expressed purpose of the ark (Gen. 6:19, 20; 7:3).

These twice repeated affirmations bracket a grim forecast of the desperation that will overwhelm lands which have no stores of grain; the famine, the severity of which has sent Jacob's sons to Egypt twice already, is still young; in the five years remaining, chances for survival outside Egypt will become increasingly bleak. The bounding of the forecast by the assertions that life will yet be preserved throws into relief the meagre chance of survival but for the intervention of a God who seeks to safeguard the life of this otherwise inconsequential clan.

Two significant terms are used to describe the purpose God has in mind for Jacob's clan—שארית and פליטה. Hamilton notes that these two occur in combination not infrequently, and in a variety of relationships—in the construct state, in syndetic parataxis, in parallelism and as name and its adjective.[290] The noun פליטה, occurring twenty-eight times in the OT, is primarily used to refer to the remnant of God's chosen people; but the escaped do not owe their survival to fortuitous circumstances or luck. Rather, their survival is an unquestionable display of divine mercy.[291] Thus, most EVV render פליטה as "deliverance" in 2 Chron. 12:7, implying a deliverer. In the usage of the term, the goodness of God in letting a part of the whole escape, rather than liquidating the whole, is emphasized.[292] When פליטה is associated with שארית, which as we have noted earlier also bears overtones of divine mercy, grace or providence, the terms reinforce the associations.[293] Here, the words are clearly indicative of the sovereign act of God in carefully

---

290. 1 Chron. 4:43 ("they destroyed the remnant of the escaped—"שארית הפלטה"); Ezra 9:14 ("so that there should be no remnant nor any to escape—"שארית ופליטה"); Isa. 10:20 ("the remnant of Israel and the survivors of the house of Jacob—"שאר ישראל ופליטת בית יעקב"); Exod. 10:5 ("and they shall eat that which is escaped, which remains to you—"הפלטה הנשארת"). See Hamilton (1995), 576.
291. Hasel (2001), 551-567.
292. E.g., Ezra 9:8, 13-15.
293. The two nouns occur frequently as parallels, פליטה being firmly linked to the OT notion of the remnant. Hasel (2001), 560, 562-65.

designing the endurance of all twelve families in the household of Jacob.

Westermann challenges this rendering of שארית as "remnant": "How can Jacob's family be described as a 'remnant'? A remnant of what?" Thus "descendants" would suit the context of the story better, because all members of Jacob's family have been kept alive.[294] Exactly such a meaning for שארית may be found in 2 Sam. 14:7; the woman of Tekoa laments that should her one remaining son be killed, her late husband will be with "neither name nor remnant—שם ושארית—on the face of the earth."[295]

Certainly, the context of 2 Sam. 14:7 moves the reading of שארית to most naturally mean "descendants." In Gen. 45:7, however, one must take into account the context of the remnant motif, as seen in the Flood story or elsewhere in the prophets. There is a world-scale calamity in progress. Jacob's family has escaped it. Joseph belabours the point that but for divine design, such a remnant would not have been possible. The survivors, as in the Flood story, are the seed from which a perfect whole will emerge, in this case, a twelve-tribed nation. Thus, the family of Jacob "in narrowly escaping destruction is like a remnant which is the bearer of hopes for the future existence;"[296] in this sense this שארית *is* a remnant. In fact, precisely by using the loaded term שארית in a context that would not normally justify its use (in that there is no clearly defined whole from which the "remnant" is separated), the narrator may have succeeded in drawing attention to the enormous significance of this act of God. "[I]t is not possible," von Rad stresses, "to overlook the great theological and programmatic significance of [Joseph's] statements, for through this guidance that family was preserved which was heir of the promise to the fathers."[297]

Having identified the common features of the remnant motif in these two narratives, we return to see if the motif may be picked up in the Elijah narrative.

3.3.2.3. An Israel Within Israel

Scholars propose several passages in the Elijah cycle as carrying the remnant motif.[298] Hasel, among others, is of the opinion that the remnant terminology in these sections, if any, is tenuous except for two key texts in the Carmel and Horeb scenes.[299] The first is found

---

294. Westermann (1987), 144; Cf. Skinner (1910), 487; Driver (1926), 362.
295. Westermann (1987), 144.
296. Hasel (1980), 154.
297. Von Rad, (1963), 393.
298. See Hasel (1980), 159.
299. Hasel (1980), 159-60.

repeated in two places, and uses the verb √יתר, often used synonymously with √שאר in articulating the remnant theme.³⁰⁰ "I, even I only, am left (√יתר) a prophet of the LORD" (1 Kgs 18:22); "I alone am left (√יתר), and they are seeking my life, to take it away" (1 Kgs 19:10b).

We have previously addressed the issue of whether Elijah here is referring to himself as the last of the faithful in all Israel, or the only prophet in the field, and concluded the argument in favour of the latter. Hasel reads the text similarly, and goes on to find here a new development to the remnant motif in that "Elijah represents a remnant of the prophets of Yahweh, i.e., a remnant of one loyal to Yahweh within apostate Israel." One must test this possibility by checking for markers common to the other two instances of motif studied. First, there is here a large-scale threat to life. Jezebel's programme of elimination (1 Kgs 18:4, 13), which is made possible by apostate Israel's collusion (1 Kings 19:10), has driven the Yahwist prophets into hiding and left Elijah the last one in open opposition. Secondly, one looks for the preservation of the remnant through the threat of death. Here, Elijah is still alive, but by no means safe. By his own statement, Israel is still hunting him, to kill him. He is not yet, if at any point he can be considered to be one, a remnant in the technical sense. One must keep in mind too, that the remnant in its technical sense "concentrates in itself the life and promise of the community" and as such, concerns a corporate whole, rather than an individual.³⁰¹ Thirdly, one seeks the most theologically significant component of the remnant motif, namely, the controlling hand of God. This was evident at Cherith and Zarephath, but hardly at Horeb. Elijah's escape strategy is clearly of his own devising and even that reached its terminus in a suicide bid. Thus, neither the Carmel nor the Horeb texts make a natural fit for the motif.

The other text that Hasel presents for the remnant motif, is 1 Kgs 19:18, which contains the root שאר: והשארתי בישראל שבעת אלפים. Checking for markers: first, there is no doubt about the magnitude of the approaching calamity. This time it is neither a flood nor a famine; Israel will be diminished from without and from within by a politico-military operation. The rhythmically recurring words of the oracle pattern a carefully calculated strategy for a triple phase purge that cuts off all possibility of escape.³⁰²

---

300. See BDB, יתר, 451; שאר, 983.
301. Rowley (1956), 118. He mentions also, however, that individuals may represent the community, e.g., the Suffering Servant. In such a case Elijah fails to qualify, since in his statement here it is clear that he represents no one but himself.
302. The grimly systematic sequence is similar to that described in Isa. 24:17-18: "Terror, and the pit, and the snare are upon you...whoever flees the sound

Secondly, there is a remnant that will survive this bloodbath. Seven thousand are mentioned, an idiomatic figure denoting adequacy;[303] the remnant spared, though small, will still be a number meaningful enough for Israel to continue as a nation under God. More importantly, it is sufficient to perform as the seed that will re-establish decimated Israel. Here, as in the technical sense of the root שאר, "remnant" is a word of expectation and hope. Thirdly, there is no ambiguity that the LORD is in control of the operation; he conceives this solution, he formulates the strategy, his anointing is on the wielders of the sword, and he selects those knees and mouths that death will pass over; והשארתי—he is the causal force. Though the seven thousand are faithful they are an integral part of a whole that has breached the covenant stipulations and as such, come under judgement by default. It is God's gracious will for salvation that separates them to life: "The Remnant is always presented as a mark of the mercy of God."[304]

The text contains all three elemental components of the remnant motif. A point of discontinuity with the motif as seen in the Noah and Joseph narratives is that while these two speak of remnant saved, "on Mt. Horeb we have for the first time a remnant spoken of as a future entity."[305] Hasel concurs with Jeremias, "this is the *locus classicus* of the promised remnant in the sense that we meet in this passage for the first time in the history of Israel the promise of a future remnant that constitutes the kernel of a new Israel."[306] Further, a watershed is defined here in that for the first time an "Israel" is sifted out from Israel, and that along ethico-religious lines.[307] The significant point of continuity, however, is that just as in early history, as against the later forms of the remnant concept where the emphasis becomes distinctly eschatological, the LORD's leaving of the seven thousand is incorporated into salvation history.[308]

To return briefly to the idea of an Israel within Israel: Hitherto, the entire nation had borne joint responsibility for sin, and had been both punished and pardoned corporately. This is best seen in the cycles of apostasy, bondage and deliverance in the book of Judges. Looking further back to the first act of rebellion post-covenant, we find that the LORD at first decides to consume all Israel (Exod.

---

of the terror shall fall into the pit; and whoever climbs out of the pit shall be caught in the snare."
303. Walsh (1996), 278.
304. de Vaux (1933), 528.
305. Hasel (1980), 171.
306. See Hasel (1980), 172.
307. Hasel (1980), 172.
308. Hasel (1980), 402.

32:10); then, he relents but still punishes by sending a plague on the people (Exod. 32:35). In Exod. 33 he decides to withdraw his presence from Israel altogether. In Exod. 34, pardon is awarded to the people as a whole and the covenant renewed. Yet, even as God forgives Israel as a nation and renews his covenant with her, the individual is warned of his personal responsibility. The covenant word חסד is promised to the faithful; the iniquity of the idolater will be personally visited on him (Exod. 20:5-6; 34:6-7).

The narrative in 1 Kgs 18 opens with a drought being announced on all Israel, on account of Israel's turning to other gods, at the encouragement of the crown. At Horeb, there is a proposal to retributively abandon the covenant with Israel. The alternative, in 1 Kgs 19:15-18, is the playing out of both the promise and the warning of Exod. 20 and 34. The LORD separates the faithful from the apostate. The LORD himself will preserve the faithful, presumably so that they may enjoy a continued covenant relationship, since they are identified by the same criterion as in the context of the making of the covenant; "all those whose knees have not bowed to Baal, and every mouth that has not kissed him" (cf. Exod 20:5-6). Meanwhile, the apostate comes under the sword, and is literally "cut off" from the covenant. From this point on, as Israel inexorably moves towards the ultimate disaster of the exile, it will be a spared remnant through which the covenant relationship will be perpetuated.[309]

This discussion on the significance of the root שאר serves as useful background as we return to examine if, as we have proposed, 1 Kgs 19:15-18 is indeed an alternate response to Elijah's statement of problem in 19:10, 14. If this is to be so, the former text must respond to the latter, and we must check if this is the case.

Elijah opens with an expression of his zeal and follows up with an explanation of the context of that zeal—Israel's abandoning of the covenant as evidenced by her treatment of the LORD's altars and prophets. He addresses the LORD by his military title, underlining the gravity of the politico-religious threat against Israel's covenanted faith. The LORD ratifies Elijah's ardour by carrying it further in his

---

309. Perhaps this is not the first instance of such alteration to the operation of the covenant. Moberly suggests that the wording of the declaration in Exod. 34:27—"I have made a covenant with you and with Israel"—"with Israel in secondary position points to an understanding of the renewed covenant as being not only mediated through, but in some sense necessarily dependent upon, Moses." This, he argues, is in line with Exod. 33:12-17 and 34:9, where it is upon Moses' special merit that God's decision against Israel is reversed. "So the position of Israel in the restored covenant is not identical to what it would have been had the people never sinned. Henceforth their life as a people depends not only on the mercy of God but also upon the intercession of God's chosen mediator." Moberly (1983), 105-6.

own reaction to Israel's apostasy. The energy that pulses through the formula recalls the Song of the Sword in Ezek. 21:14-22 (EVV 21:8-17):

> Let the sword fall twice, thrice;/It is a sword for killing.
> A sword for great slaughter—/It surrounds them...
> Ah! It is made for flashing,/It is polished for slaughter.
> Attack to the right!/Engage to the left!/Wherever your edge is directed.

If, as Terrien observes, this prophecy required of the prophet "a mimetic portrayal of the Deity," then one can readily imagine his "choreographic stance interpret[ing] visually and kinesthetically the prophetic oracle couched in the first person singular."[310] The Horeb oracle calls up just such a picture of God stirred into action by an avenging zeal.

The LORD's sword(s) adequately answer(s) the crisis Elijah articulates. In keeping with the order of responsibility for covenant keeping as established in the book of Kings, the first action is against the apostate head of the state;[311] Jehu will replace Ahab, and in turn, Jehu aided by Hazael and Elisha, will act to purge Israel of the Baalist faction.

The second half of Elijah's statement (according to the punctuation of the MT), concerns his position (as we have previously argued) as the only active prophet remaining. If there is here a shade of concern for personal safety, and there may well be, it is answered implicitly by the promise that the prophet slayers will themselves be slain in the great purge. Still, one notes that Elijah's concern for himself is unlikely to be a major issue since on the one hand, there is neither explicit guarantee of safety, nor the familiar "Do not be afraid" formula usually offered a fearful respondent by way of reassurance; on the other hand, there is no rebuke for anxiety unbecoming of a prophet. Instead, the promise of remnant is given, indicating that Elijah's concern is not so much himself but the continuing of Israel within the covenant, and to mediate this, the continuing voice of true prophecy. God lays his fears to rest with an unprecedented directive—he is to anoint a prophetic successor even while in office.

One more response is anticipated in the LORD's answer here, and that is to clarify whether he will still abandon Israel as a nation. When he finally addresses this issue, one finds that it is the very penalty that awaits Israel that performs as the instrument by which

---

310. Terrien (1978), 267.
311. Cf. 1 Kgs 6:11-13 where the LORD's relationship with Israel depends on Solomon's obedience.

true Israel will be saved.³¹² A remnant has already been identified, and will come through the upheaval unharmed. In his grace, the LORD separates and spares these seven thousand who have loyally kept the faith, and with them the covenant continues in operation. Thus, the alignment of opposites is not Elijah's "I alone" with the "seven thousand," as most commentators make out. In the context of covenant, so crucial to this narrative, the contrast is between the covenant-breakers and the seven thousand covenant-keepers.

With this we may reasonably conclude that the LORD's speech does answer the various concerns raised by Elijah, and as such, may be the alternative that Elijah had pressed for.

One further and final comment: when God re-engages with Israel, he does so with a burst of energy. He briskly commissions the prophet using the verb √הלך characteristic of authoritative and formal sending of his representative to inaugurate a new task.³¹³ In this, there is a critical interlacing of divine and prophetic endeavour in the interest of Israel, and this is in keeping with the pattern established since the commissioning of the archetypal prophet, Moses.³¹⁴ The triple directive "you shall anoint" is seamlessly conjoined with "I will leave" (19:15-18). Without an appreciation of this mechanism, one might wrongly read the LORD's declaration of a remnant as a rebuff aimed at Elijah's statement that he alone remains.³¹⁵

3.4. Comparing the Story Outlines of Exodus 32-34 and 1 Kings 19

Having worked through the account of Elijah at Horeb, we may now juxtapose its outline with that of the Moses narrative that it has been shown to recall at various levels, to see if the Elijah story is told generally keeping the plot and development of the Moses one in mind. One finds that there is a striking correspondence of episodes, even if they are not in exactly the same order. One bears in mind, of course, that the implications of these events are different in the different narratives (points 3, 6, 9); many, however, have significant conceptual overlaps (points 1-2, 4-5, 7-8).

	Exodus	1 Kings
1. Israel turns to another god	32: 1	implied in 19:17-18
2. Israel dismisses the true prophet	32:1	19:1, 10, 14
3. The prophet considers death	32:32	19:4
4. The prophet presents Israel before God	32:30	19:10

---

312. Cf. Ellul (1972), 76.
313. Cf. Exod. 4:19; Judg. 6:14, Isa. 6:8, Jer. 1:7.
314. Cf. "I have come to deliver...so come, I will send you" (3:8-10).
315. E.g., Robinson (1991), 528; Provan (1995), 147; Walsh (1996), 278; Brueggemann (2000), 241.

5. God proposes to withdraw his presence	33:1-6	19:11-12
6. God grants a personal theophany at Horeb	33:19-34:7	19:11-12
7. God involves prophet in decision	32:10; 33:5	19:13
8. The prophet presses the case for Israel	33:12-16; 34:8	19:14
9. The covenant comes into operation in a new way	34:10ff	19:15-18
(10. The prophet is affirmed before Israel	34:29-35	19:19-21)[316]

There seems to be here collusion between the narrator and his principal character in the telling of the story of Elijah at Horeb. As for Elijah, at this critical point in Israel's history when apostasy threatens the distinctive relationship of the people with their God, Elijah models himself after the archetypal prophet, Moses. Like him, Elijah approaches the place of the making of the covenant, seeking a solution; like him, he pleads Israel's case, even though they have rejected him. The outcome is that in the tradition of the great intercessor and covenant mediator, he plays a part in the emerging present: Israel remains within the covenant, even if only as a remnant. The narrator, for his part provides the setting necessary for a Mosaic event, working in the exodus motif, as pointed out, at all levels from the verbal to the conceptual.

However the postulate that Israel has fallen away in the interim between Carmel and Horeb needs to be supported. The account reads that at Carmel the people fall down in awe before the theophanic fire and confess the LORD as God indeed. The next we hear of Israel is in Elijah's report at Horeb, which portrays her seriously and systematically attempting to break free of the covenant. Scholars who privilege the received text have limited choices for reconciling these passages. In fact, as interaction with scholarship has shown, there is only one way out, and that concerns the reliability of the character Elijah; at this point in the narrative, he is either reliable or he is not.

3.5. The Reliability of the Character Elijah

If one argues that Elijah is not reliable in his statement re Israel, a problem is created: his unreliability has to be reconciled at multiple points with the narrative that follows, namely, the lack of criticism either by the narrator or by the character God, the high-profile commissions he is entrusted with, the fact that he leaves Horeb to continue in office as before, and the undeniable acclamation that the manner of his departure is. As already observed, scholarship has not engaged with this task to any significant degree.

---

316. Elijah promptly returns to Israel and engages with Elisha. Elisha's positive response, which is a public one, will be argued as an affirmation of Elijah's status as prophet and spiritual leader in Israel.

1 Kings 19: Horeb

On the other hand, if one argues Elijah's reliability, the problem described above does not arise, and the Horeb story joins seamlessly with the further narrative in 1 Kgs 19, 21 and 2 Kgs 1-2. However, it immediately puts the story at odds with the narrative that precedes it, namely, the Carmel episode. The dissonance between Carmel and Horeb boils down to two narrative features. First, at no point does the narrator inform the reader of Israel's backsliding, if any. Secondly, narrated time seems not to allow for it, since Jezebel's threat appears immediately to follow the incidents at Carmel. These two issues require discussion.

3.5.1. LEVELS OF KNOWLEDGE

The narrator, in choosing how to tell the story, manipulates not only the characters within the world of the story, but also the reader, who, like him, is outside it. One way he does this is by creating and controlling levels of knowledge. "Manipulation of the data stream," Fokkelman explains, "is at the same time manipulation of knowledge. The writer may decide to give us the same amount of insight as the character he introduces, or more, or less."[317] He offers Gen. 22 as an example where the reader has a head start over Abraham who does not know that the experience that will shortly come upon him is a test. Judg. 8, the story of Gideon, is given as an example in which the reader is at a disadvantage re knowledge.[318] The latter case may prove instructive to discerning the narrative technique in 1 Kgs 19.

The postlude to the war against Midian contains a most unexpected twist, unexpected, that is, for the reader. Gideon, in his pursuit of Zebah and Zalmunna the two Midianite kings, stops at Succoth and, stating his mission, requests refreshment for his exhausted 300. Succoth refuses with the taunt, "Do you already have in your possession the hands of Zebah and Zalmunna, that we should give bread to your army?" (v.6). The scene is repeated at the next stop, Penuel. To both, Gideon makes a reply that appears unnecessarily severe (vv.7, 9). After he defeats and captures the two enemy kings, he returns to these two cities, takes particular pains to obtain information about the leadership, and brutally avenges himself on the elders of Succoth and the male population of Penuel just as he had threatened to.

After this, a conversation ensues between Gideon and the captive kings on an issue that the reader has no knowledge of up to this moment. Gideon asks, "What manner of men [were they] whom you killed at Tabor?" "The question," remarks Boling, "is intended to be

---

317. Fokkelman (1999), 130.
318. Fokkelman (1999), 126-129.

as startling as it sounds."³¹⁹ It turns out from their reply and Gideon's further response that Midian has been responsible for the deaths of Gideon's brothers. The very same Zebah and Zalmunna, it appears, had either killed them in battle, or more probably, publicly executed them perhaps in retaliation for acts of resistance or as an intimidation strategy.³²⁰ At this point in the narrative the identity of their captor is revealed with reference to their victims. They catch up with Gideon's level of knowledge, and simultaneously, the reader, who suddenly realizes he has been at the lowest level all along, catches up with the Midianites and with Gideon. The narrator, who always operates at the highest level of knowledge, shared it with Gideon, and opted to keep the reader at the lowest.

This disclosure of information at the very end of the narrative impels the reader to review the previous events, particularly the character Gideon. Unbeknown to the reader, he has carried with him the recent loss of his blood brothers. Sharing in this knowledge, the reader at once evaluates him from an entirely new perspective; he reassesses Gideon's instinctive objection to the commission, the request of the messenger for a sign, his operating under cover of darkness to pull down a Baalist altar, the need for him to be reassured repeatedly by sign and finally, the vengefulness with which he deals with his own countrymen because they do not aid him in his cause against the Midianite chieftains.

Sternberg, in a section titled "Surprise and the Dynamics of Recognition" comments that such "manipulation of antecedents thus launches a surprise chain reaction from the point of retrospective (dis)closure"; in the more dramatic cases, "antecedents unexpectedly arise not to clinch an initial impression (portrait, response, assessment) but to qualify and complicate it, sometimes to the point of reversal."³²¹

---

319. Boling (1975), 157.
320. The seven years of hostilities alluded to in Judg. 6:1-5 may provide a context for "Tabor."
321. Thus Gideon, post Zeba and Zalmunna, may strike the reader as less admirable than before, driven as he is by considerations of personal vendetta. Sternberg (1985), 312, 315. Sternberg has several other interesting examples, among them 2 Kgs 4:8-16, the story of the Shunamite woman. When the disclosure is made that she is childless, "the surprise involves a retrospective illumination of all that has gone before, notably of the woman's character as well as her state. No ulterior motive, the discovery establishes, has lain behind her 'taking all this trouble.'…[W]here an anticipatory disclosure of the Shunamite's plight would first render her motives suspect and then her scepticism implausible…its temporary withholding and abrupt emergence maintain throughout an attractive yet credible portrait of a woman who deems virtue its own recompense." Sternberg (1985), 310.

The possibility is that in 1 Kgs 19 the narrator employs a similar narrative technique in that he has the characters Elijah and God operating at his level of knowledge, letting the reader do the catching up at the end of the story. The reader is uninformed as far as the falling away of Israel post Carmel is concerned, and thus the conversation between prophet and God at Horeb puzzles him. Elijah's statement that Israel has abandoned the covenant is as unanticipated and befuddling as Gideon's question about men killed at Tabor. To the reader, the prophet appears to engage in falsifying facts against Israel, which in itself does not quite fit with his consistent integrity thus far. Odder still, the LORD does not reprimand this untruth. Alarmingly odd is that the LORD bases his programme for Israel on this misrepresentation and decides to wipe out the entire nation but for a remnant. With this the episode ends, forcing the reader to rethink the story in order to make sense of it.

Let us suppose he works backwards from the last speech he has heard. The reliability of the character God is a given in biblical narrative, and that is a safe place to start. "Judgement by God," remarks Bar-Efrat, "is not like that by one of the characters in the plot, and is far more effective and convincing even than judgement by the narrator; for God is the absolute and supreme authority, and this naturally reflects upon the value and importance of His judgements (although it should not be forgotten that we know what God's attitude is only on the narrator's authority)." Thus, for example, in the case of David's adultery with Bathsheba (2 Sam. 11), a reader may judge David as an ancient eastern king, not subject to the limitations imposed on ordinary citizens; thus he is entitled to any woman he desires and as supreme military commander he controls deployment of soldiers in war. The narrator counters this royal canon by attributing the final judgement on the case to God, a system of absolute norms to which the king is also subject.[322]

If the LORD's decision re Israel reflects his absolute justice (in bringing the sword against faithless Israel), then Elijah's statement about Israel's falling away must be true. And if Israel has fallen away, this must have happened somewhere between Elijah's triumphant arrival at Jezreel and the arrival at his door of Jezebel's messenger. 1 Kgs 18:45b informs the reader "Ahab rode and went to Jezreel." The verse following describes how Elijah was enabled to run so as to reach Jezreel before Ahab. 19:1 tells how Ahab narrates the incidents at Carmel to Jezebel. Let us suppose that this rounds

---

322. Bar-Efrat (1989), 19-20. For this reason the narrator often cedes the judgement to God rather than present it as his own. For example, within the Ahab-Elijah material itself: The sentence on Ahab for his treaty with Ben-hadad (1 Kgs 20:42); the incident of Naboth's vineyard (1 Kgs 21:17-24 and 29); and the death of Ahaziah (2 Kgs 1:16).

off the Carmel episode. The next episode would then open with 19:2, where Jezebel sends a messenger to Elijah. Between the two episodes the reader must interpolate a time lapse long enough for the effect of Carmel to have worn out on Israel. This brings us to the second issue raised, namely, the issue of narrated time as against narration time.

3.5.2. TIME—OBJECTIVE AND INTERNAL

Two time systems meet and mesh in a narrative. There is objective or narration time, which is the time required for reading or telling the narrative, and there is internal or narrated time, time as it flows within the world of the story. The latter may flow faster or slower than the former, or be coterminous with it. A variety of temporal markers may be used to indicate the pace of narrated time. Within the Elijah corpus itself (1 Kgs 17-2 Kgs 2) there are several,[323] so it does seem odd that if there is a significant time lapse between the incidents of Carmel and Horeb, the narrator should not mention it. But before the case is shut, one may look for indicators other than temporal to see if there is a case for inserting a time period where the narrator has not mentioned one. Here, three possible non-temporal indicators may be discussed.

The first consideration is the framework that the narrator uses for his telling of the story. Alter comments: the "intersection of characters…does not take place in a trackless void…[a] stylising convention like the type-scene can offer thematic clues to the road that will be taken in the larger progress of the narrative and its implicit values."[324] What we have here is not merely a type-scene; the narrator plays off his characters against each other within one of the most significant motifs of all—that of the exodus.

Fishbane argues "[t]he simulataneous capacity of the exodus paradigm to elicit memory and expectation, recollection and anticipation discloses…its deep embeddedness as a fundamental structure of biblical historical imagination."[325] It further discloses that, as Daube explains, "[t]he kind of salvation portrayed in the exodus was not, by its nature, an isolated occurrence, giving rise to nebulous hopes for similar good luck in the future: it had its root in, and set the seal on, a permanent institution—hence it was something on which absolute reliance might be placed."[326] He rightly

---

323. See "after a while" (17:7), "many days" (17:15), "after many days" (18:1), "in a little while/meanwhile" (18:45), "a day's journey" (19:4), "forty days and forty nights" (19:8), "spent the night" (19:9), "in the spring" (20: 26), "seven days" (20:29), "as soon as" (21:15, 16), "for three years" (22:1), "until evening," "about sunset" (22:35, 36), and "for three days" (2:17).
324. Alter (1981), 87.
325. Fishbane (1979), 122.
326. Daube (1963), 14.

concludes, "Surely, this particular quality must have greatly contributed to the coming into existence and popularity of the pattern. By being fashioned on the exodus, later deliverances became manifestations of this eternal, certainty-giving relationship between God and his people."[327]

Indeed, the exodus motif has at its heart, not Moses, but Israel. As much as it says about Moses and his remarkable relationship with God, the fundamental theme is God's dealings with a wayward people. The narrator seizes these events of history and uses them as "prismatic openings to the transhistorical"[328] because his story is about the people of the exodus paradigm. Therefore, it is not an unreasonable proposition that as much as the Exod. 19-20 and 32-34 are about the covenant and the faithfulness of the signatory parties thereto, 1 Kgs 18-19, in using the exodus stories as template, is re-creating the story for a new but disappointingly comparable generation, and herein lie the "thematic clues" that Alter speaks about. Both stories end on a similar note of hope—the covenant is to remain; thus the likelihood is that both stories begin similarly, with the covenant endangered. In Exod. 32, the narrator gives an explicit account of Israel's faithlessness. In 1 Kgs 18, Israel's divided loyalty has already been described at length, and when the reader next hears of it at Horeb, he hears it within the paradigm of the exodus story; the inference is that Carmel has been another "Sinai," and within not too long a period, Israel has returned to her Baals.

Secondly, there is the consideration that the biblical storyteller does not always insert temporal indicators. Sometimes, he leaves it to the commonsense of the reader to recognize where narrated time overtakes narration time and fill in the gap as required; meanwhile he gets on with the more crucial parts of the storytelling. For example, Gen. 38 opens with the account of Judah making himself a family. In the space of five short verses, he settles in a new place, chooses a woman, marries, and has three sons by her. In v.6, Judah gets his eldest son Er a wife. In v.7 Er dies by the hand of LORD for some unnamed wickedness. The narrated time slows down only when Tamar emerges as a player in the drama, making it clear that the narrative up to this point is largely background and the narrator does not wish to spend too much time over it. Thus, the reader must interpolate between verses 5 and 6 enough time for Er to grow to a marriageable age and in the course of that period, offend the LORD in some way, the details of which are unimportant to the story; the fact that he died for it is sufficient to move the plot forward.

A different case is when a story is told twice and the reader finds that one account may be longer than the other in terms of internal

---

327. Daube (1963), 14.
328. Fishbane (1979), 122.

time. This means that the shorter story, for reasons of its own, has edited out a time period. The account of the golden calf is a case in point. After he has broken the tablets (Exod. 32:19), the furious prophet immediately turns his attention to the idol, reducing it to dust (v.20). Then he confronts Aaron. It might occur to the reader that God seems to have overlooked Aaron's culpability in this affair. It is only in another account of this episode that the reader is informed that God had indeed taken note of Aaron's role, and only Moses' intercession had saved him. Reviewing the incident from a different perspective in Deuteronomy (9:15ff), the sequence of events includes a forty-day period of fasting and intercession for Israel and Aaron on the part of Moses, interpolated between the breaking of the tablets and the destroying of the golden calf.

The point is that the absence of a temporal marker need not necessarily mean that the narrated time is flowing more or less in synchrony with narration time. In 1 Kgs 19 itself, it appears that there is need for the reader to insert a time adjustment between Horeb and Abel-meholah, to give Jezebel's death warrant enough time to lapse. Otherwise, the apparent openness that marks the appointment of Elisha as successor and their safety thereafter would be hard to reconcile with the kind of situation that sent Elijah on the run.[329] Thus there is no compelling reason why we may not insert time post Carmel and prior to Jezebel's warrant.

A third possible non-temporal indicator of a time gap may be found in Jezebel's modus operandi. In the matter of Naboth's vineyard, what impresses is her careful planning. It appears that she is careful not to turn public opinion against the crown, for she devises a sophisticated stratagem to gain her ends. It involves elders, the declaring of a fast, the convening of the city council, the hiring of false witnesses, a trial, and a stoning to death. It takes time, and Jezebel is prepared to wait to win. If this is in any way indicative of her method, then it is very likely that in the matter of the elimination of a person of Elijah's standing she plays her cards with care. It is not so probable that she would choose to threaten Elijah on the heels of his victory at Carmel, when the nation has demonstrated by the slaughter of her prophets that it is on his side. She would choose rather to wait till the revival has cooled off and Israel has relapsed into their old ways.

Let us suppose that this is what has happened. Elijah is now disadvantaged; his loss of territory is Jezebel's gain; and as Jezebel

---

329. One may argue that Jezebel's threat was an empty one, and that Elijah's panic-fuelled run was unnecessary. However, one recalls that the LORD himself saw reason to hide Elijah from the crown after the announcement of the drought, and that Jezebel did actually kill off prophets till possibly only those who had gone underground remained alive.

gains, Elijah's position becomes particularly precarious because he stands responsible for emptying her table of 450 prophets. Let us say Jezebel makes her move now. She sets the assassination in place and so confident is she that he cannot escape, that she sends him a twenty-four hour notice of death. It is not entirely unreasonable then that Elijah, receiving a death warrant under such circumstances from a queen who is no amateur at killing off prophets, flees.

As in the Gideon story, the reader is admitted into the narrator's level of knowledge only at the close of the episode, and from the point of the reliability of the character God, he undertakes an informed review of the story. He is in a position to make a more sympathetic judgement on Elijah's fear-fed flight, his deep, suicidal depression and his unusual pilgrimage to find God. The covert narrator of 1 Kgs 19 creates suspense, for "the order of suspense is the order of self-effacement," and he channels this suspense towards "the closural point of vantage" from which "details as well as contours assume new shape, meaning, determinacy."[330]

3.5.3. Conclusion

In conclusion, any attempt to read in sequence the narratives of 1 Kgs 18 and 19 must engage with the issue of Elijah's reliability, and in this exercise, one looks for help from the narrator and finds the usual intimations missing—there is neither a summary narration of Israel's falling away, nor is there comment on Elijah's integrity. This is not an unusual situation, for, as Fokkelman points out, biblical writers employ a range of tools with which to convey their values to the reader, so that the story may not be reduced to didactics; "these forms and techniques may be arranged along a scale that runs from very clear and explicit to vague, implicit and well-hidden."[331] The narrator in 1 Kgs 19 is in his covert manifestation rather than his overt one, letting his reader work at discovering where a judgement has been incorporated, and thus effectively draws him into the story.

The submission here is that the narrator *has* addressed the issue of Elijah's reliability. He has chosen not to state it in terms of his own evaluation; rather he embeds Elijah's reliability in the absolute reliability of God, by showing God taking Elijah's word as basis for drastic, programmatic action. By this he awards Elijah the highest possible endorsement. Working back from this last speech of the scene, the reader mulls over the story, making the adjustments necessary for a fresh understanding of what has gone on at Horeb, among these, making the necessary insertion of a time period during the course of which Israel returns to their folly.

---

330. Sternberg (1985), 266, 316.
331. Fokkelman (1999), 149; also Bar-Efrat on the overt and covert manifestations of the narrator, (1989), 23-45.

4. 1 Kings 19:19-21: Elisha becomes Elijah's Minister

19 So he set out from there, and found Elisha son of Shaphat, who was plowing. There were twelve yoke of oxen ahead of him, and he was with the twelfth. Elijah passed by him and threw his mantle over him.
20 He left the oxen, ran after Elijah, and said, "Let me kiss my father and my mother; and then I will follow you." Then Elijah said to him, "Go back again; for what have I done to you?"
21 He returned from following him, took the yoke of oxen, and slaughtered them; using the equipment from the oxen, he boiled their flesh, and gave it to the people, and they ate. Then he set out and followed Elijah, and became his servant.

4.1. The Question of Elijah's "Lapses"

At the conclusion of the LORD's speech, the reader expects that Elijah will (given his record of implicit obedience in 1 Kgs 17-18) proceed to the wilderness of Damascus to anoint Hazael, and follow up with the anointing of Jehu and Elisha. He does not, and some critics see this as a further mark against Elijah. We may take Walsh's summing up of the issues as representative:

> ...as the stories of 1 and 2 Kings unfold, Elijah will carry out only one of these commissions, and that only in terms that differ from Yahweh's command. Elisha, not Elijah, will visit Damascus and nominate Hazael to the throne (2 Kgs 8:7-15); Elisha, not Elijah, will send a disciple to anoint Jehu king of Israel (2 Kgs 9:1-13). Elijah will choose Elisha as his servant (1 Kgs 19:19-21) and eventual successor (2 Kgs 2:1-14), but both events involve investing Elisha with Elijah's mantle rather than anointing him.[332]

There are two matters raised here for consideration; first, the seeming non-compliance of Elijah re the appointments of Hazael and Jehu; secondly, the issue of "anointing."

4.1.1. THE APPOINTMENTS OF HAZAEL AND JEHU

Let us consider first, the "unfinished" business. The manner of its execution suggests that it is neither simple nor straightforward a matter.

It is significant that Elisha does not rush into these tasks immediately following his succession to Elijah's place. He engages in "calculated opportunism."[333] In 2 Kgs 8, his trip to Damascus is timed to coincide with Ben-hadad's illness (v.7). He is recognized as an important visitor, for his arrival is immediately reported to the

---

332. Walsh (1996), 278.
333. Ellul (1972), 80.

king, and he is honoured by the state with gifts as a "man of God" who may be consulted for an oracle (vv.7-8). Hazael addresses Elisha as "lord" (אדון), refers to Ben-hadad as Elisha's "son" and to himself as but a "dog." It appears that it would not have been easy for a prophet of Elisha's standing to visit Damascus unnoticed.

Ben-hadad's choice of Hazael as emissary perfectly suits Elisha's purposes, and the reader wonders if this is exactly as Elisha expected. Elisha's communication to Hazael is open to two readings, the regular one being that a falsehood is conveyed to the ailing king, while the truth is revealed to Hazael, namely, that he will succeed to the throne of Aram.[334] Labuschagne's is one of the several suggested solutions;[335] he reads לו (as in some Hebrew mss and most LXX mss) rather than לא, and reads the first pronoun as referring to Hazael rather than Ben-hadad. Thus: "Go say to him [that] you [Hazael] shall certainly live, and [that] Yahweh has shown me that he [Ben-hadad] shall certainly die." Hazael does not understand it till Elisha plainly tells him (vv.11-13). Hazael then cunningly uses the *ipsissima verba* of the prophet in his response to Ben-hadad: "He said to me, 'You shall certainly live (v.14).'" The king understands this as indirect narration, and is falsely reassured.[336] Both readings are possible; both reinforce the covert nature of the operation.

Hazael works the fulfilment of the oracle himself, and that without much delay. By the next day, Ben-hadad has been suffocated to death. The manner of the murder suggests that Hazael intends the death to seem natural, and his succession to the throne appears spontaneous, suggesting he was the most likely candidate in any event.

The next appointee is Jehu and here again, the procedure is opportunely timed (2 Kgs 8:25-9:37).[337] Elisha chooses a time when Joram of Israel (the son of Ahab) has retired wounded from the battlefield, and repaired to Jezreel to recover, a situation grave enough to prompt a visit from Ahaziah of Judah. Meanwhile Jehu is at the battlefront, Ramoth-gilead, in a key position of command. The reader notes that Elisha sends one from among "the sons of the prophets," with very specific instructions to perform the anointing privately, maintaining the utmost secrecy; he is to say no more than a line to explain the anointing, and then he is to flee before he can be apprehended for further questioning (9:1-3). The urgent need for stealth bespeaks the hazardous nature of the mission.[338] Again, the

---

334. E.g., Nelson (1987), 193; House (2001), 283; Fretheim (1999), 164; Brueggemann (2000), 372.
335. See Montgomery (1951), 393; Gray (1964), 477-78.
336. Labuschagne (1965), 327-28. Cf. Provan (1995), 207-08.
337. See Ellul (1972), 99-100.
338. Cf. e.g., Schulte (1994), 137.

anointed is not given any directive on how he will come into power. Once he is spontaneously "crowned" by the military officers, Jehu moves very quickly and decisively. He seals off Ramoth-gilead so that the news may not reach Jezreel. Then he sets off to Jezreel, kills two kings, and eventually wipes out Ahab's seventy sons and all those in any way connected to the house of Ahab.

The two cases—Jehu's and Hazael's—are marked by similarities: (1) Elisha chooses a time when the incumbent monarch is gravely ill, and the appointee is in a position of strength. (2) The operation is indubitably tactical and undercover, and risks severe consequences on discovery. (3) The appointment of the king-to-be directly instigates a coup; the immediacy and speed of the revolts affirms that timing is absolutely critical. These suggest that carrying out the directive of the LORD to "anoint" Hazael and Jehu is not quite as straightforward as it would seem. The possibility needs to be kept open that in being entrusted with these strategic tasks, Elijah is privileged with the responsibility of planning and executing them.[339] This possibility gains some support from the usage of תחת in 1 Kgs 19:15-16. As mentioned in an earlier discussion, the word is regularly employed in Kings as part of the formulaic expression for succession to a position, and the likelihood is great that this is the usage with respect to Elisha's appointment. In this case, one notes that the formula is not used with respect to Hazael and Jehu; whom Hazael and Jehu are to displace is left unsaid. If by this we are to understand that Elijah, by prophetic discernment, is to fill in these gaps himself, Elijah's modus operandi could be interpreted thus: he makes the installation of Elisha the immediate priority—"The missions are dangerous. In case Elijah should be killed, Elisha will fulfil that which is undone."[340] The other two appointments, one supposes then, are not made during the course of his life because the expedient moment does not arrive. In Ahab's case, one must consider that he "humbled himself" before the LORD with sackcloth and fasting; his response to the message of rebuke earns him a waiver—the disaster to come will strike only in the days of his son (1 Kgs 21:27-29).

Thus these tasks of appointment pass from Elijah to his successor Elisha (reminding of the tasks that Joshua inherits from his predecessor Moses). Elisha, in turn, bides his time and strikes when the chance of success is optimum. As Miscall remarks: "Divine commissions can be carried out in circuitous and incomplete fashion because of the circumstances at the time of execution and because of the character of the one or ones who carry out the commission."[341]

---

339. Also Fretheim (1999), 110-11.
340. Scolnic (1987), 333.
341. Miscall (1989), 77.

1 Kings 19: Horeb

This harmonious working in tandem of prophets and God towards a given goal is demonstrated at several points in these two Elisha narratives. To begin with, in the case of the Aramean succession, Elisha's authority in the matter is significant. He is certain of Ben-hadad's impending death and Hazael's coming to power because "the LORD has shown (√ראה) me" (2 Kgs 8:10, 13); the verb, with its prophetic connotations, reinforces the oracular. He foretells the catastrophe that Hazael will bring on Israel in graphic detail, weeping in the knowledge of its certainty (vv.11-12). The reader sees that this is an expansion of the summary prophecy granted Elijah at Horeb on the sword of Hazael. Elisha acts, not on secondary and devolved authority, but as one fully cognisant of and participating in the future, as God will direct it.

In the Jehu episode, though it is from Elisha that the initiative and authority to anoint Jehu originates, he may send a "young prophet" in his stead, losing nothing of the force and validity of the anointing. The highest level of military command accepts his action as sound enough basis for an immediate coup. Further, the young prophet is ordered to say "Thus says the LORD: I anoint you king over Israel" (2 Kgs 9:3). One notes that his position is that of direct representative of the LORD, even though he acts at Elisha's behest. What is of even greater interest is that the young prophet appears to overstep his brief. He adds in a prophetic commission—"You shall strike down the house of your master Ahab, so that I may avenge on Jezebel the blood of my servants the prophets, and the blood of all the servants of the LORD (v.7)"—and follows it with a prophecy that recalls Elijah's pronouncements on the house of Ahab (1 Kgs 21:21-24). The fact that the whole speech flows from the introductory "thus says the LORD" eclipses any tenor of the second-hand; he speaks with his own prophetic authority; he "places himself in a line of great prophets: Ahijah of Shiloh, Jehu son of Hanani and Elijah the Tishbite" who "respectively pronounce annihilation for the first three royal dynasties of Israel."[342] The oracle he brings Jehu meshes perfectly with the purposes of the LORD as the reader knows has been revealed to Elijah and is being acted on by Elisha.

The way the narrator tells the story directs our understanding of the working out of the LORD's commission. He repeatedly recalls Elijah's oracles at key points in the narrative of Jehu's rise to power. He inserts the detail that Joram and Ahaziah meet Jehu at the property of Naboth of Jezreel (2 Kgs 9:21). This immediately creates recall of the murder and the associated curse, and anticipates Jehu's dealing with Joram. Jehu's summary statement (2 Kgs 9:25-26) recalls 1 Kgs 21: 17-19, for this is the only other account of the LORD rebuking Ahab on the death of Naboth. Though Elijah is not

---

[342] Miscall (1989), 77-78; Cf. Scolnic (1987), 334.

mentioned by name, and the cited oracle is not exactly the same as in 1 Kgs 21, the intention of retribution is identical, and Joram's dead body on Naboth's field is "in accordance with the word of the LORD." Then again, at the description of Jezebel's death, Jehu makes another summary statement, and this time he explicitly recalls Elijah, citing what appears to be a longer version of the oracle in 1 Kgs 21:23 (2 Kgs 9:36-37). On the slaughter of Ahab's seventy sons, Jehu categorically evokes Elijah with "Know then that there shall fall to the earth nothing of the word of the LORD, which the LORD spoke concerning the house of Ahab; for the LORD has done what he said through his servant Elijah (2 Kgs 10:10; cf. 1 Kgs 21:21)." The word of the LORD and of Elijah are one and the same, and Jehu's acts bring it to pass. Even the word Jehu uses to describe his attitude towards the crown and the state-patronised religion is a key point of recall of Elijah at Horeb; like Elijah, he reacts with "zeal for the LORD," announcing it as the motivation for his acts (וראה בקנאתי ליהוה; 2 Kgs 10:16).

The reliability of Jehu's use of Elijah to justify his deeds is affirmed at the two highest levels in Hebrew narrative—by the narrator, and then by the ultimate authority, the LORD himself. In his summary statement, the narrator recalls Elijah for the last time: "he...wiped them out, according to the word of the LORD that he spoke to Elijah (2 Kgs 10:17)." In the final statement the LORD affirms that Jehu's actions were "in accordance with all that was in my heart" and as reward, his line is assured Israel's throne to the fourth generation (2 Kgs 10:30).[343]

It appears then, that there is a surprisingly wide ownership both of Elijah's oracles and commission. There is no rebuke of Elijah within the narrative for unfinished business. ("God has not only refrained from punishing him for his failure to complete the assigned missions, but has obviously honoured him" in the manner of his departure.[344]) Rather, the commission smoothly moves into Elisha's hands, and at every key point in the narrative, as the sword of Jehu moves in its deadly arc wiping out Baalism and the house that promoted it, Elijah is recalled. Miscall sums it up well:

> The word of the Lord has been spoken by himself and others; it has been repeated and declared fulfilled, all in a series of interpretations and reinterpretations that involve the great and not-so-great, the named and

---

342. We note the problem of reading this in relation to Hos. 1:4-5. See Miller (1967), 322, who attempts a solution within the context of the divine curses against the house of Omri.
343. Scolnic (1987), 334.

the unnamed...never is it a matter of a one-to-one mechanical correspondence.³⁴⁵

4.1.2. THE "ANOINTING" OF ELISHA

The second issue Walsh raises concerns the order from the LORD on Elisha's anointing.

The verb √משׁח when used with a person as its accusative object, involves solemn setting apart to an office; it is an act with sacral effectiveness and legal force, made tangible with oil poured on the head. While it is mostly used with respect to the installation of kings and the consecration of priests, √משׁח appears with respect to prophets in 1 Kgs 19:16 and Isa. 61:1. The frequent construction of the verb with ל (as in 1 Kgs 19:15, 16) shows that the process signifies a change in status. From 1 Sam. 16:1-13, one derives the theological implications associated with the act of such anointing: it is a visible sign of divine election; a representative of the LORD performs the symbolic ritual; the anointed one is empowered with the spirit of the LORD.³⁴⁶ In 1 Kgs 19, Elijah does not anoint with oil, but rather, uses his mantle on Elisha.³⁴⁷ (Here, we will restrict our consideration of the role of the mantle to this particular text, and deal with its role in 2 Kgs 2 when we come to that episode.) What are the implications?

Walsh explains that with the mantle, "we are probably dealing with a cultural convention familiar to ancient audiences concerning the prophet's mantle as a distinctive badge of office."³⁴⁸ In support he cites 2 Kgs 1:8 where Elijah is identified as a אישׁ בעל שׂער (more probably "a man with a garment of skin" rather than "a hairy man")³⁴⁹, Zech. 13:4 (false prophets put on hairy mantles— אדרת שׂער—to pass as true prophets), and Mark 1:6 and Matt. 3:4 (John the Baptist's camel-hair garment).³⁵⁰ This mantle is cast on Elisha.

---

344. Miscall (1989), 81. Also von Rad (1965), 211-12, on the Elijah stories as demonstrative of the "self-fulfilling relationship between the divinely inspired prophecy and the historical occurrence."
345. BDB, משׁח, 602-03; Seybold (1998), 45-49.
346. A conventional approach ascribes this section (1 Kgs 19:19-21) to a different hand from the section earlier, thereby settling the non-anointing of Elisha. See DeVries (1978), 112-13. Even if so, we will see that the redacted text clearly construes √משׁח in a non-literalist way.
347. Cf. e.g., Gray (1964), 368; Montgomery (1951), 316.
348. BDB, שׂער, 972.
349. Walsh (1996), 279.

It is striking that Elijah performs the action hardly breaking stride, as the MT would suggest: ויעבר אליהו אליו וישלך אדרתו אליו.[351] Rice suggests, quite plausibly, that in wordlessly continuing on his way, "Elijah both tests Elisha's readiness to serve and allows him to respond in freedom."[352] But, the fact that there is no "anointing" (in the usual sense) gives rise to the possibility that Elijah is not being faithful to the mandate given at Horeb.[353] In answer to this, one notes that the factors that define the significance of √משח as seen earlier from 1 Sam. 16:1-13 are present in the Elisha narratives: 1 Kgs 19 makes explicit that the LORD himself makes the appointment, and it is his representative Elijah who is to install Elisha; the empowering by the spirit of the LORD occurs in 2 Kgs 2, and the gap between installation and empowerment is explained by the circumstance that Elisha succeeds Elijah only at his departure. Further, the significance of Elijah's act becomes apparent as the narrative unfolds, by way of the reaction it elicits from Elisha. Elisha immediately recognizes a call here, for he directly leaves his ploughing, runs after Elijah and requests permission to take leave of his parents properly, after which, he says, he will follow Elijah. Elisha seems quite certain that he has been "invested" into service by the mantle[354] in a manner that loses none of the weight and burden of an "anointing."

Elijah's reply to this is, however, not so clear to us. Walsh holds that Elijah's answer "cannot be merely rhetorical, as if Elijah were saying, 'After all, I haven't done anything to you.' Investment into Yahweh's prophetic service, as Elijah well knows, is no light thing. It is more likely that Elijah intends the question literally. What does Elisha think this investiture means?"[355] The LXX may also move the reading in this direction with its ἀνάστρεφε ὅτι πεποίηκά σοι—"return, for I have done (a work) for you." Again, the issue is clarified by Elisha's response. Rice sums up well: "Whatever the precise meaning, it is clear from the context that Elisha understands that he

---

350. Recognizing the oddness, the LXX modifies it to read that Elijah came up to Elisha—καὶ ἐπῆλθεν ἐπ' αὐτόν.
351. Rice (1990), 165.
352. E.g., Provan (1995), 147.
353. Thus Eissfeldt concludes that the command was used "im übertragenen Sinne"—in a figurative sense. (1922-23), 329. Cf. Fretheim (1999), 110; Rice (1990), 165; House (1995), 225; Brueggemann (2000), 242; DeVries (1985), 239. Gray suggests that the verb is used in the weak sense of "set apart." (1964), 411.
354. Walsh (1996), 279. Cf. Wiseman (1993), 174-75; cf. Provan (1995), 148; contra Fretheim, who agrees that "[w]hether Elijah rebukes him is unclear," but suggests that "he appears to tell Elisha (a rich man) to return to what he was doing as if the call had not occurred." (1999), 111.

may follow Elijah and that he may also take leave of his parents."[356] Elisha returns and straightaway engages in activity that makes it unquestionably clear that he is making a decisive and enthusiastic break with his current occupation. He slaughters one yoke of oxen and uses the tackle to cook "the people" a meal, presumably in farewell,[357] for immediately following he arises, follows after Elijah and ministers to him. Thus Elijah's non-verbal communication via mantle, and his spoken statement are both elucidated by Elisha's prompt responses; even if there is no literal anointing, Elijah "sets apart" Elisha to an office as in the sense of √משח, and Elisha himself seems to have no difficulty at all in discerning and appreciating the high honour accorded him.

4.2. Mosaic Resonances

The final scene of 1 Kgs 19 not only flows from the Horeb episode, but recalls the concluding section of the story of the golden calf, namely, Exod. 34:29-35. Both narratives, one recollects, had opened with the prophet in some way losing credibility (Exod. 32:1; 1 Kgs 19:3-4). (We must stress the difference here—Moses loses reliability in the eyes of the misguided Israelites; Elijah, however, loses credibility with himself, and consequently with the reader.) Thereafter, there is a resolution of crisis via an encounter between prophet and God at Horeb (Exod. 34:4-28; 1 Kgs 19:8-18); following this, the prophet returns to the people, and is affirmed. In the case of Moses, this affirmation takes the shape of a face that shines "because he had been talking with God" (Exod. 34:29). The awed withdrawal of the people recalls their retreat from the closeness of deity at Sinai (Exod. 20:18-21). The narrator positions Moses as the LORD's undeniable and incontestable representative.[358] "If Moses should remain discredited, both the repetition of Yahweh's revelation and

---

355. Rice (1990), 165.
356. Walsh sees a "deeper meaning of the meal" in the verb √זבח, since it "generally means to kill an animal *as a sacrifice*." He also thinks that the phrase בשלם—"he boiled them"—evokes a שלם, the "communion sacrifice, in which a person offers an animal to Yahweh in thanksgiving for divine blessings and uses the sacrificial meat to host a meal for family and friends." (e.g., the זבח of Exod. 24:5 and 1 Sam. 11:15 is also a שלם; also, Lang (1980), 11, 22-24; BDB, שלם, 1023. He concludes, "Elisha's action, therefore, combines elements of separation from his old life, cultic thanksgiving upon undertaking the new, and ritual solidarity with 'the people' among whom he will pursue his prophetic service." (1996), 279-80. If this is so, it would nicely clarify the direction of the exchange between Elijah and Elisha (the verbal and non-verbal components included).
357. So, for example, Morgenstern (1925), 5; Durham (1987), 466; Moberly (1983), 108-09.

instruction given already and also the continuing revelation and instruction to be given through him would be compromised. Moses' authority must therefore be re-established in the eyes of the very people who have rejected him..."[359]

In the case of Elijah also, there is a similar narratorial affirmation. Here, the role of the people is taken over by one individual, namely, Elisha. Elijah's wordless gesture is authority enough to make Elisha drop his work and run after him in implicit obedience. In the presence of the people who eat the leave-taking meal, it is established that Elijah is a prophet of God, whom a rich man may count it a privilege to serve, renouncing all.[360]

The story of the golden calf ends with Moses passing on to Israel the instruction he had received from the LORD at Sinai (Exod. 34:32), for their obedience; so also, 1 Kgs 19 ends with Elijah executing an order received at Horeb.

Elisha becomes Elijah's "minister." Provan points out that though √שרת is used to describe Joshua's relationship with Moses and Joshua does go on to become Moses' successor, √שרת has already been used in Kings of Abishag the Shunammite (1 Kgs 1:4, 15) and will be later used of Elisha's servant (2 Kgs 4:43; 6:15), neither of which cases involves succession of any sort.[361] However, considering the Mosaic tenor of the entire chapter, the word takes on significance. As was pointed out in detail previously (under the discussion of תחת in 1 Kgs 19:16), the prophet, in anticipation of his death, makes known his concern for Israel's future leadership and is directed to install a successor. That successor is publicly invested, and then serves till such time as the prophet is removed, upon which he becomes prophet in his master's place.

5. Concluding Summary to 1 Kings 19

With 1 Kgs 19, the story makes a dramatic shift; the intrepid and triumphant Elijah makes himself a fugitive. Assessing himself as a failure, he asks the LORD to take his life. The answer takes the form of sustenance, and when Elijah eats in obedience to the messenger, the command-compliance pattern so characteristic of the narrative thus far reasserts itself and the reader may understand this as a reversal of Elijah's lapse. Elijah's subsequent move is to travel to Horeb. Reading his death wish under the broom tree and his complaint at Horeb alongside the two death wishes of Moses (at Sinai and at Kibroth-hattaavah), we located a verbal and conceptual

---

358. Durham (1987), 466.
359. It is of passing interest that Moses' veil carries associations of his most intimate encounters with God, as does Elijah's mantle.
360. Provan (1995), 150.

intersection in the phrase אנכי לבדי. The expression identifies the common theme of the loneliness of the leader that runs through the Kings, Exodus and Numbers stories. Further, we noted that the contours of Elijah's complaint at Horeb resemble those of Moses' at Kibroth-hattaavah. This led to the tentative proposal that Elijah, seeking divine guidance in his situation of crisis, sought God at a place associated with Israel's paradigmatic prophet, making a verbal presentation modelled on the Mosaic. We noted that Elijah's speech turns on Israel's abandoning of the covenant; this is information that takes the reader by surprise, and casts a shadow of doubt on Elijah's reliability, considering Israel's confession at Carmel.

The LORD's answer is graphic, coming in earthquake, wind, fire, and the translation-defying קול דממה דקה. Studying this phrase with reference to Job 4:16, the inference was that it signifies a natural phenomenon in the same sense as the other three elements of the theophany are "natural"; but as much as the latter are (explicitly) empty of the presence of deity, the former (implicitly) contains it. A clue to the absence of the divine presence may be found in the verb √עזב, which Elijah uses to describe Israel's forsaking of the covenant. We noted that a principle of retribution (stated in language not unlike the *lex talionis*) is frequently encountered in the event of Israel's unfaithfulness to the covenant. Here, God's withdrawing of his presence could be read as a proposal to abandon Israel in punitive reciprocation. When dialogue resumes, Elijah indicates his resistance to the proposal; his device of deliberately repeating his earlier indictment returns the conversation to a point prior to the "empty" theophany. The LORD is forced into considering an alternative solution to Israel's apostasy; this takes the form of a strategy to create an Israel within Israel, a faithful remnant. From this the reader infers that the narrator embeds Elijah's reliability in the absolute reliability of the character God, by showing God taking Elijah's word as basis for drastic, programmatic action; Israel has indeed relapsed since Carmel.

The story reprises the events at Sinai; it does not take long for Israel to lapse from confession into apostasy; and, as at Israel's first instance of unfaithfulness, the LORD allows his prophet a role in fickle Israel's emergent future. Once more, because of that prophet persevering in "loyal opposition," as God expects of him, Israel's covenant relationship is recovered, albeit this time in an unprecedented form, namely, in terms of a remnant.

CHAPTER 5

1 Kings 22:51-2 Kings 1:18: Elijah and Ahaziah

Sirach's paean in celebration of Elijah's life and work recalls the events recorded in 2 Kgs 1, "…also three times brought down fire…You sent kings down to destruction, and famous men, from their sickbeds" (Sir. 48:3, 6). These deeds earn him fulsome praise: "How glorious you were, Elijah, in your wondrous deeds! Whose glory is equal to yours?" (Sir. 48: 4). Reading the text in another age, the reader is not so sure that these are exploits meriting applause. Indeed, Montgomery and Gehmann note "the preposterousness of the miraculous element."[1] Since our interest is in following the characterisation of Elijah, our study of this narrative will require us to engage with this issue and resolve it as best as we may. However, the more important business is to keep on the track of any resonance between this story and the Moses narratives. One may safely say at the outset that in this aspect 2 Kgs 1 is not as rich as other sections of the Elijah corpus. However, there may be material here that furthers the argument we have been building up for Elijah as a second Moses, and this possibility directs our reading.

1. 1 Kings 22:51-53: Regnal Resumé

Ahab has made his dramatic exit from the stage of Israel's history and his son Ahaziah takes his place. The introductory regnal summary is bleak. He walks "in the way of his father and mother" — a doubly damning indictment, given he has Jezebel for a mother. Other than the brief opening notice on the loss of Moab (2 Kgs 1:1), and the closing personal detail that Ahaziah had no heir (necessary to explain his brother's accession to the throne; 2 Kgs 1:17), the story of this king's reign is curious in that it is restricted to a single incident, namely, his ultimately fatal accident. If in this, it is the narrator's intention to revisit the themes that dominated his telling of the story of Ahab in 1 Kgs 17-18,[2] the incident is well chosen. We turn first to the theme of Baal versus the LORD.

---

1. Montgomery (1951), 348.
2. This is regularly noted. E.g., Robinson (1976), 19; Smend (1975[1]), 178. Cf. Cogan and Tadmor (1988), 27.

2. 2 Kings 1: The Themes Revisited

2.1. Baal versus the LORD

Here is another king who chooses Baal over the LORD, and once more, Elijah is commissioned to demonstrate the folly of the choice. A contest-like confrontation ensues, and a show of power through word and deed both proves the LORD's exclusive position as God of Israel and affirms Elijah's position as his representative. As in 1 Kgs 17-18, the confrontation is at multiple levels. On the highest plane is the struggle for Israel's allegiance (here represented by that of the king), covenanted to the LORD but skewed towards Baal of Ekron. The characters in the narrative, human and otherwise, are more or less clearly distributed between the two divine parties, and are themselves brought into conflict in various combinations.

Events are set into motion with Ahaziah's choice of deity in his hour of need. He sends[3] messengers to Baalzebub of Ekron, believing that this god holds the answer to the pressing question of his survival. It is noted that the usage of √דרש here is specifically in the technical sense, that of seeking divine revelation by consulting an oracle (cf. Amos 5:5).[4] This is no small sin, since Ahaziah ignores the fundamental tenet of Israel's faith system, which precludes the possibility of appealing to any other deity. "Ahaziah clearly violates any belief that Yahweh is the sole God for Israel, and the specific prohibition for such activity is found in the writer's blueprint for the perfect Israelite society" (cf. Deut. 12:30).[5] In the more immediate context, that of the chronicles of the Omrides, Ahaziah's foolishness is set against the point made repeatedly in 1 Kgs 17-22, that the LORD is in control of matters of healing, and life and death.[6]

The LORD immediately counters Ahaziah by sending *his messenger* (מלאך) with the answer to Ahaziah's enquiry.[7] Baal is

---

3. Supporting his argument for the unity of the narrative, Begg sets out the verb √שלח as one of the motifs. "The various sendings cited in the course of the narrative emanate from two distinct 'sources', namely, Ahaziah (vv.2, 9, 11, 13) and Yahweh acting through his *mal'āk* (vv.3, 15). These two sources stand in sharpest opposition...[and] intersect...[T]he narrative...can be seen as revolving around the question of which 'source' will have his commissions carried to completion by those he sends." (1985), 76-77.
4. Gray (1964), 413; Cogan and Tadmor (1988), 24-25.
5. Hobbs (1985), 9.
6. House (1995), 243.
7. The equivalence between messengers is regularly noted. It is also observed that while previously, the word of the LORD came unmediated to Elijah, the divine messenger here appears to be occasioned by the intention to set up a counterpart to the royal messengers. Skinner (n.d.), 273-74; Cogan and Tadmor (1988), 25; Wiseman (1993), 193; Hobbs (1985), 9; Provan (1995),

brusquely removed from the equation; unlike Carmel, he is not even accorded the dignity of a chance to speak. The implication is that he simply does not matter, since Ahaziah's quest may be satisfied within Israel, and by Israel's God. By this act of pre-emption, Baal loses even before he has entered the game. Baal's defeat immediately reflects onto his adherent Ahaziah. He becomes a victim of his unfortunate choice; *because* he chose Baal (we note that the sentence of death flows from the indictment of his action: "now therefore"— ולכן), he is must share in Baal's defeat. This knowledge, which only the reader and Elijah share, must now filter down to the remaining characters.

The next encounter is between the prophet and the king's messengers; as at Carmel, the numbers are against Elijah. Again as at Carmel, the opposing party is unresisting, lapsing submissively into obedience. The telescoping of the narrative sharpens the irony,[8] since we do not hear Elijah pronounce the word of the LORD. Rather, the message moves directly from the mouth of the LORD's messenger into the mouths of Ahaziah's messengers; the ones that were sent to bring back word from Baal return with word from the opposing deity.

Fretheim makes an insightful contribution on the question that dominates, and reverberates through, the narrative. It is theological in content, and at the first glance, rhetorical in nature. Fretheim argues that both affirmative and negative replies to the question would concede the inadequacy of Baal (as also of the LORD). If "no," it would admit to the inferiority of the Baals already being worshipped in Israel under royal sponsorship. If "yes," it would reduce these Baals to nonentities. "And by not addressing the question at all, they admit its force. The purpose of the question is not simply to make a claim for the Lord, but to get these individuals themselves explicitly or implicitly to downgrade the godness of Baal."[9] Considering that both times in the question אלהים is used, the question may be read to embrace both the god and the God in Israel; at once the question communicates both sarcasm and severity. The proper answer to the question, Fretheim rightly observes, is to be found in Naaman's mouth: "Now I know that there is no God (אלהים) in all the earth except in Israel" (2 Kgs 5:15). "Ahaziah has

---

168-69; Nelson (1987), 155; Montgomery (1951), 349; Brueggemann (2000), 284, 287.

8. The ellipsis is sometimes read as an omission (Gray (1964), 411), but more often as a case of deferring a key scene to a later sequence in order to heighten dramatic effect (Cogan and Tadmor (1988), 26, citing Gen. 42:21 and Exod. 14:12).
9. Fretheim (1999), 134.

forfeited that source of healing by looking elsewhere and hence cannot live."[10]

With this the plot moves to the central triplet sequence. That interpreting this sequence is no small puzzle is clear in the range of readings. Skinner, for example, comments: "The calling down of fire from heaven on the presumptuous soldiery is the only painful episode in all the histories of Elijah; and it is difficult to think that the author of ch. xvii-xix would have lowered the moral grandeur of his hero by so extravagant a display of superhuman power."[11] The opposing view may be represented by Cogan and Tadmor: "…there is nothing uncharacteristic about Elijah's behaviour that does not fit his appearance in other parts of the cycle as a staunch fighter for the exclusive worship of YHWH in Israel."[12] Fortunately, the narrative itself is not unforthcoming as regards clues for interpretation.

Like his father before him, Ahaziah turns his energies to locating Elijah. His intention is not made explicit. Fretheim thinks it was probably to placate Elijah and thus neutralize the oracle, or to see what healing the prophet might offer.[13] However, the narrative suggests that Ahaziah's intentions are not honourable, for Elijah must later be divinely assured of his safety before the king (2 Kgs 1:15). Thus, Hobbs is probably more on the mark when he comments that Ahaziah's actions echo "a common theme in prophetic literature, namely, the desire of those in authority to silence an unfavourable prophetic word."[14] Thus, the companies that Ahaziah successively sends out to escort Elijah to him become, by association, doomed to the same failure as Baal, the king, and the messengers to Ekron. Further, because they are trained militia on a specific mission, by their very nature and numbers (a captain with his full contingent) they are a belligerent and hostile move against Elijah.[15] By introducing them into the ongoing confrontation between pro-Baal and pro-Yahwist parties, Ahaziah notches it up to "battle" mode. Under such circumstances, the reader may expect mortal danger to the weaker combatant. From the experience of 1 Kgs 17-18, the reader also appreciates that a party that aligns itself against the LORD of Hosts is, to say the least, unwise, and anticipates for these

---

10. Fretheim (1999), 134.
11. Skinner (n.d.), 274.
12. Cogan and Tadmor (1988), 28.
13. Fretheim (1999), 133.
14. Hobbs (1985), 10; Cf. Provan (1995), 169; Wiseman (1993), 194; House (1995), 243-44; Robinson (1976), 20.
15. Cf. Brueggemann (2000), 285.

soldiers a fate as dire as that which befell the Baalist prophets at Carmel.[16]

When the "battle" is joined, Elijah is unarmed and alone; arrayed against him is a show of military power. The king's message is terse. "It might be an invitation to parlay. The flat imperative, however, suggests it is a command, designed to apprehend, perhaps silence, perhaps eliminate the prophetic threat."[17] If so, it sits uneasily with the honorific the captain uses, "man of God."[18] Elijah seizes the implicit contradiction and turns it into a weapon. In the prevailing military context (and we remember that Ahaziah has created it), undisputed victory comes with the annihilation of the enemy. For a battle cry, Elijah throws out a jussive;[19] it releases God to act as Yhwh Sebaoth. As in the Elijah corpus thus far, the command-compliance pattern is indicated by the fulfilment following hard upon the command, and by the parallel phrasing between the two. The captain's order is overthrown by Elijah's as, instead of the prophet having to descend (√ירד), the fire of God does (√ירד). As at Carmel, this is a fire that "devours" (√אכל) and functionally there is overlap in purpose, namely, to prove Elijah's point on the superiority of his God over Baal. Indeed, as Fretheim notes, the question of whether there is a God in Israel is directly answered: "The fire is less a divine means to protect the prophet than a public demonstration of the power of Israel's God in a situation where that power (to heal) has been called into question and a public verification of Elijah as mediator of this power."[20]

The second captain and his regiment follow. As with most cases of repetition in Hebrew narrative, the variations make a significant contribution and thus, merit examination.

---

16. Regarding Elijah's part in these parallel narratives, there is room for a fairly straightforward equivalence, such as made by Cogan and Tadmor: "As in the other narratives of this cycle, Elijah is portrayed as an uncompromising man of God, zealous in his demand for exclusive loyalty to YHWH and terrifying in his acts of retribution (cf. 1 Kgs 18:40)." (1988), 28. One recognizes however, that the two narratives handle the prophet's role in complexly different ways.
17. Brueggemann (2000), 285.
18. On the regular use of the term, see Hobbs (1985), 11; Bratsiotis (1974), 1:222-35, esp. 233-35.
19. The LXX rather presents Elijah's words as prophetic oracle: καταβήσεται πῦρ ἐκ τοῦ οὐρανοῦ καὶ καταφάγεταί σε...; "fire *shall come down* out of heaven and *shall devour* you..." This adds to the characterization of Elijah as possessing awesome power, but detracts somewhat from the dynamic of interdependence and cooperation that marks the prophet-God relationship.
20. Fretheim (1999), 133.

v.9:

ויעל אליו...וידבר אליו איש האלהים המלך דבר רדה

v.11:

ויען וידבר אליו איש האלהים כה אמר המלך מהרה רדה

It is noted that this time, the verb "ascend" (עלה√) is replaced by "answer" (ענה√). Reading without emendation, Cogan and Tadmor suggest that perhaps this officer did not even risk coming up to Elijah, and rather preferred to shout up from the bottom of the hill.[21]

The captain's order has an added note of urgency, reflecting perhaps the royal pressure he operates under; he wants Elijah to come down "quickly." Also, the information that the directive comes from the king is phrased differently. In the second instance it strongly echoes the formulaic introduction to a message from the LORD as delivered by a prophet. The captain's כה אמר המלך opposes Elijah's כה אמר יהוה already delivered to the king by messenger (vv.4, 6). It represents Ahaziah's stubborn resistance to the word of the LORD, and his determination to confront it. The reader now sees the captain and Elijah shift into the roles of counterpart messengers, the former's authority being Ahaziah and the latter's, the LORD. It is inevitable that the LORD and his word should prevail, and thus, even more than the first captain, the second one invites disaster upon himself and his men.

With the third time, Ahaziah loses all pretensions to power as his representative is literally brought to his knees. The captain entreats for life, quite abandoning his responsibility to serve the royal summons. Here, at last, is a character who discerns Elijah's position and power vis-à-vis that of the crown. In contrast to his master who would resist Elijah, this captain demonstrates that acceptance is the only appropriate response to the man of God as a representative of God's will.[22] With this end Ahaziah's various commissions. Begg rightly notes: "[A]ll his messengers either turn actively disloyal to him, or suffer destruction trying to carry out his instructions."[23]

When Elijah relents and accompanies the captain, it is a decision independent of the king, prompted by the only messenger who commands his allegiance, viz., the angel of the LORD. The angel encourages Elijah with "Do not be afraid of him." The formula is regularly used in the context of war and/or threat to life. The "him" referred to could not be the captain for only in the previous speech he has been begging on bended knee for his life. Thus, it must be the king that posed a threat to Elijah, the nature of which warranted Elijah tactically seeking out the safety of a hill, and protecting

---

21. Cogan and Tadmor (1988), 26.
22. Fritz (2003), 231. Cf. Skinner (n.d.), 275; House (1995), 244.
23. Begg (1985), 77.

himself with combat measures. With the capitulation of the captain, the rout of the Baal camp is almost complete.

Elijah sets out the indictment to the king's face, making it clear that because of his seeking Baal rather than Israel's God, he is to die; his injury was not necessarily fatal.[24] The silence with which Elijah's words are met implies the crushing of all resistance. Like his father Ahab at Carmel, Ahaziah hears and "obeys." The narrative is telescoped once more, again with dramatic effect. Elijah speaks death to the king, and he simply expires.[25] The emphasis on the "dead" certainty of the event (מות תמות) is vindicated, and the word of the LORD and of Elijah echoes in the silence of the halls of the departed Baalist Ahaziah.[26]

There may be a postscript to this the LORD's routing of Baal, and Brueggemann notices it in the annalistic notice of succession. Ahaziah dies without an heir, and is followed by his brother Jehoram.

> Perhaps the court record only gives us a fact. But when the narrative is loaded, as is this one, with talk of Baal, we notice. Baal is the one who allegedly fructifies and is expected to give new life. But of course, Baal does not, yet another evidence that Baal is a futile force…The royal family never understood, but the narrative permits us to notice what it failed to grasp.[27]

2.2. The Affirmation of the Prophet

A second theme from the Elijah cycle thus far that 2 Kgs 1 revisits is that of the affirmation of the prophet. The narrator directs the reader to Elijah's position and authority in several ways, some more explicit than others.

First, we note what Begg identifies as one of the unifying factors of the narrative—the development in the appreciation of Elijah's identity.[28] The reader gets to see Elijah from the point of view of the characters, and there is a gradual progression till he is recognized in the measure the reader of Kings already knows him.

---

24. Cf. Brichto (1992), 157.
25. Cf. Brueggemann (2000), 287; Begg (1985), 77.
26. It must also be recognized that the pitting of king against prophet is of much wider and deeper significance. As Hobbs perceptively points out, "In the broader view of the history of Israel presented in the OT, this cannot be construed as a power struggle, but rather as a conflict over the very survival of Israel as the people of God and the role of the prophets in that crisis." (1985), 13.
27. Brueggemann (2000), 287.
28. Begg (1985), 78-79. Nelson recognizes that "the revelation of Elijah's identity is an important step in the plot." (1987), 157.

The first to encounter him are the king's messengers, and their knowledge of him is virtually non-existent; he is "a man." This makes his impact on them all the more astonishing: "simply at his word, the messengers had broken off their royal mission to place themselves at his disposal."[29]

When pressed for detail, the messengers can only describe him by physical appearance. The king's level of awareness is more adequate, and he instantly matches the description to "Elijah the Tishbite." His immediate action of sending to fetch Elijah by show of force implies either his ignorance or his defiance of Elijah's status.

The first two captains do address Elijah in keeping with who he fundamentally is—a "man of God"—but their intentions betray a woeful gap in perception. The only other usage of the term for Elijah was in the context of an epistemological crisis, by the Sidonian widow, newly cognisant of Elijah's incredibly powerful status as described by this term. In contrast, the captains' use of it is in woeful ignorance,[30] as they attempt the misguided task of taking this "man of God" by force. The challenge before Elijah, then, is to authenticate his position as this God's representative, and he sets up the most effective route for this, by calling on the LORD to act on his behalf. Burney may be right in noting the force of the ו (2 Kgs 1:10, though omitted in v.12) in Elijah's comeback: "The ו, by emphasis of 'if,' imparts a grim sarcasm to the prophet's words; the implication being, 'You glibly term me 'man of God,' while overlooking my power to withstand the king's command."[31]

The third captain wisely harnesses the experiences of his predecessors to protect himself against the awful power Elijah commands. We may read in his address of Elijah as "man of God" a new note of discernment and recognition. But the culmination of the portrayal of Elijah as a man of extraordinary authority is at the bedside of the sick king. The royal silence may be read as a neutralizing of all resistance as he comes into a full knowledge of Elijah as a "man of God." Certainly, Ahaziah's wordlessness affirms the potency of Elijah and his word.

A corollary to this scheme, Begg notes, is the opportunity given the reader to note the stances of the various characters towards the prophet, and their consequences. Thus, the first two captains with their fifties offend against Elijah's status as man of God and suffer instant obliteration, just as does Ahaziah who had instigated their threatening stances. The third captain escapes destruction only because he abandons his mission. Similarly, the envoys to Ekron

---

29. Begg (1985), 78.
30. It may even be derogatory, Gray proposes. (1964), 414.
31. Burney (1903), 236.

defect to Elijah's camp, and "as his messengers they participate in his own inviolability."[32]

A second affirmation of Elijah at the story level is his characterization as the obedient prophet, familiar from the stories of 1 Kgs 17-18. The chapter is bracketed by the appearances of the divine messenger, and so the story begins and ends with a showcasing of the prophet's compliance. Indeed, 2 Kgs 1, more than the preceding Elijah narrative, makes a point of this characteristic, and it does this by juxtaposing his instantaneous and total "submissiveness to Yahweh's directives" with his "total superiority to all human coercion."[33]

Thirdly, there is the word of death that Elijah speaks to the king. Straightaway (in the telescoped narrative) the king dies. Nelson notes a significant point here: "The exact and immediate correspondence between what the word announces and what follows is emphasized in regard to both the fire from heaven and the death of Ahaziah."[34] The parity drawn between God's word and Elijah's word flags the status of the latter.

The narrator then brings the story to a close with a final testimony, partly to Elijah, as if this were the natural resting point of the narrative: as the narrator notes the passing of Ahaziah he emphatically draws attention to the circumstances of his death. Elijah is presented as the reliable channel of the word of the LORD;[35] "The focus is as much on the prophet's own authority as on the efficacy of the word."[36] Thus, both prophet and divine word are vindicated in the untimely closure of the reign of yet another Omride.

Other narratorial affirmations of Elijah are at the verbal level. First, the heavenly fire: in terms of function with respect to the prophet, the fire from heaven in 2 Kgs 1 shares common ground with that in 1 Kgs 18; in both places, there is the intent to prove Elijah's position as representative of the one true God. Fretheim remarks: "It is almost as if in approaching Elijah (on a hill) they [the militia] approach the reality of God himself."[37] This testimony to Elijah's integrity in service prepares for the iconic affirmation to follow in 2 Kgs 2, when all of Elijah's life and work will be summed up in one glorious epithet and event. In anticipation of the

---

32. Begg (1985), 80-81.
33. Begg (1985), 79.
34. Nelson (1987), 157.
35. This is in keeping with the history narrated in the Books of Kings, where the fulfilment of the prophetic word is the hallmark of the prophet. Cf. e.g., von Rad (1962), 334-46.
36. Nelson (1987), 157.
37. Fretheim (1999), 133.

theophany to come, aural associations are set up as the phrase "man of God" (איש אלהים) is juxtaposed with the description "fire of God" (אש אלהים).[38] The former occasions the latter, both on this anonymous hill and in the wilderness beyond the Jordan. The fire from heaven legitimates Elijah at the highest possible level, that of God, who as a character ranks highest in the scale of reliability.

Secondly, there is the variation in the third repeat of the question that recurs through the narrative—"…is it because there is no God in Israel *to inquire of his word*?" Nelson sees in this the narrator's desire "to avoid monotony."[39] Fretheim, probably more on track, compares this formulation of the question to Jehoshaphat's in 2 Kgs 3:11, and suggests that it "stress[es] the royal infidelity to the God of Israel. Only in the word of the LORD through the prophet can healing and true life be found."[40] Indeed, a fresh factor—namely, the prophet—is introduced into this question of condemnation the third time the reader hears it. As it falls on the ears of the king directly from the mouth of Elijah, it carries not only redoubled force, but sets out the second component of the offence—Ahaziah has not only marginalized the LORD, but also done disrespect to his representative. As Begg observes, the author has "deliberately left his fullest articulation of the word against Ahaziah until the moment of its final employment."[41]

Thus, though 2 Kgs 1 is another chapter in the long and disheartening story of covenant violation in high places, and concerns itself at the deepest level with the continuing struggle for Israel's loyalty, it presents the prophet so strikingly that he appears set "in the foreground as a wonder-working 'man of God' to whom respect is due."[42]

3. 2 Kings 1 in the Context of the Elijah-Elisha Cycles

2 Kgs 1, the last but one story in the Elijah corpus, has been read as preparation for the Elisha cycle. For example, Hobbs notes the similarities between this story and others in the Elisha narratives. He finds overt parallels in the account of Elisha's visit to Damascus (2

---

38. The association is sometimes noted (e.g., Gray (1964), 414; Robinson (1976), 21; Nelson (1987), 155), but sometimes dismissed as inconsequential (e.g., Wiseman (1993), 194). Cogan and Tadmor suggest that אלהים may be added in description of the fire to express the superlative—"an awesome fire," cf. Gen. 30:8; Jon. 3:3; Job 1:16. (1988), 26-27. See Thomas (1953), 209-24.
39. Nelson (1987), 155.
40. Fretheim (1999), 134.
41. Begg (1985), 83.
42. Steck (1967), 547.

Kgs 8:7-15);[43] in the stories of the war with Moab (2 Kgs 3:11-12), he hears an echo of the theme of the presence of God and his prophet in Israel,[44] as also in the story of Naaman's healing (2 Kgs 5:15);[45] he reads the story of Elijah's departure and Elisha's investiture as part of a chiastic pattern covering 2 Kgs 1-2.[46] There is something in this, but, as we have seen, 2 Kgs 1 reaches back as well, to engage with the earlier themes of the Elijah corpus. Like any chapter in a book, it maintains its own integrity while, Janus-like, keeping connected with what has gone before and what is still to come.

If the Elijah-Elisha narrative is dominated by one crucial concern, it is the LORD's covenanted position as sole recipient of Israel's fidelity. As Childs sets out: "the essence of Israel's idolatry is reflected in Elijah's contest on Mount Carmel…The issue is not that Israel wanted to reject Yahweh and choose Baal, but rather to serve them both."[47] Of key significance in this concern are the king, and his religious allegiance. Thus, the Elijah cycle opens with him challenging the king and his people so as to bring them to reconsider their choice not to choose. This theme recurs insistently, playing out in "contests," some overt, some subtle, till finally under Elisha Baalism is wiped out by Jehu, at least for a time. The LORD is proved, in nearly all instances vis-à-vis Baal, as the controller of rain (1 Kgs 17-18), as the sustainer and restorer of life (1 Kgs 17), the one who is and therefore can answer (1 Kgs 18), and as the God who can grant his king victory whether in the hills or in the valleys (1 Kgs 20). By picking out the incident of Ahaziah's illness and death to fill his regnal record, the theme of theological infidelity is visited once more, and again this is done by pitting God against god in "contest." Besides its didactic value, it adds to the case being built up for the wiping out and replacement of the house of Omri, and in the wider context, prepares for the end of the Northern Kingdom.

Echoes of the Moses narratives may be found if one is particularly looking for them, but these are hardly as distinct as in some other parts of the Elijah corpus. There are the evocative motifs of the prophet on the "mountaintop" (ראש ההר recalling Exod. 19:20; 34:2) and the theophanic fire.[48] There is too, the familiar theme of prophet

---

43. The thrice-occurring question of Benhadad to Elisha via Hazael; the linguistic form of the question mirroring that of 1 Kgs 1:2; the similar expression used in the death oracles to emphasize the certainty of the event. Hobbs (1985), 6.
44. "Is there no prophet of the LORD here, through whom we may inquire of the LORD?"
45. "Now I know that there is no God in all the earth except in Israel."
46. Hobbs (1985), 17-19.
47. Childs (1986), 65.
48. Wiseman (1993), 194.

against establishment, particularly, against an idolatrous king who, Pharaoh-like, would send his army against the faithful, and the theme of the vindicated word of God as spoken through his obedient servant and representative. By association, 2 Kgs 1 borrows from the stronger resonance of 1 Kgs 18 with the Moses narratives, and prepares the reader for the re-emergence of that resonance with full force in the closing episode of the Elijah cycle, namely, 2 Kgs 2.

CHAPTER 6

2 Kings 2: Elijah's Ascension and Elisha's Succession

2 Kgs 2 dovetails the closing episodes of the life and work of Elijah with the incidents that mark the start of Elisha's ministry. This is the one other text, beside 1 Kgs 19, in which the resonance between the Elijah-Elisha corpus and the Mosaic narratives is at its richest, a factor which needs to be taken into account in any close reading. As in 1 Kgs 19, this resonance is complexly layered, making for intricate intertextuality. Chief among the earlier texts recalled (as regards canonical order) are the two great crossings, that of the Red Sea under the leadership of Moses and that of the Jordan under Joshua. Other texts evoked are those that narrate the appointment of Joshua, the death of Moses, and the succession of Joshua to the leadership of Israel.

In the first section of this essay, we shall read 2 Kgs 2:1-18, noting, in the process, the parallels with the earlier stories at the verbal and story levels. The second section will examine the resonance at these same levels between the two crossings, that of the Red Sea and the Jordan, so as to establish the intertexuality between these two narratives. This provides the rationale for the exercise undertaken in the third section, namely, to study two key themes that run through the Red Sea and the Jordan crossings that 2 Kgs 2 picks up and appropriates in such a way as to significantly influence its reading: (a) The theme of war, as fought on the twin planes of the historical and the "cosmic." (b) The subject of prophetic status, and its significance to the complex interrelationship between the LORD and his people.

1. 2 Kings 2

1.1. Elijah's Ascension and Elisha's Succession

1.1.1. 2 KINGS 2:1-6: ELISHA ACCOMPANIES ELIJAH

1 Now when the LORD was about to take Elijah up to heaven by a whirlwind, Elijah and Elisha were on their way from Gilgal.

2 Elijah said to Elisha, "Stay here; for the LORD has sent me as far as Bethel." But Elisha said, "As the LORD lives, and as you yourself live, I will not leave you." So they went down to Bethel.

3 The company of prophets who were in Bethel came out to Elisha, and said to him, "Do you know that today the LORD will take your master away from you?" And he said, "Yes, I know; keep silent."

4 Elijah said to him, "Elisha, stay here; for the LORD has sent me to Jericho." But he said, "As the LORD lives, and as you yourself live, I will not leave you." So they came to Jericho.

5 The company of prophets who were at Jericho drew near to Elisha, and said to him, "Do you know that today the LORD will take your master away from you?" And he answered, "Yes, I know; be silent."

6 Then Elijah said to him, "Stay here; for the LORD has sent me to the Jordan." But he said, "As the LORD lives, and as you yourself live, I will not leave you." So the two of them went on.[1]

As regularly noted, 2 Kgs 2 is placed outside the regnal chronology—"the material fills a 'pausal moment' between the sequentially rehearsed reigns."[2] The action progresses from the mundane to an unnamed and uninhabited space, where time itself fractures, temporality cracking open to become continuous with eternity, and then action reverses gradually to the mundane. The literary device of bracketing off this material highlights its thematic importance to the larger Elijah-Elisha corpus, a point we shall return to examine at the end of the reading of the narrative.

2 Kgs 2 opens with a statement that gives away what might well be the high point of the story. This choice of introduction has drawn comment, with scholars divided as to whether this underscores the ascension of Elijah as the climax of the story, or proves that this

---

1. The LXX shows significant variation in v.1. It has Elijah being taken up "as if/as it were" into heaven. Similarly, Tg. Jon. renders it, "And at the Lord's taking up Elijah in the whirlwind toward the heavens..." (2:1; cf. 2:11); Sir. 48:9 reads that he was taken "upwards" rather than heavenward—ὁ ἀναλημφθεὶς ἐν λαίλαπι πυρός. There is agreement that Elijah was bodily removed from the earth while still alive, but where precisely he went is left ambiguous. (The concern here is possibly the sanctity of the barrier between the divine and human spheres.) The LXX rendering "in a whirlwind, as it were into heaven" is not much help in deciphering what exactly it is that happened to Elijah. The ambiguity sets the tone for an enigmatic narrative, rich with intertextual resonance and symbolism, but which to the very end never explicitly resolves the issue.
2. Long (1991), 19. Cf. e.g., Fretheim (1999), 140; Nelson (1987), 158.

event cannot be the climax.³ This argument closely relates to the debate over which of the two prophets is the focus of the narrative, Elijah or Elisha; in other words, which of the two events supersedes the other—the ascension of Elijah or the succession of Elisha.⁴ Both questions are perhaps best addressed at the end of the discussion of the text.

One notes that "storm wind" is prefaced with the definite article (as in v.11 later), and this could (though not necessarily) mean that the writer is alluding to a tradition that the readers are familiar with, re the departure of Elijah.⁵ With this, the narrator sets the scene by way of dramatis personae and locale, and lets the plot advance largely by way of the ensuing dialogues. In the course of these, the reader begins to wonder if, the giveaway opener notwithstanding, he must be on the disadvantaged end of the "knowledge" spectrum; the interactions between the characters are startling, and the reader finds himself trying to keep up; through the entire section he is never sure of having caught up.

To begin with, Elijah discloses that on the LORD's command, he must go to Bethel, and so Elisha should stay behind (causative כי). There is no indication that the divine command particularly excludes a companion. The request is repeated twice more, citing the destinations Jericho and the Jordan. The regular usage of נא as a particle of entreaty⁶ is the best fit here, and makes Elijah's statement an appeal rather than a command, one that Elisha may refuse, as he promptly does. Why does Elijah want to make this last journey alone? Interpreters provide varied answers.

There is the regular reading of this request as a "test."⁷ Elisha is being tested for faithfulness, perseverance, and staying power. A test must have a purpose, and the one regularly proposed is that if he passes he will have proved himself worthy to be Elijah's successor.⁸ Given Elisha's alacrity to abandon everything (√עזב) to follow Elijah (הלך אחר√) at Abel-meholah, it is not unexpected that he doggedly

---

3. Thus, Gunkel: "This clause cannot be meant to indicate the climax of the narrative, for no skilful storyteller would thus reveal his secret at the very start, and that too in a subordinate clause!" (1929), 182.
4. Critics who see the ascension as the climax include: Long (1991), 24-26; Hobbs (1985), 17. Those who read prophetic succession as the highpoint include: Gunkel (1929), 185; Nelson (1987), 157; Jones (1984²), 387; Robinson (1976), 23; Rofé (1970), 436.
5. E.g., Gray (1964), 423; Hobbs (1985), 21; Rofé (1970), 436. See discussion on "the cave"—המערה—in 1 Kgs 19:9 earlier.
6. BDB, נא, 609.
7. E.g., Robinson (1976), 24; Nelson (1987), 159; Brichto (1992), 161. Contra, Fretheim (1999), 136.
8. So, e.g., De Vries (1978), 82-83; Nelson (1987), 159.

refuses to abandon Elijah (√עזב), at Bethel and Jericho. Further, the reader recalls that the two terms √עזב and הלך אחר √ appear as the elements of an opposing pair at key points in the Elijah narratives of 1 Kgs re the options of king (18:18) and people (18:20 and 19:10, 14) with respect to God. This significantly nuances the terms when they are used of the decisions of Elisha with respect to Elijah, moving the interpretation towards a commendation of Elisha.[9] If there is a further test of his faithfulness to his calling here, Elisha is doing well.

If Elijah's request is not a "test," then it may be a request. But what is its purpose? Gunkel proposes:

> Elijah is unwilling to have his disciple with him. The reason is not given, but we are meant to guess it. It is not fitting that the ordinary man should be a witness of the Divine secret that is about to be revealed. Besides, Elijah is anxious to spare his young friend. Jahveh is terrible, and how easily can His nearness prove destructive to one who rashly and unbidden intrudes on His revelation.[10]

Gunkel's "guess" might well be on the mark, but one cannot be sure since the text is not forthcoming on how much of the manner of his departure Elijah knows. All it gives away is that once he crosses the Jordan Elijah knows that he has arrived at the place from which he will be "taken."[11]

---

9. This is supported by the Moses-Joshua parallel: Joshua is measured by his faithfulness to Moses, which is counted as faithfulness towards God (e.g., Josh. 1:7; 11:15). This arrangement, of the prophet representing the LORD to his successor, is perhaps suggested in the Elijah-Elisha relationship as well, right at the start. Walsh observes the "peculiar analogy" set up in 1 Kgs 19:19-21, in that Elijah's encounter with Elisha echoes of the LORD's with Elijah. Like the LORD, Elijah "passes by" Elisha; the mantle that covered Elijah's face now covers Elisha; Elijah's first words to Elisha are identical to the LORD's command to Elijah – "Go, return" (לך שוב). Walsh (1996), 281.
10. Gunkel (1929), 182.
11. O'Brien (1998), 7, puts a less positive slant on Elijah's motives: Elijah suspects that Elisha wants something from him that he cannot, or does not want to give, and so attempts to leave him behind by appealing deceptively to the authority of God. Cf. Provan (1995), 172. Along similar lines, Nelson calls it a "silly journey," "pointless and roundabout," a journey with no quest other than that "Elijah is trying to shake off his tail in the person of Elisha." (1987), 158-59.
    This is hard to sustain in the event that it is Elijah who eventually initiates the proposal that Elisha should ask of him a favour. Further, even when the request proves to be a "hard thing," Elijah does not turn it down but sets up a situation by which Elisha may obtain it. Thus, Brueggemann probably reads Elijah's motives for the journey right: "Elijah is still

Considering the strongly Mosaic tenor of this narrative, we may legitimately look to the pentateuchal texts for further illumination. The parallel passages are in the closing chapters of Deuteronomy, which describe Moses' departure. His briefing is as geographically specific as Elijah's: "Ascend this mountain of the Abarim, Mount Nebo, which is in the land of Moab, across from Jericho…you shall die there" (Deut. 32:49-50; cf. 3:27; 34:1-6). Moses dies alone, and is buried in an unmarked grave the whereabouts of which remain unknown, leaving behind a mission that must be carried to completion by a divinely nominated successor whom he has installed (Num. 27:15-23; Deut. 31:1-23). Elijah too has a successor in place, and the following narrative will tell how he completes the execution of the Horeb commission to install two kings who will wipe out Baalism from Israel. We have proposed that in 1 Kgs 19, Elijah models himself after Moses in his journey to Horeb and in his presentation before the LORD. It is not improbable that here, considering the similarities in circumstance, Elijah would pattern this journey to the place of his departure, after Moses'. Thus, he would go unaccompanied.

If Elijah invoked the LORD in his command, Elisha invokes the LORD in order to refuse. Elisha swears using an oath particle. Greenberg argues that in oath forms where חֵי/חַי is joined to, say, יהוה, נפשׁ or פרעה (e.g., 2 Kgs 2:2, 4, 6; Gen. 42:15), חי is often read as a participle and thus the translation, "As truly as X lives." Difficulties with this arise in the forms חיך and חי נפשך, since the former is most naturally taken as a noun and if the latter be a participial construction, it is not only anomalous in having the participle in the construct state in a nominal sentence, it is bad grammar since נפשׁ, being feminine, requires a feminine participle. Thus, he argues, חי should be taken as a noun in the construct and read as appealing to "the life of X." In this way the Israelite customarily validated his oath by invoking the life of God or some sacred/powerful substitute, "not merely to witness the truth and sincerity of the statement, but chiefly to punish the swearer if he spoke falsely."[12]

Reading the oath particle as Greenberg suggests has the effect of increasing the intensity of the oath, and Elisha joins his to not just one, but two parties, further doubling its asseverative force: "By the life of יהוה and by the life of your soul." In so swearing, he is invoking the highest possible authorities to testify to his determination not to abandon Elijah, and putting himself at double jeopardy should his oath be insincere.

---

commanded by Yahweh and until the last is obedient. He goes where he is sent." (2000), 294.

12. Greenberg (1957), 34-39.

Elisha's persistence is urgent. Considering the strong parallels between Elisha and Joshua that the narrative will evoke, this could well be the first of these parallels, the one that introduces the theme. Joshua comes through as the one most closely associated with Moses: at the first military encounter in the desert, it is Joshua that Moses chooses to organize the battle (Exod. 17:9); the LORD's decision on Amalek has to be rehearsed in the ears of Joshua (Exod. 17:14); he alone accompanies Moses to the mount of God, waiting there till he returns (Exod. 24:13, 32:17); he is with Moses in the tabernacle (33:11); he takes objection on behalf of Moses to Eldad and Medad (Num. 11:28). In his continuing close to Elijah, Elijah's משרת may be seen playing out the role of Moses'.

The third party in this section is made up of "the sons of the prophets." There is much debate on the nature and functions of this group, and since this discussion is largely historical-critical in approach, it does not contribute much to our literary reading.[13] Our interest is in the role that the group בני הנביאים plays in the narrative. They possess information, correct (Elijah will be taken) and detailed (Elijah will be taken that very day). Closer examination of this information shows up interesting details, and here we may begin with Beek's comments on the verbs used of Elijah's disappearances:

> It is possible that the author of the cycle of Elijah-Elisha-stories already made an intentional allusion in 1 Kings xviii. Obadiah is afraid to convey a message of the prophet to his king and says: 'What will happen? As soon as I leave you the רוח יהוה will carry you away, who knows where?' (xviii 12). This 'carry away' (העלות) is realized as 'take up' (נשא) when the רוח יהוה makes use of the whirlwind (סערה)."[14]

There may be more here than Beek recognizes. One notices that the prophetic group uses the verb √לקח, and they understand that Elijah

---

13. Widespread in Old Testament scholarship is the hypothesis of a continuing prophetic party of "amphictyonic orientation," which preserved the traditions of authentic Mosaic Yahwism, and that the בני הנביאים stood in, and maintained, this prophetic succession. Thus they often posed a charismatic corrective to a monarchy which sought to establish itself as autonomous. So, e.g., Rendtorff (1967), 21-28; Porteous and Newman (1962), 11-25, 86-97. Contra Porter, for example, who argues that the בני הנביאים were a phenomenon of the Omride period and there is no warrant for tracing the group forwards or backwards. Porter (1981), 423-28. For a succinct survey see Bergen (1999), 58-60; Hobbs (1985), 25-27.
14. Beek (1972) 1.

will be taken (away) from being Elisha's master.¹⁵ Elijah will later use the same verb (2:9) to describe his departure, and he speaks of being taken (away) from Elisha. The narrator, however, uses the verb √עלה (2:1; cf. 2:11), making clear that Elijah will be taken up in a storm wind.¹⁶ This leaves open the possibility that that the awareness of the characters re the coming event may differ somewhat from that of the narrator.¹⁷ It is not improbable that the בני הנביאים understand being "taken" (לקח√) in the most natural sense, namely, as dying,¹⁸ and that the verbal clue points to death being Elijah's expectation as well.¹⁹ Post-event, the בני הנביאים move up a notch in clarity re the manner of "taking (away)" and use √נשא (2 Kgs 2:16) in a sense similar to Obadiah's usage of it; only, here, as we shall discuss later, they seem to understand that the process of being taken (up) has worked his death.

As for Elisha, when the בני הנביאים present their information and ask if he knows this (ידע√), he replies with, גם אני ידעתי. As an

---

15. Tg. Jon. has it: "Do you know that this day the Lord is taking your master *from you*?"
16. It appears that the LXX also maintains some demarcation in the levels of knowledge: it has the prophetic group use "taken (away)"—λαμβάνω (vv.3, 5)—and Elijah use "taken (up)"—ἀναλαμβάνω (v.10), in line with the narrator (v.11).
17. See O'Brien's discussion of the possibility that the characters in the story do not enjoy the same level of knowledge. He agrees that initially one would understand the unusual phrase "the LORD is taking your master from over your head" to refer to Elijah's permanent disappearance, and that as the story evolves, Elisha is shown as understanding it in that sense from the start (as also Elijah), while the prophetic group are not sure if it is a temporary or permanent departure and the narrative of the search party leaves the uncertainty unresolved. (1998), 6-7, 8-10, 13-14. It seems odd that two different prophetic groups should give the matter of Elijah's being "taken" such close attention if it was only another of his regular temporary disappearances. The concern is obviously much deeper and has to do with Elisha's status in the event of his master being permanently displaced from his position over Elisha. In reverently declaring that Elijah's spirit rests on Elisha, it is clear, as we shall argue, that the community has accepted Elisha as successor in Elijah's stead, and any further searches are for the body of the departed erstwhile leader. Our reading is more in line with that of Bergen, who notes that it is only in the voice of the narrator that the phrase השמים is heard. Thus only the reader knows exactly what will happen to Elijah. (1999), 65.
18. Cf. Ezek. 24:15-18.
19. It must also be noted, however, that the verb is לקח√ is used of the one other instance of translation, namely, that of Enoch. Like Elijah, he too suddenly "is not" because the LORD "took" him. ואיננו כי לקח אתו אלהים; Gen. 5:24.

emphatic particle, גַם is often used to express correspondence (the גַם *correlativum*)—"I also, as well as yourself."[20] In having Elisha use the same verb √ידע to affirm the information he has, and in having him use emphasis to say that he knows what the בני הנביאים know, the possibility is that the narrator (and/or the character himself) is signalling that Elisha is on the same level of knowledge as the prophetic group. (It is, of course, possible that he knows more but will not be drawn into discussion, but this is never resolved.) So, when the verb √לקח comes up for the third time (implicitly for the fifth time, taking Elisha's two acknowledgements into account), this time in Elijah's speech, the impression created is that Elijah too is included in that level of knowledge.

So, perhaps the reader is not as disadvantaged as he thinks he is. It may be that the narrator has favoured him with a head start with his very opening statement. If this is so, then one of the roles of the בני הנביאים in this section is that they sort out the players along levels of knowledge—God, the narrator and the reader on the higher level, and Elijah, Elisha and the בני הנביאים on the lower—though this will be recognized only in retrospect.

Another role of the בני הנביאים could be that they help to identify which of the two prophets is the focus of the narrative.[21] The בני הנביאים make an effort to get in touch with Elisha: the first lot "came out to Elisha" (√יצא; 2:3) and the second "drew near to Elisha" (√נגש; 2:5) in order to dialogue with him. Their exertions are directed at Elisha, not Elijah. Meanwhile, Elijah interacts only with Elisha. Taken together, it appears that Elisha is the central character. However, one must take into consideration too, that the topic of the exchange between the בני הנביאים and Elisha is "your master," Elijah. The effort expended is so as to discuss a pressing matter of which Elijah is the subject. The strategy seems to be to first assess if what they know is what Elisha also knows, and then to probe further, for Elisha pre-empts the latter by brusquely terminating the dialogue with the imperative "Be silent." So, by having two groups deliberately bringing up the topic, the reader's attention is increasingly focused on Elijah's departure. But since it is Elisha who is the respondent, a subtle balance is maintained between the two prophets, allowing neither to dominate the narrative.

If not for the בני הנביאים, Elijah would have literally taken over as the "leading" actor, with Elisha passively following him from place

---

20. BDB, גַם, 168-69. A helpful parallel is the LORD's response to Abimelech's defence of himself, "In the integrity of my heart...have I done this": "I also know (גַם אנכי ידעתי) that in the integrity of your heart you have done this." Gen. 20: 5, 6.
21. See O'Brien for a note on debate on the subject. (1998), 8-9, n.20.

to place. Because of the בני הנביאים the reader appreciates Elisha as one who is sought out by his colleagues, as one who shows himself as informed as they, and as one who may issue an imperative to, and be obeyed by, them. This adds character to his refusal to be parted from Elijah,[22] in that he is seen, not as just tagging along, but as asserting himself and his decision.[23]

To sum up, this section opened with the reader informed of one of the events that is to take place in the narrative following—the departure of Elijah. The plot is advanced by means of two series of dialogues, for all purposes verbatim repetitions. "The literary device of repeated dialogue rivets one's attention to the *fact* of movement, and builds the chilling impatience of steady, inevitable closure with mystery."[24] The point becomes increasingly clear that it is Elijah's departure that is the background against which the actors play out their roles. Elijah sets his face towards it, following a divinely prompted route, desiring, it appears, to meet it alone like his model, Moses. Elisha, fully aware that the journey leads to this event, resolutely follows Elijah, and in his decision is recalled Joshua's constant presence with Moses. The event is the consuming concern of the בני הנביאים, who with their question intensify the reader's anticipation of it. They may serve two literary purposes, that of distributing the participants in the narrative along levels of knowledge, and that of holding in equilibrium the twin focal points of the section—the characters Elijah and Elisha.

1.1.2. 2 KINGS 2:7-8: ELIJAH PARTS THE JORDAN

7 Fifty of the company of prophets also went, and stood at some distance from them, as they both were standing by the Jordan.

8 Then Elijah took his mantle and rolled it up and struck the water; the water was parted to one side and to the other, until the two of them crossed on dry ground.

The בני הנביאים shift into performing a new function now, namely, that of witnesses.[25] Perhaps they want definitive proof of

---

22. Gunkel observes: "In order to exhibit the heroism of Elisha's resolve to abide by his master, the narrator...introduces other persons as a foil. These are the sons of the prophets...filled with amazement that Elisha is determined to follow his master even on *this* journey." (1929), 183.
23. Considering the strong parallels that the narrative will shortly draw between Elisha and Joshua, this delineation of Elisha's character helps recall Joshua's. He does not quietly tag along behind Moses either; he voices his opinion (Exod. 32:17) and urgently advises him (Num. 11:28).
24. Long (1991), 26.
25. Bergen observes that v.7 breaks the chain of waw-consecutive verbs by beginning with a noun. "This disjunction informs the reader that a new episode of the story is about to begin. This is evidenced also by the new role

Elisha's succession;[26] or, perhaps it is just a continuation of their consuming curiosity, as evidenced in their questioning of Elisha.

Meanwhile, the prophet and his minister have reached the river and are standing at its brink (or in it). Elijah's actions are precisely described. He takes his mantle, rolls it up, and strikes the water with it. The river parts. The point of view intended here seems to be that of the watching בני הנביאים. What effect could the miracle have on them? Given Elijah's life and work thus far, there is no necessity for a final act of power to reiterate his authority. Beside the practicality of helping the prophet and his minister get across the river (which perhaps could have been forded even otherwise), the miracle would serve two purposes. First, it would set up a means by which Elisha may later be favourably compared with Elijah when he too is able to accomplish the same task, and thus validate the succession.[27] Secondly, it immediately recalls the two great events of the Exodus and Conquest. Going by the verbal and story details, it is an interpretative framework that the text itself appears to recommend.[28]

At the verbal level, details bring to mind the Jordan crossing. The two are said to stand upon the river (עמדו על הירדן), presumably at the edge of the water. In the Jordan crossing under Joshua, the instructions are for the priests to come right to the edge of the waters of the Jordan (עד קצה מי הירדן) and then stand in it (בירדן תעמדו). (Josh. 3:8; cf. vv.13, 15) When the waters part, Elijah and Elisha cross over (√עבר). Between Josh. 3:1 and 5:1, √עבר in various meanings occurs 24 times[29]; √עמד unites the activity of the priests with the stoppage of the waters.[30] In fact, Nelson sees this word pair as key in holding together the whole composition of the narrative of the crossing of the Jordan.[31] Be that as it may, the occurrence of the verb

---

which the sons of the prophets play in the story...as witnesses." (1999), 61. Cf. Long (1991), 26.
26. Gertel (2002[1]), 77.
27. So, e.g., Gunkel (1929), 185.
28. These are not exact correspondences. For one thing, the resonances are drawn from two different events in the history of Israel. Secondly, the correspondences with the River crossing cannot be precise, because in 2 Kgs 2 there are two crossings made, one by each prophet, and only the second is in the same direction as Joshua's crossing. However, the overall effect is what counts, for these verbal and story level resonances set the scene for the emergence of important conceptual implications.
29. Hertzberg (1965), 24.
30. Josh. 3:8, 13, 16, 17; 4:10.
31. Nelson (1997), 59.

pair in 2 Kgs 2 does recall their usage in describing the previous Jordan crossing.³²

Two other verbal details summon up the Sea crossing. The water parts "to the one side and to the other/hither and thither" (הנה והנה) recalling the description of the parting of the Red Sea which was to the Israelites "as a wall to them on their right and on their left" (להם חמה מימינם ומשמאלם; Exod. 14:22, 29). Just as the Israelites crossed over on dry land (חרבה; Exod. 14:21), so do Elijah and Elisha.

At the story level also both Sea and River crossings are evoked. Elijah and Elisha cross in the vicinity of Jericho, which compares with Israel crossing over "opposite Jericho" (Josh. 3:16; cf. 4:13, 19). The conceptual significance of the associations with Jericho (and Gilgal) will apply strongly to Elisha's crossing later on in the narrative, as we shall discuss. Hess stresses Israel's role as observer (Josh. 4:11);³³ indeed, they are to be witnesses of the miracle to future generations (Josh. 4:22-24). This finds a parallel in the prophetic group of watchers in 2 Kgs 2.³⁴

The mantle evokes the other great crossing. This is the reader's third encounter with the garment. On other occasions it has been used to shield Elijah at the moment of theophany, and later, to invest Elisha into office as successor. As such, it reminds powerfully of Elijah's prophetic status, demonstrated in these two occasions by his unique privilege of conversing with deity face to face, and in his authority to install a representative of God. Both instances recall Moses (Num. 12:8; 27:15ff.). In the context of water parting the Sea event is immediately recalled, especially since the narrator inserts the small detail that Elijah rolls up the mantle;³⁵ the reader remembers the comparable role of Moses' rod.³⁶

---

32. Bergen traces this verbal resonance even further back, to 1 Kgs 19:19, where Elijah crosses over (√עבר) to Elisha. (1999), 49-50. This may be too early for the introduction of the theme, and besides, it takes the context of a river crossing to prompt the Sea-River crossing associations.
33. Hess (1996), 112.
34. There are looser correspondences: the three legs of the journey covered by Elijah and Elisha, and the three days that lead up to the Jordan crossing (Josh. 1:11; 3:2); the בני הנביאים standing at a distance to watch, and the command to Israel to keep a specified distance from the ark that leads the way into the river (Josh. 3:4).
35. The verb √גלם (cf. Ezek. 27:24; Ps. 139:16) found only here in biblical Hebrew is found in rabbinic Hebrew with the same significance. Burney (1903), 265.
36. Cf. Fretheim (1999), 137. The spontaneous association of water-parting miracles with Moses, in rabbinic tradition, is exemplified by the exclamation that follows the account of the stream parting thrice for Pinchas Ben Yair: "How great is this man! Greater than Moses...For the latter [the

We will argue at length, later, that one of the overarching themes of the two great crossings—Sea and River—is military. In recalling these crossings in the telling of the 2 Kgs 2 river parting, an anticipation is being created towards the introduction of the war theme into this story. This is not unexpected, because it has already been threaded into the larger narrative, emerging at key points: the title set the tenor of the Carmel contest (1 Kgs 18:15) and the events following (19:10, 14) in the course of which the LORD declared war against apostate Israel (19:17). Here, as the scene being set evokes the other crossings, it will be seen in retrospect that it anticipates the military overtones in Elijah's ascension and in the apostrophe that Elisha will award him.

1.1.3. 2 KINGS 2:9-10: ELISHA ASKS A "HARD THING"

9 When they had crossed, Elijah said to Elisha, "Tell me what I may do for you before I am taken from you." Elisha said, "Please let me inherit a double share of your spirit."

10 He responded, "You have asked a hard thing; yet, if you see me as I am being taken from you, it will be/let it be granted you; if not, it will not."

When the two have reached the final point on the itinerary, Elijah introduces into the conversation the subject of his imminent departure. Elijah speaks as if he knows that Elisha knows that they are now close to the end. Thus, there is no prefatory remark about his being "taken"; instead, he introduces it into another issue. He asks what he may do for Elisha before the event.[37] Does he ask because he thinks Elisha has a request in mind that has motivated him to follow Elijah to the place of his departure? Is it a reward for Elisha's fidelity?[38] Or is he following a conventional pattern of granting a final oracular blessing, perhaps still modelling himself on Moses,[39] modifying it here by inviting Elisha's participation?[40] Any

---

sea divided itself] but once, whilst for the former thrice!" *Hullin* 7a. *The Babylonian Talmud: Seder Kodashim, Hullin I.*

37. Tg. Jon.: "Ask what I will do for you while I am still not taken from your presence."
38. So Gunkel (1929), 184. This reminds of Elisha's request of the Shunammite in appreciation of her hospitality, set out in identical language: מה לעשות לך (2 Kgs 4:13).
39. Cf. Deut. 31:7-8.
40. Elisha himself later gives Joash an ("interactive") oracle from his deathbed, which is launched from Joash's concern that Israel will lose its most powerful defence. 2 Kgs 13:14ff.

or all could be true, though in the light of tradition,[41] the last possibility appeals.

Elisha surprises even Elijah with his request. He desires פִּי שְׁנַיִם of Elijah's spirit. Gertel wonders if it is Elijah's Mosaic miracle that emboldens Elisha to ask for a transfer of spirit (cf. Num. 11).[42] However that may be, Elisha's reply shows: (a) He is already aware of his position as "son" and heir to the prophetic inheritance.[43] Thus, it is not the request in general that is significant, as much as the appeal for פִּי שְׁנַיִם of Elijah's spirit. If פִּי שְׁנַיִם is indeed the operative term here, what exactly does it mean? The term is widely understood as "double portion," though sometimes it is read as "two-thirds," based on the reading of the expression in Zech. 13:8.[44] Thus, Elisha is thought to transfer the material law to the realm of the "spirit" and asks to be given a firstborn's share[45], twice as much as any other son would receive,[46] from the one he addresses as "my father." Hobbs sees this allusion to Deut. 21:17 as keeping to the fore the motif of rightful succession that runs through this narrative.[47]

Skinner reads "double portion" to mean twice as great a prophet as Elijah;[48] this is debatable, but he smooths over the thorny issue

---

41. Cf. the pre-death speeches of Isaac (Gen. 27:1ff.), Jacob (Gen. 49), Moses (Deut. 31:7-8) and David (1 Kgs 2:1-9) — all examples of exhortation and assurance given to successors (in different senses of the word).
42. Gertel (2002²), 177, n.20.
43. Rofé sees a father-son relation between master and devotee, cf. the Mishnah (Baba Mesia 2.11) which decrees that the relationship of rabbi and student precedes, in some respects, that of father and son. (1970), 439.
44. E.g., Cogan and Tadmor (1988), 32; Gunkel (1929), 184. Brown, (1971), 90, citing Ginzberg (1913), 239, notes that Jewish tradition translates "two-thirds." Burney resists this reading, arguing that in Zech. 13:8, the expression has that meaning only through being brought into relationship with הַשְּׁלִשִׁית, "the third part"; thus the term does not apply to 2 Kgs 2:9, which he translates: "Let there now be a share of two in thy spirit upon me!" (1903), 265.
45. Cf. Deut. 21:15-17, which discusses the case of the inheritance of a man's first-born born of the less favoured wife. Carroll finds in this request a parallel to the reference to Israel as God's "firstborn." Carroll (1969), 405, n.5.
46. E.g., Robinson (1976), 25; Gray (1964), 425; Nelson (1987), 159.
47. Hobbs (1985), 21.
48. Skinner (n.d.), 279. Cf. some Talmudic authorities, e.g., *Sanhedrin 47a. The Babylonian Talmud: Seder Nezikin, Sanhedrin I*. Following some strands of rabbinic tradition, Levine argues that Elisha's miracles repeat and multiply elements of the miracles of his teacher from whom he requested and gained twice as much as his spirit. He picks out common themes, motifs and wordplay in the two sets of narratives to demonstrate that Elisha's miracles

with, "[T]he burden of Elisha's petition is that he may be worthy to succeed Elijah as head of the prophetic body."[49] We may reasonably infer that in specifying the פִּי שְׁנַיִם, Elisha is requesting that he will be endowed with a grant of a "double portion" in his inheritance of Elijah's spirit; and this request springs, not from a desire to be Elijah's successor, for that has been sealed from the moment the mantle was laid on him, but from his dissatisfaction with his giftedness as concerns his taking Elijah's place.[50]

(b) Elisha seems to think that Elijah can give him this gift, or at least, arrange for it in some way. We shall return to this after briefly considering the only other passage in which רוח is transferred from one person to another, namely, Num. 11.

In Num. 11, the LORD addresses Moses' problem of bearing the burden of the people alone. According to the instructions given, Moses gathers seventy "elders" of the people to the tent of meeting. The LORD comes down, takes "from the spirit that is on him" (מִן הָרוּחַ אֲשֶׁר עָלָיו; 11:25, cf. v.17) and puts it on the seventy. "When the spirit rests on them" (כְּנוֹחַ עֲלֵיהֶם הָרוּחַ; 11:25), they prophesy. Drawing from Ashley, we make the following observations: The spirit is not simply the "spirit of Moses" (רוּחַ מֹשֶׁה) but the "spirit which is upon Moses" (רוּחַ אֲשֶׁר עַל מֹשֶׁה). Taking as a general guideline that out of the forty Old Testament instances of רוח used with עַל, twenty-five refer to the LORD's spirit, this instance too may fall within this category.[51] Secondly, it is common in the OT that mighty deeds, including prophesying, were the result of the LORD's spirit coming upon a person (e.g., 1 Sam. 10:10). Thirdly, within the story itself, Moses indicates that the spirit being given out has a divine source, and is given at divine pleasure (Num. 11:29). However, Ashley concludes that this instance of the transfer of spirit is only partially parallel to the incident in 2 Kgs 2, and this is because of the phrasing in the latter,[52] that is, the watching prophetic group testifies, נָחָה רוּחַ אֵלִיָּהוּ עַל אֱלִישָׁע ("*The spirit of Elijah* rests on Elisha"; 2 Kgs 2:15), and because 2 Kgs 2 deals with prophetic

---

are more complex than Elijah's. (1999), 25-46. Cf. Sirach: "Elisha was filled with his [Elijah's] spirit. He performed twice as many signs..." (48:12).

49. Skinner (n.d.), 279. Cf. e.g., Gray (1964), 426; Carroll (1969), 405.
50. Cf. House: "Perhaps...Elisha...simply ask[s] for the spiritual power to do the job he has known he would someday assume." (1995), 258.
51. Seven refer to other spirits sent by God, eight to other spirits, and six clearly to the human spirit. Ashley (1993), 211.
52. Contra Weisman, who argues that "an examination of the dynamics of the construct state...permits an interpretation of 'the spirit that was on Elijah'." (1981), 226, n.3. Cf. the objective genitive, Joüon-Muraoka, §129 e.

succession, which is not the concern of the Numbers text.[53] This conclusion is debatable.

Even though there is a difference in phrasing, the argument common to both 2 Kgs 2 and Num. 11 is that it is by the enabling of the spirit of God bestowed on a human that the said human is able to perform acts of power. It is clear that Elijah's and Elisha's acts of power originated from beyond themselves;[54] thus, the accounts of some of their miracles specifically include a record of prayer (1 Kgs 17:20ff.; 18:36ff.; 2 Kgs 4:32; 6:18ff.). Further, the telling of Elisha's parting of the Jordan (which we shall discuss) makes it clear that the act that accredits him as prophet is God-enabled, and the comment that Elijah's spirit is to be given the recognition for it is a specific way of making the larger assertion that the LORD has affirmed Elisha as prophet in Elijah's stead. In the case of the seventy elders, they behaved in a manner that accredited them as prophets in the eyes of watching Israel; this accreditation was necessary if they were to function in the role the LORD intended for them, namely, to share the burden of Moses in leading Israel.

That the "spirit" appears to have a secondary, human origin is also clear. Fretheim rightly asserts "The 'spirit' is a theological and anthropological reference, linking God's spirit and the human spirit, issuing in authority, wisdom and power."[55] However, the anthropological dimension can lead to misreading of the text. For example, Gray comments that in Num. 11, the רוח "is conceived materially and, as in 2 K. 2:9f., quantitatively" and if Moses has enough רוח to spare for seventy it is a measure of his close relationship with the LORD and of his superiority.[56] Setting aside the quantification of a material רוח as the superimposition of modern distinctions over the exegesis of these texts, one tackles the more legitimate issue of the point that these two texts are trying to make

---

53. Ashley (1993), 210-11.
54. Contra Weisman, who makes a lengthy argument for the phenomenological difference between the "personal spirit" in the 2 Kgs 2 and Num. 11 stories, and the "personal spirit" in the recurring formula "and the LORD stirred up the spirit of…" (e.g., 1 Chron. 5:26; 2 Chron. 36:25; Hag. 1:14). The latter is an object that changes to an active factor only through the LORD's intervention, while the former is a subject that has the power to affect others, and thus is akin to (but clearly distinguished by origin from) the transcendental spirit that appears as "the spirit of the LORD/God" which, when it encounters certain individuals stirs them to special tasks (e.g., Judg. 3:10; 1 Sam. 10:5). (1981), 226-28. Cf. Gertel (2002[1]), 78, n.6.
55. Fretheim (1999), 137-38.
56. Gray (1964), 110-11. Cf. Binns (1927), 69: That the seventy receive *part of the spirit* that was already on Moses, and not a direct unction from the LORD is seen as a sign of their subordination, as also is the case in 2 Kgs 2.

in linking the spirit with human sources. In Num. 11, the elders are to share Moses' very exclusive task of leadership; it would seem logical that in publicly linking the task to Moses', the enabling for the task must also be clearly linked back to him, and in this case, it is the רוח that enables (whether Moses or the elders).[57] The case is even stronger in 2 Kgs 2, because it concerns succession; thus, that Elisha is able to replicate Elijah's miracle of river parting is what explicitly links the element that enables him, back to the one that enables Elijah. In these contexts, the question of superiority and/or subordination is not really the issue, except perhaps in Joshua's mind, for which he is soundly reproached. And neither is it implied anywhere that the elders' (or Elisha's) gain is in any way Moses' (or Elijah's) loss.

It is of crucial importance, as Noth points out re Num. 11, that the LORD himself sees to the dispensation of his רוח—apparently only he can do it.[58] Moses makes this clear when Joshua mistakenly assumes that Moses somehow has control over who may or may not receive the רוח: "Would that all the LORD's people were prophets, and that the LORD would put his spirit on them!" (Num. 11:29). The implication then, is that Eldad and Medad are as equally endowed as the elders at the tent of meeting, and that neither the decision nor the ability to endow them was Moses'. Noth's point applies even more forcefully to 2 Kgs 2, as we shall discuss. Elisha's request is just as misinformed as Joshua's zealous urging to "stop them," and he too learns that it is not the prophet who commands this רוח.

We conclude then, contra Ashley, that the two cases are manifestly comparable: The critical issue is that of divine affirmation of a certain role of leadership, and that affirmation is made by a certain enabling, which comes by the bestowing of the spirit of God by God himself; such bestowing is beyond the scope of the prophet even though that spirit is associated with him.

Returning to the narrative of 2 Kgs 2, we note that Elijah's answer to Elisha's request is hesitating, and neither a "yes" nor a "no." He can neither grant the request nor can he arrange for it. The best he can do is set up a situation—Gunkel calls it a "sign"[59]—by which the LORD himself will operate on the request, and either grant or refuse it in such a way that Elisha will know the result. Here, Moberly draws attention to the irregularity that most modern EVV translate

---

57. Cf. Young (1952), 69: "In order that the seventy might work with Moses in one spirit and purpose, they were equipped with the same Spirit which had filled him."
58. Noth (1968), 87.
59. Gunkel (1929), 184. It is indeed a sign of divine approval that a human should see God and still live. (e.g., Gen. 32:30; Exod. 33:18-23.) Cf. Robinson (1976), 25.

both יהי and יהיה as the indicative "it will be."[60] If Elisha sees Elijah being taken, then, יהי לך כן; "let it be to you thus." However if Elisha does not see, then לא יהיה; "it will not be." That Elijah cannot firmly assure the reception of the gift of "spirit" is in line with our discussion of רוח above. Elijah "can set up the appropriate test, but cannot pre-empt God's response even to a successful outcome."[61]

What are the implications of Elisha being able to see the event? The episode in 2 Kgs 6 bears conspicuous parallels and so, may be of help. Elisha prays/intercedes (√פלל) for his servant: "O LORD, please open his eyes that he may see (√ראה)." So the LORD opened the eyes of the servant, and he saw (√ראה); the mountain was full of horses and chariots of fire all around Elisha (2 Kgs 6:17)." Three points immediately become clear. First, there is a desire that the servant may see (expressed by the prophet). Secondly, as expressed by the fact that the desire must be addressed to God as prayer, and by the fact that it is the LORD who must cause the servant to see, it is clear that "seeing" beyond what normally can be seen is by the divine unction alone. Thirdly, "to see" is not merely to spectate, but to perceive and to understand.

Applying this situation to 2 Kgs 2, Skinner rightly asserts, as is generally agreed, that since God is the one who withholds and discloses "heavenly realities," "if that gift should be bestowed on Elisha, it will be the sign that God has answered his prayer."[62] On the other hand it is also agreed, as for example Jones observes, that Elisha's status as successor depends on his ability to see and comprehend the spiritual world—it is a condition he must meet.[63] Modifying Jones to keep in line with our argument: Elisha's status as a worthy successor depends on his ability to pierce through the temporal and human to that which is eternal and divine.[64] The two assertions are not mutually exclusive. Elisha's seeing will be neither completely up to him, nor will it be totally independent of him and dependent on the sovereignty of divine will. This is in line with 2 Kgs 6, where the desire that the servant should see prompts the gift of sight. In Elisha's case, there is the added complexity that the seeing will be concomitant with Elisha's desire to be a true and potent prophet, one who can discern beyond what can normally be discerned. He will see because he desires the prophetic gift of

---

60. See Moberly (2006), 135.
61. Moberly (2006), 135, n.12.
62. Skinner (n.d.), 277, 279. Cf. Robinson (1976), 25; Montgomery (1951), 354. The question of Elisha being "found worthy of the sight of the mysterium" (Montogmery (1951), 354) may not be relevant.
63. Jones (1984²), 385-86.
64. Thus the close association of the verbs of perception √חזה and √ראה with the prophet, נביא. BDB, חזה, 302; ראה, 906-09. Jepsen (1980), 280-90.

discernment as befits a successor of Elijah, and he will see also because the gift is divinely bestowed on him. Thus, his seeing will coalesce two features into one—the sign that his request has been granted, and the granting of the request itself. Elijah's role then, *mutatis mutandis*, would be that of Elisha's in 2 Kgs 6, namely, that of mediator.

1.1.4. 2 KINGS 2:11-12: ELIJAH IS "TAKEN"

11 As they continued walking and talking, a chariot of fire and horses of fire separated the two of them, and Elijah ascended in a whirlwind into heaven.
12 Elisha kept watching and crying out, "Father, father! The chariots of Israel and its horsemen!" But when he could no longer see him, he grasped his own clothes and tore them into two pieces.[65]

As Elijah and Elisha continued to walk on, and converse, their privacy is invaded dramatically by רכב אש וסוסי אש which part the two, and Elijah ascends into the heavens in a storm wind. רכב being more often used as a collective noun, it is better read "chariots" (contra LXX),[66] especially since this brings it in line with the image of Dothan's hills thick with fiery celestial hosts (סוסים ורכב אש; 2 Kgs 6:17); we shall argue that both visions have a common theological function.[67]

The general agreement is that the fiery elements are symbols of God's presence since fire is a regular feature of divine manifestation (e.g., Exod. 3:2; 13:21; 19:18) and is of the divine essence (cf. Deut. 4:24).[68] In fact, unearthly fire has been a motif of the Elijah narrative, seen at Carmel, Horeb, and one other unnamed hilltop. So vivid are the associations of Elijah and fire that Sirach's eulogy refers to him as "a prophet like fire" whose "word burned like a torch"; he "three times brought down fire," and was eventually "taken up by a

---

65. The LXX describes Elijah being "taken up" with the verb ἀναλαμβάνω, synonymous with the ἀνάγω of v.1. It is the way he has described his departure in v.9. Elijah's removal is still "as it were" into heaven. Refer to Chapter 1 (p.2) for Josephus' preferential use of the verb ἀφανίζομαι, "to disappear," and the associations he sets up between Enoch, Moses and Elijah with the singular expression πρὸς τὸ Θεῖον ἀναχωρῆσαι, he "returned to the divinity" (*Ant.* 1.85; 4.326; 9.28).

Both these preferences, Begg holds, are "typical for Hellenistic *Entrückung* accounts" and Josephus' accounts bear parallels with the telling of the disappearances of apotheosized Roman heroes Aeneas, Romulus and Oedipus. (1990), 692. See *Rom. Ant.* (1937), 213; Sophocles (1982), 364. Cf. Tabor (1989), 237-38; Feldman (1984), 407-8; Thackeray (1967), 116-17.
66. BDB, רכב, 939. Cf. Gray (1964), 426, who recommends "chariotry."
67. √רכב with the meaning of "chariots/chariotry" in the context of cosmic hosts occurs elsewhere – Ps. 68:18 (EVV 17); Hab. 3:8.
68. Jones (1984²), 386; Cogan and Tadmor (1988), 32; Skinner (n.d.), 279.

whirlwind of fire, in a chariot with horses of fire" (Sir. 48:1, 3, 9). The misrepresentation of the ascension aside, Sirach correctly matches Elijah's end to his life work, the literal with the figurative.[69]

The storm wind, since it is associated with both theophany (Job 38:1; 40:6) and divine punishment (Jer. 23:19; Zech. 9:14; Ps. 83:16), also conveys a sense of the numinous.[70] Both at Carmel and at Horeb, there was violent wind, the latter part of a theophany. We shall incorporate the discussion of the significance of these symbols and images into our comment on the following verses.

In v.12, the participial forms suggest an iterative sense, thus "Elisha kept watching and kept calling out," and, as at the theophany at Horeb (1 Kgs 19:11) insert a note of immediacy and urgency. The apostrophe Elisha accords Elijah appears drawn from the images that his eyes are recording.[71] All indications are that Elisha has seen Elijah's departure and in doing so, received his request.[72]

The content of Elisha's calling out deserves attention. Elisha addresses his master as אב; we shall briefly comment on this title, before moving on to the more significant designation רכב ישראל ופרשיו. Historical critics propose that the spiritual leader of the בני הנביאים was accorded the honorific title אב, and the plural in בני הנביאים refers to the long tradition and succession of prophetic leaders whose authority the group recognized.[73] Perhaps Elisha is using it in that sense.[74] Phillips takes this further and makes a case for אב being used as a technical term for any person who possessed special powers of wisdom in that he was able to reveal what was hidden to ordinary men. He draws this conclusion from the usage of the term in several OT narratives, of which we shall cite two.

---

69. Bronner treats the implications of fire in the Baal myths for the Elijah narratives. (1968), 54-65.
70. Cogan and Tadmor (1988), 31.
71. Cf. Burney (1903), 265. Lundbom arrives at the same inference but by a very different route. His hypothesis is that Elisha's cry described what was literally happening before his eyes—Elijah was being kidnapped and taken to his death by Jehoram's chariots and horses in revenge for his brother Ahaziah's death. (1973), 39-50. Long rightly dismisses it as a reading that "misses the literary point and completely ignores the characteristic language of visionary experience." (1991), 27.
72. So, regularly (e.g., Nelson (1987), 160); contra, e.g., O'Brien, who sees ambiguity and a lack of resolution re Elisha's succession till he performs his first miracle using the prophetic formula "thus says the LORD," at Jericho. (1998), 10-14.
73. Williams (1966), 344-48.
74. Tg. Jon. has Elisha address his master as רבי.

Joseph is elevated to the position of אב פרעה (Gen. 45:8) and the events that lead to his rise include his ability to interpret dreams, the meaning of which was hidden to everyone else. Then, in Judg. 17:7ff. Micah requests a young Levite to remain with him and be to him "a אב and a priest" (17:10). As in Joseph's case the term אב here is not relevant to age, nor is it merely a title of honour; it has to do with his special abilities to reveal information not accessible ordinarily, and it is for this reason that Micah installs in his shrine the necessary oracular instruments, the ephod and the teraphim. Thus the Danite spies ask the Levite for information about the future (Judg. 18:5), and when the Danites take away the contents of Micah's shrine, it was only natural that they should persuade the Levite to go with them in order that he may continue this special function of being to them "a אב and a priest" (18:19), since without an אב the oracular instruments would have been of little use to them.

Phillips applies his conclusions from these two narratives to the usage of the term for Elisha. Appealing to Elisha's extraordinary powers to obtain knowledge ordinarily inaccessible (2 Kgs 6:12; 7:1), he proposes that Elisha occupied the special position of royal אב to successive kings of Israel (2 Kgs 6:21; 13:14) to whom he was freely available for consultation. The possibility extends to his being regarded in that capacity by the Aramean king Ben-hadad as well, for he sends to ask of him an oracle regarding his survival of an illness, placing himself in the position of Elisha's "son" (2 Kgs 8:9).

Phillips goes on to relate the term אב to the בני הנביאים (1 Kgs 20:35; 2 Kgs 2; 4:1, 38; 5:22; 6:1; 9:1) and "bands of prophets" (1 Sam. 10:10ff.) From these and other usages, Phillips infers that the term applied technically to persons capable of revelatory powers re dreams, the use of oracular instruments, the future and even ecstatic utterances. The hypothesis is not implausible. However, Phillips' hypothesis leaves no room for Elijah genuinely being addressed as אב, since, he argues, Elijah was never involved in politics as Elisha was, and because of his hostile relations with the crown. Thus, Elisha's address of Elijah is a "transferred exclamation" (taken from Joash's description of Elisha in 2 Kgs 13:14), introduced by a later compiler so as to serve as the basis for the introduction of the fiery chariot and horses.[75]

As we have noted, Phillips' premise is generally conceivable, and within its framework, the likelihood is that Elijah does fit the description of an אב. He certainly had access to extraordinary knowledge—he predicted a lengthy drought and its end (1 Kgs 17:1; 18:44), and foretold the fall of the house of Ahab (1 Kgs 21:17ff.) and the death of Ahaziah (2 Kgs 1:16). His stormy relationship with the royal house makes it all the more impressive how implicitly he was

---

75. Cf. e.g., Gray (1964), 422, 542; Rofé (1970), 436-37; Phillips (1968), 183-194.

obeyed—Ahab took orders from him without demur (1 Kgs 18:17ff.; 18:41-42; 18:45-45), and repented with fasting and sackcloth at his reprimand (1 Kgs 21:27). Even if in hostility, both Ahab and Ahaziah sought him in a crisis (1 Kgs 18:10; 2 Kgs 1:9ff.), the latter to hear if he would survive his injury. Thus, even if he is not addressed as אב by the king, he qualifies for the position and apparently holds it, both with respect to the royal house, and the בני הנביאים who stand in awe of his "spirit"; it is this high standing that Elisha's exclamation vocalizes.

If Phillips' proposal from the traditio-historical approach is valid, and if our reading of Elijah within the parameters of that proposal stands, it informs our literary reading of the text insofar as it sharpens the implication of Elisha's request in that he could be said to ask for a double share in his אב's legacy of extraordinary access to knowledge; in other words, to be the next אב in Israel, which indeed he goes on to become. Since this knowledge manifestly has its source in God, this does not detract from our earlier argument that it is the prophetic gift of discernment that Elisha values and is seeking after. In fact, considering the heavy risk this position carried for Elijah, Elisha's request is to his merit.

This brings us to the description of Elijah as רכב ישראל ופרשיו. The consensus is that Elisha means that the prophet stands for the LORD's invisible forces, which are more Israel's safeguard than her own army, and conveys the apprehension that his removal may leave the nation defenceless.[76] For further comment, an economical approach will be to examine this expression in the context of the motif words אש, סוס, פרש and רכב which recur in the string of stories between 2 Kgs 2:1 and 13:14, and in the context of the larger theme of cosmic hosts.

The parallel story that the motif words immediately recall is that found in 2 Kgs 6:13-17. Significantly, a major element in this story is the verb √ראה, "to see." The Aramean king orders his men to "Go and see where he [Elisha] is" (v.13); Elisha prays for his servant "that he may see," and his servant "saw" (v.17); Elisha prays for the blinded Arameans, "that they may see," and they "saw" (v.20). The "blindness" of both servant and soldiers underscores Elisha's superiority in this regard, and recalls his desire for prophetic discernment that had brought about the extraordinary endowment of seeing, and recalls also, what he saw—the fiery chariotry and horses.

---

76. E.g., Burney (1903), 265; Skinner (n.d.), 279-80; Robinson (1976), 26; Gray (1964), 426; Brueggemann (2000), 297. Some propose that the term is a "standard cliché," but that discussion is of little help in determining the significance of the title in the context. E.g., Gaster (1969), 512; von Rad (1958), 100.

Here, it is the servant through whose eyes we see both the Aramean and cosmic hosts. LaBarbera makes the interesting observation that the Aramean host, which consists of an army with horses and chariots (חיל...וסוס ורכב) is balanced by the heavenly host which shows itself as horses and chariots of fire around Elisha (סוסים ורכב אש סביבת אלישע); the implication is that the חיל of the LORD is concentrated in one man, Elisha.[77] To borrow from Galling, it is a "Kontrastparallele."[78]

Indeed, as LaBarbera rightly observes, Elisha's prayer is the celestial hosts' order to attack, for his words function as a military command: the LORD "struck them with blindness according to the word of Elisha" (v.18). By the end of the story Elisha is seen to completely outmanoeuvre the military establishment of both sides. He provides the king of Israel with military intelligence his own men cannot gather; and he helps the Arameans fulfil their king's mandate to "go and see," becoming their ironic leader. LaBarbera reminds that the following story reinforces Elisha's unique military role vis-à-vis the defence of Israel. In the episode of the Aramean siege, it is Elisha who predicts the victory; "his" horses, chariots and army discomfit the enemy (קול רכב קול סוס קול חיל גדול; 2 Kgs 7:6). There is not one military person who succeeds in the two stories – be it soldier, adjutant or king.[79] It is in appropriate metaphor, therefore, that Joash should bewail his impending death with the exclamation, "My father, my father! The chariots of Israel and its horsemen!"[80] Even from that deathbed, Elisha gives the king a war oracle. (2 Kgs 13:14-19)

In 2 Kgs 2, it is the image of Elijah with "his" celestial horses and chariots, which evokes the military title.[81] Considering he was never directly involved in matters of war in a manner comparable to Elisha, how may this title be justified? Beek approaches this problem

---

77. LaBarbera (1984), 640-41.
78. He uses the term with reference to Elisha's name as contrasted against the name of an Aramaic war-god. Galling (1956), 131-35.
79. LaBarbera (1984), 642, 645, 651.
80. Josephus develops a much more elaborate scene than in the Old Testament. Joash remarks that because of Elisha, the Israelites never had to use arms against the enemy, and that through his prophecies they had actually overcome the enemy without a battle. Joash goes so far as to remark that Elisha's death would leave him unarmed before the Syrians and that consequently, since it was no longer safe for him to live, he would do best to join Elisha in death. *Ant.* 9. 179-80.
81. For discussion on the relationship of סוס (2 Kgs 6) with פרש ("horse/horseman"; 2 Kgs 2 and 13), see Beek (1972), 4; Ap-Thomas (1970), 135-51. Cf. Arnold (1905), 45-53; Gesenius (1846), 693; Koehler and Baumgartner (1993), 783; Mowinckel (1962), 278-99.

through the recurrence of the motif words סוס, רכב and פרש in the tradition of the Sea crossing.⁸² In Exod. 14, the narrative of the incident, the first mention of them is in v.9: "all the horses and chariots of Pharoah, and his horsemen and his army" (כל סוס רכב פרעה ופרשיו וחילו). The elements of this war machine recur in combinations in vv.18, 23, 26 and 28. The victory poem in Exod. 15 propagates the strain with its refrain, "Horse and rider he has thrown into the sea" (סוס ורכבו 15:1; cf. vv.4, 19, 21). The literal סוסים, רכב and פרשים take on a symbolic meaning in formulas of liturgy. The Sea crossing demonstrated the impotence of these elements of warfare, and the image of defeated Egypt that they evoke is exploited in reminders, warnings and exhortations.⁸³ Thus Israel's kings are forbidden from acquiring horses in large numbers (Deut. 17:16); Joshua is specifically instructed to burn the chariots and in some way disable (√עקר) the horses of the defeated Canaanites (Josh. 11:6; cf. v.9), an act repeated by David (2 Sam. 8:4); Solomon's building up of chariotry and cavalry (1 Kgs 9:19, 22; 10:28-29) eventually comes to nothing; and Israel confesses: "Some take pride in chariots, and some in horses, but our pride is in the name of the LORD our God" (Ps. 20:7).⁸⁴

סוסים, רכב and פרשים have no place in the defence of Israel; they represent a power that repeatedly proved itself to be powerless. In their place are the LORD and his representatives, the prophets. Tg. Jon. brings this out in its exegetical rendering of Elisha's ejaculation: "רבי, רבי, who did more good for Israel by his prayer than chariots and horsemen." Thus, as Beek emphasizes, the title applies to Elijah, as it applies to "the function…of every prophet in the light of Israel's faith."⁸⁵ Von Rad, who arguably reads this as "obviously a standard quotation," agrees that "in any case it is a polemic expression, a very radical slogan, which concerns the most elementary question of the very existence of Israel…Protection and help for Israel are guaranteed only by the prophet."⁸⁶ In the Elijah-Elisha corpus the more critical foe is the lure of Baalism, rather than the Aramean armies, and it is against the former that their swords are employed

---

82. Beek (1972), 4-10.
83. For e.g., Isa. 31:1: "Alas for those who go down to Egypt for help and who rely on horses (סוסים), who trust in chariots (רכב) because they are many and in horsemen (פרשים) because they are very strong, but do not look to the Holy One of Israel…"
84. Cf. Ps. 30:17; 147:10; Hos. 14:3. Also Mic. 5:10; Hag. 2:22.
85. Beek (1972), 10. Cf. Nelson (1987), 162.
86. Von Rad's line of argument leads him to the interesting, even if debatable, conclusion that prophecy, seen as the guarantor of the protection of Israel, "pushed with its guarantee exactly into the place where previously the institution of holy war stood." (1958), 100.

(1 Kgs 18:40; 19:17) much more than against the latter (cf. 2 Kgs 6:21-23). Both prophets make it their lifework to protect Israel against these enemies, and in doing so, become the true "chariotry and horsemen of Israel."

Here at Elijah's passing, Elisha proves by his penetrating understanding of the critical role and function of the prophetic office that he is worthy of succeeding to it in its highest degree.[87]

Elisha's cry is passionate, bursting out of the depth of his grief. The double expression "My father, my father!" carries the personal dimension of the lament;[88] the spontaneous epithet describes Israel's loss. Elisha keeps his eyes on Elijah till he can see him no more, and then tears his clothes in the standard symbolic gesture of dismay and/or grief (cf. 2 Kgs 5:7; 6:30 within the same cycle of stories).[89] With this the reader is informed that Elisha understands Elijah's departure as equivalent to the latter's death;[90] he is irretrievably lost to Israel and to Elisha.

1.1.5. 2 KINGS 2:13-15: "THE SPIRIT OF ELIJAH RESTS ON ELISHA"

13 He picked up the mantle of Elijah that had fallen from him, and went back and stood on the bank of the Jordan.

14 He took the mantle of Elijah that had fallen from him, and struck the water saying, "Where is the LORD, the God of Elijah?" When he had struck the water, the water was parted to the one side and to the other, and Elisha went over.

15 When the company of prophets who were at Jericho saw him at a distance, they declared, "The spirit of Elijah rests on Elisha." They came to meet him and bowed to the ground before him. [91]

---

87. Brichto (1992), 163.
88. Cf. David's "My son, my son!" at the news of Absalom's death; 2 Sam. 19:4.
89. Long observes that the usual expression of tearing the garments is heightened here in that Elisha tears his garments in two. The phrase (לשנים קרעים) recalls the two prophets in each other's company (שניהם; 2:6, 11) and "suggests the depth of change wrought by the trajectory from Gilgal to Transjordan." (1991), 27.
90. As, for example, at the "death" of Joseph (Gen. 37:34) and the deaths of Nadab and Abihu (Lev. 10:6), Abner (2 Sam. 3:31), David's sons (2 Sam. 13:31) and Saul (2 Sam. 1:2, 11).
91. In the LXX, Elisha's cry addresses "the God of Elijah" (omitting the preceding word יהוה), and reads הוא אף as אפוא. This last is left transliterated, perhaps recognizing the difficulties. Its being connected by accentuation to the following clause is syntactically awkward. Most moderns follow אפוא, the expletive meaning "then/indeed," and connect the term back to the previous clause. One of the several usages of אפוא (איפוא/אפו) is in connection with interrogative adverbs, and when combined with איה it is read, "Where, then...?" (Judg. 9:38; Isa. 19:12; Job.

Elisha picks up the fallen mantle (רום√), which the reader is reminded fell from off Elijah.[92] Skinner suggests that Elisha connects the fallen mantle with the personal significance of the vision, in that the garment is indication that the sight of the vision was a sign of his empowerment.[93] More than that, it carries connotations of prophetic status,[94] and if Elisha had understood its being laid on him as an investiture into the position of Elijah's successor, its presence here makes it clear to him that Elijah's place is his for the taking, as much as the mantle is. "[W]ith a truly graphic touch, it is now shown that Elisha has actually inherited his master's 'Spirit'."[95] Not only his "spirit" but also his unfinished mission has Elisha inherited;[96] the narrative will go on to tell how he accomplishes this mission.

Elisha retraces his steps to the bank of the Jordan and stands there. Then he takes (לקח√) the mantle, (and again the reader is reminded that the mantle has fallen from off Elijah), and at this point the sequence of actions and speech becomes debatable. Does Elisha strike the water once or twice, and at what point does he speak? The LXX (Lucianic) constructs a sequence with the help of an exegetical gloss—καὶ οὐ διέστη.[97] It has Elisha strike the water, and when it does not part, he calls on the God of Elijah (presumably, to prove himself) and then strikes again;[98] with this, the water parts and Elisha crosses over. One implication of this sequence, as Cogan and Tadmor point out, would be a casting of doubt on the rank achieved by Elisha vis-à-vis Elijah;[99] the former has not quite made the grade. In this vein, Nelson, for example, comments that Elisha "repeats Elijah's power deed, albeit with a little extra effort."[100]

However, the LXX's exegetical insertion may not be necessary, for there is another possible construction. Burney refers to the use of the verb "to bless" (ברך√) in Gen. 27:23, 27 as a comparable literary

---

17:15). If this is the reading of the translators of the Hebrew into Aramaic also, then, as Harrington and Saldarini suggest, perhaps they read a tone of scepticism into the question, and so, replace it with a petition: "And he took the cloak of Elijah that fell from him, and he struck the waters and said: 'Accept my petition, Lord God of Elijah.'" Tg. Jon. (1987), 267.
92. The LXX has the mantle fall off Elijah *onto Elisha*, making the symbolism of transfer of power even more explicit.
93. Skinner (n.d.), 277.
94. Elsewhere, in Zech. 13:4.
95. Gunkel (1929), 185.
96. Cf. Nelson (1987), 158.
97. MSS of Vulgate follow: "et non sunt divisae."
98. So, e.g., Nelson (1987), 159.
99. Cogan and Tadmor (1988), 33.
100. Nelson (1987), 160.

device.[101] The narrative has a series of "tests" by the vulnerable Isaac, after which he blessed Jacob (וַיְבָרְכֵהוּ; v.23), Then, Isaac continues into further "tests" and he blesses him (וַיְבָרְכֵהוּ; v.27) again. Of the several approaches to solving this puzzle, two appeal to the literary critic. The first possibility is that the first "and he blessed him" is proleptic – "so that is why he (eventually) blessed him" (cf. NEB, NAB).[102] The argument raised against this is that it would work against the logic of the plot, which continues to build up a second series of tests by Isaac. The tension released, the literary purpose of these further tests is hard to see. Thus, the suggestion that the imperfect of √ברך in v.23 should be read as an ingressive, an action about to take place, sits better with the development of the plot – "he was about to bless him."[103] This reading of the phrase not only sustains the drama but also notches it up significantly.

This could well be the device employed in 2 Kgs 2. The logic of the narrative demands that Elisha must cross the Jordan to return to his community. Will he be able to replicate his master's miracle, and so confirm to the watching prophetic group, the reader and to himself that he is a worthy successor? The narrative slows down, as in the case of the first parting of the water, and with every move of Elisha, the reader's anticipation increases, especially since the narrator's description of this second parting closely follows his description of the first.

v.8

A וַיִּקַּח אֵלִיָּהוּ אֶת־אַדַּרְתּוֹ
B וַיִּגְלֹם
C וַיַּכֶּה אֶת־הַמַּיִם
D וַיֵּחָצוּ הֵנָּה וָהֵנָּה
E וַיַּעַבְרוּ שְׁנֵיהֶם בֶּחָרָבָה׃

A* וַיִּקַּח אֶת־אַדֶּרֶת אֵלִיָּהוּ
B* אֲשֶׁר־נָפְלָה מֵעָלָיו
C* וַיַּכֶּה אֶת־הַמַּיִם
וַיֹּאמֶר אַיֵּה יְהוָה אֱלֹהֵי אֵלִיָּהוּ אַף־הוּא וַיַּכֶּה אֶת־הַמַּיִם
D* וַיֵּחָצוּ הֵנָּה וָהֵנָּה
E* וַיַּעֲבֹר אֱלִישָׁע׃

We note that the verbs used are identical, as is the depiction of the parting of the water. By delaying the striking of the water at the last

---

101. Burney (1903), 265-66; cf. Cogan and Tadmor (1988), 32-33.
102. E.g., Wenham (1994), 209.
103. E.g., Speiser (1964), 209; Fokkelman (1975), 103; Hamilton (1995), 218, n.6.

possible moment, the narrator not only ratchets up suspense, but also highlights the extra sequence of speech and action in an otherwise perfectly matched sequence.

The careful construction would implicitly signal that Elisha is no less a prophet than Elijah; he proves himself able to replicate Elijah's miracle. However the unmatched detail, namely Elisha's question, serves the crucial purpose of explicitly connecting Elisha's miracle back to Elijah.[104] Elisha clearly expects that the wonder will take place, if at all, as a concrete and tangible affirmation by God of his position as Elijah's successor; the LORD, Elijah's God, must perform the miracle by the hand of the rightful successor.[105] Thus, when the river parts, it tangibly proves the legitimacy of his position to himself;[106] it realizes the share of the firstborn that he had requested. Thus the point is made that the replication of the nature miracle means more than just that Elisha is as divinely gifted a prophet as Elijah; beyond that, and enormously critical to the continuing narrative, is the assurance that though Elijah has departed, another has picked up the standard, and the battle continues without pause.[107] This is immediately plain to the other players within the world of the story, namely, the watching בני הנביאים, and they, like a chorus, confirm what Elisha and the reader have worked out: "The spirit of Elijah rests on Elisha." Elisha's new status changes their own; they are henceforth his "servants" (עבד; 2 Kgs 2:16).[108] Thus, to seek in this piece of narrative a statement concerning Elisha's rank as prophet with reference to Elijah's (cf. Nelson above) would be misguided.

There is one last item, and this concerns the sections B-B* diagrammed above. We noted that the verb √גלם in 2 Kgs 2:8 possibly links Elijah back with Moses in that it recalls the latter's rod, held out over the Sea in dividing it. The corresponding segment in 2 Kgs 2:14 (B*) could well be read as a parallel in that it links Elisha

---

104. Cf. Fretheim (1999), 138.
105. Bergen, ("Where is the God of Elijah, even he?") finds in it "a challenge of the impatient." (1999), 64. Contra Gunkel ("Where is Jahveh? The God of Elijah, where is he?"), to whom it is a pious supplication: "Jahveh, who did marvels by Elijah, turn now to me." (1929), 185. Hobbs sees no need to read any tone of anxiety into the prayer, and suggests that a link with Deut. 32:37 is implied in the question. (1985), 22.
106. "The symbolic value of a comparable succession is central here, not the 'miraculous' character of what occurs." Fretheim (1999), 137. Cf. Rofé (1970), 438; Coote (1992), 29.
107. Cf. Hobbs (1985), 27-28; Provan (1995), 175; Fretheim (1999), 139-40.
108. Coote observes that Elisha's reception of the "spirit" is validated in three places – by the act of "seeing," by the parting of the waters and by the affirmation of the prophetic community. (1992), 29. Elisha

back with Elijah, since it reiterates that the mantle Elisha holds had fallen off Elijah. Thus, looking back over this portion of the text, we see that one theme that gets picked up constantly is that of Elisha as successor to Elijah. The mantle itself, the two explicit references to the ownership of the mantle, the words with which Elisha sets about his first miracle, and the patterning of the report of the second water-parting on the first are all explicitly summed up in the decisive declaration of the בני הנביאים.[109]

Certainly, the text evokes Mosaic parallels. The statement of the prophetic group recalls Deut. 34:9 on three details. First, immediately following the telling of the death of Moses, the reader is informed of the "spirit of wisdom" that Joshua was full of. Secondly, this gift is associated back with Moses, from whose laying on of hands it came. Thirdly, within the same statement, the reader is told that Israel hearkened to Joshua, as if in consequence to his derived charisma.

The other narrative recalled is Joshua's crossing of the Jordan. This requires a lengthier engagement and we will return to it at the end of the discussion on the 2 Kgs 2 narrative.

1.1.6. 2 KINGS 2:16-18: THE SEARCH FOR ELIJAH

16 They said to him, "See now, we have fifty strong men among your servants; please let them go and seek your master; it may be that the spirit of the LORD has caught him up and thrown him down on some mountain or into some valley." He responded, "No, do not send them."

17 But when they urged him until he was ashamed, he said, "Send them." So they sent fifty men who searched for three days but did not find him.

18 When they came back to him (he had remained at Jericho), he said to them, "Did I not say to you, Do not go?"

Gertel comments on the בני הנביאים: "If these Disciples of the Prophets were to be compared to a Greek chorus, they would have to be characterized as a rather annoying one. They give Elisha no privacy and show no restraint. They have all the subtlety of modern-day tabloid reporters. They offer him a party of 50 to go searching for the departed Elijah…"[110] This is amusingly true, and only emphasizes the literary purpose of this group. Their role as witnesses is not over.

---

109. Later in 2 Kgs 2, Jericho's waters will be healed "according to the word of Elisha," recalling the comment regarding the word of Elijah (1 Kgs 17:16; 2 Kgs 1:17), and a curse against the youth of Bethel will be fulfilled, recalling the word that comes from Elijah's mouth (1 Kgs 17:24). These may be read as narratorial affirmations that Elisha is Elijah's true and worthy successor.

110. Gertel (2002¹), 77.

The request of the בני הנביאים provokes the question—What is the purpose of the search? The reader notes that they now use a different verb to describe Elijah's being taken, not √לקח as before, but √נשא. It appears that their knowledge of what has happened to Elijah has become a little clearer; in being taken away, he was taken up. We noted that this is the same verb that Obadiah uses in describing Elijah's disappearances. Obadiah seems quite familiar with the phenomenon; "As soon as I have gone from you, the spirit of the LORD will carry you (ורוח יהוה ישאך) I know not where; so when I come and tell Ahab and he cannot find you, he will kill me..." (1 Kgs 18:12). The בני הנביאים too speak the same language: "perhaps the spirit of the LORD has caught him up" (פן נשאו רוח יהוה). However, the latter party continues to explain that the selfsame spirit may have cast him down (√שלך). The verb has usage in Kings and elsewhere with the disposal of dead bodies,[111] and the likelihood that this is the sense here as well is sustained by the further possibilities the בני הנביאים sketch – Elijah may have been thrown down onto one of the hills or into one of the valleys.

Thus, adding together the understanding of the בני הנביאים that Elijah was to be taken (away) from over Elisha, the evidence to them from Elisha's torn garments of Elijah's departure, their declaration that Elijah's spirit now rests on Elisha his successor, and that Elijah may have been carried up and hurled down again to earth, the picture that emerges is of a request to send out a search party for the body, so that the corpse may receive a proper burial.[112] The LXX moves the interpretation in this direction with the insertion that Elijah may have been thrown into the Jordan.

If we assume (as argued earlier) that the בני הנביאים and Elisha started off at the same level of knowledge re Elijah's being "taken," the gap between them at the end of the narrative is more a yawning chasm. Without having asked and received, Elisha's level of prophetic discernment may have been no keener than that of his fellow prophets.[113] Publicly invested as Elijah's successor, as he had

---

111. 2 Kgs 9:25, 26; 13:21; Josh. 8:29; 10:27; Amos 8:3; Jer. 22:19. BDB, שלך, 1021.
112. So, e.g., Robinson (1976), 27; Provan (1995), 174; Wiseman (1993), 196-97.
113. Nelson's deduction is that the narrator shows the prophetic group to regress from correct predictions (2:3, 5) and accurate interpretation (2:15), when they insist on the search for Elijah – it shows "they are less perspicacious at the end of the story than they were at the start." (1987), 159. It seems to me that this regression is an illusion created by *Elisha's* journeying on, while they have remained "standing" on the "far side" (2:7, 15). Moberly rightly concludes from his study of 2 Kgs 2, "Seeing God…is something that exists unequally among those called to serve God" (2006),

2 Kings 2: Elijah's Ascension and Elisha's Succession

already been, Elisha might still have literally and/or figuratively been awarded the mantle of his master. In fact, it is possible that nothing else in the "succession story" would have been different, except, of course, for the crucial difference that Elisha would have been a poorer "seer," much to Israel's loss. Like Solomon before him, Elisha seized the opportunity to ask for special enabling in the task that he was succeeding a great predecessor into. "It pleased the LORD that Solomon had asked this" (1 Kgs 3:10), and that appears to be the case with Elisha as well.

Meanwhile, Elisha maintains an enigmatic silence on the issue of what it is that has really happened to Elijah. In this, he is consistent with his earlier behaviour, where he had sharply hushed the בני הנביאים rather than discuss with them what he knew of the imminent event. Perhaps the matter is far too personal and beyond that, too sacred to be commonly shared. At any rate, this suits the narrator, because he can orchestrate it into a concluding flourish in his Mosaic composition of the life and work of Elijah.

The detail that the search party consists of fifty strong men (בני חיל) emphasizes both the competence and the futility of the search. Elijah is not to be found – dead or alive. As Provan observes, finally, the narrative never resolves what exactly it is that has happened to him – whether he died in the process of being taken up or was translated into another life without experiencing death. We are only given pointers towards what the various actors believed about his disappearance, while the narrator carefully guards the mystery at the heart of the event, never quite letting on what he means by that verb only he uses (√עלה) of Elijah's disappearance.

This concluding section of the narrative is not only necessary, but also enormously significant to the narrator; with it he consummates the Mosaic theme carried through his telling of the life story of this prophet. In his departure too, Elijah resembles Moses. Both prophets know the time and place of their departure (Deut. 32:48-50). Moses dies while still full of "sap,"[114] meaning to say that he did not die of old age but rather because the LORD willed it so, and because his work was done and his service fulfilled. Elijah too remains in active service to the end. Both are last seen journeying towards their end. Deut. 34 reviews Moses in terms of his intimacy with the LORD (v.10) and his deeds on behalf of Israel (vv.11-12). The symbols of divine presence at Elijah's translation are a reminder of a similar intimacy, recalling as they do, the wind and fire of his encounter with deity at Horeb; and, in celestial fiery images and human

---

138. This inequality has arisen, in part, because Elisha made the right moves towards seeing.
114. לח is used of the freshness and moisture of growing or freshly cut wood. Cf. Gen. 30:37; Eze. 17:24; 21:3 (EVV 20:47).

exclamation his significance to Israel is proclaimed. Both departures are mediated by God, and shrouded in mystery; Moses dies at God's command and is buried by him, none knows where; Elijah is caught up by God and is never seen again. The manner of each one's "death" speaks God's approval – a "Well done, good and faithful servant!"[115]

Meanwhile, the reader recalls that the account of the death of Moses is separated from his epitaph by a quick but insistent mention that "Joshua the son of Nun was full of the spirit of wisdom, because Moses had laid his hands on him; and the Israelites obeyed him, doing as the LORD had commanded Moses" (Deut. 34:9). Like his namesake and counterpart, Elisha has demonstrated himself to be wise and discerning.

Like Joshua too, Elisha has seen a military vision in the environs of Jericho (Josh. 5:13-15), though the plot progression in the latter story demands that the vision happen before the parting of the Jordan. In both cases it is the water crossing that affirms them as successors worthy of their predecessors. Like Joshua, Elisha will follow the Jordan miracle with a miracle at Jericho. Both Joshua and Elisha have a "purge" to perform, via the herem and the metaphorical "sword," respectively. Each procedure functions in its own way to accomplish a comparable purpose, namely, the securing of the land for the LORD's people; in the process it destroys and/or dispossesses those who are outside the covenant. As we shall see in our examination of Exod. 15, the conquest creates a sanctuary for the LORD, and establishes his kingship. This is significant when applied to the context of Elisha's work since he will catalyse the deconstruction of the political structures of Israel to make way for a king who will represent the LORD.

1.2. Structure and Focus of the 2 Kings 2 Narrative

We may conclude this close reading of 2 Kgs 2 by standing back to observe the larger picture.

Commenting on the many attempts to map 2 Kgs 2 into a geographical chiasm,[116] Bergen comments: "The common feature that all share is their near success. Near success is certainly a sign

---

115. Maccabees reads the manner of Elijah's departure as reward for work well done: "Elijah, because of great zeal for the law, was taken up into heaven" (1 Macc. 2:58). Cogan and Tadmor offer that this non-death "invested his with the qualities of eternal life, surpassing even Moses, the father of all prophets, who dies and was buried (albeit by God himself: Deut. 34:5-6)." (1988), 33-34.
116. The itinerary runs thus: Gilgal (v.1); Bethel (v.2); Jericho (v.4); Jordan (vv.6-14); Jericho (v.15); Bethel (v.23); Mt. Carmel/Samaria (v.25). E.g., Lundbom (1973), 41-42; O'Brien (1998), 3-4; Long (1991), 20-21.

that something is happening..."[117] Of these attempts, we may mention Hobbs'; his pattern is event-based rather than geographical, and embraces both chapters 1 and 2 of 2 Kgs with a climax at 2:11, the ascension of Elijah. On either side, in 2:10 Elisha's receiving of his request is dependent on seeing and in 2:12, Elisha "saw"; in 2:9 Elisha requests for the firstborn's share and in 2:13 he picks up the mantle of Elijah, the symbol of succession; 2:8 and 2:14 describe the two crossings in almost identical terms; in 2:7 and 2:15 mention is made of the watching sons of the prophets"; in 2:2-6 this group asks Elisha if he knows of the departure of his master and in 2:16-18 they request permission of him to confirm that departure. 2:19-22 balances with 1:1-8, 16-17, the common theme being sickness and healing, the seeking out of a deity/prophet for help, the word of judgement/healing and a fulfillment formula. Ahaziah dies without progeny and Elisha heals a city of its barrenness. 1:9-15 is balanced by 2:23-24 in that in both, the status of the prophet is challenged ("Come down!"/"Go up!"), and drastic judgement executed by a third party (described in identical syntax).[118] Elisha's brief stop at Carmel (2:25) before he moves on to the political centre, Samaria, is seen as bridging back to Elijah's great work on that mountain.[119]

The events are so ordered that they form a literary retracing of Elijah's steps by Elisha in what Hobbs calls a "succession narrative."[120] Thus: "The 'copy' of Elijah found in the figure and activity of Elisha—although it is by no means a perfect copy—serves to emphasize the perpetuation of prophetic tradition, even after the disappearance of the prophetic giant, Elijah."[121] This is not improbable.[122] The other narrative of prophetic succession also

---

117. Bergen (1999), 56.
118. Hobbs (1984), 327-34.
119. E.g., Nelson (1987), 158; Long (1991), 20.
120. Hobbs (1985), 19.
121. Hobbs (1984), 333.
122. Certainly, as we shall discuss later, authority is a key issue in the corpus Joshua-Kings, and the schema here could well demonstrate that. The three sets of episodes (the two river crossings, the death of Ahaziah/the healing of Jericho's waters, the fire/the bears) voice this theme each in its own way. Carroll compares the fire from heaven incident to that of Nadab and Abihu in that the authority of the prophet was questioned and the detractors punished by divine fire. (1969), 412. Woods makes out an interesting argument for קרח in the jeer of the youths recalling Num. 16—קרח stands for either "baldhead" or "Korah" (the type of a usurper of authority), or, paranomastically, both. (1992), 47-58. In trying to unlock this difficult text, it seems more probable that a consequence as serious as death should follow the sin of questioning the authority of the prophet, rather than that of heckling. (Cf. the other narrative of prophetic succession, where death is promised those who rebel against or disobey the new leader; Josh. 1:18).

makes continuity its refrain, as our discussion of Joshua 1-5 later will remind. The two figures of Elijah and Elisha, their charisma, and their role as Israel's leaders are seamlessly conjoined. In this endeavour, perhaps the other literary device, that of setting the narrative of 2 Kgs 2 outside the regnal records, also helps. Long suggests that this "pausal moment" creates the necessary space for "analogical image making"; the Moses-Joshua model of transition is reworked for another critical period of Israel's history, and setting the narrative in such relief compels the reader to make new associations with the paradigm.[123]

In bringing the reading of 2 Kgs 2 to a close, we must revisit the related questions of which prophet is the protagonist of the narrative (Elijah or Elisha), and which of the two events its climax (the ascension or the succession). We may briefly scan the argument of one proponent from each camp, Long and Gunkel.

Long sees the giveaway opening of 2 Kgs 2 as a "typical anticipatory device of Hebrew narration" of which there are other examples within the Kings material, namely, the accounts of the adversaries of Solomon—Hadad, Rezon and Jeroboam (1 Kgs 11:14a, 23a, 26a). He understands such anticipatory statement to establish a hierarchy among possible readings of the narrative and defines at the outset the narrator's preferred view, somewhat imposing this view on the reader.[124] It is interesting then, that while the other three comparable stories revolve entirely around the character named in the introductory summary, 2 Kgs 2 works differently. It is the character of Elisha that steals the focus; he is the one with whom the other characters dialogue; his is the radical transformation from a dependent protégé to self-assured prophet. Elijah moves through the narrative with a strange detachment, and actually leaves the narrative mid-way, as against Hadad et al.

Gunkel's approach is more through hypothesizing on sources and redaction.

> The purpose of the original story was to show how Elisha became Elijah's successor. The hero of it is Elisha, not Elijah...In order to set forth his conception of Elisha, the narrator has utilized an older tradition of Elijah's ascension. Of course, in that narrative Elijah was the centre of interest, but our author has ventured so to adapt the story that his own hero, Elisha, plays the chief part. He has succeeded beyond measure...Without detracting from the greatness of Elijah, he has made Elisha the central figure of his narrative.[125]

Along the same lines, Bakon sees a denial of Elisha's prophetic authority, in that he was called bald in deliberate contrast to the hairy Elijah. (2001), 248.
123. Long (1991), 31-32.
124. Long (1991), 25-26.
125. Gunkel (1929), 186.

The "original story," according to Gunkel, ends at v.15; vv.16-18 are a "supplement" added by a later hand, the purpose being to furnish proof of Elijah's non-death. As for the incidents that immediately follow it, they are not part of the narrator's scheme and "completely destroy its symmetry." Gunkel is not comfortable with the "supplement" either, since, judged from the aesthetic standpoint, "it again diverts the attention of the reader from Elisha, who is the chief figure, to Elijah, about whom everything needful has been told."[126]

The questions of redaction aside, Gunkel's observations only reiterate the point we have been making that the narrative sustains a remarkably fine twin focus right through vv.1-18, if not to the end of the chapter. In the received form of the text, Elisha is seen to detract in no way from Elijah's moment of glory; rather, he actively contributes to it with the arresting and graphic epitaph. The character of Elijah, meanwhile, allows room for Elisha from the start, withdrawing to the point of seeming removed from the action. Even the ascension is not Elijah's moment alone, since Elijah intentionally meshes it with Elisha's successorship.

We conclude then, that the unresolved debates only testify to the difficulty of locating which, if any, is the climax of the narrative, and who, if either prophet, is the "hero." The continuing argument is a tribute to the skill of the narrator.

1.3. Interim Conclusion

The close reading of 2 Kgs 2 shows it to be one that continuously challenges the reader to engage with it. The reader must work out where he has been placed re level of knowledge, and in doing so, attempt to resolve where the other players stand. To the very end he can never be quite sure, though the probability is that he has been privileged from the start, while the prophetic group, at the lowest level, is still groping for answers at the close of the story. In the course of events, it is the character of Elisha that develops, not only in terms of knowledge of the anticipated departure of Elijah, but also in terms of maturing from dependent disciple to authoritative leader; from seeker to possessor of the gift of the highest degree of prophetic discernment— the gift of being able to see the divine. The narrator skilfully weaves his two concerns into the climactic moment towards which the first half of the story moves, and from which the second half moves away, namely, the theophany. In that one instant of time encountering eternity, Elijah's life and work is brought to a splendid consummation, and Elisha is established as a divinely legitimated and gifted successor.

The narrator throws these twin concerns into relief by setting up an analogy at different levels with the only other prophetic

---

126. Gunkel (1929), 85-86.

"succession narrative," that of Moses and Joshua; considering the Mosaic tenor of the larger narrative, this is but logical. The fulcrum on which this analogy turns is the miracle of water parting, invoking, as it does, the two great crossings in Israel's history and liturgy, rich with overlapping themes. In order to discern which of these themes the narrator is seeking to evoke in 2 Kgs 2, we need to study first the resonance between the Sea and River crossings, and to this task we turn.

2. Exodus 14-15 and Joshua 1, 3-5

2.1. The Two Great Water Crossings

Exod. 15, commonly called the Song of Sea, is often the starting point for discussion on how the two crossings, that of the Red Sea under Moses' leadership and that of the Jordan under Joshua's, resonate with each other. Tradition history regularly reads Exod. 15:11, 12 as a transition between the two themes of the song—the celebration of the Sea crossing and the entry into the Promised Land.[127] Common concepts and choice of words in the two texts (namely, Exod. 14-15 and Josh. 3-4) fuel the debate over which tradition has influenced the other, and in what way. A common consensus is that the River tradition is extrapolated back into the Sea tradition and hence the twin themes of Exod. 15.[128] Alternatively, the Sea crossing is seen to influence the River crossing: this influence is seen in the Sea motif being imported into the River account,[129] or, more forcefully, the crossing of the Jordan is seen as a cultic re-enactment of the Sea crossing.[130] An added dimension discussed in scholarship is that of the influence on the water-separation motifs from the mythic patterns of Canaan, namely, the Baal myths re Yamm, god of the Sea.[131]

These considerations aside, let us note the resonance at the verbal and story levels between the two texts, namely, Exod. 14-15 and Josh. 3:1-5:1, as extensively noted by scholarship.

2.1.1. VERBAL PARALLELS

In this section we list words, phrases and constructions that link the Jordan crossing with that of the Sea.

---

127. See, e.g., Noth (1962), 124-25; Coats (1969), 1-17.
128. E.g., Coats (1969), 11; Hulst (1965), 167-68; Hay (1964), 402.
129. E.g., Noth (1953), 33.
130. E.g., Kraus (1951), 181-99; cf. Childs (1970), 406-418: Cross (1966), 11-30, esp. pp. 26-27; Winjgaards (1969).
131. E.g., Cross (1968) 1-25, esp. 22; Eakin (1967), 378-84.

Josh. 3:5:
Joshua describes the miracle to come as "miraculous works" (פלא√) which the LORD will perform among Israel
Exod. 15:11:
The Red Sea crossing is attributed to the LORD, who does "miraculous works" (פלא√)

Josh. 3:13, 16:
The waters stand in a "single heap"—נד אחד
Exod. 15:8:
The waters stand up "like a heap"—כמו נד

Josh. 3:16:
The waters flowing down from above the crossing heap up at Adam, cutting off, on the other side of the crossing, the waters flowing down to the Salt Sea.
Exod. 14:22, 29:
The waters form a wall on the right and left of the crossing.

Josh. 3:17; 4:22:
Israel crosses over on dry ground—חרבה (3:17)/יבשה (4:22), while the priests stand in the middle of the Jordan—בתוך הירדן (cf. 4:10, 18).
Exod. 14:21-22, 29:
The sea is turned into dry land—חרבה (14:21)/יבשה (14:22, 29). Israel goes into the midst of (בתוך) the sea.

Josh. 5:1:
The kings of the cis-Jordan nations hear (שמע√) of Israel's miraculous crossing (עבר√) of the river with dismay. Their hearts melt (מסס√).
Exod. 15:16:
The peoples hear (שמע√) and are dismayed as Israel crosses over (עבר√) into the land. The Canaanites melt away (מוג√).

Josh. 4:14:
The crossing causes Israel to "fear" (ירא√) Joshua as they had "feared" (ירא√) Moses.
Exod. 14:31:
The crossing causes Israel to believe (אמן√) in the LORD and his servant Moses.

Josh. 4:24:
The purpose of the miraculous river crossing is that Israel may "fear" (ירא√) the LORD.

Exod. 14:31:
The crossing inspires Israel to "fear" (√ירא) the LORD.

Josh. 4:24:
The crossing demonstrates that the hand of the LORD is mighty
(יד יהוה כי חזקה היא).
Exod. 13:9:
The Song of the Sea makes reference to the LORD's right hand (ימין —15:6, 12) participating in the event; 13:9 uses "with a strong hand" (ביד חזקה) to describe the LORD's bringing Israel out of Egypt.

Significantly, the Joshua account itself also sets up resonance between the two crossings at the verbal level, affirming the relevance and significance of the exercise we are engaged in. Rahab's description of the Sea crossing parallels the narrator's description of the River crossing:

Josh. 2:9-11:
The inhabitants of the land hear (√שמע)
that the LORD dried up the water of the Red Sea
(אשר הוביש יהוה את מי ים סוף)
and how Israel dealt with the two kings of the Amorites beyond the Jordan
(שני מלכי האמרי אשר בעבר הירדן), i.e., the trans-Jordan
and "our" hearts melt (וימס לבבנו)
and there is no longer any spirit left in any man (לא קמה עוד רוח באיש)
Josh. 5:1:
All the kings of the Amorites beyond the Jordan to the west
(כל מלכי האמרי אשר בעבר הירדן ימה)
hear (√שמע)
that the LORD has dried up the waters of the Jordan
(אשר הוביש יהוה את מי הירדן)
their hearts melt (וימס לבבם)
and there is no longer any spirit left in them (ולא היה בם עוד רוח)

Further, Rahab describes the effect of the Sea crossing on the Canaanites, recalling the language of Exod. 15:
Josh. 2:9:
the inhabitants of the land melt (כל ישבי הארץ נמגו);
Exod. 15:15:
the inhabitants of Canaan melt (נמגו כל ישבי כנען)

Josh. 2:9:
dread of "you" falls on "us" (נפלה אימתכם עלינו)

Exod. 15: 16:

dread falls on them (תפל עליהם אימתה)

In conclusion, one notes the two *explicit* parallels the Joshua text draws between the two crossings; the phrasing is pointedly equivalent.

Josh. 4:14:

On that day the LORD exalted Joshua in the sight of all Israel; and they stood in awe of him as they had stood in awe of Moses, all the days of his life.

וייראו אתו כאשר יראו את משה

Josh. 4:23:

For the LORD your God dried up the waters of the Jordan for you until you crossed over, as the LORD your God did to the Red Sea, which he dried up for us until we crossed over...

אשר הוביש יהוה אלהיכם את מי הירדן מפניכם עד עברכם
כאשר עשה יהוה אלהיכם לים סוף אשר הוביש מפנינו עד עברנו

2.1.2. STORY LEVEL PARALLELS

This wealth of intertextuality at the verbal level is replicated at the next wider level, namely that of story. Both crossings are marked by the symbolic presence of the LORD. At the Red Sea, the "angel of God"/"pillar of cloud" covers Israel's vulnerability as they cross, by taking up position as Israel's rear guard, separating them from the Egyptians who follow hard at their heels. At the end of the crossing *"the LORD* in the pillar of fire and cloud" glares down on the Egyptians and throws them into panic. (Exod. 14:19-20)

At Jordan (Josh. 3:2-6), Joshua is given instructions re "the ark of the covenant of the LORD your God"; the reason for it making up the vanguard of the crossing is that the Israelites have not been this way before and the ark will guide them; they are to "follow it." Presumably it will "carry" the priests along; (cf. 3:11—"the ark of the covenant of the LORD of all the earth is going to pass before you into the Jordan"). However, care must be taken to keep a specified distance between "you and it." The implication of these directions is reinforced by Joshua's orders to Israel—"Sanctify yourselves; for tomorrow the LORD will do wonders among you."

The ritual preparations and the setting of boundaries (and the inclusion of the minor detail re the "third day") recall similar preparations before Israel meets the LORD at Sinai (Exod. 19:10-12, 14-15, 21, 23-24). Soggin draws attention to the resonance here with Num. 10:35-36, a passage where the ark and the LORD are wholly identified, remarking that the ark "still" carries out the functions of a guide, and is a sign of the presence of the LORD.[132] Thus, the ark

---

132. Soggin (1972), 56.

becomes the locus of divine power and presence. In fact, the narrative does not fail to connect regularly the miracle with the ark – the parting and closing of the waters is consistently linked to it (Josh. 3:13; 15-17; 4:10; 4:18).[133]

Further, both crossings are closely associated with the celebration of the Passover. The night of the observance of the first Passover, on the fourteenth day of the first month, is followed by the day of Israel's exit from Egypt—"this very day"— בעצם היום הזה. Further, the ordinance for the Passover specifically includes a directive for circumcision of any foreigner who wants to join in its celebration, so that he may "be regarded as a native of the land." (Exod. 12:6, 41-51) At Gilgal, "the disgrace of Egypt" is finally removed from Israel, as they are circumcised. They keep the Passover on the fourteenth day of the (first) month, and the very day—בעצם היום הזה—following it, manna ceases and they eat the produce of the land. A wandering generation becomes natives of the land. (Josh. 5:2-12)[134]

There are a couple of loose correspondences, where the Jordan crossing evokes Mosaic elements from stories other than that of the Red Sea event. Joshua sets up twelve stones on the riverbed; these are piled up over the "standing place" (מצב) of the feet of the priests who bore the ark of the covenant (Josh. 4:9). At Sinai, Moses erects twelve pillars (sg. in Exod. 24:4—מצבה) under the mountain of the covenant making. In both cases, the number twelve explicitly represents the tribes of Israel; in Exod. 24, the monument marks Israel's affirmation of obedience to the LORD; at the Jordan too, the stone pile commemorates a crossing made possible by obedience (Josh. 4:10; cf. 1:17-18).

Another instantly recognizable resonance is that of the theophanic encounter (Exod. 3:2 ff; Josh. 5: 13 ff). Joshua, like Moses, sees a divine being and is instructed (in language almost identical to the earlier story) to take his shoes off in deference to the sanctity of the place. In both cases, explicitly or implicitly, the message is that deity is ready to intervene in history on Israel's behalf.

2.2. Interim Conclusion

Our examination of the Exodus and Joshua texts at the verbal and story levels clarifies that the River crossing recapitulates the crossing of the Red Sea. We have also seen in our reading of 2 Kgs 2 that the parting of the Jordan by Elijah and Elisha, by the very nature of the miracle, immediately calls up associations with the Sea and River

---

133. See Miller and Tucker (1974), 35; Soggin (1972), 56.
134. Soggin comments on Josh. 3-5: "The first thing one notices is a striking analogy with the account of the Passover and the crossing of the Red Sea, Exod. 12-15, to the extent that it seems safe to affirm a substantial unity of content between these two passages." Soggin (1972), 51.

partings in Israel's history. Further, we noted that the 2 Kings account carries echoes of the earlier miracles at the level of words, expressions and story detail. These, in themselves, would be of little value, unless we examine how these associations direct the reading of the Elijah-Elisha cycle, especially at this point in narrative. This is the undertaking in the section that follows.

3. The Red Sea Crossing, the Jordan Crossing and 2 Kings 2: Conceptual Parallels

The resonance at the verbal and story levels between the Exodus and Joshua texts sets the scene for overarching conceptual parallels. Our intention here is to examine those themes that unite the crossings of Moses and Joshua which appear to have been exploited by the narrator of 2 Kgs 2. The two we will discuss are (1) the theme of authoritative prophetic leadership and (2) the war theme, both concepts being overtly treated and being a significant concern in all three texts.

3.1. The Dynamics of Authoritative Leadership: Moses and Joshua; Elijah and Elisha

The narrative of Joshua's succession and the Jordan crossing is interlaced with threads that extend back into the past, coordinating Joshua with Moses. Joshua's commission comes in the context of Moses' death; his coming into leadership has been contingent on Moses vacating that position (Josh. 1:1, 2). The most immediate issue concerns Joshua's authority and the commissioning speech is quick to address it. The LORD assures Joshua that both his position as leader and portfolio as the leader of the conquest of the land are backed by him: God will be with Joshua as he was with Moses (1:5) and consequently, God will give him the land as promised to Moses (1:3).

However, Israel needs demonstration that Joshua's authority is in no way lacking when compared to Moses', and this comes out in the dialogue between Joshua and the trans-Jordan tribes. The latter express their willingness to obey Joshua just as they obeyed Moses, "Only, may the LORD your God be with you as he was with Moses (1:17). The use of רק introduces a note of hesitation. As Nelson notes: "The syntax asserts: 'A is true, but B is even more important'."[135] It usually stands between two assertions and normally signals an exception, restriction or limitation. After an affirmative statement, it

---

135. Nelson (1997), 36. The second רק in the speech is with respect to Joshua's courage, and in time, it will be Joshua who will exhort Israel with exactly the same words (Josh. 1:18; 10:25).

usually signals a strong disjunction and draws particular attention to what follows.[136] This inserts a subtle note of contingency into the pledge of obedience, Moses serving as the yardstick by which Joshua is measured. True authority requires, as Nelson rightly observes, both legal warrant and the LORD's favour, for leadership may be legitimate, yet devoid of the LORD's support, and evil.[137] With the LORD, this reservation is a serious issue, one that he duly addresses. As with Moses (Exod. 14:31), the proof of legitimisation to the people is via what Overholt calls an "act of power."[138] In the narrative of the river crossing, Joshua's position re Moses' is affirmed at the highest levels—by the LORD (Josh. 3:7) and by the narrator (4:14).

This concern with legitimacy and divine favour as regards leadership is reflected in the Elijah-Elisha narrative. Privately, Elijah is "proved" to the widow of Zarephath; in being able to restore her son to her he demonstrates himself to be a genuine "man of God" (1 Kgs 17:24). Publicly, he is "proved" to "all Israel"; at his request fire descends from heaven, demonstrating simultaneously that the LORD is God and that Elijah is the one he has chosen to serve his purposes (1 Kgs 18:36ff). 2 Kgs 2, as we have discussed in our close reading, is even more focussed in its concern to affirm Elisha as Elijah's divinely chosen successor. As with Joshua, Elisha's position is "proved" vis-à-vis Elijah's by acts of power—he replicates Elijah's miracle at the Jordan, and at Jericho his "word" proves to be as potent as Elijah's was. He is affirmed by God (in that he is granted the vision of Elijah's ascension), by the characters (in the prophetic band's declaration, and in the deferential phrasing of the request of the people of Jericho) and by the narrator (at the micro-level of words and phrases, and at the macro-level of the parallel he sets up with Moses and Joshua).

The effect of Joshua's legitimisation is initially awe, and this leads to the desired end, the obedience of Israel. The stones that Joshua sets up as memorial at the riverbed verbally recall the "pillars" Moses set up at Sinai, as we observed earlier, and the overlap between the two separate episodes is the obedience that unifies the tribes of Israel. Moses' twelve pillars stand as testimony to the covenant between a respectfully complying Israel and God (Exod. 24:3-8). Joshua's pile of twelve stones stands as memorial to the

---

136. Hawk (2000), 16.
137. Cf. Saul, contra David (1 Sam. 18:12). Nelson (1981), 538-39. Along similar lines, McCarthy argues that a theology of legitimate leadership is a concern that runs through Deuteronomistic History, the assertion being that "Yahweh accomplishes his designs through a leader he chooses and sustains." (1971¹) 175.
138. Overholt (1982), 23. Cf. Long (1977), 10-11, 15.

crossing made possible because "everything was finished that the LORD commanded Joshua to tell the people" (Josh. 4:10).

The effect of Elisha's act of power is a similar awe, demonstrated by the witnesses bowing before him. They are immediately bound by his authority, and so, would rather persuade him at length to send them rather than undertake a mission without his permission. Eventually, Elisha's authority is established in the larger community, and the symbolism of his guiding the twelve yoke of oxen translates into his directing the prophetic community, the people and kings.

Since the narrator goes to great lengths to present Joshua as a leader who is correctly and completely endorsed, the constant harking back to Moses in the telling of the story of the conquest and settlement in no way detracts from Joshua. In the run-up to the crossing itself, Moses' words and authority are recalled by God (Josh. 1:7), by the author (4:10, 12), and by Joshua himself (1:12-15; cf. Deut. 3:18-20). Towards the end of the conquest narrative, the narrator concisely portrays the synergy of the interrelationships between God, Moses and Joshua: "As the LORD had commanded his servant Moses, so Moses commanded Joshua, and so Joshua did; he left nothing undone of all that the LORD had commanded Moses." (Josh. 11:15) Rather than read a hierarchy here, one does better to appreciate a harmonious working in tandem towards the accomplishment of the great task of bringing God's people out of Egypt and into Canaan. Joshua's authority is not second-hand; he is directly commissioned by God, as much as Moses was. However, the task that Joshua brings to consummation began with Moses. Thus, like warp and weft, the process by which Canaan is taken possession of meshes the lifework of both leaders.

This corresponds remarkably with the picture the narrator presents of the interlocked missions of Elijah and Elisha, discussed in detail in our reading of 1 Kgs 19:19-21. Two of the three directives Elijah receives at Horeb become Elisha's tasks. Elijah himself is allowed but a proleptic glimpse of the extermination of Baalism and the promise of a remnant; it is through Elisha that the enemy is vanquished and the land repossessed. At every turn in the telling of this tale, Elijah is recalled, both by the characters and by narratorial comment.

Joshua, at his death, is given the same appellation as that of Moses at his death and after—"the servant of the LORD" (Josh. 24:29; Judg. 2:8; cf. Deut. 34:5). Elijah and Elisha too earn the same title at their departures—"the chariotry of Israel and its horsemen." In both cases, the identical designations function to unify the life and work of these two pairs of prophets, which is to bring the people within the covenant into possession of the land.

Another feature that may have bearing on the resonance between the characters of Joshua and Elisha is the possibility of the narrator's depiction of the figure of Joshua as essentially royal, as noted by several scholars.[139] Nelson's summary lists the major arguments in support, and of these the following may be relevant to our study:[140] (1) Joshua takes up office immediately following the death of Moses, recalling the royal pattern of smooth succession, and contrary to the charismatic pattern of judges or prophets (Josh. 1:2, cf. 1 Kgs 2:2). (2) To authenticate transfer of power, the LORD gives Joshua a special sign of favour (Josh. 3:7) and the people respond with awe (4:14), cf. Solomon (1 Kgs 2:12; 3:12-13, 28). (3) Joshua undergoes a double installation,[141] first by Moses (Deut. 31:7-8) and then by the LORD (Josh. 1:1-9).[142] A two-stage process may be claimed for Saul (1 Sam. 10:1; 10:20 ff), David (1 Sam. 16:12-13; 2 Sam. 5:1-3), Solomon (1 Kgs 1:17; 1:32 ff), Jeroboam (1 Kgs 11:29-39; 12:20) and Jehu (2 Kgs 9:6-10; 9:13). Nelson concludes: "Joshua, therefore, is pictured by Dtr as a royal figure. He could hardly have made his point clearer without committing a serious anachronism: Joshua is a sort of proto-king sketched out along the lines of the ideal deuteronomic monarch."[143] Porter notes the points listed above with respect to Elisha and concludes that the two groups Moses-Joshua and Elijah-Elisha reflect a common royal pattern.[144] Though this is arguable, the common elements in the two procedures of succession (whether derived from the royal model or otherwise) may not be denied; at least, they add to the general evocation of Elisha's literary counterpart.[145]

---

139. Östborn (1945), 65-66; Widengren (1957), 14-16; Porter (1970), 102-32.
140. Nelson (1981), 531-40.
141. Some of the texts cited to illustrate this point vary from Nelson.
142. Lind examines the various texts in Deuteronomy and Josh. 1 to conclude that "the chain of texts on the replacement of Moses by his successor, Joshua...never say the same thing...Each tells us something new...it is the sum total that constitutes the sharp and differentiated portrayal of the transfer of office." (1994), 235-36. This is true of the Elijah-Elisha case, as we have argued.
143. Nelson argues this monarch to be Josiah. (1981), 534. McCarthy argues that Josh. 1:1-9 falls into an installation genre which has most of its examples connected with Davidic monarchy. (1971²), 31-41.
144. Porter (1970), 120-21, adds two other details from Elisha's case which may carry the royal motif: the mantle, which he likens to the robe of state, properly worn by kings, cf. Montgomery (1951), 316, and the royal feature in the heavenly chariots, cf. L'Orange (1953), 48-79. See Widengren for the general possibility of features borrowed from the royal pattern in the call and appointment of prophets. (1950), 33, n.3.
145. Both may be understood as succession to a prophetic office, cf. Sir. 46:1. Even though the canonical traditions do not explicitly refer to Joshua as a prophet, one notes that he speaks the prophetic formula כה אמר יהוה (Josh. 7:13; 24:2) and 1 Kgs 16:34 records the fulfilment of "the word of the LORD, which he spoke by the hand of Joshua the son of Nun."

3.2. The War Theme in Exodus 14-15 and Joshua 1-5; Implications for 2 Kings 2

Both crossings plainly carry military themes. The Sea event is depicted as a battle. Miller identifies war vocabulary in Exod. 13-14: Israel goes out of Egypt חמשים, "in battle array" (13:18). The verb "to encamp" and its cognate "camp" are used both of Israel and the Egyptians (√חנה; 13:20; 14:2, 9, 19, 20). He acknowledges that these terms are not necessarily military, but draws attention to the balancing of the "camp of Egypt," explicitly a military encampment, with the "camp of Israel" in 14:20. 14:14 uses √לחם, "to fight/battle." "Discomfited," √המם, is a term that recurs in the later battles of Israel (14:24; e.g., Josh. 10:10; Judg. 4:15). The Egyptian call for a retreat is again a military procedure, and occurs in the context of the verb "to fight." The summary statement is in the language of victor and vanquished: "The LORD overthrew/shook off (√נער) the Egyptians in the midst of the sea" (14:27).[146] Exod. 15 so explicitly defines the event as a battle that we need not stop to examine the details; the overarching theme is the LORD as a warrior (איש מלחמה; 15:3) against whom Egypt has presumptuously taken up position as enemy (אויב; 15:6, 9).

At the Jordan, the objective of the crossing is to occupy the land, first having defeated the inhabitants; thus the trans-Jordan tribes cross over armed for battle, and a detail of their number is recorded – about forty thousand (Josh. 4:12-13). Mitchell observes that just as their joining in marks the beginning of the war, so their departure marks the end of the conquest. Symmetry is created by the wording of Josh 1:15 being echoed in 22:4, and with the account of the taking of provisions (Josh. 1:11) matched with a booty report (Josh. 22:8; a narrative marker signalling the end of a campaign).[147] He also points out the military connotations associated with √עבר: an advance by an invading army,[148] and an invasion which sometimes involved an armed crossing of the Jordan,[149] could be described thus. Further, he points out, "[c]rossing territory also means encroachment into on someone else's property and implies a claim to its ownership."[150] Therefore, "the crossing of the Jordan may be understood as a juridical act" that marks the beginning of the offensive against Canaan.[151]

---

146. Lind (1980), 54.
147. Mitchell (1993), 105-06.
148. Josh. 6:7; 2 Sam. 29; 1 Kgs 8:21; Isa. 10:28-29; Hab. 1:11; Ps. 48:5, etc. Mitchell (1993), 32.
149. Judg. 6:33; 12:1, etc. Mitchell (1993), 32.
150. Gen. 31:52; Judg. 11:18-20; 2 Sam. 19:41-43, etc. Mitchell (1993), 32.
151. Mitchell (1993), 32-33.

There are yet other elements in the military motif of these two crossings, some less obvious than others. First, the ark is presented as the locus of the LORD's power and presence among the people. In the context of goal of the mission – to dispossess the Canaanites, and inherit the land, the function of the ark as described in Num. 10:33-36 is readily recalled: "So they set out...with the ark of the covenant of the LORD going before them...to seek out a resting place (נוח√) for them...Whenever the ark set out, Moses would say, 'Arise, O LORD, let your enemies be scattered, and your foes flee before you.' And whenever it came to rest, he would say, 'Return, O LORD of the ten thousand thousands of Israel'."[152] Joshua speaks of Moses describing Canaan as "[a place of] rest" (נוח√; Josh. 1:13), and the ark itself is positioned as a scout that Israel is to follow (Josh. 3:2-4) into that rest. One recalls here, too, the defeat that befell the previous generation when they rebelled and presumed to go out to do battle "even though the ark of the covenant of the LORD...had not left the camp" (Num. 14:44-45).

Secondly, there is the discussion on whether Josh. 1:1-9 may exemplify an "installation genre," used for the installation of a person into an official role and charging him with a specific task (or set of tasks) to carry out. This genre is said to consist of three elements: an exhortation to be bold, a statement of task and an assurance of divine presence and support.[153] Rowlett argues at length that each time this schema occurs in the Deuteronomistic History, it appears in the context of military action; thus, the three-element formula finds its earliest and most complete expression as a war oracle where the warrior is commanded to be bold in executing the military task before him since divine presence and help in battle are promised, thereby assuring a victorious outcome.[154]

Thirdly, there is the schema of "holy war." On examining a spectrum of "ritual Conquest" texts and traditions, Cross concludes: "...it becomes apparent that the normal locus of holy warfare is discovered in the Exodus-Conquest..."[155]; this pairing is of interest in our discussion of the Sea and River crossings, so we visit this complex and much-debated concept briefly.

Though Schwally was one of the first of the modern scholars to examine the concept of "holy war," the classic presentation remains that of von Rad, a study which bears the stamp of form-critical concerns. Basing his investigation on the use of formulaic language

---

152. From a tradition history approach, Cross comments of this text: "Evidently these are liturgical fragments rooting in holy war ideology, used also in the re-enactment of the wars of Yahweh." (1966), 24-25.
153. E.g., McCarthy (1971²), 31-41; Porter (1970), 109-17.
154. Rowlett (1996), 122-155.
155. Cross (1966), 25.

in the text, he identified a set of features associated with "sacral warfare" of the "tribal amphictyony" stage of the pre-monarchial period. Among them are: the mustering of the tribes; the consecration of the men; the divine oracle; the formalized exhortation including assurance of divine presence; the LORD moving out ahead of the army; terror falling on the enemy; the LORD's being awarded exclusive credit for the victory; the חרם; the dismissal of the militia with the cry, "To your tents, O Israel!"[156] Since von Rad, the focus has changed from the search for a cultic institution to the search for the characterisitics of warfare conducted in the LORD's name, with or without formal cultic involvement; further, the terms "wars of Yahweh"/"Yahweh war" have been favoured over "holy war," the former terms being biblically derived (מלחמות יהוה; Num. 21:14; 1 Sam. 18:17; 25:28; cf. Exod. 17:16; 1 Sam. 17:47).[157] Still, von Rad's schema makes a reasonable checklist for rhetoric associated with warfare, sacral or otherwise (distinctions between the two being nebulous, if not non-existent), and we may use it on the narratives of the two crossings as we examine the war motif running through each.

At the Red Sea, the people are assembled into a specific campsite by the sea (Exod. 14:2, 9); the divine oracle is given, assuring victory (14:3-4, 15-18); the "angel of the LORD" goes before Israel partway before moving to the rear for tactical reasons (14:19); the Egyptians are discomfited and attempt to flee (14:24-25). As for the Jordan crossing, Miller notes that "[t]he journey of the Israelites into the land of Canaan appears to have been viewed throughout Israel's history from a very early time as the holy war or Yahweh war *par excellence*."[158] The people move from Shittim to the Jordan in preparation for the crossing; there is an emphasis on representation from all twelve tribes in that the fighting men from the trans-Jordan tribes are called to join the crossing so as to "help" their brothers (Josh. 1:12-16). The people are commanded to sanctify themselves in readiness for the event.[159] The divine oracle pronounces victory (1:2-9; 3:7). The ark, the palladium of war, associated with the LORD in eight out of the fifteen occurrences in Josh. 3-4, moves ahead (3:3-4). The opposition loses spirit (5:1).[160]

---

156. Von Rad (1958), 41-51.
157. Smend (1963); Stolz (1972); Jones (1975), 642-58.
158. Miller (1973), 160.
159. Cf. Josh. 7:13; 1 Sam. 21:6; 2 Sam. 11:11; Deut. 23:13-15. "Because the war was sacral, a sphere of activity in which Israel's God was present, the camp and the warriors had to be ritually purified." Miller (1973), 157.
160. At the end of the narrative of conquest, Joshua dismisses the fighting men from the trans-Jordan tribes with "go to your tents"—ולכו לכם לאהליכם. Cf. 1 Kgs 12:16, 2 Chron. 10:16.

Related to the concept of "holy war" is the concept of "cosmic war." Here, our narrative critical reading of texts may profit from being informed by comment from the study of the history of Israelite religion in its Canaanite context.

There is warrant for arguing that Exod. 15 is not to be read via the familiar motif of chaos, death, sea or the like. Cross and Freedman, for example, point out that the Sea is never personified in the Exodus text, rather it performs as the LORD's passive tool. The opposition is a human host, a "historically limited foe." Neither is the Song a mythologically derived conflict nor a result of "historicizing" myth.[161] On the other hand, Cross also agrees that "the ideology of holy war...was characterized by a number of cosmic elements...[which] gave mythic depth to the historical events of the Exodus and Conquest."[162] Thus, the Song of the Sea, he affirms, preserves a familiar Canaanite creation myth pattern: the combat of the divine warrior and his victory at sea, the building of a sanctuary on the mount of inheritance won in battle, and the god's manifestation of eternal kingship.[163] Miller observes that the LORD's incomparability is made vis-à-vis the "gods" (Exod. 15:11).[164] Plausibly, it is this cosmic dimension that is picked up in the retelling of these crossings in later periods, where cosmological conflict is used to describe what was conflict on a historical plane (e.g., Ps. 77:16-20; Ps. 114).[165] "It is proper," says Cross, "to speak of this...as the tendency to mythologize historical episodes to reveal their transcendent meaning."[166]

Cross also notes that the episode at the sea was chosen as symbolic of Israel's redemption and creation as a community, over other possible episodes, and specifically, myths of creation came to be identified with the historical battle in which Yahweh won salvation for Israel. This, he emphasizes, was no chance: "In choosing the event of the sea, Israel drew upon available symbols and language which retained power and meaning even when the old mythic patterns which gave them birth had been attenuated or broken by Israel's austere historical consciousness."[167]

---

161. Cross and Freedman (1955), 237-250.
162. Thus, for example, Isa. 40:3-6, which opens with an apostrophe to the arm of the Divine Warrior and with allusion to cosmogonic myth, but then is suddenly penetrated by the historical memory of the redemption from Egypt. Cross (1966), 28-29.
163. Cross (1968), 142; Cross and Freedman (1955), 240, 249-50.
164. Miller (1973), 115.
165. E.g., Geller (1990), 179-94.
166. Cross (1968), 144.
167. Cross (1968), 137-38.

It can hardly be contested that the narrative of the Jordan crossing used the episode of the Red Sea as paradigm, a recapitulation that reinforced that though it was the Jordan that was being crossed, it was the same mighty saving and guiding hand of the LORD of the Red Sea event that was bringing them through it. The overt military tenor of the river crossing would then conceptually parallel the battle at sea, and take on the latter's theme of the LORD as divine warrior. Thus, though the trans-Jordan tribes cross over armed for battle, it is "the living God who without fail will drive out" the inhabitants of the land, and the ark is guarantor and sign of this (Josh. 3:10, 11). The centrality of the LORD's role in the wars to come is climaxed in the episode of the vision (Josh. 5:13-15).

The incident happens when Joshua is ביריחו;[168] reading from the previous note that Israel was encamped on the plains of Jericho (5:10), and from the note following that Jericho was shut up (6:1), the plainest reading would place the episode in the region of Jericho, and chronologically at the start of the campaign. A man stands before Joshua with a drawn sword, and the latter's question—"Are you one of us, or one of our adversaries?"—suggests some ambiguity to the vision. Miller considers it significant that the being identifies himself with a very specific and unusual designation, different from the more familiar מלאך יהוה, the "angel of the LORD." This שׂר צבא יהוה "links the heavenly cosmic army with Israel's earliest holy wars."[169]

There are multiple indicators towards the possibility that the vision is a manifestation of divine presence, and though each in itself need not necessarily indicate deity, their cumulative effect does move the interpretation in that direction: Joshua falls facedown to the ground and pays homage; he addresses the vision as "my lord" and positions himself as his "servant"; the place is rendered holy by the presence of the being and this demands that Joshua, like Moses before him, must take off his shoe. This last takes the reader back to the parallel episode in Exod. 3, and the reader notes that there, the distinction between messenger and the LORD is blurred to the point of disappearing altogether.

The commander's לא may be rendered a positive "Indeed!" reading with an emphatic lamedh; it would then answer positively the first half of Joshua's question, that is, הלנו אתה אם לצרינו, and would be implicitly negative with respect to the second half of the question.[170] Or, the לא could be read as a negative, and mean

---

168. We are considering here only those readings that see this section as not necessarily incomplete.
169. Miller (1973), 131. Cf. Josh. 10:12-13a; Judg. 5:20. שׂר הצבא is found elsewhere only in Dan. 8:11.
170. E.g., Soggin (1972), 76-78.

"Neither one!" since the shape of Joshua's question gives two mutually exclusive choices. This answer would show the commander as representing a third force, namely, the army of the LORD, in the conflict to come; this independent and neutral party will judge which side to support in the coming battles.[171]

The general agreement is that this episode, though enigmatic, serves the literary purpose of marking the start of and authorizing the hostilities in Canaan, and may even be read as a guarantee of its success, should the divine host align itself with Israel. The drawn sword speaks of combat readiness; the forces of the LORD have already been mobilized. [172]

Thus, in both narratives, the LORD is the key actor. He dominates the story both directly and with reference to the theologoumena of cloud or ark,[173] he sets the agenda and pronounces the oracles, the decisive action is his, and the miraculous nature of the event makes redundant any human role. The events are described, in fact, as נפלאות (Exod. 15:11; Josh. 3:5), the word used of all that befalls Egypt before Pharaoh finally lets Israel go (Exod. 3:20), and of the deeds that the LORD will do to put Israel in possession of Canaan (Exod. 34:10). The LXX translates with אתסמאָק, which Soggin observes "is often used for miracles when they provoke the reactions of astonishment and marvelling" thus putting the emphasis on the supranormal nature of the event.[174] Thus, victory is not by might of numbers and weapons but by terror (אימה: Exod. 15:16, cf. Exod. 23:27 f; Josh. 2:9) and dread (פחד: Exod. 15:16, cf. Deut. 2:25; 11:25), establishing among the nations the LORD's supremacy.

It is clear, then, that there is a discernible "cosmic" undertone to the two narratives, though always subordinate to and fused with the more political, historical aspect of the Warrior God's activity,

---

171. E.g., Nelson (1997), 73-74; Boling and Wright (1982), 197. Thus, Israel succeeds at Jericho (Josh. 6) and is defeated at Ai (Josh. 7). Hawk arrives at this reading from a third angle. He sees the לא as evasive, in that it constitutes a refusal to choose between two alternatives. What he finds most significant is what is *not* said following the command re shoes. The identical command in Exod. 3 had been followed by comment on Israel's occupation of Canaan (3:8). Since the speech here is terminated at precisely that part which pertains to the present situation, Hawk sees in this failure to affirm the promise of the land, taken with the commander's refusal to commit for Israel, an ambiguity re the LORD's position in the conflict. Thus, the wars to come will be the LORD's wars for the LORD's own purposes. Hawk (1991), 21-24.
172. E.g., Nelson (1997), 83; Woudstra (1981), 106.
173. Lind makes a case counting up the number of times the various characters are mentioned in the narratives of the crossings. (1980), 58-59, 81.
174. Soggin (1972), 57.

namely, the defeat of Israel's enemies. Miller sums up the concept vis-à-vis the Canaanite context:

> By and large, there existed a separation between the historical battles of the kings aided by the god or gods and the mythological battles of the gods against the gods. The gods acted to save men, but at the centre of the religious concern was the battle for order over chaos, life over death, fertility over sterility. At the center of Israel's faith, however, lay the battle for Israel's deliverance, a conflict involving the theophany of Yahweh and his mighty armies to fight with and for Israel. This encounter took place on a definitely historical level, but the forces of the cosmos were involved. Insofar as the mythological battle of the gods existed in normative Yahwism it was brought into this complex.[175]

This is the rationale for the prime place that these two crossings occupied in the national consciousness—as embodied by the memorials (e.g., Josh. 4) and by liturgy (e.g., Exod. 15). In both categories, the conceptual linkage is made between the event of the sea and that of the river: the stone piles set up in Josh 4 stand testimony to the fact that the LORD acted on behalf of a later generation just as he had for the one that participated in the Red Sea miracle (v.20-23); in liturgy (e.g., Ps. 66:6; 114:3, 5), as Nelson observes, the correlation extends beyond the typological to the mythic as a mode of affirming that the Jordan crossing was a prototypical and foundational event for Israel.[176] Thus, even though the Jordan event is rarely found in confessional summaries other than Josh. 24:11 and Ps. 114,[177] Micah 6:5 puts the events that transpired between Shittim and Gilgal on a par with the Sea crossing by counting them among the LORD's "saving acts" (צדקות יהוה; cf. 1 Sam. 12:7).

These are the many nuances that are evoked when the narrator of 2 Kgs 2 embeds his story into the matrix of the two great crossings in Israelite history. The fiery chariotry of the theophany presents the LORD in his established function as a man of war, and gathers together the many implications of the hostilities between the LORD and Baal in the narrative thus far; here, discernible to the human eye, are the symbols of the יהוה צבאות whom Elijah has thrice invoked. The enemy has been routed once at Carmel, and now may expect a final, decisive defeat by the swords of two kings and a prophet. If on a "cosmic" level that enemy is Baal,[178] on the ground, it is those

---

175. Miller (1973), 164-65.
176. Nelson (1997), 71.
177. See Thomson (1981), 346.
178. There is much comment on the possible polemic against the Baal myths in the Elijah-Elisha corpus. As regards the story in 2 Kgs 2, Bronner (1968), reads hints of a polemic against Baal in the ascension of Elijah. She argues

knees that bow to Baal and those lips that kiss his image. Miller rightly reminds:

> Judgement...is the other side of the coin, the negative dimension of the activity of the divine warrior. As he fought for Israel to deliver her, so he could and did fight against her to punish. The prophets especially drew this obvious conclusion from Israel's theology. And it was this important assumption that kept the theology of Yahweh's wars from being purely ideological or a naïve and simple 'God is on our side' faith. To speak about the judgement of God in the Old Testament is to be confronted again with the imagery of the divine warrior.[179]

The divine warrior intervenes in history, as at the Red Sea and in the Conquest, with salvific intent; here, he saves a faithful remnant. The end point of that salvation is regularly God's people dwelling in the land promised to their ancestors. Thus, the Red Sea crossing, and more pointedly, the Jordan crossing, had as its key purpose the occupation of Canaan. "[T]he Jordan," comments Soggin, "is not any river but the traditional frontier of the promised land to the east, which is now crossed in order to take possession of this land. Thus the crossing of the river is synonymous with the conquest and the beginning of the fulfilment of ancient promises."[180] In this context, Elisha's miraculous crossing becomes the symbol that anticipates the victory promised at Horeb, whereby God's people will once more possess the land and dwell in safety. Joshua's military associations and the militant nature of the task he succeeds to colour Elisha's "inheritance."[181]

---

that √רכב can mean "to ascend." This may be used in allusion to Baal, the one who mounts clouds. However, unlike Elijah, he dies, and again unlike Elijah whose body cannot be located, his is found lying on the earth. 123-27. Again, she reads the miracle of the parting of the Jordan by Elijah and Elisha as polemical; Baal too splits a river. 127-33. Also, Battenfield (1988), 19-37; Miller (1973), 24-48.

179. Miller (1973), 173-74.
180. Soggin (1972), 54.
181. Moore finds in the Elisha stories a store of detail that fits with the schema of "holy"/"cosmic" war: Elisha's "Fear not, for those who are with us are more than those who are with them" to his servant (2 Kgs 6:16) can be identified with the language and function of the holy-war call to faith." The divinely-wrought deliverance that follows is the tradition's most essential characteristic, one that is repeated in the story of the Aramean siege (2 Kgs 7). In the latter, the sudden panic of the army is another distinctive feature of the schema. In the Moabite war a formulaic oracle is delivered and an enemy-confounding miracle occurs (2 Kgs 3). Joash is awarded a battle oracle (2 Kgs 13). (1990), 132-34.

As in the former events, the "unique relationship of the Israelite prophet to Yahweh's holy war" is asserted in that the prophet-leader, "as God's messenger dare[s] to engage the enemy political leader";[182] Elijah has done as much, and Elisha will follow. Victory is possible because the Divine Warrior, the LORD of Hosts, participates side by side with the prophet. The Jordan crossing by Joshua had had as one of its purposes the demonstration that God was with Joshua (Josh. 3:7). Elisha's question—"Where is the LORD…?"—is answered to say that the LORD is with Elisha.

The historical and liturgical dimensions appealed to in the 2 Kgs 2 narrative dramatically and unambiguously extrapolate into the present, with pointed relevance, the ancient and celebrated triumphs of Israel. Since these triumphs rest on the legal and promissory relations between the LORD and Israel, their being recalled, at this point in the Elijah-Elisha stories, anticipates an ultimate deliverance from the bondage of Baalism and the possession of the land by the faithful.

4. Conclusion

2 Kgs 2 skilfully treats two important themes, that of the ascension of Elijah and that of the succession of Elisha, with impeccable impartiality. Thus the narrator achieves the twin ends of according Elijah a departure that pointedly glorifies his life work as Israel's great defence, and assuring that Elijah has been replaced by a fully worthy successor. Simultaneously, the narrative sets up resonance with the great historical paradigm of continuity in discontinuity re leadership, that of Moses and Joshua. This is accomplished using as axis the defining experiences in the history of Israel under these leaders, namely the crossing of the Red Sea and the Jordan. This automatically imports into the 2 Kgs 2 narrative the salvific overtones so relevant to faithful Israel in her critical struggle against another enemy, this time from within. The story of the transition from Elijah to Elisha speaks the hope that as at that key era when Israel was forged into a landed nation against daunting odds, the LORD of Hosts has raised up leaders through whom he will repeat that ancient, miraculous victory.

---

182. Miller (1973), 63.

CHAPTER 7

Is Elijah a Prophet Like Moses?

Standing back from our close reading of the texts, we study the larger picture, to see how it informs us on the question that directed this study: is, and if so, how is, Elijah a prophet like Moses? To aid the exercise, we set out the full contours of the resonance, as we have argued it. In this, we cannot avoid a mix of levels; considering the key nature of the conceptual parallels, we will emphasize these over the verbal and story level resonances.

The Elijah Stories

1 Kings 16:29-34-18:19
1. Ahab's forsaking of the LORD invites drought on Israel; he continues resistant to correction.

2. Elijah confronts Ahab; hides at Cherith.

3. Elijah is miraculously sustained with bread and meat in the wilderness.

4. Elijah mediates the miracle of the oil and flour, enabling the household to survive the drought.

1 Kings 18
1. All Israel is assembled at a mountain, Carmel.

2. The issue is covenant loyalty, as evidenced by
- the accusation against Ahab (17:18)

The Moses Stories

Exodus 2; 5-14; 16
Pharaoh puts Israel in bondage; later, his refusal to acknowledge the LORD brings plagues on his people.

Moses resists the establishment, and incurs Pharaoh's wrath; He flees to Midian (2:11-15).

Israel is fed with manna and quails in the desert (Exod. 16).

Elijah's miracle verbally echoes the description of manna (Num. 11:8), the staple of the nation's wilderness years.

Exodus 19-20; 24
All Israel is assembled at a mountain, Horeb (Exod. 19).

The issue is covenant making, as seen in

- the symbolic altar of 12 stones (18:31-32)	- the altar and symbolic 12 pillars (24:4)
- the possible covenant-sealing ritual meal by Ahab (18:41-42).	- the ritual meal by the institutional representatives (24:9-11).
3. Elijah sets out the choice between the LORD and Baal.	Moses is instructed to proscribe the worship of other gods alongside the LORD (20:23).
4. Elijah mediates between the LORD and Israel, the former making himself known in a fire that "eats" (√אכל).	Moses mediates between God in the "devouring (√אכל) fire" and Israel (19:18; 20:18ff; 24:17)
5. Israel confesses allegiance to the LORD in words identical to Elijah's, implying their acceptance of his authority as God's representative.	Israel confesses acceptance of and obedience to the covenant with God as laid out by Moses (Exod. 24:3-7).
6. The theophany proves - that the LORD is God alone, vis-à-vis Baal	The theophany is - sufficient reason for Israel to serve the LORD alone (Ex. 20:2-4; 22-23)
- that Elijah is his obedient servant.	- affirmation of Moses' position as the LORD's representative (19:9).
1 Kings 19 1. Israel returns to apostasy (as divinely judged in vv.17-18).	**Exodus 32-34** Israel turns to another god (32:1).
2. The crown and Baalist Israel seek Elijah's life (vv.1, 10, 14).	Israel dismisses Moses as prophet/leader (32:1).
3. Elijah is discouraged by failure and desires to die (v.4).	Moses desires to die if he should fail to obtain Israel's pardon (32:32).
4. Elijah presents sinful Israel before the the LORD at Horeb (v.10).	Moses presents sinful Israel before LORD at Horeb (32:30-34).
5. The LORD uses a personal theophany to propose symbolically that he should reciprocally forsake Israel (vv.11-12).	The LORD proposes to withdraw his Presence from among Israel (33:1-6); Moses requests, and is

	granted, a personal theophany (33:19-34:7).
6. The LORD invites feedback from Elijah (v.13b).	The LORD involves Moses in deciding what he should do with Israel (32:10; 33:5).
7. Elijah returns the conversation to pre-proposal stage, in effect rejecting the proposal, and pressing for an alternative for Israel (v.14).	Moses refuses the LORD's proposal, and presses for an alternative (33: 12-16; 34:8).
8. The LORD presents an alternative operation of the covenant—a remnant "Israel" within Israel (vv.15-18).	The LORD renews his covenant with Israel, with a new element of dependence on Moses (34:10-28).
9. Elijah's prophetic authority in Israel is affirmed by Elisha's response to his mantle (vv.19-21).	Moses' prophetic authority in Israel is affirmed by the people's response to his shining face (34:29-35).

2 Kings 1
Faint echoes of Moses here, in that Elijah is once more on a mountaintop, is pitted against the crown and militia, and is theophanically affirmed as the LORD's representative.

2 Kings 2
Regarding succession, we note that the Moses-Joshua and Elijah-Elisha prophetic succession narratives are the only two of their kind in the OT. Key comparable features are:

	Deuteronomy 34; Joshua 1-6
1. Elijah leaves with his mission against Baalism only partly completed; Elisha carries it to the finish.	Moses dies while Israel is still to enter Canaan; it falls to Joshua to complete this leadership task (Deut. 34).
2. Elijah's "spirit" rests on his successor, Elisha.	Moses' "spirit" may likewise be imparted (Num. 11:16-30); he mediates the "spirit of wisdom" to his successor Joshua (Deut. 34:9).

3. Elisha's first miracle replicates Elijah's parting of the Jordan; with this, the prophetic community accepts him as legitimate successor to Elijah.	Joshua's first miracle recalls Moses' parting of the Red Sea; with this, all Israel accepts him as worthy successor to Moses (Josh. 4:14).
4. The circumstances of the investiture have "holy/cosmic war" overtones, viz., the vision of heavenly chariots.	Joshua's task is clearly military; this is enhanced by the "holy/cosmic war" connotation at the outset of hostilities, viz., the encounter with the commander of the LORD's host (Josh. 5:13-15).
5. Post Jordan, Elisha opens his prophetic career with a miracle in Jericho.	Post Jordan, Joshua begins the conquest of Canaan with the miraculous victory over Jericho (Josh. 6).

As relates to the exits of Moses and Elijah:

	Deuteronomy 32; 34
1. Elijah is aware of the day and place of his departure.	Moses is informed of the time and place of his death (Deut. 32: 48-50).
2. Elijah leaves the earth from the wilds east of the Jordan, across from Jericho.	Moses dies and is buried in the mountains east of the Jordan, across from Jericho (Deut. 32:49; 34:1).
3. The LORD takes Elijah up in a whirlwind; he is never seen again.	The LORD commands Moses' death and buries him; the whereabouts of the grave are unknown (Deut. 34:5-6).

As comment on this table, we borrow Walsh's conclusion on his own brief comparison of the geographical, and the life-and-work frameworks of Elijah and Moses: "The congruence of the frameworks shows that we are to compare the whole Elijah story with the whole Moses story, not simply the isolated episodes alluded to in the individual narratives about Elijah." Walsh continues: "In other words, Moses is the paradigm by which Elijah is to be measured." Whether this is the intention of the resonance it is not possible to be dogmatic about, but the setting up of parallels does invite comparison. Indeed, the extraordinary and exceptional intertextuality between these two sets of prophetic narratives warrants Walsh's question: "Is Elijah, in the words of Deuteronomy 18:15-19, the 'prophet like Moses' whom Yahweh promised to raise up?"[1]

Walsh's answer is representative. He agrees that through 1 Kgs 17-18 "Elijah corresponds quite closely to the Moses paradigm," in that he and those in his care are miraculously provisioned, in that he intercedes for both individuals and all Israel, and in that he mediates a powerful theophany which becomes the basis of a covenant renewal. In 1 Kgs 19, he argues, the parallels become contrasts. While Moses' complaints of solitude are tied to his leadership role, Elijah's preoccupation is with himself; while Moses intercedes for Israel, Elijah accuses them; the personal theophany granted Moses (Ex. 33-34) is a scene of cooperation and harmony, while with Elijah it is one of stubborn resistance between God and a prophet who desires to abandon his ministry.[2] This view is in line with that of the literary critics we have engaged with at length in the course of arguing our thesis, for example, Provan, Fretheim, Robinson, Nelson, DeVries, Brueggemann and Hauser; all are agreed that at Horeb Elijah's prophetic career is at its ebb. Robinson is particularly articulate in his criticism of Elijah as a "latterday Moses": "He is a figure devoured by egotism...a *propheta gloriosus*...He falls far short of Moses' example." The LORD dismisses Elijah, "not interested in continuing to employ this tetchy and arrogant prima donna of a prophet...the future lies with Hazael, Jehu and Elisha." "Elijah has Mosaic aspirations, does he?" asks Robinson. "Well, has he forgotten that Moses, great prophet as he was, was removed from the scene before the climax of the Exodus story was reached, and had to hand over the leadership to another...? In this respect at least he resembles Moses."[3]

However, as Walsh commends, any assessment of Elijah as a second Moses would require us to compare the "whole Elijah story with the whole Moses story." That comparison, when plotted, yields an uneven graph. 1 Kgs 17 and the first half of chapter 18 are, at most, preparatory. The parallels begin to pick up with the Carmel episode, but undeniably, it is at 1 Kgs 19 that the resonance peaks, following which it falls away with chapter 21 and 2 Kgs 1. The second peak, again undisputed, is at 2 Kgs 2, on which point the narrative ends.

If we follow the proposal that the first peak, namely the Horeb episode, discredits Elijah, we run into problems with respect to the immediate context, the context of the Elijah cycle and the wider context of Mosaic resonance. First, as concerns the episode itself,

---

1. Walsh (1996), 287.
2. Walsh (11996), 287-88.
3. Robinson (1991), 528-30, 535.

there is the matter of the reliability of the character, the LORD, which is of course, in Hebrew narrative, absolute. The reader notes the LORD's radical action on Elijah's presentation of Israel's sin; he proposes a bloody purge so as to birth an Israel within Israel. This moves the reader to appreciate that the narrator embeds Elijah's reliability in the absolute reliability of God, and to rethink a negative evaluation of Elijah.

Secondly, as regards the larger narrative, any unreliability on the part of Elijah at Horeb must be reconciled at multiple points with the narrative that follows, namely, the high-profile commissions he is entrusted with; his return to business as usual in faithfully discharging his duty in confronting Ahab (1 Kgs 21) and more powerfully, Ahaziah (2 Kgs 1); and, the undeniable commendation granted him by way of his departure. Especially considering that there is no mention of any rehabilitation, one questions that there was any act by which the prophet discredited himself in the first place.

Thirdly, as concerns the intertexuality with the Moses stories, there is the issue of penalty for bad behaviour, particularly stringent as regards Moses. The divine displeasure Moses incurs over a single act debars him from carrying his commission to completion. If Elijah, in his capacity as prophet, has twice misrepresented Israel at Horeb, surely this qualifies him for reprimand, if not outright dismissal. That none is forthcoming either from the LORD or the narrator weakens the case against him.

Thus, what contrasts are depicted in 1 Kgs 19 apply to the contexts rather than to the prophetic characters; that is, the phenomena of the Exodus theophany (Exod. 19-20) unambiguously portend the presence of the LORD, but the earthquake, wind and fire of 1 Kgs 19 are explicitly empty of his presence; the קול of Exodus comes in the context of God covenanting himself to Israel, but the קול of Kings is set in the context of God proposing to abandon the covenant. However, as concerns the characters Moses and Elijah, we conclude that the Horeb episode, peaking the resonance chart as it does, does not contrast Elijah with Moses, but rather climaxes the build up of the similarity. There are several ways to argue for this.

First, from the resonance graph vis-à-vis the plot progression: the reader would expect Carmel to make a natural resting point for the Mosaic comparisons being drawn, especially since it resolves the rain issue with which the plot opened. However the peak of the resonance lies beyond Carmel, at Horeb, and this alerts the reader that *this* is where the climax lies, as far as the setting up of parallels is concerned. It is here that the defining strokes of a Moses *redivivus* are painted. Once the narrator establishes Elijah as a second Moses, he continues with two other stories of his prophetic authority, building up to a second peak in resonance. It is the Horeb depiction of Elijah that legitimises this final representation of him, east of the Jordan. Without the affirmative parallelism drawn at Horeb, 2 Kgs 2 would be too extravagant a compliment when paid to a would-be Moses who failed the crucial test for a prophet, namely, that of prioritising Israel over self.

Secondly, when the frameworks of the two sets of narratives are set side by side, the Carmel story, with its themes of confession and covenant renewal, is seen to evoke Exod. 19-20, 24. Though the Horeb story also recalls elements from this stretch of the Moses narratives, the themes that dominate the Horeb story belong to Exod. 32-34, namely, the themes of a backslidden and covenant-breaking Israel, a prophet's personal theophany at Horeb, and an angry God announcing punishment on a catastrophic level. Israel's story in the Exodus texts turns on the covenant—its making, breaking and coming back into operation. If this is the story template for 1 Kgs 19, then the demand is for Elijah's profile to match Moses' re the task of reconciling Israel with God. Since the Horeb episode does conclude with the covenant in operation with the true Israel within Israel, it may be argued that Elijah is set up in favourable comparison, rather than contrast, with Moses.

Thirdly, one considers the relevance of the Exodus event in the telling of this story. Fishbane argues the exodus motif as "one that emphasizes the temporal-historical paradigm in whose image all future restorations of the nation are to be manifest." Kept alive through historical sermons, national liturgies and individual prayers, "a more penetrating means of preserving the exodus in national consciousness was its reuse as a literary motif" especially "as a hedge against despair and a catalyst towards renewed hope."[4] The Omride rule under Ahab, strengthened by its Sidonian connection, not only plumbed the depths of apostasy, but more dangerously, also intended the wiping out of Yahwism—the permanent alienation of Israel from their covenanted God. The narrator, it would appear, seizes this story of kings, prophets (named and anonymous), people, God and gods and, within the parameters of a regnal chronicle, tells it in the fashion of Israel's deliverance story *par excellence*. In such a tale, told for such a need, the likelihood is that the resonances with the transhistorical paradigm would be strongest where that resonance spells hope. Thus, setting up Elijah as a prophet like Moses, especially at Horeb, is a step in this direction, as is recording Elijah's departure from the Transjordan.

To conclude: the Elijah narratives portray a prophet who models Deut. 18:18—"I will raise up for them a prophet like you from among their brethren; and I will put my words in his mouth, and he

---

4. Fishbane (1979), 121-22.

shall speak to them all that I command him." Elijah obediently represents the LORD, be it to hostile kings or a contrary people; is fiercely zealous for the sanctity of the covenant; intercedes for and protects sinful Israel; and departs in a blaze of divine approval. To the reader who responds to the richly nuanced resonance of this prophetic narrative with the Exodus stories, it appears that Kings recreates for a new generation in dire need of deliverance—from their own king and from their own waywardness—a prophet like Moses.

Appendix

Piska 4.2, *Pesikta Rabbati*. Translated by William G. Braude. Vol. 1. Yale Judaica Series 18. London: Yale Univ. Press. 1968.

R. Tanhuma Berabbi began his discourse as follows: *And by a prophet the* Lord *brought Israel out of Egypt* (Hos. 12:14), that prophet being Moses; *and by a prophet he was preserved* (*ibid.*)—that is, by Elijah.
You find that two Prophets rose up for Israel out of the tribe of Levi; one the first of all the Prophets, and the other the last of all the Prophets: Moses first and Elijah last, and both with a commission from God to redeem Israel: Moses, with his commission, redeemed them from Egypt, as is said *Come now, therefore, and I will send thee unto Pharaoh* (Exod. 3:10). And in the time-to-come, Elijah, with his commission, will redeem them, as is said *Behold, I will send you Elijah the prophet* (Mal. 3:23). As with Moses, who in the beginning redeemed them out of Egypt, they did not return to slavery again in Egypt; so with Elijah, after he will have redeemed them out of the fourth exile, out of Edom, they will not return and be enslaved—theirs will be an eternal deliverance.

You find that Moses and Elijah were alike in every respect: Moses was a prophet; Elijah was a prophet. Moses was called *man of God* (Deut. 33:1); and Elijah was called *man of God* (1 Kings 17:18). Moses went up to heaven: *And Moses went up to God* (Exod. 19:3); and Elijah went up to heaven, as it is said *And it came to pass when Elijah would go up...into heaven* (2 Kings 2:1). Moses slew the Egyptian; and Elijah slew Hiel, as it is said *But when [Hiel] became guilty through Baal, he died* (Hos. 13:1). Moses was sustained by a woman, by the daughter of Jethro: *Call him, that he may eat bread* (Exod. 2:20); and Elijah was sustained by the woman of Zarephath in Zidon: *Bring me, I pray thee, a morsel of bread* (1 Kings 17:11). Moses fled from the presence of Pharaoh; and Elijah fled from the presence of Jezebel. Moses fled and came to a well; and Elijah fled and came to a well, as it is written *he arose, and went...and came to Beer-sheba* [the well of Sheba] (1 Kings 19:3). Moses: *And the cloud covered him six days* (Exod. 24:16); and Elijah went up in a whirlwind: *And it came to pass, when the Lord would take up Elijah by a whirlwind* (2 Kings 2:1). The power of Moses: *If these men die the common death of all men,* etc (Num. 16:29); and the power of Elijah: *As the Lord, the God of Israel, liveth, before whom I stand, there shall not be dew not rain these years, but according to my word* (1 Kings 17:1). Of Moses: *And the Lord passed by before him* (Exod. 34:6); and of Elijah: *And, behold the Lord passed by* (1 Kings 19:13). Moses gathered Israel about Mount Sinai; and Elijah gathered them about Mount Carmel.

Moses exterminated idolaters: *Put ye every man his sword upon his thigh,* etc. (Exod. 32:27); and Elijah exterminated idolatry, when he seized the prophets of Baal and slew them. Moses was zealous for the Lord: *Whoso is on the Lord's side, let him come unto me* (Exod. 32:26); and Elijah was zealous for the Lord: *Elijah said unto all the people: "Come near, I pray ye, unto me"...And he repaired the altar of the Lord that was thrown down* (1 Kings 18:30). Moses hid in a cave: *I will put thee in a cleft of the rock* (Exod. 33:22); and Elijah hid in a cave, spending a night there: *And he came unto a cave, and lodged there* (1 Kings 19:9). Of Moses: *he...came to the mountain of God* (Exod. 3:1); and of Elijah: *And came to...the mount of God* (1 Kings 19:8). Moses went to Horeb, and Elijah went to Horeb. Moses went into the wilderness: *He led the flock to the farthest end of the wilderness* (Exod. 3:1); and Elijah went into the wilderness: *But he himself went into the wilderness* (1 Kings 19:5). Moses spent forty days and forty nights, during which he did not eat and did not drink; so too, Elijah *went in the strength of that meal forty days* (1 Kings 19:8). Moses made the orb of the sun stand still: *by means of this day will I begin to put the dread of thee...upon the peoples that are under the heaven* (Deut. 2:25); and Elijah made the orb of the sun stand still; *By means of this day let it be known that thou art God in Israel* (1 Kings 18:36). Moses prayed in [sic] behalf of Israel: *Destroy not Thy people and Thine inheritance* (Deut. 9:26); and Elijah prayed in [sic] behalf of Israel: *Hear me, O Lord, hear me...for Thou didst turn their heart backward* (1 Kings 18:37). Moses, when he prayed in [sic] behalf of Israel, seized upon the merit of the Fathers: *Remember Abraham, Isaac and Israel* (Exod. 32:13); so, too, Elijah: *O Lord, the God of Abraham, of Isaac, and of Israel* (1 Kings 18:36). Moses—through him Israel accepted love for God, saying: *All that the Lord hath spoken we will do, and obey* (Exod. 24:7); and Elijah— through him they accepted love for God, saying: *The Lord, He is God* (1 Kings 18:39). Moses made the Tabernacle in an area in which two sĕ' ah of seed might be sown; and Elijah made a trench about the altar in an area in which two sĕ' ah measure of seed might be sown.

In only one way do we find Moses presented as greater than Elijah. For God said to Moses: *But as for thee, stand thou here by Me* (Deut. 5:28); whereas God said to Elijah: *What doest thou here, Elijah?* (1 Kings 19:9).

Moses brought down fire; and Elijah brought down fire. Moses— when he brought down fire, all Israel stood by and saw it, as is said *There came a fire from before the Lord...which, when all the people saw, they shouted* (Lev. 9:24); and Elijah, when he brought down fire, all Israel stood by and saw it: *When all the people saw it, they fell on their faces* (1 Kings 18:39). Moses built an altar; and Elijah built an altar. Moses called the altar by the name of the Lord: *Moses...called the name of it Adonai-nissi* (Exod. 17:15); and Elijah—the name of his altar was the Lord: *And with twelve stones he built an altar in the name of the Lord* (1 Kings 18:32). Moses, when he built the altar, built it with twelve stones, according to the number of the children of Israel; and Elijah, when he built the altar, built it according to the number of the Tribes of Israel, as is said *And Elijah took twelve stones,* etc (1 Kings 18:32).

Bibliography

Primary Sources

A. Biblical

BHS   *Biblia Hebraica Stuttgartensia.* K. Elliger and W. Rudolph (eds). Stuttgart: Deutsche Bibelgesellschaft. 1997.
LXX   *Septuaginta.* A. Rahlfs (ed.). Stuttgart: Deutsche Bibelgesellschaft. 1979.
NRSV   *The Holy Bible: New Revised Standard Version.* Oxford: Oxford Univ. Press. 1989.

B. Other

Dionysius
1937   *The Roman Antiquities of Dionysius of Halicarnassus.* Translated by Earnest Cary. Vol. 1. London/ Cambridge, Mass.: Wm. Heinemann/ Harvard Univ. Press.

Josephus
1926-65   *Josephus.* Translated by H. St. J. Thackeray et al. 10 vols. LCL. Cambridge: Harvard Univ. Press/London: Heinemann.

Philo
1993   *The Works of Philo.* Translated by C. D. Yonge. New updated edn. USA: Hendrickson.

Pseudepigrapha
1985   *The Old Testament Pseudepigrapha.* Translated by James H. Charlesworth. Vol. 2. London: Darton, Longman and Todd.

Pseudo-Philo
1971   *Liber Antiquitatum Biblicarum.* Translated by M. R. James. The Library of Biblical Studies. New York: Ktav.

Sophocles
1982   *Oedipus at Colonus* in *The Three Theban Plays.* Translated by Robert Fagles. London: Allen Lane.

Talmud
1935   *The Babylonian Talmud: Seder Nezikin, Sanhedrin I.* Translated by I. Epstein. London: Soncino.
1938   *The Babylonian Talmud: Seder Mo'ed.* Translated by I. Epstein. London: Soncino.
1948   *The Babylonian Talmud: Seder Kodashim, Hullin I.* Translated by I. Epstein. London: Soncino.
1963   *The Babylonian Talmud: Seder Nashim.* Translated by I. Epstein. London: Soncino.

Targums
1987 *Targum Jonathan of the Former Prophets*. Daniel J. Harrington and Anthony J. Saldarini (eds). The Aramaic Bible. Vol. 10. Edinburgh: T & T Clark.
1988 *The Targum Onqelos to Exodus*. Bernard Grossfeld (ed.). The Aramaic Bible. Vol. 7. Edinburgh: T & T Clark.
1991 *The Targums of Job, Proverbs, Qoheleth*. Céline Mangan, O. P., John F. Healey, Peter S. Knobel (eds). The Aramaic Bible. Vol. 15. Edinburgh: T & T Clark.
1994 *Targum Neofiti 1: Exodus*. Martin McNamara and Robert Hayward (eds). *Targum Pseudo-Jonathan: Exodus*. Michael Maher (ed.). The Aramaic Bible. Vol. 2. Edinburgh: T & T Clark.

Other Judaica
1968 *Pesikta Rabbati*. Translated by William G. Braude. Vol. 1. Yale Judaica Series 18. New Haven: Yale Univ. Press.
1987 *Sifre to Deuteronomy: An Analytical Translation*. Jacob Neusner. Vol. 2. Brown Judaic Studies 101. Atlanta, Ga.: Scholars.

Secondary Sources

Ackerman, Susan
1993 "The Queen Mother and the Cult in Ancient Israel," *JBL* 112:385-401.
Aejmelaeus, Anneli
1986 "Function and Interpretation of כי in Biblical Hebrew," *JBL* 105:193-209.
Albrecht, Karl
1896 "Das Geschlecht der hebräischen Hauptworter," *ZAW* 16:41-121.
Allen, R. B.
1979 "Elijah the Broken Prophet," *J Ev Th Soc* 22:195-201.
Alsop, John E.
1985 "Atonement," in Paul J. Achtemeier (ed.), *Harper's Bible Dictionary*. USA, San Francisco: Harper and Row. P. 80.
Alt, Albrecht
1966 "The Monarchy in the Kingdoms of Israel and Judah," in Albrecht Alt, *Essays on Old Testament History and Religion*. Translated by R. A. Wilson. Oxford: Basil Blackwell. Pp. 239-59.
Alter, Robert
1981 *The Art of Biblical Narrative*. USA: Basic Books.
1996 *Genesis*. London: W. W. Norton.
1999 *The David Story*. New York: W. W. Norton.
Appler, Deborah A.
1999 "From Queen to Cuisine: Food Imagery in the Jezebel Narrative," *Sem* 86:55-71.
Ap-Thomas, D. R.
1960 "Elijah on Mount Carmel," *PEQ* 92:146-55.
1970 "All the King's Horses?," in J. I. Durham and J. R. Porter (eds), *Proclamation and Presence: Old Testament Essays in Honour of Gwynne*

Henton Davies. London: SCM. Pp. 135-151.

Arndt, William F. and F. Wilbur Gingrich
1957 *A Greek-English Lexicon of the New Testament and other Early Christian Literature. A translation and adaptation of Walter Bauer's Griechisch-Deutsches Worterbuch zu den Schriften des Neuen Testaments und der übrigen urchristlichen Literatur.* 4th ed. Cambridge: Cambridge Univ. Press/Chicago: Univ. of Chicago Press.

Arnold, William R.
1905 "The Word פָּרָשׁ in the Old Testament," *JBL* 24:45-53.

Ashley, Timothy R.
1993 *The Book of Numbers.* NICOT. Grand Rapids, Mich.: Eerdmans.

Auld, A. Graeme
1994 *Kings Without Privilege.* Edinburgh: T & T Clark.

Bailey, R. C.
1990 *David in Love and War. The Pursuit of Power in 2 Samuel 10-12.* JSOTSup 75. Sheffield: Sheffield Acad. Press.

Bakon, Shimon
2001 "Elisha the Prophet," *JBQ* 29:242-48.

Balentine, Samuel
1983 *The Hidden God: The Hiding of the Face of God in the Old Testament.* Oxford: Oxford Univ. Press.

Bar-Efrat, Shimon
1989 *Narrative Art in the Bible.* Sheffield: Almond.

Barr, J.
1963 "Expiation," in James Hastings (ed.), *Dictionary of the Bible.* Revised by Frederick C. Grant and H. H. Rowley. 2nd edn. Edinburgh: T &T Clark. Pp. 280-83.

Battenfield, James R.
1988 "YHWH's Refutation of the Baal Myth through the Actions of Elijah and Elisha," in Avraham Gileadi (ed), *Israel's Apostasy and Restoration.* Grand Rapids, Mich.: Baker. Pp. 19-37.

Baumann, A.
1978 "דמה II," in G. Johannes Botterweck and Helmer Ringgren (eds), *TDOT.* Translated by John T. Willis, Geoffrey W. Bromiley and David E. Green. Vol. 3. Grand Rapids, Mich.: Eerdmans. Pp. 260-61; 64-65.

Beek, M. A.
1972 "The Meaning of the Expression 'The Chariots and the Horsemen of Israel' (2 Kings 2:12)," *OTS* 17:1-10.

Begg, Christopher T.
1985 "Unifying Factors in 2 Kings 1.2-17a," *JSOT* 32:75-86.
1990 " 'Josephus' Portrayal of the Disappearances of Enoch, Elijah and Moses': Some Observations," *JBL* 109:691-93.

Bergen, Wesley J.
1999 *Elisha and the End of Prophetism.* JSOTSup 286. Sheffield: Sheffield Acad. Press.

Binns, L. E.
1927 *The Book of Numbers.* WC. London: Methuen.

Bird, Phyllis
1989 " 'To Play the Harlot': An Enquiry into an Old Testament Metaphor," in P. L. Day (ed.), *Gender and Difference in Ancient Israel*. Minneapolis, Minn.: Fortress. Pp. 75-94.
Blank, S. H.
1950/51 "The Curse, the Spell and the Oath," *HUCA* 23:73-95.
Blommerde, A.
1969 *Northwest Semitic Grammar and Job*. Biblica et Orientalia 22. Rome: Pontifical Biblical Institute.
Boling, R. G.
1975 *Judges: Introduction, Translation and Commentary*. New York: Doubleday.
Boling, Robert G. and G. Ernest Wright
1982 *Joshua*. AB. New York: Doubleday.
Bratsiotis, N. P.
1974 "איש אשה," in G. Johannes Botterweck and Helmer Ringgren (eds), *TDOT*. Translated by John T. Willis. Vol. 1. Grand Rapids, Mich.: Eerdmans. Pp. 222-35.
Bright, J.
1981 *A History of Israel*. 3rd edn. Philadelphia: Westminster.
Bronner, Leah
1968 *The Stories of Elijah and Elisha as Polemics against Baal Worship*. Leiden: Brill.
Brown, Francis, S.R. Driver and Charles A. Briggs
1906 *The Brown-Driver-Briggs Hebrew and English Lexicon*. Boston: Houghton, Mifflin and Company. Reprint, Peabody, Mass.: Hendrickson. 2000.
Brown, Raymond
1971 "Jesus and Elisha," *Per* 12:85-104.
Brueggemann, Walter
1985 *David's Truth in Israel's Imagination and Memory*. USA: Fortress.
1990 *First and Second Samuel*. Louisville, Ky.: Westminster/John Knox.
2000 *1 and 2 Kings*. Macon, Ga.: Smith & Helwys.
Budd, Philip J.
1984 *Numbers,* WBC. Vol. 5. Waco, Tex.: Word.
Burney, C. F.
1903 *Notes on the Hebrew Text of Kings*. Oxford: Clarendon.
Carlson, R. A.
1969 "Élie à L'Horeb," *VT* 19:416-39.
Carroll, R. P.
1969 "The Elijah-Elisha Sagas: Some Remarks on Prophetic Succession in Ancient Israel," *VT* 19:400-15.
Cartledge, Tony W.
2001 *1 and 2 Samuel*. Smyth and Helwys Bible Commentary. Macon, Ga.: Smyth & Helwys.
Cassuto, U.
1967 *A Commentary on the Book of Exodus*. Translated by Israel Abrahams. Jerusalem: Magnes.
Childs, B. S.
1970 "A Traditio-Historical Account of the Reed Sea Tradition," *VT* 20:406-

Bibliography

418.
1974   *Exodus: A Commentary*. London: SCM.
1986   *Old Testament Theology in a Canonical Context*. Philadelphia: Fortress.

Chinitz, Jacob
1997   "Two Sinners," *JBQ* 25:108-113.

Claassen, Walter T.
1983   "Speaker-Orientated Functions of *kî* in Biblical Hebrew," *JNSL* 11:29-46.

Clements, R. E.
2004   "שׂאר," in G. Johannes Botterweck, Helmer Ringgren and Heinz-Josef Fabry (eds), *TDOT*. Translated by Douglas W. Stott. Vol. 14. Grand Rapids, Mich.: Eerdmans. Pp. 272-286.

Clines, J. A.
1989   *Job 1-20*. WBC. Vol. 17. Dallas, Tex.: Word.

Coats, George W.
1969   "The Song of the Sea," *CBQ* 31:1-17.
1977   "The King's Loyal Opposition: Obedience and Authority in Exodus 32-34," in George W. Coats and Burke O. Long (eds), *Canon and Authority: Essays in Old Testament Religion and Theology*. Philadelphia: Fortress. Pp. 91-109.
1993   *The Moses Tradition*. JSOTSup 161. Sheffield: Sheffield Acad. Press.

Cogan, Mordechai and Hayim Tadmor
1988   *2 Kings: A New Translation with Introduction and Commentary*. AB. Vol. 11. USA: Doubleday.

Cohn, R. L.
1982   "The Literary Logic of 1 Kings 17-19," *JBL* 101:333-50.

Conroy, Charles
1996   "Hiel Between Ahab and Elijah-Elisha: 1 Kgs 16, 34 in Its Immediate Literary Context," *Biblica* 77:210-18.

Cook, F. C. and T. E. Espin
1871   *The Fourth Book of Moses called Numbers*, The Holy Bible according to the Authorized Version Vol. 1/2. London: Murray.

Coote, Robert B.
1981   "Yahweh Recalls Elijah," in Baruch Halpern and Jon D. Levenson (eds), *Traditions in Transformation: Turning Points in Biblical Faith*. Winona Lake, Indiana: Eisenbrauns. Pp. 115-120.
1992   *Elijah and Elisha in Socio-Literary Perspective*. Atlanta, Ga.: Scholars.

Cross, F. M.
1966   "The Divine Warrior in Israel's Early Cult," in Alexander Altmann (ed.), *Biblical Motifs: Origins and Transformations*. Cambridge, Mass.: Harvard Univ. Press. Pp. 11-30.
1968   "The Song of the Sea and Canaanite Myth," *JTC* 5:1-25.
1973   *Canaanite Myth and Hebrew Epic: Essays in the History of the Religion of Israel*. Cambridge, Mass.: Harvard Univ. Press.

Cross, Frank M. and David Noel Freedman
1955   "The Song of Miriam," *JNES* 14:237-250.

Dahood, M.
1960   "Textual Problems in Isaia," *CBQ* 22:400-09.

1967 "S'RT "Storm" in Job 4,15," *Bib* 48:544-45.
Daube, David
1963 *The Exodus Pattern in the Bible*. London: Faber and Faber.
de Vaux, Roland
1933 "Le "reste d'Israël" d'apres les prophètes," *RB* 42:526-39.
De Vries, Simon
1978 *Prophet Against Prophet*. Grand Rapids, Mich.: Eerdmans.
1985 *1 Kings*. WBC. Vol. 12. Waco, Tex.: Word.
Deem, Ariella
1978 "...And the Stone Sank into his Forehead: A Note on 1 Samuel XVII 49," *VT* 28:349-51.
Dhorme, E.
1967 *A Commentary on the Book of Job*. London: Nelson.
Driver, S. R.
1918 *Book of Exodus*. Cambridge: Cambridge Univ. Press.
1926 *The Book of Genesis: With Introduction and Notes*. London: Methuen.
Driver, S.R. and G. B. Gray
1921 *The Book of Job*. ICC. Edinburgh: T & T Clark.
Durham, John I.
1987 *Exodus*. WBC. Vol. 3. Nashville, Tenn.: Thomas Nelson.
Eakin, Jr., Frank E.
1967 "The Reed Sea and Baalism," *JBL* 86:378-84.
Edelman, Diana Vikander
1991 *King Saul in the Historiography of Judah*. JSOTSup 121. Sheffield: Sheffield Acad. Press.
Eichrodt, Walther
1961 *Theology of the Old Testament*. Translated by J. A. Baker. Vol. 1. London: SCM.
1967 *Theology of the Old Testament*. Translated by J. A. Baker. Vol. 2. London: SCM.
Eissfeldt, Otto
1922-23 *Könige*. 4th ed. HSAT. Tübingen.
1967 "Bist du Elia, so bin ich Isebel," *VTSup* 16:65-70.
Ellul, Jaques
1972 *The Politics of God and the Politics of Man*. Translated by Geoffrey W. Bromiley. Grand Rapids, Mich.: Eerdmans.
Emerton, J. A.
1997 "The House of Baal in 1 Kings xvi 32," *VT* 47:293-300.
Enns, Peter
2000 *Exodus*. NIV Application Commentary. Grand Rapids, Mich.: Zondervan.
Feldman, L. H.
1984 *Josephus and Modern Scholarship (1937-1980)*. Berlin: de Gruyter.
1992 "Josephus' Portrait of Ahab," *ETL* 68:368-84.
Fensham, F. C.
1980 "A Few Observations on the Polarisation between Yahweh and Baal in 1 Kings 17-19," *ZAW* 92:227-236.

Fishbane, Michael
1979   Text and Texture: Close Readings of Selected Biblical Texts. New York: Schocken.
1985   Biblical Interpretation in Ancient Israel. Oxford: Clarendon.
1989   "Israel and the 'Mothers'," in The Garments of Torah. Bloomington: Indiana Univ. Press.
Flanagan, James W.
1976-77 "The deuteronomic meaning of the phrase 'kol yiśrā'ēl'," SR 6:159-68.
Fohrer, George
1957   Elia. ATANT 31. Zurich: Zwingli.
Fokkelman, J. P.
1975   Narrative Art in Genesis. Amsterdam: Van Gorcum.
1986   The Crossing Fates. Vol. 2 of Narrative Art and Poetry in the Books of Samuel. Maastricht: Van Gorcum.
1999   Reading Biblical Narrative: A Practical Guide. Translated by Ineke Smit. Leiden: Deo.
Fox, Everett
2002   "The Translation of Elijah: Issues and Challenges," in Athalya Brenner and Jan Willem van Henten (eds), Bible Translation on the Threshold of the 21st Century: Authority, Reception, Culture and Religion. JSOTSup 353. Sheffield: Sheffield Acad. Press.
Frank, Richard M.
1963   "A Note on 3 Kings 19:10, 14," CBQ 25:413.
Fretheim, Terence E.
1991   Exodus. Louisville, Ky.: John Knox.
1999   First and Second Kings. Louisville, Ky.: Westminster/John Knox.
Fritz, Volkmar
2003   1 and 2 Kings. Translated by Anselm Hagedorn. CC. Minneapolis: Fortress.
Galling, Von Kurt
1956   "Der Ehrenname Elisas und die Entrückung Elias," ZTK 53:129-48.
Garsiel, Moshe
1985   The First Book of Samuel: A Literary Study of Comparative Structures, Analogies and Parallels. Ramat Gan, Israel: Revivim.
Gaster, Theodor H.
1969   Myth, Legend and Custom in the Old Testament. London: Duckworth.
Geller, S. A.
1990   "The Language of Imagery in Psalm 114," in Tzvi Abusch, John Huehnergard, Piotr Steinkeller (eds), Lingering over Words: Studies in Near Eastern Literature in Honour of William L. Moran. Winona Lake, Ind.: Eisenbrauns. Pp. 179-94.
Gerstenberger, E.
1999   "עזב," in G. Johannes Botterweck, Helmer Ringgren and Heinz-Josef Fabry (eds), TDOT. Translated by Douglas W. Stott. Vol. 10. Grand Rapids, Mich.: Eerdmans. Pp. 584-92.
Gertel, Elliott B.
2002[1] "Moses, Elisha and the Transferred Spirit: The Height of Biblical Prophecy? Part 1," JBQ 30:73-79.

2002² "Moses, Elisha and the Transferred Spirit: The Height of Biblical Prophecy? Part 2," *JBQ* 30:171-77.

Gesenius, W.
1846 *Hebrew and Chaldee Lexicon*. Translated and edited by S. P. Tregelles. London: Bagster.

Gesenius, William and E. Kautzsch
1898 *Gesenius-Kautzsch Hebrew Grammar*. Translated by Collins, G. W. Revised by Cowley, A. E. Oxford: Clarendon.

Ginzberg, Louis
1910 *Bible Times and Characters from Joseph to the Exodus*. Translated by Henrietta Szold. Vol. 2 of *Legends of the Jews*. 7 vols. Philadelphia: JPSA.
1911 *Bible Times and Characters from the Exodus to the Death of Moses*. Translated by Paul Radin. Vol. 3 of *Legends of the Jews*. 7 vols. Philadelphia: JPSA.
1913 *Bible Times and Characters from Joshua to Esther*. Translated by Paul Radin. Vol. 4 of *Legends of the Jews*. 7 vols. Philadelphia: JPSA.

Gooding, D. W.
1964 "Ahab according to the Septuagint," *ZAW* 76:269-80.

Gordis, R.
1943 "The Asseverative *Kaph* in Ugaritic and Hebrew," *JAOS* 63:176-78.
1978 *Book of Job*. New York: JTSA.

Gowan, Donald E.
1994 *Theology in Exodus: Biblical Theology in the Form of a Commentary*. Louisville, Ky.: Westminster/John Knox.

Graupner, M. and Heinz-Josef Fabry
2004 "שׁוּב," in G. Johannes Botterweck, Helmer Ringgren and Heinz-Josef Fabry (eds), *TDOT*. Douglas W. Stott. Vol. 14. Grand Rapids, Mich.: Eerdmans. Pp. 461-522.

Gray, John
1964 *1 and 2 Kings: A Commentary*. OTL. London: SCM.

Greenberg, Moshe
1957 "The Hebrew Oath Particle "Hay/He," *JBL* 76:34-39.
1983 *Biblical Prose Prayer as a Window to the Popular Religion of Ancient Israel*. Los Angeles: Univ. of California Press.
1995 *Studies in the Bible and Jewish Thought*. Jerusalem: JPS.

Gunkel, Hermann
1929 "Elisha – The Successor of Elijah (2 Kings ii:1-18)," *ExpTim* 41:182-86.

Habel, N.
1965 "The Form and Significance of the Call Narratives," *ZAW* 77:297-323.

Halpern, B. and D. S. Vanderhooft,
1991 "The Editions of Kings in the 7th-6th Centuries B. C. E.," *HUCA* 62:179-244.

Hamilton, Victor P.
1990 *The Book of Genesis; Chapters 1-17*. NICOT. Grand Rapids, Mich.: Eerdmans.
1995 *The Book of Genesis: Chapters 18-50*. NICOT. Grand Rapids, Mich.: Eerdmans.

Hartley, John E.
1988   *The Book of Job.* NICOT. Grand Rapids, Mich.: Eerdmans.
Hasel, Gerhard F.
1980   *The Remnant: The History and Theology of the Remnant Idea from Genesis to Isaiah.* 3rd edn. Berrien Springs, Mich.: Andrews Univ. Press.
2001   "פלט," in G. Johannes Botterweck, Helmer Ringgren and Heinz-Josef Fabry (eds), *TDOT.* Translated by David E. Green. Vol. 11. Grand Rapids, Mich.: Eerdmans. Pp. 551-67.
Haupt, Paul
1909   "Some Assyrian Etymologies," *AJSL* 26:1-26.
Hauser, Alan J. and Russell Gregory
1990   *From Carmel to Horeb.* Sheffield: Almond.
Hawk, L. Daniel
1991   *Every Promise Fulfilled: Contesting Plots in Joshua.* Louisville, Ky.: Westminster/John Knox.
2000   *Joshua.* Berit Olam. Collegeville, Minn.: Liturgical Press.
Hay, Lewis S.
1964   "What Really Happened at the Sea of Reeds?," *JBL* 83:397-403.
Hayward, Robert
1978   "Phinehas – the same is Elijah: The Origins of a Rabbinic Tradition," *JJS* 29:22-34.
Henton, E. W.
1952   "The Root שאר and the Doctrine of the Remnant," *JTS* 3:27-39.
Hertzberg, H. W.
1965   *Die Bücher Josua, Richter, Ruth.* Göttingen: Vandenhoeck and Ruprecht.
Hess, Richard
1991   "Yahweh and His Asherah? Epigraphic Evidence for Religious Pluralism in Old Testament Times," in Andrew D. Clarke and Bruce W. Winter (eds), *One God, One Lord in a World of Religious Pluralism.* Cambridge: Tyndale. Pp. 5-33.
1996   *Joshua.* TOTC. Leicester: Inter-Varsity Press.
Hobbs, T. R.
1984   "2 Kings 1 and 2: Their Unity and Purpose," *SR* 13:327-34.
1985   *2 Kings.* WBC. Vol. 13. Waco, Tx.: Word.
Holt, Else K.
1995   " '...urged on by his wife Jezebel.' A Literary Reading of 1 Kgs 18 in Context," *SJOT* 9:83-96.
House, Paul R.
1995   *1, 2 Kings.* The New American Commentary. Vol. 8. USA: Broadman and Holman.
Hulst, A.R.
1965   "Der Jordan in den alttestamentlichen Überlieferungen," *OTS* 14:162-188.
Hvidberg, Fleming Friis
1962   *Weeping and Laughter in the Old Testament.* Leiden: Brill.
Imschoot, P. van
1954   *Théologie de L'Ancien Testament.* Bibliothèque de Théologie Série 3. Vol. 1. Tournai: Desclée.

Janzen, Waldemar
2000 *Exodus*. Waterloo, Ontario: Herald.
Jepsen, A.
1971 "Elia und das Gottesurteil," in Hans Goedicke (ed.), *Near Eastern Studies in Honour of William Foxwell Albright*. Baltimore: John Hopkins. Pp. 291-306.
1980 "חזה," in G. Johannes Botterweck and Helmer Ringgren (eds), *TDOT*. Translated by David E. Green. Vol. 4. Grand Rapids, Mich.: Eerdmans. Pp. 280-90.
Jeremias, Jörg
1965 *Theophanie: Die Geschichte einer altentestamentlichen Gattung*. WMANT. Neukirchen-Vluyn: Neukirchener Verlag.
Jobling, David
1978 *The Sense of Biblical Narrative: Three Structural Analyses in the Old Testament*. JSOTSup 7. Sheffield: JSOT Press.
1998 *1 Samuel*. Berit Olam Series. Collegeville, Minn.: Liturgical Press.
Johnson, Aubrey R.
1962 *The Cultic Prophet in Ancient Israel*. Cardiff: Univ. of Wales Press.
Jones, G. H.
1975 " 'Holy War or 'Yahweh War'?," *VT* 25:642-58.
1984[1] *1 and 2 Kings*. NCB Commentary. Vol. 1. Grand Rapids, Mich.: Eerdmans/London: Marshall, Morgan and Scott.
1984[2] *1 and 2 Kings*. NCB Commentary. Vol. 2. Grand Rapids, Mich.: Eerdmans/London: Marshall, Morgan and Scott.
Joüon, Paul
1993 *A Grammar of Biblical Hebrew*. Translated and revised by T. Muraoka. Vol. 1. Reprint of 1st edn. with corrections. Subsidia biblica 14/1. Rome: Pontifical Biblical Institute.
Keil, C. F.
1869 *The Book of Numbers*. Translated by J. D. Martin et al. Edinburgh: T & T Clark.
Kidner, Derek
1967 *Genesis*. TOTC. Chicago: Inter-Varsity Press.
Kirsch, Jonathan
1998 *Moses: A Life*. New York: Ballantine.
Kissling, Paul J.
1996 *Reliable Characters in the Primary History: Profiles of Moses, Joshua, Elijah and Elisha*. JSOTSup 224. Sheffield: Sheffield Acad. Press.
Klein, Ralph W.
1983 *1 Samuel*. WBC. Vol. 10. Waco, Tex.: Word.
Koch, Klaus
1969 *The Growth of Biblical Tradition: The Form Critical Method*. Translated by S. M. Cupitt. London: Adam and Charles Black.
Koehler, Ludwig and Walter Baumgartner
1994 *The Hebrew and Aramaic Lexicon of the Old Testament*. Revised by Walter Baumgartner and Johann Jakob Stamm. M.E. J. Richardson (ed.). Vol. 1. Leiden: Brill.

Kraus, H.-J.
1951 "Gilgal; Ein beitrag zur Kultusgeschichte Israels," *VT* 1:181-99.
1966 *Worship in Israel*. Translated by Geoffrey Buswell. Richmond, Va.: John Knox.

L'Orange, H. P.
1953 *Studies in the Iconography of Cosmic Kingship in the Ancient World*. Oslo: Aschehoug.

LaBarbera, Robert
1984 "The Man of War and the Man of God: Social Satire in 2 Kings 6:8-7:20," *CBQ* 46:637-51.

Labuschagne, C. J.
1965 "Did Elisha Deliberately Lie? – A Note on 2 Kings 8.10," *ZAW* 77:327-28.

Lambdin, T. O.
1971 *Introduction to Biblical Hebrew*. New York: Scribner.

Lang, B.
1990 "זבח," in G. Johannes Botterweck and Helmer Ringgren (eds), *TDOT*. Translated by David E. Green. Vol. 6. Grand Rapids, Mich.: Eerdmans. Pp. 8-29.

Le Maire, A.
1984 "Who or What was Jahweh's Asherah?" *BAR* 10:42-51.

Lehmann, M. R.
1969 "Biblical Oaths," *ZAW* 81:74-92.

Levine, Baruch
1993 "Silence, Sound and the Phenomenology of Mourning in Biblical Israel," *JANESCU* 22:89-106.

Levine, Nachman
1999 "Twice as much of your spirit: Pattern, Parallel and Paronomasia in the Miracles of Elijah and Elisha," *JSOT* 85:25-46.

Licht, Jacob
1978 *Storytelling in the Bible*. Jerusalem: Magnes.

Lind, Millard C.
1980 *Yahweh is a Warrior: The Theology of Warfare in Ancient Israel*. Scottdale, Pa.: Herald.
1994 "The Deuteronomistic Picture of the Transfer of Authority from Moses to Joshua: A Contribution to an Old Testament Theology of Office," in Norbert Lohfink (ed.), *Theology of the Pentateuch: Themes of the Priestly Narrative and Deuteronomy*. Translated by Linda M. Maloney. Edinburgh: T & T Clark. Pp. 234-47.

Long, Burke O.
1984 *1 Kings: With an Introduction to Historical Literature*. FOTL. Vol. 9. Grand Rapids, Mich.: Eerdmans.
1977 "Prophetic Authority as Social Reality," in G. W. Coats and B. O. Long (eds), *Canon and Authority: Essays in Old Testament Religion and Authority*. Philadelphia: Fortress. Pp. 3-20.
1991 *2 Kings*. FOTL. Vol. 10. Grand Rapids, Mich.: Eerdmans.

Lundbom, Jack R.
1973 "Elijah's Chariot Ride," *JJS* 24:39-50.
Lust, J.
1975 "A Gentle Breeze or a Roaring Thunderous Sound? Elijah at Horeb: 1 Kings xix 12," *VT* 25:110-15.
McCarter, Jr., P. Kyle
1987 "Aspects of the Religion of the Israelite Monarchy: Biblical and Epigraphical data," in Patrick D. Miller, Jr., Paul Hanson and S. Dean McBride (eds), *Ancient Israelite Religion: Essays in Honour of Frank Moore Cross*. Philadelphia: Fortress. Pp. 137-55.
McCarthy, D. J.
1971[1] "The Theology of Leadership in Joshua 1-9," *Bib* 52:165-175.
1971[2] "An Installation Genre?," *JBL* 90:31-41.
1981 *Treaty and Covenant: A Study in the Form of Ancient Oriental Documents and in the Old Testament*. Analecta Biblica 21A. New edn. Rome: Biblical Institute Press.
McClellan, W. H.
1940 "Dominus Deus Sabaoth," *CBQ* 2:300-307.
McNeile. A. H.
1908 *The Book of Exodus: With Introduction and Notes*. London: Methuen.
1911 *The Book of Numbers: With Introduction and Notes*. Cambridge: Cambridge Univ. Press.
Meek, T. J.
1959/60 "Translation Problems in the Old Testament," *JQR* 50:45-54.
Milgrom, J.
1990 *Numbers*. JPS Torah Commentary. New York: JPS.
Miller, J. M.
1967 "Fall of the House of Ahab," *VT* 17:307-24.
Miller, J. Maxwell and Gene Tucker
1974 *The Book of Joshua*. CBC. Cambridge: Cambridge Univ. Press.
Miller, Patrick D.
1973 *The Divine Warrior in Early Israel*. Cambridge, Mass.: Harvard Univ. Press.
1994 *They Cried to the Lord: The Form and Theology of Biblical Prayer*. Minneapolis: Fortress.
Miscall, Peter D.
1983 *The Workings of Old Testament Narrative*. Philadelphia, Pa.: Fortress/Chico, Calif.: Scholars.
1989 "Elijah, Ahab and Jehu: A Prophecy Fulfilled," *Proof* 9:73-83.
Mitchell, Gordon
1993 *Together in the Land: A Reading of the Book of Joshua*. JSOTSup 134. Sheffield: Sheffield Acad. Press.
Moberly, R. W. L.
1983 *At the Mountain of God: Story and Theology in Exodus 32-34*. JSOTSup 22. Sheffield: JSOT Press.
2006 *Prophecy and Discernment*. Cambridge: Cambridge Univ. Press.
Montgomery, James A.
1951 *A Critical and Exegetical Commentary on the Books of Kings*. Edited by

Henry Snyder Gehman. ICC. Edinburgh: T & T Clark.

Moore, Rick Dale
1990 *God Saves: Lessons from the Elisha Stories.* JSOTSup 95. Sheffield: Sheffield Acad. Press.

Morgenstern, J.
1925 "Moses with the Shining Face," *HUCA* 2:1-44.
1942-43 "The Ark, the Ephod and the Tent of Meeting," *HUCA* 17:153-265.
1943-44 "The Ark, the Ephod and the Tent of Meeting," *HUCA* 18:1-52.

Mosis, R.
2001 "עכר," in G. Johannes Botterweck, Helmer Ringgren and Heinz-Josef Fabry (eds), *TDOT*. Translated by David E. Green. Vol. 11. Grand Rapids, Mich.: Eerdmans. Pp. 67-71.

Mowinckel, Sigmund
1962 "Drive and/or Ride in O. T.," *VT* 12:278-99.

Muilenberg, James
1961 "Usages of Particle כי in the Old Testament," *HUCA* 32:135-160.

Na'aman, Nadav
1997 "Prophetic Stories as Sources for the Histories of Jehoshaphat and the Omrides," *Bib* 78:153-73.

Nelson, Richard D.
1981 "Josiah in the Book of Joshua," *JBL* 100:531-40.
1987 *First and Second Kings.* Interpretation. Louisville, Ky.: John Knox.
1997 *Joshua.* OTL. Louisville, Ky.: Westminster John Knox.
2002 *Deuteronomy: A Commentary.* OTL. London: Westminster John Knox.

Newman, M.
1962 "The Prophetic Call of Samuel," in B. W. Anderson and W. Harrelson (eds), *Israel's Prophetic Heritage.* London: SCM.

Noordtzij, A.
1983 *Numbers.* Translasted by E. van der Maas. BSC. Grand Rapids, Mich.: Zondervan.

Nordheim, Eckhard von
1978 "Elia am Horeb," *Bib* 59:153-73.

Noth, Martin
1953 *Das Buch Josua.* HAT. Vol. 7. Tübingen: Mohr Siebeck.
1962 *Exodus: A Commentary.* Translated by J. S. Bowden. London: SCM.
1968 *Numbers: A Commentary.* Translated by J. D. Martin. OTL. Philadelphia: Westminster.

O'Brien, Mark
1998 "The Portrayal of Prophets in 2 Kings 2," *ABR* 46:1-16.

Olley, John W.
1998 "YHWH and his Zealous Prophet: The Presentation of Elijah in 1 and 2 Kings," *JSOT* 80:25-51.

Olson, Dennis T.
1996 *Numbers,* Interpretation. Louisville, Ky.: John Knox.

Olyan, Saul M.
1988 *Asherah and the Cult of Yahweh in Israel.* SBLMS 34. Atlanta, Ga.: Scholars.

Organ, Barbara E.
2001   "Pursuing Phinehas: A Synchronic Reading," *CBQ* 63:203-18.
Östborn, G.
1945   *Törä in the Old Testament*. Lund: Hakan Ohlsons.
Overholt, Thomas W.
1982   "Seeing is Believing: The Social Setting of Prophetic Acts of Power," *JSOT* 23:3-31.
Parzen, Robert
1940   "The Prophets and the Omri Dynasty," *HTR* 33:69-96.
Patai, Raphael
1939   "The 'Control of Rain' in Ancient Palestine," *HUCA* 14:251-86.
Paul, Shalom M.
1983   "Job 4:15 – A Hair Raising Encounter," *ZAW* 95:119-21.
Pedersen, Johannes
1926   *Israel: Its life and Culture*. Vols. 1-2. London: Oxford Univ. Press.
Peterson, Eugene H.
1999   *First and Second Samuel*. Westminster Bible Companion. Louisville, Ky.: Westminster/John Knox.
Phillips, Anthony
1968   "The Ecstatics' Father," in Peter R. Ackroyd and Barnabas Lindars (eds), *Words and Meanings: Essays Presented to David Winton Thomas*. Cambridge: Cambridge Univ. Press. Pp. 183-94.
Polzin, Robert
1980   *Moses and the Deuteronomist: A Literary Study of the Deuteronomic History*. Part 1. New York: Seabury.
Porteous, Norman W.
1962   "The Prophets and the Problem of Continuity," in Bernhard W. Anderson and Walter Harrelson (eds), *Israel's Prophetic Heritage: Essays in Honour of James Muilenberg*. London: SCM. Pp. 11-25.
Porter, J. R.
1970   "The Succession of Joshua," in J. I. Durham and J. R. Porter (eds), *Proclamation and Presence: Old Testament Essays in Honour of Gwynne Henton Davies*. London: SCM. Pp. 102-32.
1981   "בני הנביאים," *JTS* 32:423-28.
Porúbcan, Stefan
1963   *Sin in the Old Testament: A Soteriological Study*. Rome: Herder.
Provan, Iain W.
1995   *1 and 2 Kings*. NIBC. Peabody, Mass.: Hendrickson/Carlisle, Cumbria: Paternoster.
Rad, Gerhard von
1953   "The Deuteronomistic Theology of History in the Books of Kings," in *Studies in Deuteronomy*. Translated by D. M. G. Stalker. SBT. Vol. 9. London: SCM. Pp. 74-91.
1958   *Holy War in Ancient Israel*. Translated by Marva J. Dawn. 1991. Grand Rapids, Mich.: Eerdmans.
1962   *Old Testament Theology: The History of Israel's Historical Traditions*. Translated by D. M. G. Stalker. Vol. 1. Edinburgh: Oliver and Boyd.
1965   *The Problem of the Hexateuch and Other Essays*. Translated by E. W.

         Trueman Dicken. Edinburgh: Oliver and Boyd.
1972   *Genesis: A Commentary.* Translated by John H. Marks. 3rd rev. edn. London: SCM.
1975   *Old Testament Theology: The History of Israel's Prophetic Traditions.* Translated by D. M. G. Stalker. Vol. 2. London: SCM.

Rand, Herbert
1996   "David and Ahab: A Study in Crime and Punishment," *JBQ* 24:90-97.

Reif, Stephan C.
1971   "What Enraged Phinehas?," *JBL* 90:200-06.

Rendtorff, Rolf
1967   "Reflections on the Early History of Prophecy in Israel," *JTC* 4:14-34.

Rice, Gene
1990   *Nations Under God: A Commentary on the Book of 1 Kings.* Edinburgh: Handsel/Grand Rapids, Mich.: Eerdmans.

Riggans, Walter
1983   *Numbers.* The Daily Study Bible. Edinburgh: St. Andrew Press/Philadelphia: Westminster.

Roberts, Kathryn L.
2000   "God, Prophet and King: Eating and Drinking on the Mountain in First Kings 18:41," *CBQ* 62:632-44.

Robinson, J.
1976   *The Second Book of Kings*, CBC. Cambridge: Cambridge Univ. Press.

Robinson, Bernard P.
1991   "Elijah at Horeb, 1 Kings 19:1-18: A Coherent Narrative?," *RB* 98:513-36.

Rofé, Alexander
1970   "The Classification of the Prophetical Stories," *JBL* 89:427-40.

Ross, J. P.
1967   "Jahweh Sebaot in Samuel and Psalms," *VT* 17:76-92.

Rowlett, Lori L.
1996   *Joshua and the Rhetoric of Violence: A New Historicist Analysis.* JSOTSup 226. Sheffield: Sheffield Acad. Press.

Rowley, H. H.
1952   *The Servant of the Lord and Other Essays on the Old Testament.* London: Lutterworth.
1956   *The Faith of Israel: Aspects of Old Testament Thought.* London: SCM.
1970   *Job.* NCB. London: Nelson.

Ruppert, L.
2003   "פרר," in G. Johannes Botterweck, Helmer Ringgren and Heinz-Josef Fabry (eds), *TDOT*. Translated by Douglas W. Stott. Vol. 12. Grand Rapids, Mich.: Eerdmans. Pp. 114-21.

Sarna, Nahum M.
1989   *Genesis.* JPS Torah Commentary. Philadelphia: JPS.
1991   *Exodus.* JPS Torah Commentary. Philadelphia: JPS.

Schick, George V.
1913   "The stems dûm and damám in Hebrew," *JBL* 32:219-243.

Schniedewind, William M.
1993   "History and Interpretation: The Religion of Ahab and Manasseh in the

Book of Kings," *CBQ* 55:649-61.
Schoors, A.
1981 "The Particle כי," *OTS* 21:240-76.
Schulte, Hannelis
1994 "The End of the Omride Dynasty: Social-Ethical Observations on the Subject of Power and Violence," *Sem* 66:133-48.
Scolnic, Benjamin Edidin
1987 "The Flexible Word of God: Thoughts on the Other Pole of Biblical Authority," *Judaism* 36:331-38.
Seebass, Horst
1973 "Elia und Ahab auf dem Karmel," *ZTK* 70:121-36.
Seybold, Klaus
1973 "Elia am Gottesberg," *EvT* 33:3-17.
1998 "משח," in G. Johannes Botterweck, Helmer Ringgren and Heinz-Josef Fabry (eds), *TDOT*. Translated by David E. Green. Vol. 9. Grand Rapids, Mich.: Eerdmans. Pp. 43-54.
Simon, Uriel
1997 *Reading Prophetic Narratives*. Translated by Lenn J. Schramm. Bloomington and Indianapolis: Indiana Univ. Press.
Skinner, John
n.d. *1 and 2 Kings*. The Century Bible. Edinburgh: T. C. and E. C. Jack.
1910 *A Critical and Exegetical Commentary on Genesis*. Edinburgh: Clark.
Smend, R.
1963 *Jahwekrieg und Stämmebund*. Göttingen: Vandenhoeck and Ruprecht.
1975[1] *Der Biblische und der Historische Elia*. VTSup 28:167-84.
1975[2] "Das Wort Jahwes an Elia," *VT* 25:525-43.
Smith, Henry P.
1899 *Samuel*. ICC. Edinburgh: T & T Clark.
Smith, Mark S.
2002 *The Early History of God: Yahweh and the Other Deities in Ancient Israel*. 2nd edn. Grand Rapids, Mich.: Eerdmans.
Snaith, Norman
1975 "The verbs zabah and sahat," *VT* 25:242-46.
Soggin, J. Alberto
1972 *Joshua*. OTL. London: SCM.
Speiser, E. A.
1964 *Genesis*. AB. New York: Doubleday.
Stamm, J. J.
1966 "Elia am Horeb," in *Studia Biblica et Semitica: Festschrift for T. C. Vriezen*. Wageningen: Veenman and Zonen.
Steck, O. H.
1967 "Die Erzählung von Jahwes Einschreiten gegen die Orakelbefragung Ahasjas (2 Kön 1, 2-8)," *EvT* 27:546-56.
1968 *Überlieferung und Zeitgeschichte in den Elia-Erzählungen*. Neukirchen-Vluyn: Neukirchener Verlag.
Sternberg, Meir
1985 *The Poetics of Biblical Narrative: Ideological Literature and the Drama of Reading*. Bloomington: Indiana Univ. Press.

Stolz, F.
1972   *Jahwes und Israels Krieg: Kriegstheorien und Kriegserfahrungen im Glauben des alten Israel.* Zürich: Zwingli Verlag.
Sturdy, J.
1976   *Numbers.* Cambridge Bible. New York: Cambridge Univ. Press.
Tabor, James D.
1989   "'Returning to the Divinity': Josephus' Portrayal of the Disappearances of Enoch, Elijah, and Moses," *JBL* 108:225-38.
Terrien, Samuel
1978   *The Elusive Presence: Toward a New Biblical Theology.* Religious Perspectives. Vol. 26. San Francisco: Harper & Row.
Thackeray, H.
1967   *Josephus the Man and the Historian.* New York: Ktav.
Thomas, D. Winton
1953   "A Consideration of Some Unusual Ways of Expressing the Superlative in Hebrew," *VT* 3:209-24.
Thomson, Leonard L.
1981   "The Jordan Crossing: Cidqot Yahweh and World Building," *JBL* 100:343-58.
Tov, Emmanuel
1992   *Textual Criticism of the Hebrew Bible.* Minneapolis: Fortress/Maastricht: Van Gorcum.
Trible, Phyllis
1995   "Exegesis for Storytellers and Other Strangers," *JBL* 114:3-19.
Waldman, Nahum M.
1988   "Ahab in Bible and Talmud," *Judaism* 37:41-47.
Wallace, H. N.
1986   "The Oracles Against the Israelite Dynasties in 1 and 2 Kings," *Bib* 67:21-40.
Walsh, Jerome T.
1996   *1 Kings.* Berit Olam Series. Collegeville, Minn.: Liturgical Press.
Waltke, Bruce K. and M. O'Connor
1990   *An Introduction to Biblical Hebrew Syntax.* Winona Lake, Ind.: Eisenbrauns.
Wambacq, B. N.
1947   *L'épithète divine Jahvé Seba'ôt: Étude Philologique, Historique et Exégétique* Bruges: Desclée.
Warne, D. M.
1958   "The Origin, Development and Significance of the Concept of the Remnant in the Old Testament." Ph. D. Dissertation, Univ. of Edinburgh.
Weinfeld, Moshe
1972   *Deuteronomy and the Deuteronomic School.* Oxford: Oxford Univ. Press.
1991   *Deuteronomy 1-11.* AB. Vol. 5. London: Doubleday.
Weisman, Ze'ev
1981   "The Personal Spirit as Imparting Authority," *ZAW* 93:225-34.

Wenham, Gordon J.
1981   *Numbers: An Introduction and Commentary*. TOTC. Downers Grove: Inter-Varsity Press.
1987   *Genesis 1-15*. WBC. Vol. 1. Waco, Tex.: Word.
1994   *Genesis 16-50*. WBC. Vol. 2. Dallas, Tex.: Word.
Werblowsky, R. J.
1956   "Stealing the Word," *VT* 6:105-06.
Westermann, Claus
1984   *Genesis 1-11: A Commmentary*. Translated by John J. Scullion. London: SPCK.
1987   *Genesis 37-50: A Commmentary*. Translated by John J. Scullion. London: SPCK.
Widengren, G.
1950   *The Ascension of the Apostle and the Heavenly Book*. Uppsala: Lundequistska Bokhandeln/Leipzig: Harrassowitz.
1957   "King and Covenant," *JSS* 2:1-32.
1984   "Yahweh's Gathering of the Dispersed," in W. Boyd Barrick and John R. Spencer (eds), *In the Shelter of Elyon: Essays on Ancient Palestinian Life and Literature in Honour of G. W. Ahlström*. JSOTSup 31. Sheffield: JSOT Press.
Widmer, Michael
2004   *Moses, God, and the Dynamics of Intercessory Prayer*. FAT 2. Reihe 8. Tübingen: Mohr Siebeck.
Wiener, A.
1978   *The Prophet Elijah in the Development of Judaism: a Depth-Psychological Study*. London: Routledge and Kegan Paul.
Wildberger, H.
1997   "שׂאר," in Ernst Jenni and Claus Westermann (eds), *TLOT*. Translated by Mark E. Biddle. Vol. 3. Peabody, Mass.: Hendrickson.
Williams, James G.
1966   "The Prophetic 'Father': A Brief Explanation of the Term 'Sons of the Prophets'," *JBL* 85:344-48.
Williams, R. J.
1976   *Hebrew Syntax: An Outline*. 2nd edn. Toronto: Univ. of Toronto Press.
Winjgaards, J. N. M.
1969   *The Dramatization of Salvific History in the Deuteronomic Schools*. OTS 16.
Wiseman, Donald J.
1993   *1 and 2 Kings: An Interpretation and Commentary*. Leicester: Inter-Varsity Press.
Woods, Fred E.
1992   "Elisha and the Children: The Question of Accepting Prophetic Succession," *Brigham Young University Studies* 32:47-58.
Woudstra, M. H.
1981   *The Book of Joshua*. NICOT. Grand Rapids, Mich.: Eerdmans.
Wright, Christopher J. H.
1998   *Deuteronomy*. NIBC. Peabody, Mass.: Hendrickson.
Wurthwein, Ernst
1970   "Elijah at Horeb: Reflections on 1 Kings 19:9-18," in John I. Durham

and J.R. Porter (eds), *Proclamation and Presence: Old Testament Essays in Honour of Gwynne Henton Davies*. London: SCM.

Young, E. J.
1952 *My Servants the Prophets*. Grand Rapids, Mich.: Eerdmans.

Zakovitch, Yair
1982 "A Still Small Voice: Form and Content in 1 Kings 19," *Tarbiz* 51:329-46.

AUTHOR INDEX

Aejmelaeus, A., 63–64, 65
Allen, R.B., 48
Alter, R., 108, 141
Ap-Thomas, D.R., 34
Ashley, T.R., 179, 181

Bailey, R.C., 8
Bakon, S., 198
Balentine, S., 96–97
Bar-Efrat, S., 139, 143
Barr, J., 44
Baumann, A., 88
Baumgartner, W., 78
Beek, M.A., 171, 187, 188
Begg, C.T., 155, 159, 160, 161–162, 163, 183
Bergen, W.J., 171, 172, 174–175, 176, 192, 196–197
Binns, L.E., 180
Boling, R.G., 137–138
Bratsiotis, N.P., 158
Bronner, L., 10, 184, 215–216
Brown, R., 178
Brueggemann, W., 8, 32, 39, 61, 119, 160, 169–170, 222
Burney, C.F., 48, 49, 161, 178, 190–191

Carroll, R.P., 178, 197
Cartledge, T.W., 61
Cassuto, U., 43, 44
Charlesworth, J.H., 43–44
Childs, B.S., 37, 164
Coats, G.W., 116–117
Cogan, M., 157, 158, 159, 163, 190, 196
Cohn, R.L., 26, 42
Conroy, C., 7–8
Coote, R.B., 52, 67, 69, 76, 192
Cross, F.M., 210, 212

Dahood, M., 81
Daube, D., 140
De Vries, S., 19, 25, 41, 222
Deem, A., 62
Dhorme, E., 79, 83
Driver, S.R., 44
Durham, J.I., 151

Edelman, D.V., 61
Eichrodt, W., 50, 91–92
Eissfeldt, O., 150

Feldman, L.H., 39
Fensham, F.C. 13
Fishbane, M., 3, 4, 140, 224
Flanagan, J.W., 26
Fohrer, G., 90
Fokkelman, J.P., 62, 108, 137, 143
Fox, E., 70, 73, 74–76, 77, 79, 84, 86
Frank, R.M., 62
Freedman, D.N., 212
Fretheim, T.E., 9, 11, 27, 37, 43, 49, 52, 55, 110, 150, 156–157, 158, 162, 163, 180, 192, 222

Gertel, E.B., 178, 193
Ginzberg, L., 178
Gordis, R., 81
Gowan, D.E., 110–111
Gray, J., 150, 161, 180, 183
Greenberg, M., 170
Gregory, R., 10
Gunkel, H., 168, 169, 174, 181, 192, 198–199

Habel, N., 119
Hamilton, V.P., 127, 129
Harrington, D.J., 190
Hartley, J.E., 80
Hasel, G.F., 127–128, 130, 131, 132

Author Index

Haupt, P., 77
Hauser, A.J., 10, 48, 52, 222
Hawk, L.D., 214
Hayward, R., 57
Hobbs, T.R., 157, 158, 160, 163, 171, 178, 192, 197
Holt, E.K., 31, 39
House, P.R., 34, 39–40, 48, 52, 179

Jeremias, J., 88–89, 132
Jobling, D., 30, 37
Jones, G.H., 182

Kissling, P.J., 120
Koehler, L., 78

LaBarbera, R., 187
Labuschagne, C.J., 145
Levine, N., 178–179
Lind, M.C., 208, 214
Long, B.O., 8, 17, 19, 24, 184, 189, 198
Lundbom, J.R., 184
Lust, J., 87

McCarthy, D.J., 206, 208
McClellan, W.H., 61
McNeile, A.H., 44, 59
Milgrom, J., 123
Miller, J.M., 148
Miller, P.D., 60, 211, 213, 215, 216
Miscall, P.D., 146, 148–149
Mitchell, G., 209
Moberly, R.W.L., 43, 56, 133, 151, 181–182, 194
Moore, R.D., 216
Morgenstern, J., 57, 151
Montgomery, J.A., 33, 154, 182
Muilenburg, J., 65

Nelson, R.D., 28, 33, 38, 41, 49, 160, 162, 163, 169, 175, 190, 192, 194, 205, 206, 208, 215, 222

Noth, M., 181

O'Brien, M., 172, 173, 184
Olley, J.W., 54
Organ, B.E., 58
Overholt, T.W., 206

Parzen, R., 39
Paul, S.M., 82
Pedersen, J., 62
Phillips, A., 184–186
Porter, J.R., 171, 208
Provan, I.W., 17, 25, 52, 152, 195, 222

Rad, G. von, 86–87, 128, 130, 149, 188, 210–211
Reif, S.C., 58
Rice, G., 150–151
Roberts, K.L., 38–39
Robinson, B.P., 67, 71–72, 73, 88, 89, 90, 91, 92, 93, 102, 103–105, 112–113, 114, 115, 116, 117, 118, 120, 121, 222
Rofé, A., 178
Ross, J.P. 61
Rowlett, L.L., 210
Rowley, H.H., 80, 131

Saldarini, A.J., 190
Schick, G.V., 77–79
Schoors, A., 63
Seybold, K., 53
Simon, U., 51, 53, 73, 90, 119
Skinner, J., 10, 157, 178, 182, 190
Smend, R., 5
Soggin, J.A., 203, 204, 214, 216
Steck, O.H., 42
Sternberg, M., 138

Tadmor, H., 157, 158, 159, 163, 190, 196
Terrien, S., 87, 100, 134

Thomas, D.W., 163
Trible, P., 27

Waldman, N.M., 39
Walsh, J.T., 1–2, 11–12, 14, 16, 18, 22, 23, 25, 27, 29, 31–32, 33, 34, 35–36, 37, 49–50, 72, 73, 84–85, 104, 144, 149, 150, 151, 169, 221–222
Weinfeld, M., 55
Weisman, Z., 179, 180

Wenham, G.J., 124, 127
Werblowsky, R.J., 80
Westermann, C., 130
Widengren, G., 208
Widmer, M., 109–110
Wiener, A., 87
Woods, F.E., 197
Wright, C.J.H., 28
Wurthwein, E., 71, 89, 90

SCRIPTURE INDEX

Scripture references **in bold** indicate a longer discussion. Square brackets indicate the reference in the English version, as against the reference in the Hebrew text.

Genesis
1:11, *126*
1:28, *126*
2:7, *126*
2:21, *80*
3:9, *53*
4:25, *120*
5:24, *172*
6:5-7, *127*
6:7, *127*
6:19-20, *129*
7:1-5, *125*
7:3, *129*
7:4, *127*
7:17-24, *126*
7:18, *126*
7:19, *126*
7:23, *125*
8:7-8, *51*
8:15-19, *125*
8:21, *127*
15:12, *80*
15:16, *81*
16:8, *53*
16:9, *119*
20:5-6, *173*
21:7, *54*
22, *137*
27:1, *178*
27:23, *190, 191*
27:27, *190, 191*
30:1, *55*
30:8, *163*
30:37, *195*
31:52, *209*
32:30, *181*
34:30, *25*
36:33-39, *121*
37:11, *55*
37:19-34, *108*
37:20, *108*
37:33, *108*
37:34, *189*
38:5, *141*
38:6, *141*
38:7, *141*
41:3-7, *75*
41:23-24, *75*
42:15, *170*
42:21, *156*
44:33, *120*
45:3, *128*
45:4b-8a, *128*
45:5, *129*
45:7, *125, 129, 130*
45:8, *185*
46:3, *13*
49, *178*
50:20, *129*

Exodus
2–6, *20*
2, *218*
2:11-15, *11, 218*
2:15, *11*
3, *92, 103, 104, 213, 214*
3:1, *51*
3:2, *183, 204*
3:2-3, *87*
3:6, *91*
3:6b, *103*
3:8, *214*
3:8-10, *135*
3:20, *214*
4:3, *12*
4:6-7, *12*
4:10-16, *3*
4:13, *115*
4:19, *135*
4:20, *51*
4:22, *46*
5–14, *218*
5, *45*
5:22, *18, 45*
5:23, *45*
6:18, *57*
7–12, *20*
7, *12*
7:1-5, *34*
7:11, *41*
7:17-18, *12*
7:20-21, *12*
7:22, *41*
8:3, *41*
8:5-6, *12*
8:12-13, *12*
8:14, *41*
8:15, *41*
8:18, *20*
9:4-6, *20*
9:8-10, *12*
9:13-21, *73*
9:14, *40*
9:26, *20*
10:5, *129*
10:21-22, *12*
10:23, *20*
10:28, *20, 26, 48*

10:28-29, *40*
11:7, *20*
11:12, *20*
12–15, *204*
12:6, *204*
12:12, *20, 40*
12:35, *59*
12:39, *64*
12:41-51, *204*
13–14, *209*
13:9, *202*
13:18, *209*
13:20, *209*
13:21, *183*
14–15, *200, 209*
14, *12, 40, 188*
14:2, *209, 211*
14:3-4, *211*
14:9, *188, 209, 211*
14:12, *156*
14:14, *209*
14:15-18, *211*
14:16, *12*
14:18, *188*
14:19, *211*
14:19-20, *203, 209*
14:20, *209*
14:21, *12, 176*
14:22, *176, 201*
14:23, *188*
14:24, *209*
14:24-25, *211*
14:26, *12, 188*
14:27, *12, 209*
14:28, *188*
14:29, *176, 201*
14:31, *41, 201, 202, 206*
15, *196, 200, 202, 209, 212, 215*
15:1, *188*
15:3, *209*
15:4, *188*

15:6, *202, 209*
15:8, *201*
15:9, *209*
15:11, *201, 212, 214*
15:11-12, *200*
15:12, *202*
15:15, *202*
15:16, *77, 201, 203, 214*
15:19, *188*
15:21, *188*
15:22, *11*
15:25, *45*
16, *12, 14, 18, 20, 218*
16:3, *12, 14*
16:8, *12*
16:12, *12, 45*
16:12-13, *12*
16:14, *75, 76*
16:15, *50*
16:16, *15*
16:20, *45*
16:21, *12*
16:31, *14*
16:35, *12, 15*
17:1-7, *11*
17:4-6, *45*
17:9, *171*
17:14, *126, 171*
17:16, *211*
18:11, *18*
19–20, *70, 71, 91, 92, 93, 99, 100, 104, 141, 218, 223, 224*
19, *34, 74, 85, 93, 218*
19:5, *93, 96*
19:9, *41, 85, 99, 219*
19:9-17, *85*
19:10-12, *203*
19:11, *74*
19:12, *100*
19:14-15, *203*
19:16, *74*

19:16-17, *52*
19:16-18, *85, 99*
19:17, *85*
19:18, *34, 100, 183, 219*
19:19, *74, 75, 85*
19:20, *164*
19:21, *203*
19:21-22, *100*
19:23-24, *203*
19:24, *100*
20–24, *56*
20, *98, 100, 101, 133*
20:1, *75*
20:2, *91*
20:2-4, *219*
20:4, *56, 82*
20:5, *55, 56, 64*
20:5-6, *133*
20:18, *219*
20:18-21, *90, 151*
20:19, *75, 100*
20:21, *100*
20:22, *75*
20:23, *43, 219*
22–23, *219*
22:25-26, *64*
23:20-33, *50*
23:20, *50*
23:24, *65*
24, *29, 35, 36, 37, 38, 204, 218, 224*
24:2, *37*
24:3, *37*
24:3-7, *219*
24:3-8, *37, 206*
24:4, *36, 204, 219*
24:5, *151*
24:7, *37*
24:7-8, *37*
24:9, *38*
24:9-11, *38, 219*
24:13, *171*

24:17, *35, 36, 92, 219*
29:30, *121*
30:36, *76*
32–34, *59, 100, 101, 109, 112, 116, 125, 135, 141, 219, 224*
32, *35, 36, 52, 54, 59, 68, 69, 141*
32:1, *135, 151, 219*
32:2-4, *59*
32:6, *56*
32:10, *93, 109, 111, 112, 125, 132–133, 136, 220*
32:11-13, *35*
32:17, *171, 174*
32:19, *45, 101, 142*
32:20, *76, 142*
32:24, *43*
32:25-29, *35*
32:27, *59*
32:29, *59*
32:30, *135*
32:30-34, *219*
32:31, *43, 69*
32:31-32, *42*
32:31-34, *110*
32:32, *69, 135, 219*
32:32-33, *126*
32:35, *59, 133*
33–34, *70, 71, 87, 90, 93, 99, 100, 101, 103, 104, 222*
33, *73, 133*
33:1-6, *136, 219*
33:2, *50*
33:3, *125*
33:5, *111, 220*
33:11, *87, 136, 171*
33:12-16, *136, 220*
33:12-17, *133*
33:12-23, *110*
33:16, *101*

33:18-23, *181*
33:18–34:9, *102*
33:19–34:7, *136, 220*
33:21-22a, *71*
33:21, *103, 104*
33:22, *91*
34, *54, 56, 98, 133*
34:2, *52, 71, 104, 164*
34:4-28, *151*
34:5, *87*
34:6, *71, 91*
34:6-7, *133*
34:6-9, *110*
34:8, *136, 220*
34:9, *101, 133*
34:10, *136, 214*
34:10-28, *220*
34:11-26, *56*
34:14, *55, 56, 64*
34:14-16, *56*
34:15-16, *55*
34:27, *133*
34:28, *51*
34:29, *151*
34:29-35, *136, 151, 220*
34:30-35, *102*
34:32, *152*

Leviticus
6:22, *121*
9:24, *34*
10:2, *34*
10:6, *189*
10:16, *45*
13:30, *75*
16:12, *75*
16:32, *121*
19:28, *31*
21:5, *31*
21:18, *29*
21:20, *75*
26:4, *10*

26:15-16, *97*

Numbers
3:12, *120*
4:23, *60*
5:23, *126*
7:89, *87, 93*
8:24, *60*
10:33-36, *210*
10:35-36, *203*
11, *11, 12, 14, 18, 45, 50, 68, 69, 178, 179, 180, 181*
11:4-15, *45*
11:8, *14, 18, 218*
11:9, *50*
11:10, *45*
11:10-12, *18, 69*
11:11-15, *18–19*
11:12, *46*
11:13, *69*
11:13-14, *46*
11:14, *69, 123*
11:14-15, *69*
11:15, *44, 46, 69*
11:16-17, *123*
11:16-30, *220*
11:17, *179*
11:25, *179*
11:28, *171, 174*
11:29, *179, 181*
12:8, *82, 176*
14:10, *125*
14:44-45, *210*
16, *197*
16:15, *45*
16:35, *34*
16:44, *125*
20:1-13, *11*
20:12, *122*
21:6, *125*
21:14, *211*
21:34, *13*

22:9, *53*
23:3, *81*
25, *57, 59*
25:3, *58*
25:4, *58*
25:5, *58*
25:6, *57–58*
25:8, *58*
25:13, *121*
25:14, *58*
26:1-2, *59*
26:23-24, *98*
26:27-28, *98*
26:40-41, *98*
26:44-45, *98*
26:64-65, *59*
27, *124*
27:4, *64*
27:12-14, *122*
27:12-23, *122*
27:15, *176*
27:15-23, *170*
27:16-17, *123*
27:18-23, *123*
28:1, *124*
30:1, *124*
31:1-2, *124*
31:7, *60, 66*
31:13, *124*
31:14, *45*
31:16, *58*
31:25-26, *124*
31:51, *124*
31:54, *124*
32:12, *121*

Deuteronomy
1:31, *46*
2:12, *121*
2:21-23, *121*
2:25, *214*
3:18-20, *207*
3:27, *170*
3:28, *123*
3:31, *123*
4:10, *35*
4:12, *82, 91*
4:15, *35, 82*
4:16, *82*
4:19, *60*
4:23, *82*
4:24, *55, 64, 183*
4:25, *55, 82*
4:37, *121*
5:1, *28*
5:4, *75, 91*
5:4-5, *34*
5:8, *82*
5:9, *55, 64*
5:22, *75*
5:22-26, *76*
5:22-27, *34*
5:25, *76*
6:15, *55, 64*
9:9, *51*
9:15, *142*
9:18, *51*
9:18-19, *110*
9:21, *76*
9:25, *51*
10:6, *121*
11:10-17, *10*
11:11-17, *28*
11:25, *214*
11:26-28, *28*
12:30, *155*
13:1-3, *34*
13:1-11, *27, 34*
14:1, *31*
17:16, *188*
18, *123*
18:15-19, *222*
18:15-22, *1*
18:16-17, *90*
18:18, *2, 3, 4, 30, 224*
18:20, *27, 66*
21:15-17, *178*
21:17, *178*
23:13-15, *211*
24:1, *95*
28:13-14, *26*
28:14, *10*
28:20, *9, 95, 96*
28:24, *9*
29:24, *56, 96*
29:25, *56*
30:15, *28*
30:15-20, *28*
30:16-17, *28*
30:19, *28*
31:1-23, *170*
31:2-3, *123*
31:7-8, *177, 178, 208*
31:14, *123*
31:16, *95*
31:16-17, *95, 97, 101*
31:16-21, *98*
31:17, *99*
31:20, *96*
31:23, *123*
32, *221*
32:18, *46*
32:37, *192*
32:48-50, *195, 221*
32:49, *221*
32:49-50, *170*
33:9, *96*
34, *40, 195, 220, 221*
34:1, *221*
34:1-6, *170*
34:5, *207*
34:5-6, *196, 221*
34:9, *193, 196, 220*
34:10, *195*
34:10a, *1*
34:11-12, *195*

Joshua
1–5, *198, 209*

Scripture Index

1–6, *1, 220*
1, *200, 208*
1:1-2, *124, 205*
1:1-9, *208, 210*
1:2, *208*
1:2-9, *211*
1:3, *205*
1:5, *205*
1:7, *169, 207*
1:11, *176, 209*
1:12-15, *207*
1:12-16, *211*
1:13, *210*
1:15, *209*
1:17, *205*
1:17-18, *204*
1:18, *197, 205*
2:9, *202*
2:9-11, *18, 202*
3–4, *200, 211*
3–5, *200, 204*
3:1, *175*
3:1–5:1, *200*
3:2, *176*
3:2-4, *210*
3:2-6, *203*
3:3-4, *211*
3:4, *176*
3:5, *201, 214*
3:7, *206, 208, 211, 217*
3:8, *175*
3:10, *213*
3:11, *203, 213*
3:13, *175, 201, 204*
3:15, *175*
3:15-17, *204*
3:16, *175, 176, 201*
3:17, *175, 201*
4, *215*
4:9, *204*
4:10, *175, 204, 207*
4:11, *176*

4:12, *207*
4:12-13, *209*
4:13, *176*
4:14, *124, 201, 203, 206, 208, 221*
4:18, *204*
4:19, *176*
4:20-23, *215*
4:22, *201*
4:22-24, *176*
4:23, *203*
4:24, *201, 202*
5:1, *175, 201, 202, 211*
5:2-12, *204*
5:7, *121*
5:10, *213*
5:12, *12*
5:13, *61, 204*
5:13-15, *196, 213, 221*
6, *214, 221*
6:1, *213*
6:7, *209*
6:26, *8*
7, *214*
7:13, *208, 211*
7:25, *25*
8:1, *13*
8:24, *66*
8:29, *194*
10:8, *13*
10:10, *209*
10:12-13a, *213*
10:25, *205*
10:27, *194*
11:6, *13, 188*
11:9, *188*
11:15, *169, 207*
12:4, *66*
14:11, *123*
22:4, *209*
22:8, *209*
22:17, *58*

23:12, *66*
24, *28*
24:2, *208*
24:11, *215*
24:19, *55*
24:20, *96*
24:26-27, *36*
24:29, *207*

Judges
1:14, *53*
2:1, *98*
2:8, *207*
2:11-23, *98*
2:12-13, *95, 96, 98*
2:13, *26*
2:14-15, *98*
2:15, *26*
2:20, *96*
3:10, *180*
4:2, *60*
4:15, *209*
5:20, *213*
6:1-5, *138*
6:14, *135*
6:14-16, *114*
6:22-23, *103*
6:33, *209*
7:25, *66*
8:6, *137*
8:7, *137*
8:9, *137*
9:1-3, *106*
9:3, *106*
9:3-5, *106*
9:5, *66*
9:16, *106, 107*
9:16-20, *105*
9:17, *106*
9:18, *106*
9:19, *106, 107*
9:24, *106*
9:38, *189*

9:57, *107*
10:6, *95, 96*
10:10, *96*
10:13, *96*
11:12, *16*
11:18-20, *209*
12:1, *209*
13, *95*
13:20, *34, 103*
15:2, *120*
17:2, *80*
17:7-8, *185*
17:10, *185*
18:5, *185*
18:17-18, *80*
18:19, *185*
18:23-24, *54*
18:24, *80*

1 Samuel
4:6, *75*
6:7, *49*
8:7-9, *107*
8:7a, *107*
8:7b, *107*
8:8, *95, 96*
8:9, *107*
8:9a, *107*
9, *38*
10:1, *208*
10:5, *180*
10:10, *179, 185*
10:20, *208*
11:15, *151*
12:7, *215*
12:10, *96*
12:14-15, *43*
15:23, *97*
15:26, *97, 120*
16:1, *122*
16:1-2, *121*
16:1-13, *149, 150*
16:12-13, *208*

17, *24*
17:6, *62*
17:41-51, *61*
17:43, *61*
17:45-47, *61*
17:47, *211*
17:49, *62*
18:12, *206*
18:13, *123*
18:16, *123*
18:17, *211*
21:6, *211*
22:23, *13*
25:28, *211*
26:11-16, *14*
28:6, *120*
28:15, *120*
29:6, *123*
30:13, *95*

2 Samuel
1:2, *189*
1:11, *189*
3:31, *189*
4:4, *29*
5:1-3, *208*
5:2, *123*
6–7, *38*
8:4, *188*
9:7, *13*
9:9-11, *26*
10:1, *121*
11–12, *23*
11, *139*
11:11, *211*
13:31, *189*
14:5, *53*
14:7, *130*
15:16, *95*
16:10, *16*
16:11, *111*
16:18, *121*
17:25, *121*

19:4, *189*
19:23, *16*
19:41-43, *209*
21:1, *23*
21:1-10, *10*
21:8, *34*
22:43, *76*
24, *34*
29, *209*

1 Kings
1–2, *5*
1:2, *164*
1:4, *152*
1:15, *152*
1:16, *53*
1:17, *208*
1:32, *208*
2:1-9, *178*
2:2, *208*
2:7, *26*
2:12, *208*
2:35, *121*
3:7, *123*
3:10, *195*
3:12-13, *208*
3:28, *208*
6:11-13, *134*
6:13, *101*
8:21, *209*
8:35-36, *10, 22*
9:9, *96*
9:19, *188*
9:22, *188*
10:28-29, *188*
11:1-5, *7*
11:9-13, *7*
11:14a, *198*
11:23a, *198*
11:26a, *198*
11:29-39, *208*
12:16, *211*
12:20, *208*

Scripture Index 257

13:1-10, *25*
13:11, *51*
16:29–17:24, **7–20**
16:29–33, *7, 8*
16:29-34, *218*
16:30, *7*
16:30-33, *98*
16:31–22:40, *5*
16:33b, *7*
16:34, *7, 8, 208*
17–18, *5, 10, 144,
    155, 157, 162, 164,
    222*
17–19, *5, 10, 42*
17–21, *1*
17–22, *155*
17, *10, 12, 14, 17, 18,
    19, 20, 21, 40, 89,
    164, 222*
17:1, *19, 24, 98, 104,
    185*
17:1-7, *9*
17:2-16, *19*
17:2, *85*
17:3, *24*
17:4, *13*
17:5a, *14*
17:6, *12, 13*
17:6a, *12*
17:7, *140*
17:8, *85*
17:9, *105*
17:10, *105*
17:14, *13*
17:15, *140*
17:15a, *14*
17:16, *13, 193*
17:16b, *14*
17:17-24, *19*
17:18, *218*
17:20, *180*
17:24, *3, 17, 193, 206*
18–19, *141*

18, *5, 10, 19, 20,* **21–
    41**, *28, 29, 35, 36,
    37, 38, 40, 41, 54,
    65, 74, 88, 89, 90,
    133, 141, 143, 162,
    164, 165, 218, 222*
18:1, *39, 85, 105, 140*
18:2, *105*
18:3-4, *22*
18:4, *51, 131*
18:4-5, *22*
18:9, *23*
18:10, *22, 186*
18:12, *23, 171, 194*
18:12a, *23*
18:12b, *23*
18:13, *23, 51, 131*
18:14, *23*
18:15, *9, 60, 104, 177*
18:17, *18, 186*
18:18, *10, 56, 95, 97,
    169*
18:19, *218*
18:19-21, *26*
18:20, *26, 169*
18:21, *29, 31*
18:22, *67, 131*
18:23-34, *31*
18:23, *31*
18:24, *26, 30, 31, 32,
    74, 90*
18:24-25, *30*
18:25, *30*
18:25-26, *30*
18:26, *29, 31, 74*
18:27, *31*
18:28, *31*
18:29, *31, 32, 34, 74*
18:30, *26*
18:31, *85*
18:31-32, *219*
18:36, *18, 37, 41, 92,
    180, 206*

18:37, *18, 31, 74*
18:38, *90*
18:39, *26, 37, 90*
18:40, *32, 158, 189*
18:41, *74*
18:41-42, *186, 219*
18:42, *38*
18:44, *185*
18:44-45, *186*
18:45, *140*
18:45b, *39, 139*
19, *5, 6, 16, 19, 29,
    36, 39,* **42–153**, *44,
    48, 59, 62, 68, 69,
    70, 71, 73, 74, 76,
    78, 83, 84, 85, 88,
    89, 91, 92, 93, 94,
    99, 100, 101, 103,
    105, 107, 108, 111,
    112, 115, 117, 122,
    123, 126, 137, 139,
    142, 143, 149, 150,
    151, 152, 166, 170,
    219, 222, 223, 224*
19:1, *60, 135, 139,
    219*
19:1-4, *47*
19:1-10, *47*
19:2, *140*
19:3-4, *54, 151*
19:4, *69, 135, 140,
    219*
19:5-9a, *50*
19:6, *14*
19:8, *51, 94, 140*
19:8-18, *151*
19:9, *53, 85, 103, 109,
    140, 168*
19:9-10, *112*
19:9-14, *5*
19:9-18, *94*
19:9b, *93*
19:9b-10, *53*

19:10, *10, 24, 29, 63, 64, 94, 97, 98, 102, 109, 131, 133, 135, 169, 177, 219*
19:10a*a*, *54, 62*
19:10a*a*1, *69*
19:10a*a*2-b, *69*
19:10ab, *65*
19:10ag, *65*
19:10b, *66, 69, 131*
19:11, *71, 81, 83, 84, 94, 104, 105, 184*
19:11aa, *72*
19:11ab, *71*
19:11-12, *72, 102, 109, 112, 136, 219*
19:11-13, *86*
19:11-13a, *70, 72, 73*
19:11b-12, *72, 102, 103*
19:12, *72, 74, 75, 78, 83, 84, 85, 88, 93*
19:13, *72, 74, 84, 85, 93, 102, 136*
19:13b, *72, 109, 111, 114, 220*
19:14, *29, 112, 115, 133, 135, 136, 169, 177, 219, 220*
19:15, *149*
19:15-16, *146*
19:15-18, *10, 117, 118, 125, 133, 135, 136, 220*
19:16, *74, 75, 121, 124, 149, 152*
19:17, *60, 177, 189*
19:17-18, *135, 219*
19:18, *66, 131*
19:19, *176*
19:19-21, *121, 136, 144, 149, 169, 207, 220*

19:21, *120, 124*
20, *39, 164*
20:13, *40*
20:26, *140*
20:28, *40*
20:29, *140*
20:35, *185*
20:42, *139*
21, *6, 23, 120, 137, 148, 222, 223*
21:15, *140*
21:16, *39, 140*
21:17, *125, 185*
21:17-19, *147*
21:17-20, *73*
21:17-24, *139*
21:17-29, *39*
21:21, *148*
21:21-24, *147*
21:23, *148*
21:27, *186*
21:27-29, *39, 146*
21:29, *120, 139*
22, *40*
22:1, *140*
22:19, *60*
22:19-23, *34*
22:26-27, *11*
22:35-36, *140*
22:51-53, *154*
22:51–2 Kings 1:18, **154–165**

2 Kings
1–2, *1, 137, 164*
1, *5, 41, 89, 90, 120, 154, 155, 160, 162, 163, 164, 165, 197, 220, 222, 223*
1:1, *154*
1:1-8, *197*
1:2, *155*
1:3, *155*
1:4, *159*

1:6, *159*
1:8, *149*
1:9, *155, 159, 186*
1:9-15, *197*
1:10, *41, 161*
1:11, *155, 159*
1:12, *41, 161*
1:13, *155*
1:15, *13, 155, 157*
1:16, *139, 185*
1:16-17, *197*
1:17, *8, 154, 193*
1:17-18, *5, 154*
2, *1, 6, 8, 40, 121, 149, 150, 162, 165,* **166–217**, *167, 175, 176, 177, 179, 180, 181, 182, 185, 187, 191, 193, 194, 196, 197, 198, 199, 200, 204, 205, 206, 209, 215, 217, 220, 222, 224*
2:1, *167, 172, 183, 186, 196*
2:1-6, *166*
2:1-14, *144*
2:1-18, *121, 166, 199*
2:2, *24, 170, 196*
2:2-6, *197*
2:3, *120, 172, 173, 194*
2:4, *170, 196*
2:5, *120, 172, 173, 194*
2:6, *170, 189*
2:6-14, *196*
2:7, *174, 194, 197*
2:7-8, *174*
2:8, *191, 192, 197*
2:9, *172, 178, 183, 197*
2:9-10, *177, 180*

2:10, *172, 197*
2:11, *167, 168, 172, 189, 197*
2:11-12, *183*
2:12, *9, 184, 197*
2:13, *197*
2:13-15, *189*
2:14, *192, 197*
2:15, *124, 179, 194, 196, 197, 199*
2:16, *172, 192*
2:16-18, *193, 197, 199*
2:17, *140*
2:19-22, *197*
2:21, *122*
2:23, *196*
2:23-24, *197*
2:25, *196, 197*
3, *216*
3:11, *122, 124, 163*
3:11-15, *164*
3:13, *16*
3:14, *9, 24*
4:1, *185*
4:8-16, *138*
4:13, *177*
4:32, *180*
4:38, *185*
4:43, *152*
5:7, *189*
5:15, *18, 156, 164*
5:16, *9*
5:22, *185*
6, *182, 183, 187*
6:1, *185*
6:12, *185*
6:13, *186*
6:13-17, *186*
6:15, *61, 152*
6:16, *13, 216*
6:17, *182, 183, 186*
6:18, *180, 187*
6:20, *186*

6:21, *185*
6:21-23, *189*
6:28, *53*
6:30, *189*
7, *216*
7:1, *185*
7:6, *75, 187*
8:7, *144*
8:7-8, *145*
8:7-15, *144, 163–164*
8:9, *185*
8:10, *147*
8:11-12, *147*
8:11-13, *145*
8:13, *147*
8:14, *145*
8:25–9:37, *145*
9–10, *10*
9:1, *185*
9:1-3, *145*
9:1-13, *144*
9:3, *147*
9:6-10, *208*
9:7, *147*
9:13, *208*
9:21, *147*
9:25-26, *147, 194*
9:26, *8*
9:36-37, *148*
10:10, *148*
10:16, *148*
10:17, *148*
10:30, *148*
11:18, *123*
13, *187, 216*
13:14, *177, 185, 186*
13:14-19, *187*
13:21, *194*
15:7-38, *121*
17:5-23, *26*
17:15, *97*
17:16, *95, 96*
21:22, *95, 96*

22:16, *96*
22:17, *96*
23, *38*
23:3, *38*
23:6, *76*
23:15, *76*
23:18, *111*

1 Chronicles
2:7, *25*
4:43, *129*
5:26, *180*
29:24, *119*

2 Chronicles
7:1-3, *34*
10:16, *211*
12:5, *96*
12:7, *129*
15:2, *96*
15:16, *76*
21:12, *6*
24:20, *96*
29:1–31:1, *38*
29:10, *38*
34:4, *76*
34:7, *76*
34:29–35:19, *38*
34:31-32, *38*
36:25, *180*

Ezra
9:8, *129*
9:10, *95*
9:14, *129*

Esther
2:4, *120*
3:13, *66*
5:3, *53*
7:4, *66*

Job
1:16, *163*
1:19, *81*
4, *86*
4:12-16, *77, 78, 79, 83*
4:15, *83, 84*
4:15-16, *86, 104*
4:16, *77, 78, 79, 82,
    83, 84, 88, 102,
    153*
7:14, *80*
9:11, *81*
9:17, *81*
11:10, *81*
17:15, *189–190*
20:2, *80*
20:8, *80*
26:14, *80*
28, *82*
31:34, *77*
33:15, *80*
38:1, *81, 184*
40:6, *184*

Psalms
4:5, *78*
17:15, *82*
20:7, *188*
30:13, *77, 78*
30:17, *188*
44:9, *61*
44:17, *96*
48:5, *209*
66:6, *215*
68:18 [17], *183*
76:7, *80*
77:16-20, *212*
78:37, *96*
83:16, *184*
84:4, *61*
89:31 [30], *95*
95:7, *37*
97:2, *89*

97:2-5, *71*
99:6, *1*
104:1, *92*
104:4, *92*
107:23-32, *83*
107:25, *83*
107:27, *78*
107:29, *77, 78, 79, 83,
    84*
107:30, *83*
114, *212, 215*
114:3, *215*
114:5, *215*
119:20, *81, 82*
139:16, *176*
147:10, *188*
148:8, *81*

Proverbs
19:15, *80*
21:31, *61*

Ecclesiastes
2:18, *121*

Isaiah
5:24, *97*
6:5, *61*
6:5-7, *114*
6:5-8, *3*
6:8, *135*
10:20, *129*
10:28-29, *209*
14:30, *125*
15:9, *125*
17:3, *125*
17:4-6, *125*
17:6, *80*
19:12, *189*
23:2, *78*
24:17-18, *131*
28:28, *76*
29:5, *75*

29:10, *80*
30:23, *10*
31:1, *188*
37:38, *121*
40:3-6, *212*
40:15, *75*
41:15, *76*
41:16, *81, 82*
41:21-29, *32*
42:13, *55*
44:17, *125*
47:5, *78*
49:14-15, *95*
53, *43*
61:1, *149*
63:17, *34*
65:11, *95*

Jeremiah
1:5-9, *114*
1:7, *135*
1:9, *3*
2:2, *55*
2:13, *95*
2:17, *95*
2:19, *95*
3, *55*
5:10-18, *126*
5:24, *10*
8:3, *125*
8:19, *75*
9:12 [13], *95*
10:13, *10*
11:16, *75*
12:1-6, *115, 119*
13:25, *97*
14, *10*
14:3-4, *10*
14:22, *10*
15:1, *1, 110*
15:1-4, *44*
15:10-21, *115, 119*
16:11, *95*
18:15, *97*

Scripture Index

19:4, *95*
22:9, *95*
22:19, *194*
23:3, *125*
23:3-4, *126*
23:19, *184*
23:20, *80*
30:23, *10*
31:7-9, *126*
37:1, *121*
51:16, *10*

Lamentations
2:10, *77, 78*
3:28, *78*

Ezekiel
1:4, *81*
1:26-38, *87*
1:28, *87, 103*
2:8–3:3, *3*
3:12, *75*
13:9, *43*
16, *55*
16:59-60, *99*
17:24, *195*
18:30-32, *28*
21:3 [20:47], *195*
21:14-22 [21:8-17], *134*
22:12, *97*
23, *55*
23:35, *97*
23:42, *75*
24:15-18, *172*
27:24, *176*
39:23, *97*

Daniel
8:11, *213*
8:18, *80*
10:9, *80, 103*
10:15-19, *103*
11:30, *95*

Hosea
1–3, *55*
1:4-5, *148*
2:7, *55*
2:15, *55*
4:10, *95*
4:16-17, *111*
9:17, *97*
11:8-9, *110*
14:3, *188*

Amos
1:8, *125*
2:4, *97*
4:13, *61*
5:3, *125*
5:5, *155*
5:13, *78*
5:14-15, *126*
7:1-6, *109, 112*
8:3, *194*
9:12, *125*

Jonah
1:6, *53*
1:11-12, *83*
3:3, *163*
4:8, *69*
4:9, *53*

Micah
2:12, *125*
4:6-7, *126*
4:7, *125*
4:13, *76*
5:10, *188*
6:5, *215*

Nahum
1:2, *55*
1:3, *81*

Habakkuk
1:1, *81*
1:11, *209*
3:8, *183*

Zephaniah
3:12-13, *125, 126*

Haggai
1:14, *180*
2:22, *188*

Zechariah
9:7, *125*
9:14, *184*
10:1, *10*
13:4, *149, 190*
13:8, *178*

Malachi
3:16, *43*
4:5, *6*

Sirach
10:10, *80*
18:32, *80*
45:23, *57*
46:1, *208*
48:1, *184*
48:3, *154, 184*
48:4, *154*
48:6, *154*
48:9, *167, 184*
48:12, *179*

1 Maccabees
2:26, *57*
2:58, *196*

2 Maccabees
7:30-38, *44*

4 Maccabees
6:28-29, *43*
17:12-13, *44*
18:12, *57*

Matthew
3:4, *149*

Mark
1:6, *149*

Romans
11:2-5, *66*

Paternoster Biblical Monographs

(All titles uniform with this volume)
Dates in bold are of projected publication.
Condensed details are given for volumes published before 2004.

Joseph Abraham
Eve: Accused or Acquitted?
A Reconsideration of Feminist Readings of the Creation Narrative Texts in Genesis 1–3
'A perceptive exploration of modern feminist readings', Gordon McConville.
2002 / 978-0-85364-971-7 / xxiv + 272pp

Kevin L. Anderson,
'But God Raised Him from the Dead'
The Theology of Jesus' Resurrection in Luke-Acts
This first full-scale study of the resurrection of Jesus in Luke-Acts argues that the resurrection of Jesus constitutes the focus of the Lukan message of salvation. It situates Luke's perspective on resurrection amongst Jewish and Hellenistic conceptions of the afterlife, and within the complex of Luke's theology, christology, ecclesiology, and eschatology.
Kevin L. Anderson is an Assistant Professor of Bible and Theology at Asbury College, Wilmore, Kentucky, USA.
2006 / 978-1-84227-339-5 / xx + 354pp

Octavian D. Baban
On the Road Encounters in Luke-Acts
Hellenistic Mimesis and Luke's Theology of the Way
The book argues on theological and literary (mimetic) grounds that Luke's on-the-road encounters, especially those belonging to the post-Easter period, are part of his complex theology of the Way. Jesus' teaching and that of the apostles is presented by Luke as a challenging answer to the Hellenistic reader's thirst for adventure, good literature, and existential paradigms.
Octavian D. Baban is New Testament and New Testament Greek Lecturer at the Bucharest State University and at the Bucharest Baptist Theological Centre, Bucharest, Romania.
2006 / 978-1-84227-253-4 / xviii + 332pp

Paul Barker
The Triumph of Grace in Deuteronomy
This book is a textual and theological analysis of the interaction between the sin and faithlessness of Israel and the grace of Yahweh in response, looking especially at Deuteronomy chapters 1–3, 8–10 and 29–30. The author argues that the grace of Yahweh is determinative for the ongoing relationship between Yahweh and Israel and that Deuteronomy anticipates and fully expects Israel to be faithless.
Paul Barker is Visiting Lecturer in Old Testament, Ridley College, Melbourne, and Vicar, Holy Trinity Doncaster, Victoria, Australia.
2004 / 978-1-84227-226-8 / xxii + 270pp

Jonathan F. Bayes
The Weakness of the Law
God's Law and the Christian in New Testament Perspective
'Will provoke wide-ranging and stimulating debate', William S. Campbell.
2000 / 978-0-85364-957-1 / xii + 244pp

Michael F. Bird
The Saving Righteousness of God
Studies on Paul, Justification and the New Perspective
This book presents a series of studies on contentious aspects of Paul's doctrine of justification including the meaning of 'righteousness', the question of imputation, the role of resurrection in justification, an evaluation of the New Perspective, the soteriological and ecclesiological significance of justification, justification by faith with judgment according to works, and debates over the orthodoxy of N.T. Wright. The burden of the volume is to demonstrate that reformed and 'new' readings of Paul are indispensable to attaining a full understanding of Paul's soteriology.

Michael F. Bird is New Testament Lecturer, Highland Theological College, Dingwall, Scotland, UK.

2007 / 978-1-84227-465-1 / xviii + 230pp

David Bostock
A Portrayal of Trust
The Theme of Faith in the Hezekiah Narratives
This study provides detailed and sensitive readings of the Hezekiah narratives (2 Kings 18–20 and Isaiah 36–39) from a theological perspective. It concentrates on the theme of faith, using narrative criticism as its methodology. Attention is paid especially to setting, plot, point of view and characterization within the narratives. A largely positive portrayal of Hezekiah emerges that underlines the importance and relevance of scripture.

David Bostock is a teaching fellow in Old Testament at the University of St Andrews, Scotland, UK.

2006 / 978-1-84227-314-2 / xx + 252pp

Mark Bredin
Jesus, Revolutionary of Peace
A Non-violent Christology in the Book of Revelation
'Bold and engaging', Richard Bauckham.

2003 / 978-1-84227-153-7 / xviii + 262pp

Robinson Butarbutar
Paul and Conflict Resolution
An Exegetical Study of Paul's Apostolic Paradigm in 1 Corinthians 9
The author sees the apostolic paradigm in 1 Corinthians 9 as part of Paul's unified arguments in 1 Corinthians 8–10 in which he seeks to mediate in the dispute over the issue of food offered to idols. The book also sees its relevance for dispute-resolution today, taking the conflict within the author's church as an example.

Robinson Butarbutar has served as a minister, theological lecturer and mission organizer in his homeland of Indonesia.

2007 / 978-1-84227-315-9 / xviii + 276pp

Daniel J-S Chae
Paul as Apostle to the Gentiles
His Apostolic Self-awareness and its Influence on the Soteriological Argument in Romans
'An outstanding piece of work', I. Howard Marshall.

1997 / 978-0-85364-829-1 / xiv + 378pp

Ling Cheng
The Characterisation of God in Acts
The Indirect Portrayal of an Invisible Character
Based on the plot-oriented nature of the Acts narrative, Dr Cheng shows that God's supreme saving will and mission plan determine the development of human history as well as the narrative, and his sovereign authority and power governs the movement of characters and the development of events and thus assures the fulfilment of his salvific plan. From the carrying out of the divine redemptive plan emerges a God who is invisible-yet-perceivable, dominant-yet-cogent, and continuous-yet-changing.
Ling Cheng teaches New Testament Studies at Taiwan Theological Seminary.
2011 / 978–1–84227–628–0 / approx. 300pp

Luke L. Cheung
The Genre, Composition and Hermeneutics of the Epistle of James
'A masterly study', Richard Bauckham.
2003 / 978-1-84227-062-2 / xvi + 372pp

Youngmo Cho
Spirit and Kingdom in the Writings of Luke and Paul
An Attempt to Reconcile these Concepts
The relationship between Spirit and kingdom is a relatively unexplored area in Lukan and Pauline studies. This book offers a fresh perspective of two biblical writers on the subject. It explores the difference between Luke's and Paul's understanding of the Spirit by examining the specific question of the relationship of the concept of the Spirit to the concept of the kingdom of God in each writer.
Youngmo Cho is Assistant Professor of New Testament Studies, Asia LIFE University, Daejon, South Korea.
2005 / 978-1-84227-316-6 / xviii + 228pp

Andrew C. Clark
Parallel Lives
The Relation of Paul to the Apostles in the Lucan Perspective
'Crisp and methodological elucidation of the issues', Max Turner.
2001 / 978-1-84227-035-6 / xviii + 386pp

Andrew D. Clarke
Secular and Christian Leadership in Corinth
A Socio-Historical and Exegetical Study of 1 Corinthians 1–6
This volume is an investigation into the leadership structures and dynamics of first-century Roman Corinth. These are compared with the practice of leadership in the Corinthian Christian community which are reflected in 1 Corinthians 1–6, and contrasted with Paul's own principles of Christian leadership.
Andrew D. Clarke is Senior Lecturer in New Testament, Department of Divinity with Religious Studies, University of Aberdeen, Scotland, UK.
2006^2 / 978-1-84227-229-9 / 206pp

Victor Copan
Saint Paul as Spiritual Director
An Analysis of the Imitation of Paul with Implications and Applications to the Practice of Spiritual Direction
In recent years much has been written on spiritual direction. However, confusion and at times outright contradiction exists between the aims and methodologies of various models of Christian spiritual direction. In order to develop solid criteria for evaluating and critiquing these models it is necessary to root the practice of spiritual direction in the biblical record. The intention of this study is to provide such biblical moorings by examining the Apostle Paul as a case study in his function as a spiritual director—with respect to his aims and praxis of spiritually forming the members of the congregations he founded.
Victor Copan is Associate Professor of Ministry, Palm Beach Atlantic University, Florida, USA.
2007 / 978-1-84227-367-8 / xxvi + 296pp

John C. Crutchfield
Psalms in Their Context
An Interpretation of Psalms 107–118
Psalms in their Context employs a canonical methodology to interpret Psalms 107-118. This methodology begins with a study of each poem as a separate work, but also includes consideration of each psalm in its various literary contexts, including its relation to adjacent psalms, its Psalter context, and its canonical context. The author suggests that each psalm should be understood in light of the Psalter's three-fold themes of wisdom, eschatology and worship. An Appendix reviews selected evidence from the Dead Sea Scrolls on when and how the Psalter may have been put together.
John C. Crutchfield is Associate Professor of Biblical Studies, Columbia International University, Columbia, South Carolina, USA.
2011 / 978-1-84227-396-5 / approx. 240pp

Audrey Dawson
Healing, Weakness and Power
Perspectives on Healing in the Writings of Mark, Luke and Paul
As Mark, Luke and Paul reveal major differences in their emphases and theological presentations of divine healing, the evidence for, and causes of, these variations are analysed in relation to their views of Jesus' power and weakness, and the legacy of Jesus' healing is considered briefly over the subsequent few centuries.
Audrey Dawson was a consultant physician (clinical haematologist) and senior lecturer in the University of Aberdeen, becoming OBE for services to medicine. On retirement she completed her PhD at Aberdeen on which this book is based.
2008 / 978-1-84227-524-5 / xviii + 302pp

Havilah Dharamraj
A Prophet Like Moses?
A Narrative-Theological Reading of the Elijah Stories
In evaluating Elijah as a prophet after the Mosaic paradigm, this work proposes a radically different schema for interpreting what is one of the most dramatic and difficult texts in the Old Testament, namely, the earthquake-wind-and-fire theophany at Horeb.
Havilah Dharamraj is Assistant Professor, Department of Old Testament, South Asia Institute of Advanced Christian Studies, Bangalore, India.
2011 / 978-1-84227-533-7 / approx. 300pp

Stephen Finamore
God, Order and Chaos
René Girard and the Apocalypse

Readers are often disturbed by the images of destruction in the book of Revelation and unsure why they are unleashed after the exaltation of Jesus. This book examines past approaches to these texts and uses René Girard's theories to revive some old ideas and propose some new ones.

Stephen Finamore is Principal of Bristol Baptist College, UK.

2009 / 978-1-84227-197-1 / xxviii + 290pp

David G. Firth
Surrendering Retribution in the Psalms
Responses to Violence in the Individual Complaints

Firth examines the ways the book of Psalms inculcates a model response to violence through the repetition of standard patterns of prayer. Rather than seeking justification for retributive violence, it encourages not only a surrender of the right of retribution to Yahweh, but also sets limits on the retribution that can be sought.

David G. Firth is Tutor in Old Testament, Cliff College, Calver, UK.

2005 / 978-1-84227-337-1 / xviii + 154pp

William A. Ford
God, Pharaoh and Moses
Explaining God's Actions in the Exodus Plagues Narrative

The story of the Exodus from Egypt is of fundamental importance, both in the Old Testament and beyond. However, it also contains issues that are theologically problematic for readers, especially concerning the actions of God. Why does God send a series of plagues on Egypt? How do we understand the hardening of Pharaoh's heart? What do the answers to these questions say about the character of God? Ford addresses these questions, taking a narrative theological approach, reading the story as story. He concentrates on the passages within the story that appear to present rationales for God's actions, reading these 'explanations' in their context, paying attention to speaker, addressee, purpose, and reception. The picture that emerges is of God as responsive, speaking and acting to challenge the hearer to make the appropriate response to him.

William A. Ford is a Visiting Lecturer in Hebrew and Old Testament at All Nations Christian College, Ware, and previously studied at Durham and Oxford.

2006 / 978-1-84227-420-0 / xx + 248pp

Kabiro wa Gatumu
The Pauline Concept of 'Supernatural Powers'
A Reading from an African Worldview

The study of supernatural powers is fraught with hermeneutical challenges, which increase further in the African context. While Western anthropology tends to discount the idea of supernatural powers by attempting to 'explain them away', Western biblical scholarship has mainly worked from the premise of 'demythologizing' them. But none of these approaches make sense to African scholars for whom supernatural powers constitute an integral component of the spiritual psyche. This book, based on the examination of over a thousand documentary sources (both ancient and modern), attempts to address the issue of interpreting supernatural powers from an African worldview. The author analyses, identifies, and critiques major hermeneutical errors and offers a 'bridging hermeneutic' using the method of reader-response criticism.

Kabiro wa Gatumu is Lecturer in New Testament Studies, New Testament Greek and African Biblical Hermeneutics at St Paul's University, Limuru, Kenya.

2008 / 978-1-84227-532-0 / xxvi + 300pp

Scott J. Hafemann
Paul, Moses and the History of Israel
The Letter/Spirit Contrast and the Argument from Scripture in 2 Corinthians 3
An exegetical study of the call of Moses, the second giving of the Law (Exodus 32–34), the new covenant, and the prophetic understanding of the history of Israel in 2 Corinthians 3. Hafemann demonstrates Paul's contextual use of the Old Testament and the essential unity between the Law and the Gospel within the context of the distinctive ministries of Moses and Paul.
Scott J. Hafemann is the Mary F. Rockefeller Distinguished Professor of New Testament at Gordon-Conwell Theological Seminary, South Hamilton, Massachusetts, USA.
2005 [1995] / 978-1-84227-317-3 / xii + 498pp

Scott J. Hafemann
Suffering and Ministry in the Spirit
Paul's Defence of His Ministry in II Corinthians 2:14–3:3
'A book of persuasive power', Jerome Murphy O'Connor.
2000 [1990] / 978-0-85364-967-0 / xvi + 262pp

Paul M. Hoskins
Jesus as the Fulfillment of the Temple in the Gospel of John
Interpreters often associate John 1:14, 1:51, 2:18-22 and 4:20-24 with Jesus' replacement of the Temple. Based on these texts, one can already begin to see that he fulfills and replaces the Temple in that he is the new locus of God's presence, glory, revelation, and abundant provision for his people. In particular, John 2:18-22 clearly associates Jesus' role as the Temple with his death and resurrection.
Paul M. Hoskins is Assistant Professor of New Testament, Southwestern Baptist Theological Seminary, Fort Worth, Texas, USA.
2006 / 978-1-84227-360-9 / xvi + 266pp

Barry C. Joslin
Hebrews, Christ, and the Law
The Theology of the Mosaic Law in Hebrews 7:1–10:18
Joslin seeks to fill a lacuna in studies of Hebrews, namely, the writer's theology of the Mosaic Law, which is seen most clearly in the doctrinal centre of the book, 7:1–10:18. He concludes that for the writer the work of Christ has *transformed* the Law, and that this involves both its fulfillment and internalization in the New Covenant; the Law has forever been affected christologically. As such, there are continuous and discontinuous aspects of the Law that hinge on Christ, the writer's chief 'hermeneutical principle'.
Barry C. Joslin is Assistant Professor of Christian Theology, Boyce College, The Southern Baptist Theological Seminary, Louisville, KY, USA.
2008 / 978-1-84227-530-6 / xx + 334pp

Mark Keown
Congregational Evangelism in Philippians
The Centrality of an Appeal for Gospel Proclamation to the Fabric of Philippians
Did Paul want his congregations to pick up the ministry of evangelism or did he envisage himself and other 'specialist' proclaimers continuing the ministry of the gospel? Dr Keown argues that one essential element of the rhetorical appeal of the letter is an injunction to the Philippians to continue to preach the gospel with renewed unity in the face of pagan opposition. He suggests Paul envisaged 'specialist proclaimers' leading the evangelistic mission and equipping 'general believers' to share the gospel as one dimension of living in the world.
Mark J. Keown is Lecturer in New Testament at Laidlaw College, Auckland, New Zealand.
2008 / 978-1-84227-510-8 / xxii + 360pp

Roger A. Latham
Christian Scripture and Postmodernity
Toward a Confessional Hermeneutic in Postmodern Biblical Studies
This book engages in depth with the work of pioneering postmodern scholars to explore the strongly ideological character of much postmodern biblical scholarship, and explains the failure of some confessional approaches to respond adequately to the new environment. Christian interpretation has a valid role to play as a distinct ideological perspective within the spectrum of academic approaches in Biblical Studies, and Latham proposes a multidisciplinary model for confessional interpreters which, along with a distinctively Christian ethics of interpretation, will enable Christian scholars to engage constructively with those whose methods, values and ideologies differ from theirs.
Roger Latham is a Team Vicar on the Cartmel Peninsula in the Diocese of Carlisle.
2010-11 / 978-1-84227-631-0 / approx. 300pp

Nicholas P. Lunn
Word-Order Variation in Biblical Hebrew Poetry
Differentiating Pragmatic Poetics
This study tackles the neglected subject of word order in biblical Hebrew poetry. The fact that the order of clause constituents frequently differs from that found in prose has often been noted, but no systematic attempt has been offered by way of explanation. Here two separate factors are taken into consideration: that of purely poetic variation (defamiliarisation), and that of pragmatic markedness. This work offers a new approach to the poetry of the Old Testament that will aid towards more accurate translation, exegesis, and discourse analysis of poetic texts.
Nicholas P. Lunn is a Senior Translation Consultant with Wycliffe Bible Translators, UK.
2006 / 978-1-84227-423-1 / xxii + 374pp

Douglas S. McComiskey
Lukan Theology in the Light of the Gospel's Literary Structure
Luke's Gospel was purposefully written with theology embedded in its patterned literary structure. A critical analysis of this cyclical structure provides new windows into Luke's interpretation of the individual pericopes comprising the Gospel and illuminates several of his theological interests.
Douglas S. McComiskey is Professor of New Testament, Ridley College, Melbourne, Australia.
2004 / 978-1-84227-148-3 / xviii + 388pp

Martin Mosse
The Three Gospels
New Testament History Introduced by the Synoptic Problem
Mosse combines a relentlessly logical assault on the Synoptic Problem with a radical treatment of New Testament history and chronology. Arguing for early dates and traditional authorship of the Synoptics, and against the redundant hypothesis of Q, he tackles also the major cruces in early church history, including the later career of Paul.
Martin Mosse holds degrees in classics, mathematics and theology. He currently runs a think tank called BRAINWAVES.
2007 / 978-1-84227-520-7 / xxxii + 364pp

Stephen Motyer
Your Father the Devil?
A New Approach to John and 'The Jews'
'This elegantly-written book breaks fresh ground', Graham Stanton.
1997 / 978-0-85364-832-1 / xiv + 260pp

Esther Ng
Reconstructing Christian Origins?
The Feminist Theology of Elizabeth Schüssler Fiorenza: An Evaluation
'Strongly challenges Fiorenza's rather rosy picture of egalitarianism', Ruth B. Edwards.
2002 / 978-1-84227-055-4 / xxiv + 468pp

Robin Parry
Old Testament Story and Christian Ethics
The Rape of Dinah as a Case Study
What is the role of story in ethics and, more particularly, what is the role of Old Testament story in Christian ethics? This book, drawing on the work of contemporary philosophers, argues that narrative is crucial in the ethical shaping of people and, drawing on the work of contemporary Old Testament scholars, that story plays a key role in Old Testament ethics. Parry then argues that when situated in canonical context Old Testament stories can be reappropriated by Christian readers in their own ethical formation. The shocking story of the rape of Dinah and the massacre of the Shechemites provides a fascinating case study for exploring the parameters within which Christian ethical appropriations of Old Testament stories can live.
Robin Parry is Commissioning Editor for Paternoster, UK.
2004 / 978-1-84227-210-7 / xx + 350pp

Robert L. Plummer
Paul's Understanding of the Church's Mission
Did the Apostle Paul Expect the Early Christian Communities to Evangelize?
This book engages in a careful study of Paul's letters to determine if the apostle expected the communities to which he wrote to engage in missionary activity. It helpfully summarizes the discussion on this debated issue, judiciously handling contested texts, and provides a way forward in addressing this critical question. While admitting that Paul rarely explicitly commands the communities he founded to evangelize, Plummer amasses significant incidental data to provide a convincing case that Paul did indeed expect his churches to engage in mission activity. Throughout the study, Plummer progressively builds a theological basis for the church's mission that is both distinctively Pauline and compelling.
Robert L. Plummer is Assistant Professor of New Testament Interpretation, The Southern Baptist Theological Seminary, Louisville, Kentucky, USA.
2006 / 978-1-84227-333-3 / xviii + 190pp

David Powys
'Hell': A Hard Look at a Hard Question
The Fate of the Unrighteous in New Testament Thought
'This book is an impressive and thorough discussion of a thorny question', Graham Stanton.
1997 / 978-0-85364-831-4 / xxii + 478pp

Sorin Sabou
Between Horror and Hope
Paul's Metaphorical Language of Death in Romans 6.1-11
This book argues that Paul's metaphorical language of death in Romans 6.1-11 conveys two aspects: horror and hope. The 'horror' aspect is conveyed by the 'crucifixion' language, and the 'hope' aspect by 'burial' language. The life of the Christian believer is understood, as relationship with sin is concerned ('death to sin'), between these two realities: horror and hope.
Sorin Sabou is Lecturer at Bucharest Baptist Seminary and Senior Pastor of the Romanian Baptist Church, Brasov, Romania.
2005 / 978-1-84227-322-7 / xvi + 160pp

Rosalind Selby
The Comical Doctrine
The Epistemology of New Testament Hermeneutics
This book argues that the gospel breaks through postmodernity's critique of truth and the referential possibilities of textuality with its gift of grace. With a rigorous, philosophical challenge to modernist and postmodernist assumptions, Selby offers an alternative epistemology to all who would still read with faith *and* with academic credibility.
Rosalind Selby is a lay preacher in the United Reformed Church and completed her doctorate at the University of Aberdeen, UK.
2006 / 978-1-84227-212-1 / xvi + 282pp

Kiwoong Son
Zion Symbolism in Hebrews
Hebrews 12.18-24 as a Hermeneutical Key to the Epistle
This book challenges the general tendency of understanding the Epistle to the Hebrews against a Hellenistic background and suggests that the Epistle should be understood in the light of the Jewish apocalyptic tradition. The author especially argues for the importance of the theological symbolism of Sinai and Zion (Heb. 12.18-24) as it provides the Epistle's theological background as well as the rhetorical basis of the superiority motif of Jesus throughout the Epistle.
Kiwoong Son completed his doctorate at London School of Theology and has served as a chaplain to Korean and Asian students at Royal Holloway College, University of London, UK.
2005 / 978-1-84227-368-5 / xviii + 248pp

Kevin Walton
Thou Traveller Unknown
The Presence and Absence of God in the Jacob Narrative
'A lucid and perceptive interpretation of the Jacob narratives', Gordon McConville.
2003 / 978-1-84227-059-2 / xvi + 238pp

Jason A. Whitlark
Enabling Fidelity to God
Perseverance in Hebrews in Light of Reciprocity Systems of the Ancient Mediterranean World
The primary focus of this book is to demonstrate how Hebrews represents, in view of its historical and religious context, human fidelity to God. In order to provide a fresh perspective on this issue it examines Hebrews' understanding of fidelity from the perspective of Hebrews' authorial audience. Its conclusions have far reaching implications for the soteriology of Hebrews, the author's and the auditors' presumed experience of salvation in Jesus Christ, and how the message of the supremacy of Jesus Christ was heard in the context Hebrews presupposes.

Jason A. Whitlark is a Professor in Religion, Baylor University, Waco, Texas, USA.

2008 / 978-1-84227-573-3 / xviii + 226pp

George M. Wieland
The Significance of Salvation
A Study of Salvation Language in the Pastoral Epistles
The language and ideas of salvation pervade the three Pastoral Epistles. This study offers a close examination of their soteriological statements. In all three letters the idea of salvation is found to play a vital paraenetic role, but each also exhibits distinctive soteriological emphases. The results challenge common assumptions about the Pastoral Epistles as a corpus.

George M. Wieland is Lecturer in New Testament, Carey Baptist College and Auckland University, New Zealand.

2006 / 978-1-84227-257-2 / xxii + 344pp

Alistair Wilson
When Will These Things Happen?
A Study of Jesus as Judge in Matthew 21–25
This study seeks to allow Matthew's carefully constructed presentation of Jesus to be given full weight in the modern evaluation of Jesus' eschatology. Careful analysis of the text of Matthew 21–25 reveals Jesus to be standing firmly in the Jewish prophetic and wisdom traditions as he proclaims and enacts imminent judgement on the Jewish authorities then boldly claims the central role in the final and universal judgement.

Alistair Wilson is Principal of Dumisani Theological Institute, and Extraordinary Associate Professor of New Testament, North-West University, South Africa.

2004 / 978-1-84227-146-9 / xxii + 272pp

Lindsay Wilson
Joseph Wise and Otherwise
The Intersection of Covenant and Wisdom in Genesis 37–50
This book offers a careful literary reading of Genesis 37–50 that argues that the Joseph story contains both strong covenant themes and many wisdom-like elements. The connections between the two helps to explore how covenant and wisdom might intersect in an integrated biblical theology.

Lindsay Wilson is Vice Principal and Lecturer in Old Testament, Ridley College, University of Melbourne, Australia.

2004 / 978-1-84227-140-7 / xvi + 340pp

Stephen I. Wright
The Voice of Jesus
Studies in the Interpretation of Six Gospel Parables
'A book which genuinely has something fresh to offer', I. Howard Marshall.
2000 / 978-0-85364-975-5 / xiv + 280pp

New and unscheduled titles:

Mark Bonnington
The Antioch Episode of Galatians 2:11-14 in Historical and Cultural Context
The Antioch 'incident' over table-fellowship suggests significant disagreement between the leading apostles. This book analyses its background by locating the incident within the dynamics of social interaction between Jews and Gentiles, proposing a new way of understanding the relationship between the individuals and issues involved.
978-1-84227-050-9 / approx. 300pp

Stefan Kürle
The Appeal of Exodus
The Characters of God, Moses and Israel in the Rhetoric of the Book of Exodus
978-1-84227-657-0 / approx. 300pp

Daniel W. MacDougall
The Authenticity of 2 Thessalonians
978-1-84227-433-0 / approx. 300pp

John E. Morgan-Wynne
The Cross in the Johannine Writings
978-1-84227-658-7 / approx. 300pp

Ester Petrenko
Created in Christ Jesus for Good Works
The Integration of Soteriology and Ethics in Ephesians
978-1-84227-636-5 / approx. 300pp

Jennifer M. Shepherd
Exorcising a Dead Sea Scroll
A Contextual Reading of 11QapocryphalPsalms in the Shadow of Psalm 91 and Cave 11
978-1-84227-653-2 / approx. 300pp

Lawson Stone
Holy War and Holy Hero
978-1-84227-400-2 / approx. 300pp

Paternoster Theological Monographs

(All titles uniform with this volume)
Dates in bold are of projected publication.
Condensed details are given for volumes published before 2004.

James N. Anderson
Paradox in Christian Theology
An Analysis of the Presence, Character, and Epistemic Status of Paradoxical Christian Doctrines

Dr Anderson develops and defends a model of understanding paradoxical Christian doctrines according to which the presence of such doctrines is unsurprising and adherence to paradoxical doctrines can be entirely reasonable. As such, the phenomenon of theological paradox cannot be considered as a serious intellectual obstacle to belief in Christianity. The case presented in this book has significant implications for the practice of systematic theology, biblical exegesis, and Christian apologetics.

James N. Anderson is a Research Fellow of the University of Edinburgh, Scotland, UK.
2007 / 978-1-84227-462-0 / xvi + 328pp

Emil Bartos
Deification in Eastern Orthodox Theology
An Evaluation and Critique of the Theology of Dumitru Staniloae

'This book deals with a major topic of importance—Staniloae is the greatest Romanian theologian of the twentieth century', Kallistos Ware.
1999 / 978-0-85364-956-4 / xii + 370pp

Paul H. Brazier
Barth and Dostoevsky
A Study of the Influence of Fyodor Dostoevsky on the Development of Karl Barth (1915–1922)

A work of historic and systematic theology *Barth and Dostoevsky* examines the influence of Dostoevksy on Barth. It demonstrates that the writings of Dostoevsky effected the development of Barth's theology. This influence was mediated by his friend and colleague Eduard Thurneysen and was in the form of a key element of Barth's thought: his understanding of sin and grace. This study, therefore, explicates: first, the reading of Dostoevsky by Barth 1915–16, and the influence on his understanding of sin and grace; second, a study of Thurneysen in so far as his life and work complements and influences Barth; third, Barth's illustrative use of Dostoevsky, around 1918–21, the period of the rewriting of his seminal commentary on Romans.

Paul H. Brazier originally trained in the fine arts. He holds degrees from King's College, London, where he completed his PhD on which this book is based.
2007 / 978-1-84227-563-4 / xxiv + 246pp

Graham Buxton
The Trinity, Creation and Pastoral Ministry
Imaging the Perichoretic God

In this book the author proposes a three-way conversation between theology, science and pastoral ministry. His approach draws on a Trinitarian understanding of God as a relational being of love, whose life 'spills over' into all created reality, human and non-human. By locating human meaning and purpose within God's 'creation-community' this book offers the possibility of a transforming engagement between those in pastoral ministry and the scientific community.

Graham Buxton is Director of Postgraduate Studies in Ministry and Theology, Tabor College, Adelaide, Australia.
2005 / 978-1-84227-369-2 / xviii + 310pp

Iain D. Campbell
Fixing the Indemnity
The Life and Work of George Adam Smith
When Old Testament scholar George Adam Smith (1856–1942) delivered the Lyman Beecher lectures at Yale University in 1899, he confidently declared that 'modern criticism has won its war against traditional theories. It only remains to fix the amount of the indemnity.' In this biography, Iain D. Campbell assesses Smith's critical approach to the Old Testament and evaluates its consequences, showing that Smith's life and work still raises questions about the relationship between biblical scholarship and evangelical faith.

Iain D. Campbell is Minister of Back Free Church of Scotland, Isle of Lewis, Scotland, UK.

2004 / 978-1-84227-228-2 / xx + 256pp

Daniel Castelo
The Apathetic God
Exploring the Contemporary Relevance of Divine Impassibility
This book attempts a view of God and suffering that takes the testimony of the early church seriously while also considering with equal vigour the contemporary climate. It emphasizes divine impassibility because a balance between impassibility and passibility requires establishing space within a contemporary climate that all too easily assumes passibility.

Daniel Castelo is Assistant Professor of Theology, School of Theology, Seattle Pacific University, Washington, USA.

2009 / 978-1-84227-536-8 / xvi + 152pp

Tim Chester
Mission and the Coming of God
Eschatology, the Trinity and Mission in the Theology of Jürgen Moltmann
This book explores the theology and missiology of the influential contemporary theologian, Jürgen Moltmann. It highlights the important contribution Moltmann has made while offering a critique of his thought from an evangelical perspective. In so doing, it touches on pertinent issues for evangelical missiology. The conclusion takes Calvin as a starting point, proposing 'an eschatology of the cross' which offers a critique of the over-realised eschatologies in liberation theology and certain forms of evangelicalism.

Tim Chester is part of a church planting initiative in Sheffield and was previously Research and Policy Director for Tearfund and visiting lecturer in Christian Community Development at Redcliffe College, Gloucester, UK.

2006 / 978-1-84227-320-3 / xviii + 264pp

Sylvia Wilkey Collinson
Making Disciples
The Significance of Jesus' Educational Strategy for Today's Church
This study examines the biblical practice of discipling, formulates a definition, and makes comparisons with modern models of education. A recommendation is made for greater attention to its practice today.

Sylvia Wilkey Collinson is a Visiting Lecturer, Morling College, Sydney, Australia.

2004 / 978-1-84227-116-2 / xiv + 278pp

Darrell Cosden
A Theology of Work
Work and the New Creation
Through dialogue with Moltmann, Pope John Paul II and others, this book develops a genitive 'theology of work', presenting a theological definition of work and a model for a theological ethics of work that shows work's nature, value and meaning now and eschatologically. Work is shown to be a transformative activity consisting of three dynamically inter-related dimensions: the instrumental, relational and ontological.
Darrell Cosden is Lecturer in Theology and Ethics at the International Christian College, Glasgow, Scotland, UK.
2005 / 978-1-84227-332-6 / xvi + 208pp

Oliver Crisp
An American Augustinian
Sin and Salvation in the Dogmatic Theology of William G.T. Shedd
Shedd's theology is arguably one of the richest resources in the American Reformed tradition yet it has not received the attention it deserves. Shedd was a theologian unafraid to think for himself, even if this meant he ended up with views that were not held by others with whom he had a natural affinity. His theology of sin and salvation illustrate well this creative innovation within a tradition. Crisp explores the relationship between sin and salvation in Shedd's theology, with an eye to both its philosophical and dogmatic significance for contemporary theology.
Oliver Crisp is Lecturer in Theology, University of Bristol, UK.
2007 / 978-1-84227-526-9 / xvi + 184pp

Garry J. Deverell
The Bonds of Freedom
Vows, Sacraments and the Formation of the Christian Self
This book proposes that Christian worship is a key source for any theology seeking to understand the covenant between God and human beings in the Christian tradition. Through a detailed examination of phenomenological, biblical and theological sources, the author seeks to write a theology in which the selfhood of God and human beings is seen as essentially 'vowed' or 'covenantal'. This claim is then explored through a detailed examination of eucharistic and baptismal practices within the worship life of the church. Eucharistic worship is understood as a 'non-identical performance' of the covenant established between God and human beings in baptism. Here, then, is a theology that understands Christian worship not simply as 'form' or 'event' but, more radically, as a mutual act of promising and commitment between God and human beings.
Garry J. Deverell is a minister of the Uniting Church in Australia and an Honorary Research Associate, Centre for Studies in Religion and Theology, Monash University, Victoria, Australia.
2008 / 978-1-84227-527-6 / xvi + 214pp

Paul G. Doerksen
Beyond Suspicion
Post-Christendom Protestant Political Theology in John Howard Yoder and Oliver O'Donovan
By pursuing a critical comparison of the political theologies of John Howard Yoder and Oliver O'Donovan, the present work shows how post-Christendom Protestant political theology has attempted to move beyond the suspicion that politicians corrupt morality, and that politics is corrupted by theology without putting forward some hidden attempt to reassert a contemporary version of Christendom.
Paul G. Doerksen teaches Christian Theology and Ethics in Winnipeg, Manitoba, Canada.
2009 / 978-1-84227-634-1 / approx. 300pp

Stephen M. Dunning
The Crisis and the Quest
A Kierkegaardian Reading of Charles Williams
'An invaluable contribution to our understanding of this extraordinary man', Glen Cavaliero.
2000 / 978-0-85364-985-4 / xxiv + 254pp

Keith Ferdinando
The Triumph of Christ in African Perspective
A Study of Demonology and Redemption in the African Context
'I am excited by this book', R.T. France.
1999 / 978-0-85364-830-7 / xviii + 450pp

Craig Gardiner
Melodies of Community
Christian Community through the Metaphor of Music, with Dietrich Bonhoeffer and the Iona Community
Gardiner adopts the musical metaphor of polyphony to articulate a new paradigm for exploring the nature of Christ and argues that the church can still affirm ecumenical unity while celebrating the diverse patterns of practice and belief. He weaves together Bonhoeffer, the Iona Community and a rich variety of further metaphors to suggest a 'Discipline of Counterpoint' with which the Christian community might perform divine melodies such as worship, healing, ecumenism, peace, justice and ecology.
Craig Gardiner is pastor of Calvary Baptist Church, Cardiff, a member of the Council of the Baptist Union of Great Britain and serves on its Faith and Unity Executive.
2010 / 978-1-84227-564-1 / approx. 300pp

Richard Gibb
Grace and Global Justice
The Socio-Political Mission of the Church in an Age of Globalization
What does it mean for the twenty-first-century church to conceive of itself as a community defined by the covenant of grace? *Grace and Global Justice* explores the ramifications of this central Christian doctrine for the holistic mission of the church in the context of a globalized world.
Richard Gibb is Assistant Minister of Charlotte Chapel, Edinburgh, UK.
2006 / 978-1-84227-459-0 / xviii + 248pp

Andrew Goddard
Living the Word, Resisting the World
The Life and Thought of Jacques Ellul
'The best introduction to Ellul's thought currently available', Alister E. McGrath.
2002 / 978-1-84227-053-0 / xxiv + 378pp

Andrew Hartropp
Economic Justice
Biblical and Secular Perspectives Contrasted
This book argues that a biblically-rooted account of justice in economic life has three great strengths as opposed to the confusing disarray of views evident in the secular world: it is harmonious; it is substantial; and it is contemporary. It indicates how a biblical understanding of production and exchange ('free trade' versus 'fair trade' and equality versus freedom) applies to contemporary topics such as the relationships between borrowers and lenders, and the use of monopoly power.
Andrew Hartropp has lectured in economics at Brunel University and is currently a Church of England Curate in Watford, Hertfordshire, UK.
2007 / 978-1-84227-434-7 / xvi + 222pp

Sharon E. Heaney
Contextual Theology for Latin America
Liberation Themes in Evangelical Perspective
In the context of Latin America, the theology of liberation is both dominant and world renowned. However, this context and the pursuit of theological relevance belong also to other voices. In this book, Sharon Heaney examines and systematises the thought of five evangelical theologians striving for liberation in Latin America.
Sharon E. Heaney teaches Religious Studies at Bloxham School, Oxfordshire, having completed her doctorate at Queens University, Belfast, Northern Ireland, UK.
2008 / 978-1-84227-515-3 / xx + 292pp

Timothy D. Herbert
Kenosis and Priesthood
Towards a Protestant Re-Evaluation of the Ordained Ministry
Herbert argues it is possible to re-imagine priesthood so that it becomes a useful way to understand the nature and importance of ordained ministry without undervaluing or negating the priesthood of all believers.
Timothy D. Herbert is Principal of the Carlisle and Blackburn Diocesan Training Institute, Carlisle, UK.
2008 / 978-1-84227-565-8 / xxii + 300pp

Roger Hitching
The Church and Deaf People
A Study of Identity, Communication and Relationships with Special Reference to the Ecclesiology of Jürgen Moltmann
'An excellent book', Jürgen Moltmann.
2003 / 978-1-84227-222-0 / xxii + 236pp

Mark F.W. Lovatt
Confronting the Will-to-Power
A Reconsideration of the Theology of Reinhold Niebuhr
'A constructive evaluation', Anthony C. Thiselton.
2001 / 978-1-84227-054-7 / xviii + 216pp

Neil B. MacDonald
Karl Barth and the Strange New World within the Bible
Barth, Wittgenstein, and the Metadilemmas of the Enlightenment (Revised Edition)
'Brilliant and nuanced', Christopher R. Seitz.
2001^2 / 978-0-85364-970-0 / xxvi + 404pp

Neil B. MacDonald and Carl R. Trueman (eds)
Barth, Calvin, and Reformed Theology
Barth and Calvin belong to the first rank of great theologians of the Church. Historically, Calvin's influence on Reformed doctrine has been much greater than that of Barth's. In contrast, Barth's Reformed credentials have been questioned—not least in his understanding of election and atonement. The question is: who should be of greater importance for the Reformed church in the twenty-first century in the light of recent academic research into the Bible? Who has the better arguments on the Bible? Barth or Calvin: who should carry the mantle of Reformed theology in the future? Doctrinal areas of focus are the nature of the atonement, scripture, and the sacraments.
Neil B. MacDonald is Senior Lecturer in Theology, University of Surrey Roehampton, London, UK.
Carl R. Trueman is Professor of Church History, Westminster Theological Seminary, Philadelphia, USA.
2008 / 978-1-84227-567-2 / xiv + 182pp

Keith A. Mascord
Alvin Plantinga and Christian Apologetics
This book draws together the contributions of the philosopher Alvin Plantinga to the major contemporary challenges to Christian belief, highlighting in particular his ground-breaking work in epistemology and the problem of evil. Plantinga's theory that both theistic and Christian belief is warrantedly basic is explored and critiqued, and an assessment offered as to the significance of his work for apologetic theory and practice.
Keith A. Mascord lectures in Philosophy at Moore Theological College, Sydney, Australia.
2006 / 978-1-84227-256-5 / xvi + 236pp

Gillian McCulloch
The Deconstruction of Dualism in Theology
With Reference to Ecofeminist Theology and New Age Spirituality
'McCulloch's informed and timely book fills an important gap', Christopher Partridge.
2002 / 978-1-84227-044-8 / xii + 282pp

Leslie McCurdy
Attributes and Atonement
The Holy Love of God in the Theology of P.T. Forsyth
'Skilful and nuanced', Trevor Hart.
1999 / 978-0-85364-833-8 / xiv + 328pp

David H. McIlroy
A Trinitarian Theology of Law
In Conversation with Jürgen Moltmann, Oliver O'Donovan and Thomas Aquinas
This book explores the neglected significance of the doctrine of the Trinity for the understanding of human law. Through interaction with the thought of Moltmann, O'Donovan and Aquinas, it argues that human law is called to play a positive but limited role in maintaining 'shallow justice' and relative peace. Human law is overshadowed by the work of the Son, included in the purposes of the Father, and used as an instrument by the Holy Spirit. However, the Spirit works in those who are in Christ to effect 'deep justice', a work of sanctification which culminates in glorification – the experience of perfect, free, willing obedience in heaven.
David H. McIlroy is a practising barrister and a theologian and an Associate Research Fellow of Spurgeon's College, London, UK.
2009 / 978–1–84227–627–3 / xxii + 262pp

John E. McKinley
Tempted for Us
Theological Models and the Practical Relevance of the Impeccability and Temptation of Christ
How could Christ be tempted to sin despite his divine impeccability? How could Christ experience temptation in a way that makes him truly empathetic for others who are not impeccable as he is? How could Christ resist temptation in a way that others can reasonably follow his human example? Historical theology yields several models for working out the apparent dilemmas that follow from the traditional affirmations about Jesus' temptation. In response, McKinley explores the biblical and theological evidence for Christ's impeccability and temptation with the goal of formulating a contemporary model. Doing this clarifies both the full humanity of Christ and the true relevance and implications of his earthly life for Christian sanctification in conformity to Christ.
John E. McKinley is Assistant Professor of Systematic Theology, Biola University, La Mirada, California, USA.
2009 / 978-1-84227-537-5 / xxii + 346pp

Nozomu Miyahira
Towards a Theology of the Concord of God
A Japanese Perspective on the Trinity
'A profound contribution to East–West dialogue', John Macquarrie.
2000 / 978-0-85364-863-5 / xiv + 256pp

Eddy José Muskus
The Origins and Early Development of Liberation Theology in Latin America
With Particular Reference to Gustavo Gutiérrez
'Fills a crucial gap', D. Eryl Davies.
2002 / 978-0-85364-974-8 / xiv + 296pp

Jim Purves
The Triune God and the Charismatic Movement
A Critical Appraisal from a Scottish Perspective
All emotion and no theology? Or a fundamental challenge to reappraise and realign our trinitarian theology in the light of Christian experience? This study of charismatic renewal as it found expression within Scotland at the end of the twentieth century evaluates the use of Patristic, Reformed and contemporary models of the Trinity in explaining the workings of the Holy Spirit.
Jim Purves is pastor of Bristo Baptist Church, Edinburgh, and serves on the Baptist Union of Scotland's national leadership team.
2004 / 978-1-84227-321-0 / xxiv + 246pp

Anna Robbins
Methods in the Madness
Diversity in Twentieth-Century Christian Social Ethics
The author compares the ethical methods of Walter Rauschenbusch, Reinhold Niebuhr and others. She argues that unless Christians are clear about the ways that theology and philosophy are expressed practically they may lose the ability to discuss social ethics across contexts, let alone reach effective agreements.
Anna Robbins is Lecturer in Theology and Contemporary Culture and Director of Training at the London School of Theology, UK.
2004 / 978-1-84227-211-4 / xx + 294pp

Ed Rybarczyk
Beyond Salvation
Eastern Orthodoxy and Classical Pentecostalism on Becoming Like Christ
At first glance eastern Orthodoxy and classical Pentecostalism seem quite distinct. This ground-breaking study shows they share much in common, especially as it concerns the experiential elements of following Christ. Both traditions assert that authentic Christianity transcends the wooden categories of modernism.
Ed Rybarczyk is Assistant Professor of Systematic Theology, Vanguard University, California, USA.
2004 / 978-1-84227-144-5 / xii + 356pp

Signe Sandsmark
Is World View Neutral Education Possible and Desirable?
A Christian Response to Liberal Arguments
(Published jointly with The Stapleford Centre)
'Bold, balanced and sensitive', Andrew Wright.
2000 / 978-0-85364-973-1 / xiv + 182pp

Alison Searle
'The Eyes of your Heart'
Literary and Theological Trajectories of Imagining Biblically

This book develops a theory of imagining biblically that explores the contributions scripture can make to new ways of thinking about creativity, reading, interpretation and criticism. The methodology employed in order to demonstrate this thesis consists of a theoretical exploration of current theological understandings of the 'imagination' and their implications within the field of literary studies. The biblical text locates the function generally defined as 'imagination' in the heart ('the eyes of the heart', Ephesians 1:18). This book assesses what the biblical text as a literary and religious document contributes to the concept of 'imagination'.

Alison Searle is a postdoctoral research associate on the James Shirley Project at Anglia Ruskin University, Cambridge, UK.

2008 / 978-1-84227-627-3 / xviii + 232pp

Andrew Sloane
On Being a Christian in the Academy
Nicholas Wolterstorff and the Practice of Christian Scholarship

'Accurate, meticulously researched, lucidly presented and critically sympathetic', Nicholas Wolterstorff.

2003 / 978-1-84227-058-5 / xvi + 274pp

Damon W.K. So
Jesus' Revelation of His Father
A Narrative-Conceptual Study of the Trinity with Special Reference to Karl Barth

This book explores the trinitarian dynamics in the context of Jesus' revelation of his Father in his earthly ministry with references to key passages in Matthew's Gospel. It develops from the exegeses of these passages a non-linear concept of revelation which links Jesus' communion with his Father to his revelatory words and actions through a nuanced understanding of the Holy Spirit, with references to K. Barth, G.W.H. Lampe, J.D.G. Dunn and E. Irving.

Damon W.K. So serves as an adviser of the Oxford Chinese Christian Church having studied at London Bible College and the University of Oxford, UK.

2006 / 978-1-84227-323-4 / xviii + 348pp

Daniel Strange
The Possibility of Salvation Among the Unevangelised
An Analysis of Inclusivism in Recent Evangelical Theology

'One of the best comprehensive surveys of this debate', Gavin D'Costa.

2002 / 978-1-84227-047-9 / xviii + 362pp

Scott Swain
God According to the Gospel
Biblical Narrative and the Identity of God in the Theology of Robert W. Jenson

Robert W. Jenson is one of the leading voices in contemporary Trinitarian theology. His boldest contribution in this area lies in his use of the Bible's narrative structure both to ground and explicate a panentheistic doctrine of the Trinity. *God According to the Gospel* critically examines Jenson's proposal and, through an engagement with canon and creed, outlines an alternative way of reading the biblical characterization of the Trinity.

Scott Swain teaches Theology and Biblical Interpretation at Southwestern Baptist Theological Seminary, Fort Worth, Texas, USA.

2010 */ 978-1-84227-258-9 / approx. 300pp*

Justyn Terry
The Justifying Judgement of God
A Reassessment of the Place of Judgement in the Saving Work of Christ
Terry's argument is that judgement, understood as the whole process of bringing justice, is the primary metaphor of atonement, with others – victory, redemption and sacrifice – subordinate to it. Judgement also provides the proper context for understanding penal substitution and the call to repentance, baptism, eucharist and holiness.
Justyn Terry teaches at the Trinity Episcopal School for Ministry, Ambridge, PA, USA.
2007 / 978-1-84227-370-8 / xvi + 228pp

Graham Tomlin
The Power of the Cross
Theology and the Death of Christ in Paul, Luther and Pascal
'Here is the groundwork of constructive theology at its best', Stephen Williams.
1999 / 978-0-85364-984-7 / xiv + 344pp

Steven Tsoukalas
Krsna and Christ
Body-Divine Relation in the Thought of Sankara, Ramanuja and Classical Christian Orthodoxy
This work compares the Krsnavatara (Krsna in his *avatara* state) doctrines of Sankara and Ramanuja and the incarnation of Christ as represented by classical Christian orthodoxy, and draws out comparative theological and soteriological implications. The result is a demonstration that many of the popularly held similarities between *avatara* and incarnation are superficial, and that therefore careful consideration of epistemologies and ontologies should be undertaken when comparing theologies and soteriologies pertinent to *avatara* and incarnation.
Steven Tsoukalas is Adjunct Professor of Comparative Religion and Theology, Wesley Biblical Seminary, Jackson, Mississippi, USA.
2006 / 978-1-84227-435-4 / xvi + 310pp

Adonis Vidu
Postliberal Theological Method
A Critical Study
The postliberal theology of Frei, Lindbeck, Thiemann, Milbank and others is one of the more influential contemporary options. Vidu focuses on several aspects pertaining to its theological method, specifically its understanding of background, hermeneutics, epistemic justification, ontology, the nature of doctrine and christological method.
Adonis Vidu is Associate Professor of Theology, Gordon-Conwell Theological Seminary, South Hamilton, Massachusetts, USA.
2005 / 978-1-84227-395-1 / xiv + 270pp

Adonis Vidu
Theology after Neo-Pragmatism
How are theological claims justified? What is the meaning of Christian talk about the non-empirical and the transcendent? Should Evangelical theology continue to hitch a ride with realism? These important contemporary issues are approached by way of a theological conversation with neo-pragmatic philosophers such as Davidson, Rorty, Putnam, McDowell, and others. This is an introduction to an influential philosophical trend and a critical and constructive theological proposal, at once scriptural and historicist, pragmatic and realist.
Adonis Vidu is Associate Professor of Theology, Gordon-Conwell Theological Seminary, South Hamilton, Massachusetts, USA.
2008 / 978-1-84227-460-6 / xx + 308pp

Graham J. Watts
Revelation and the Spirit
A Comparative Study of the Relationship between the Doctrine of Revelation and Pneumatology in the Theology of Eberhard Jüngel and of Wolfhart Pannenberg
The relationship between revelation and pneumatology is relatively unexplored. This approach offers a fresh angle on two important twentieth-century theologians and raises pneumatological questions which are theologically crucial and relevant to mission in a postmodern culture.

Graham J. Watts is Minister of Albany Road Baptist Church, Cardiff, Wales, UK.

2005 / 978-1-84227-104-9 / xx + 230pp

Nicholas J. Wood
Faiths and Faithfulness
Pluralism, Dialogue and Mission in the Work of Kenneth Cragg and Lesslie Newbigin
Wood offers a critical account of two key twentieth-century missionary-theologians who addressed the issue of pluralism within a confessional framework. He argues for a reconsideration of the biblical themes of fullness and fulfilment, which may offer a way of holding together the traditions of continuity, which Cragg shows can never be total, and of discontinuity, which Newbigin argues can never be absolute. He contributes to the development of an appropriate missiological approach to inter-faith issues which takes people of faith seriously while allowing faithfulness to the Christian gospel.

Nicholas J. Wood is Fellow in Religion and Culture, and Director of the Oxford Centre for Christianity and Culture at Regent's Park College, University of Oxford. He is a member of the Faculty of Faculty in the University of Oxford and a President of the National Christian Muslim Forum.

2009 / 978-1-84227-371-5 / xviii + 220pp

Nigel G. Wright
Disavowing Constantine
Mission, Church and the Social Order in the Theologies of John Howard Yoder and Jürgen Moltmann
'A strong-minded, original contribution', Alan Kreider.

2000 / 978-0-85364-978-6 / xvi + 252pp

Terry J. Wright
Providence Made Flesh
Divine Presence as a Framework for a Theology of Providence
Traditional discussions of the Christian doctrine of providence often centre on the relation between divine agency and human freedom, seeking to offer an account of the extent to which a person is free before God, the first cause of all things. Terry J. Wright argues that such riddles of causation cannot determine the content of providence, and suggests a unique and alternative framework that depicts God's providential activity in terms of divine faithfulness to that which God has made. Providence is not God as first cause acting through creaturely secondary causation, rather providence is God's sovereign mediation of the divine presence across the whole world, achieved through creaturely faithfulness made possible and guaranteed by his own faithful action in Jesus Christ.

Terry J. Wright is an Associate Research Fellow at Spurgeon's College, London, UK.

2009 / 978-1-84227-632-7 / approx. 300pp

Theodore Zachariades
The Omnipresence of Jesus Christ
A Neglected Aspect of Evangelical Christology

Omnipresence is the key to unlock the kenosis question. The popular view of the incarnation whereby Christ possesses but does not independently exercise divine relative attributes is shown to be problematic and cannot be maintained with Christ's omnipresence, which by definition demands possession and use. Drawing on historical studies from the early church and John Calvin's christological exposition utilizing such concepts as *communicatio idiomatum* and *extra calvinisticum*, this work argues for a robust Chalcedonian incarnational christology that avoids all forms of kenotic thought.

Theodore Zachariades is founding pastor of Sovereign Grace Baptist Fellowship, Tullahoma, Tennessee, and teaches for Luther Rice University's distance learning program, Lithonia, Georgia, USA.

978-1-84227-531-3 / approx. 300pp

New and unscheduled titles:

Nicholas John Ansell
The Annihilation of Hell
Universal Salvation and the Redemption of Time in the Eschatology of Jürgen Moltmann
978-1-84227-525-2 / approx. 300pp

Laurence M. Blanchard
Will God Save Us All? [Provisional title]
An Assessment of the Historical Development and Contemporary Expression of Universalism in Western Theology
978-1-84227-638-7 / approx. 300pp

David Hilborn
The Words of our Lips
Language-Use in Free Church Worship

Studies of liturgical language have tended to focus on the written canons of Roman Catholic and Anglican communities. By contrast, David Hilborn analyses the more extemporary approach of English Nonconformity. Drawing on recent developments in linguistic pragmatics, he explores similarities and differences between 'fixed' and 'free' worship, and argues for the interdependence of each.

978-0-85364-977-9 / approx. 300pp

John G. Kelly
One God, One People
The Differentiated Unity of the People of God in the Theology of Jürgen Moltmann

The author expounds and critiques Moltmann's doctrine of God and highlights the systematic connections between it and Moltmann's influential discussion of Israel. He then proposes a fresh approach to Jewish–Christian relations building on Moltmann's work using insights from Habermas and Rawls.

978-0-85346-969-4 / approx. 300pp

Robert Knowles
Anthony C. Thiselton and the Grammar of Hermeneutics
The Search for a Unified Theory
978-1-84227-637-2 / approx. 300pp

Esther L. Meek
Contact with Reality
An Examination of Realism in the Thought of Michael Polanyi
978-1-84227-622-8 / approx. 300pp

Myron B. Penner
Subjectivity and Knowledge
Self and Being in Kierkegaard's Thought
978-1-84227-406-6 / approx. 300pp

Hazel Sherman
Reading Zechariah
The Allegorical Tradition of Biblical Interpretation through the Commentary of Didymus the Blind and Theodore of Mopsuestia
A close reading of the commentary on Zechariah by Didymus the Blind alongside that of Theodore of Mopsuestia suggests that popular categorising of Antiochene and Alexandrian biblical exegesis as 'historical' or 'allegorical' is inadequate and misleading.
978-1-84227-213-8 / approx. 300pp

www.ingramcontent.com/pod-product-compliance
Ingram Content Group UK Ltd.
Pitfield, Milton Keynes, MK11 3LW, UK
UKHW021838210426
5322IPUK00021B/348